# CENTRE AND
# LABYRINTH

# Centre and Labyrinth

## ESSAYS IN HONOUR OF NORTHROP FRYE

EDITED BY Eleanor Cook, Chaviva Hošek,
Jay Macpherson, Patricia Parker,
and Julian Patrick

Published in association with
Victoria University by
UNIVERSITY OF TORONTO PRESS
Toronto  Buffalo  London

© University of Toronto Press 1983
Toronto Buffalo London
First published in paperback 1985
Printed in Canada

ISBN 0-8020-2496-3 (cloth)
ISBN 0-8020-6594-5 (paper)

---

**Canadian Cataloguing in Publication Data**

Main entry under title:
Centre and labyrinth: essays in honour of Northrop
Frye

ISBN 0-8020-2496-3 (cloth)    ISBN 0-8020-6594-5 (paper)

1. Literature – History and criticism – Addresses,
essays, lectures, 2. Frye, Northrop, 1912–    –
Addresses, essays, lectures, I. Cook, Eleanor, 1933–
II. Frye, Northrop, 1912–

PN85.C46    809    C83-094200-9

---

Design: William Rueter RCA

# CONTENTS

## PREFACE

Northrop Frye, whose work and influence this collection of essays seeks to honour, has taught at Victoria College in the University of Toronto since the beginning of the second world war. From this centre, which he has never left for long, Professor Frye has become his country's most distinguished academic presence both at home and abroad. His major publications fall into four main groups. Spanning his career are three encyclopaedic works, on Blake, on the theory of criticism, and on the Bible: *Fearful Symmetry* (1947), *Anatomy of Criticism* (1957), and *The Great Code* (1982). Equally well known are his several shorter treatments of great writers, central genres, and important literary periods of English literature: *A Natural Perspective* (1965) and *Fools of Time* (1967) on Shakespeare, *The Return of Eden* (1965) on Milton, *T.S. Eliot* (1961), *A Study of English Romanticism* (1969), and *The Secular Scripture: A Study of the Structure of Romance* (1976). Four other books have been influential in redefining the social functions of literature and criticism: *The Educated Imagination* (1963), *The Well-Tempered Critic* (1963), *The Modern Century* (1967), and *The Critical Path* (1971). There are, in addition, four collections of essays which combine theoretical, cultural, and practical criticism on a wide variety of issues: *Fables of Identity* (1963), *The Stubborn Structure* (1970), *The Bush Garden* (1970), and *Spiritus Mundi* (1976). What is remarkable about this group of books, including the *Anatomy* and *The Great Code* and almost all the shorter essays, is that they were initially occasional in nature: responses to invitations to lecture, to hold extended seminars for a term or a year, to contribute to this or that academic conference, or special project, or memorial volume. These occasions reflect a widespread excitement throughout North America and extending to many other countries about the fiery originality of Frye's teaching.

With the publication in 1982 of *The Great Code*, it is perhaps possible
to see that there have been two determining lines of force in Frye's
writing from the beginning. The first is the openly visionary nature of
his understanding of literature and of literary criticism. Throughout his
career, he has stressed the need to bring literary criticism into significant and coherent relation to the great traditions of Western culture,
from the Bible and the Greek myths, to the canonical writers of our own
tradition, to contemporary writing and the avant-garde, whose absorb-
ing pull Frye has always strongly felt. For Frye, it is true both that
literary criticism should be based upon 'what the whole of literature
actually does' and that literature as a whole reflects an organized myth
of human experience. In practice, this vision has contributed to the
virtual dismantling of literary history as it was known before the
publication of the *Anatomy* and its redefinition according to holistic
standards analogous to Aristotle's in the *Poetics*. The sweep of Frye's
vision of literature and literary criticism still challenges contemporary
writers, but it is not in itself as responsible for his vast influence as is the
second line of force in his writing, his imagination's Horatian or
civilizing power. Frye's criticism is distinguished by polished epigram-
matic brilliance, by indispensable formulations and definitions, by a
radical blend of intimacy, humour, and well-tempered indignation, and
by a capacity for broad and even savage satire, only just kept in check by
the constant need to civilize, educate, and restrain.

Accordingly, the following essays wish to honour, on the occasion of
his seventieth year, both the scope of his vision for criticism and its
special pleasures and uses. The collection is divided into four groups of
essays and a coda. The first group begins with three studies of
Aristotelian subjects: plot or narrative intelligibility, catharsis, and
metaphor. These are subjects that Frye has made especially his own in
the *Anatomy of Criticism* and elsewhere. The fourth essay studies the
'anatomy' form, which Frye largely defined. Beginning with two
extended studies of Dante and Milton, the second group takes up the
relation between the Bible and later literature, a subject Frye first made
central to modern criticism in *Fearful Symmetry* and which *The Great
Code* addresses. The third group considers forms of romance and
romanticisms. This subject has correctly been identified as close to the
centre of Frye's influence. His argument, in the *Anatomy* and elsewhere, that romance should be understood as an independent category
of literary experience, has been widely persuasive. In the next group,
the first essay describes several influential theories of truth in relation to

the claims of poetry. Another essay seeks to associate Frye's discussion of irony with later views of language and the reading process, while a third essay analyses the contentions surrounding Frye's controversial writings on Canadian culture. The last essay, Prospero-like, discovers a fresh way of staging plays scattered among Frye's more formal remarks on drama.

The unity of this volume stems from two main sources. The first, of course, is Frye himself, many of whose characteristic subjects and preoccupations are given extended discussion in the course of the volume. Virtually all the essays return explicitly to, or keep in mind, that large and still imperfectly understood book of 1957, the *Anatomy of Criticism*, and, as Frye himself has done in many of his later works, these essays branch out from the new direction Frye has given to criticism. A second subject shared by many of the essays is the state of criticism today. In a famous discussion in the *Anatomy* (118), Frye suggested that, unless there were discoverable in literature a total form, a centre to the order of words, the critic would be condemned to a series of free associations, to exploring an 'endless labyrinth without an outlet.' Now, a quarter of a century later, and with the pejorative implication removed, the labyrinths of language – of forms, structures, terms, and subjects – make up both the central preoccupation of contemporary critical writing, and its dispersal. It is thus appropriate that a volume of essays in Frye's honour should begin with a discussion of paradigmatic form and should conclude with two essays, one decoding Freud, the other on the subject of labyrinths as an image of lost direction. It is the editors' hope that, by their response to his work, these essays will express our sense of the overwhelming intellectual generosity of the man they honour, as well as our gratefulness.

ACKNOWLEDGMENTS

We should like to express our gratitude, first, to Goldwin French, President of Victoria University, for his generous and effective assistance on behalf of this volume.

For able and cheerful help, we should also like to thank Mrs. Veronica Waugh, Head of the Printing Department, Victoria College; Kim Partridge and Judy Broughton; and especially Rea Wilmshurst, who knows the mysteries of word processors. We are grateful for the use of the facilities of the *Collected Works of John Stuart Mill*. Jane Widdicombe, as always, has been indispensable.

The Office of Research Administration, University of Toronto, through its Humanities and Social Science Committee, provided funds for expenses incurred during preparation of the volume.

Finally, we should like to thank the editors of the University of Toronto Press: Ian Montagnes; Judy Williams, our helpful copy editor; and especially Prudence Tracy, who advised wisely and sped us on our way.

BIBLIOGRAPHICAL NOTE

The most extensive listing of Northrop Frye's writings through 1973 appears in Robert D. Denham's *Northrop Frye: An Enumerative Bibliography* (Metuchen, NJ: Scarecrow Press, 1974), which also includes an annotated list of 129 articles, books, and essays about Frye's criticism and a list of the reviews of his books. Denham has provided a supplement to this bibliography in *Canadian Library Journal*, 34 (1977), 181-97, and 301-2. The material in these lists is incorporated in *Northrop Frye: A Supplementary Bibliography* (Emory, Va.: Iron Mountain Press, 1979). Denham's *Northrop Frye: An Annotated Bibliography*, which will include more than 1200 references to primary and secondary sources, is forthcoming from Garland Publishing Company.

# CONTRIBUTORS

| | |
|---|---|
| HAROLD BLOOM | Yale University |
| JAMES CARSCALLEN | Victoria College, University of Toronto |
| ELEANOR COOK | Victoria College, University of Toronto |
| MICHAEL DOLZANI | University of Toronto |
| ANGUS FLETCHER | The Graduate Center, City University of New York |
| JOHN FRECCERO | Stanford University |
| GEOFFREY HARTMAN | Yale University |
| JENNIFER LEVINE | Victoria College, University of Toronto |
| ELI MANDEL | York University |
| JAMES NOHRNBERG | University of Virginia |
| PATRICIA PARKER | Victoria College, University of Toronto |
| JULIAN PATRICK | Victoria College, University of Toronto |
| JAMES REANEY | University of Western Ontario |
| PAUL RICOEUR | Université de Paris and the University of Chicago |
| W. DAVID SHAW | Victoria College, University of Toronto |
| FRANCIS SPARSHOTT | Victoria College, University of Toronto |
| DAVID STAINES | University of Ottawa |
| HELEN VENDLER | Boston University and Harvard University |
| THOMAS WILLARD | University of Arizona |
| MILTON WILSON | Trinity College, University of Toronto |

# CENTRE AND
# LABYRINTH

**PAUL
RICOEUR**

# 'Anatomy of Criticism' or the Order of Paradigms

This essay on interpreting Northrop Frye's *Anatomy of Criticism* is governed by an underlying hypothesis which I want to set forth before testing it out in the reading that follows. It is my belief that, despite its systematic aspect, this work does not belong to the same system of thought that governs the narrative theory of the French school of structuralism. I see in the latter an attempt to reconstruct, to simulate at a higher level of rationality, what is already understood on a lower level of narrative understanding, the level brought to light for the first time by Aristotle in his *Poetics*. This attempted reconstruction has the same ambitions and arises out of the same second-order rationality that we see at work in the domain of historiography; its best illustration is provided by nomological models of historical explanation. It has the same ambition and the same legitimacy, that of bringing into play in the human sciences a logic of explanation akin to the one governing the exact sciences. In this sense, the vast body of work already produced in the field of narrative studies cannot be questioned. What is philosophically disputable is the claim to substitute this form of rationality for the narrative understanding that precedes it, not just as a fact in the history of culture, but also as a rule in the epistemological order of derivation. Such a substitution depends upon forgetting how rooted semiotic rationality is in narrative understanding, for which it attempts to provide an equivalent or a simulacrum on its own level.

Yet the precedence of narrative understanding in the epistemological order can neither be claimed nor maintained unless we restore to it those features of intelligibility that serve as the original model which semiotic rationality undertakes to simulate.

It is to just this intelligibility that Aristotle attributes poetry's power to 'teach,' to present 'universals' to thought – poetry, in the context of his *Poetics*, referring to the composing of tragic, comic, or epic works. But these universals are not those of theoretical reason. Rather they are akin to the universals operative in *phronesis*, 'prudence' in the practical, ethical, and political order. Indeed, the configurational act (to use a term Louis Mink has introduced into the philosophy of history), by means of which the tragic, comic, or epic *mythos* imitates an action, is intelligible by virtue of this single fact: that the arrangement of incidents in a plot calls upon our capacity for 'grasping together' scattered events, circumstances, ends, means, interactions, contingencies, and unintended and unexpected results. It is this synthesis of the heterogenous in the configurational act that we understand as meaningful.

The multiple typologies we find in Northrop Frye's *Anatomy of Criticism* are grafted to this first order of intelligibility, without any recourse to the structuralists' narratological rationality, which begins by setting aside on principle every chronological and therefore every narrative feature in its models of the deep grammar of narration.

How then does one establish a typology that stays close to narrative intelligibility? This will be the guiding question of the remainder of my inquiry.

Two conditions for the possibility of such a typology are to be found in narrative understanding itself. First, that the creation of new plots arises from the eminently synthetic operation which Kant designated in terms of the productive imagination. Unlike the simply reproductive imagination, which is limited to representing already existing objects *in absentia*, the productive imagination brings about new syntheses without any prior models. Yet, for Kant, the productive imagination does not work in a random fashion. It is the model for all rule-governed behaviour, in the sense that it is the creative matrix for the categories that critical philosophy proceeds to constitute in following its own *Leitfaden* (or guideline) stemming from transcendental logic. Even this constructive process, however, is subterraneously guided by the order of the schematism. The schematism has such power because the productive imagination itself performs a basically synthetic function. It connects the level of understanding (in the Kantian sense of *Verstand*) with that of intuition by generating new syntheses that are both intellectual and intuitive. In the same way, emplotment, that is, the formation (or *poeisis*) of plots, generates a mixed intelligibility between what can be called the thought – the 'theme,' the topic of a story – and the intuitive presentation of situations, characters, episodes, changes of fortune, and so on. We may thus speak of a schematism of the narrative function to characterize the work of intelligibility proper to the configurational act of emplotment.

And we may say that it is thanks to such potential intelligibility that individual plots lend themselves to typologies of the kind Northrop Frye construes in his *Anatomy of Criticism*. Such typologies, I believe, reflect a sustained familiarity with the individual works of our narrative tradition or traditions, and they constitute the schematism of the narrative function, whereas individual plots express the productive imagination at work on the level of poetic composition.

In this way, we can transpose into more contemporary terms – with Kant's help! – Aristotle's thesis that poetry teaches us universals. These universals, as I said, are not those of theoretical reason. Let us now add that they are the universals of the schematism of the narrative function.

The second condition for the possibility of a typology that is not reducible to a 'logic' of narrative is close to the first one. Its universals are taught through reflection upon the structuring acts of our narrative traditions in the course of our history. In other words, the narrative schematism is constituted in and through a history that has all the features of a tradition. By this I do not mean some inert transmission of dead materials but rather the living transmission of a chain of interactions which can always be reactivated by a return to the most creative moments of poetic composition. This phenomenon of 'traditionality' is the key to the functioning of the narrative paradigms. The constituting of any tradition relies on the interplay between innovation and sedimentation; and it is to sedimentation – that is, the preservation of innovations through a cumulating time – that we can ascribe those paradigms that constitute the typology of emplotment. They – or rather their schematisms – stem from a sedimented history whose genesis has largely been obliterated.

However, sedimentation does not occur without its contrary process, innovation, just as innovation does not occur apart from sedimentation. It is easy to see why. Paradigms that are generated by some previous innovation in turn provide guidelines for further experimentation in the narrative field. These paradigms change under the pressure of new innovations, but they change slowly and even resist change by virtue of the process of sedimentation. This dialectic of sedimentation and change gives rise to a whole range of combinations, deployed between the two poles of servile application and calculated deviance, and passing through every degree of rule-governed deformation. Most folk-tales, myths, and traditional narratives in general stand close to the pole of servile application. But to the extent that we move beyond such traditional forms of narrative, deviance prevails. For example, many contemporary novels may be defined as anti-novels. A range of variations is thus delineated beyond which we should no longer speak of deviance but rather of 'schism,' to use Frank Kermode's term. But rule-governed deformation remains the axis along which the various modalities of paradigm change get distributed. These variations confer a historicity of its own upon the productive imagination, one that keeps the narrative tradition alive.

It is to this schematism of narrative understanding, considered in terms of the unity of its style of traditionality, that I attach the typologies that abound in the first essay of Frye's work, 'Historical Criticism: Theory of Modes,' and even more in the third essay, 'Archetypal Criticism: Theory of Myths.' These typologies do not justify themselves by some abstract form of coherence or by their deductive virtues, but just by their capacity for rendering an account, by an openly inductive process, of the greatest possible number of works included in our cultural heritage.

*Anatomy of Criticism*, in its very construction, poses a delicate problem of interpretation in that it seems to develop fully a theory of 'modes' (wherein tragedy, epic, and modern forms of narrative find their place) before it develops the theory of symbols that, in the final analysis, contains the profound motivation justifying the cyclic distribution of the modes. The author no doubt wanted us to be able to read his theory of modes independently of his theory of symbols. But to anyone who has read the remainder of this book, it seems as though the theory of modes is only established on the basis of the theory of symbols that follows it.

Taken alone, the theory of modes is a vast taxonomy on the level of what I have called a narrative schematism. Let us concentrate our attention on the fictional modes, here leaving aside the thematic ones. In opposition to the thematic modes, which group together all the traits that link a poem to its speaker, the fictional modes refer only to internal structural relations. Their distribution is governed by a single basic criterion, their hero's power of action, which may be, as we read in Aristotle's *Poetics*, greater than our own, less than our own, or more or less similar to our own. Frye applies this criterion along two parallel planes, that of tragedy and that of comedy, which in fact are not modes but classes of modes. In tragic modes, the hero is isolated from society (to which isolation corresponds the spectator's aesthetic distance, as we see in the 'purifying' emotions of terror and pity). In comic modes the hero is reincorporated into his society. Frye applies his criterion of the power of action along these two lines of tragedy and comedy. And he distinguishes on each line five modes divided into five columns. In the first column, that of myth, the hero is superior in kind. In the second, that of romance, he is no longer superior in kind but in degree, in relation to other people and their environment. In the third column, that of high mimetic, the hero is superior to others but not to their environment, as we see in epic and in tragedy. In the fourth column, that of low mimetic, the hero is the equal of his fellows and their surroundings. Finally, in the fifth column, that of irony, the hero is inferior to us in strength and intelligence; we look down at him from above.

If we limited ourselves to this taxonomy, there would be hardly any place for more than the little parlour game of endlessly adding new subdivisions or of proving the author wrong by 'inventing' a category that would be unclassifiable according to this taxonomy. However, the real interest lies elsewhere than in the question of completeness. Beyond the fact that Frye adds differential features to his model equal in importance to those of the fictional modes, under the title 'thematic modes,' he also adds two rules for reading which profoundly transform the simply taxonomic character of the classification. On the one side, it is said that fiction, in the West, ceaselessly displaces its centre of gravity from above to below, that is, from the divine hero toward the hero of tragedy and of ironic comedy, including the parody of ironic tragedy. This law of descent is in no way a law of decadence, as may be seen by its counterpart. To the extent that the sacred in the first column and the marvellous in the second column decrease, we see the mimetic tendency increase, first in the form of high mimetic, then of low mimetic. We also see the values of plausibility, then of resemblance increase. What is more, by means of the diminution of the hero's power, the values of irony are liberated and allowed to develop. And in one sense, irony is already potentially present as soon as we have a *mythos* or plot in the broad sense. Every *mythos* implies an 'ironic withdrawal from reality' (82). This explains the apparent ambiguity of the term 'myth': in the sense of sacred myth, the term designates the stories of heroes superior to us in every way; in the Aristotelian sense of *mythos*, it covers the entire region of fiction. The two senses are connected by irony. Irony is implicitly present in all *mythos*, but it only becomes a separate mode with the decline of sacred myth. Only thus does irony become a terminal mode, in accordance with the law of descent mentioned above. The irony inherent in plot as such appears to be connected in this way to the whole set of fictional modes. As we shall see, this first appended thesis introduces an orientation into the taxonomy.

The second thesis is still more unsettling. It states that, in one way or another, irony moves back toward myth (see 42, 48-9), for Northrop Frye is anxious to catch hold of an indication of a return toward myth underlying what he calls 'ironic myth.' This indication is the basis of the scale that runs from ironic comedy through the irony of the *pharmakos* or scapegoat, to the irony of the inevitable and the incongruous.

Now these two rules for reading – the law of descent, which orients the taxonomy, and the law of return, which gives a circular shape to the linear succession of modes – define what I would call the style of European or Western traditionality for Northrop Frye. But these two rules are incomprehensible and appear entirely arbitrary unless the theory of modes finds its hermeneutical key in the theory of symbols that informs the three other essays of *Anatomy of Criticism*.

For the purposes of our discussion, let us consider two important points of that theory: the definition of what counts as a symbol for literary criticism, and the distinguishing of phases, which is the real object of *Anatomy of Criticism*.

For Northrop Frye, literary symbolism does not imply a category of symbols in the broad sense that Cassirer gave this term. Instead the definition of literary symbolism is quite specific. It follows from a prior definition of what a poem is, namely a 'hypothetical verbal structure' (71). Correlatively, a symbol is 'any unit of any literary structure that can be isolated for critical attention' (ibid.). The three words used in defining a poem – and by implication a symbol – are equally important. It is a question of language phenomena that present a delimited, closed texture, and whose relation to external things is neutralized. This last point is most important because schematically a symbol can be considered as moving in two different directions, one toward the outside, the other toward the inside. If we follow the first direction, the symbol stands for or points toward external things. It 'represents' them (73). This class of symbols is that of 'signs.' If we follow the other direction, the symbol unifies a verbal structure. It 'connects' it and hence we can speak of a 'motif.' These two kinds of symbols appear in every form of reading, but in descriptive reading the ultimate direction is toward the outside. Conversely, 'in all literary verbal structures the final direction of meaning is inward' (74). This is why literary meaning is 'hypothetical.' A 'hypothetical or assumed relation to the external world is part of what is usually meant by the word 'imaginative' (ibid.), a term that Northrop Frye clearly distinguishes from 'imaginary,' which designates a failed assertion. Literature is made of such hypothetical verbal structures, and symbols are the units that critical interest isolates.

If Northrop Frye chooses to use the term symbol, in spite of all the risks of confusion in this overloaded concept, it is because it allows him to take up in a new way the problem of multiple meanings arising from the medieval exegetical theory of the four senses of Scripture. The polysemy of a symbol is nothing other than the possibility of placing it in a succession of contexts or networks of relations which define its 'phases.'

As in the hermeneutic of the four senses of Scripture, the first phase is the literal one. It is defined exactly by our taking the hypothetical character of poetic structure seriously. To understand a poem literally is to understand everything that constitutes it as it stands. It is to interest ourselves in the unity of its structure, to read it as a poem. A poem is then taken by the reader to represent a certain 'mood,' which is nothing other than the unifying emotion that informs it and that arises from the references from one poetic image to another. In this sense, the mood is just as hypothetical as is the *mythos* or plot. We can even say that they share the same ironic relation with regard to reality, the same 'ironic withdrawal from reality.'

With the second phase, which Frye calls the formal one to distinguish it from the literal one, the symbol begins its hermeneutic course paralleling the four senses of the medieval tradition. With this stage, the author introduces the mimetic function of the poem, whether it be a mimesis of action in narrative plots or *mimesis logou* with the *dianoia* poetically transposed. To the reader's surprise, this second phase introduces the symbol into the cycle of nature. 'The poem is not natural in form, but it relates itself naturally to nature' (82). Is the critic about to deny his allegiance to the hypothetical? No. Just as the non-literal senses of the medieval tradition presuppose the literal one, Frye's formal phase presupposes it too. But since the literal for Frye means something hypothetical, the mimetic relation to nature which constitutes the second phase must be constructed on the basis of the hypothetical one. Mimesis therefore cannot be a copy unless we abolish the difference between poetry and description. And if we wish to conserve the metaphor of a mirror, we must understand it precisely in the sense of a poem holding up a mirror to nature; 'the poem is not itself a mirror' (84). We can therefore explore this stage of the symbol as an image if we keep in mind that the image is not the replica of some natural object but rather a relation to nature based upon the hypothetical status of the poem and its symbols. Given this condition, an autonomous type of criticism is possible, one that would be the examination of the imagery recurring in this or that poem. We can then risk calling this phase an 'allegorical' one, recalling the older terminology, as long as we do not mean by 'allegory' an illustration in images of abstract ideas arising from anything but the poem itself. On the contrary, allegory is the very movement from the literal sense of the poem to another kind of sense. And in this sense, the initial irony of the literal sense puts us on guard against taking a poem's ideas too seriously in the wrong way – I mean, in a way contrary to its hypothetical status.

For myself, I understand this turn in Northrop Frye's theory of symbols as follows. Even within that state of suspension wherein fiction holds the poem, there subsists an oblique reference to the real world, either as a form of borrowing or as a subsequent resymbolization of it. Therefore I see Frye's second phase as the nexus or turning-point between suspended reference and recreated reference, what I would call, in a vocabulary close to Hans-Georg Gadamer's, reference to the world of the text. To the extent that the poem unfolds in some hypothetical dimension, it also projects a world that we might inhabit.

There is evidence for such an interpretation, I submit, in the following statements from *Anatomy of Criticism*. Literature, Frye says, must be seen

as a body of hypothetical creations which is not necessarily involved in the worlds of truth and fact, nor necessarily withdrawn from them, but which may enter into any kind of relationship to them, ranging from the most to the least explicit ... The conception of art as having a relation to reality which is neither direct nor negative, but potential, finally resolves the dichotomy between delight and instruction, the style and the message. (92-3)

The third stage, that of the symbol as archetype, marks the place for a third type of criticism, archetypal criticism. We should not rush to denounce the latent 'Jungianism' of this type of criticism. On the contrary, it is a question of following the rigorous movement inaugurated by the literal phase, that is, by the hypothetical status of the poem and continued across the second stage, that of the symbol as an image. Within this perspective, we see that the term archetype designates the genesis of a conventional and generic bond, stemming from a poem's external relations with every other poem. This bond derives from the eminently communicable character of poetic art, that is, its social or sociable character. No poem is without precedent. The new always appears within an already existing order of words. 'Poetry can only be made out of other poems; novels out of other novels. Literature shapes itself' (97). Thus to talk about an archetype is to presuppose that the order of words is not pure chaos, that it has its own recurrences. And a symbol considered as an archetype designates some communicable form of unity. 'I mean by an archetype a symbol which connects one poem with another and thereby helps to unify and integrate our literary experience' (99). In this sense, I recognize in the concept of an archetype an equivalent of what I have called the schematism issuing from the sedimentation of tradition.

It is true that Northrop Frye gives his notion of an archetype a more pregnant and at first glance a more opaque meaning. But this meaning becomes more accessible if we consider its filiation not just from the first phase, but also from the second, the mimetic dimension added to the hypothetical one. If an archetype designates a stable conventional order, this order can be established in terms of its correspondence to the order of nature and its recurrences – day and night, the seasons, the years, life and death. To see the order of nature as imitated by a corresponding order of words is a perfectly legitimate enterprise, if we know how to construct it on the basis of the mimetic conception that is itself built upon the hypothetical conception of the symbol. These two approaches to the archetype are then conjoined in archetypal criticism in which the individuality of any poem is entirely absorbed into the order of words born both from social conventionality and imitation of the natural order. Jungian or not, this way of understanding symbols from the point of view of an order that goes beyond individual creations does not betray its premises; rather, it enriches them without destroying them. Archetypal criticism in this sense is not fundamentally different from the type of criticism practised by Gaston Bachelard in his theory of a 'material' imagination governed by the 'elements' of nature – water, air, earth, fire – but operating within the realm of language. It is also akin to the way in which Mircea Eliade orders hierophanies in terms of such cosmic dimensions as the sky, water, life, and so on – dimensions that go beyond all spoken or written rituals. This is why the archetypes most laden with cosmic meaning in *Anatomy of Criticism* are still 'learned cultural archetypes' (102). It is their belonging to the sphere of language that makes them suitable for comparative and morphological study, which, by right, extends from folk-tales and legends to all the rest of literature.

Finally, the last symbolic phase is one where the symbol is a 'monad.' This phase corresponds to the anagogical sense of medieval biblical exegesis. By a monad Frye means imaginative experience's capacity to attain totality in terms of some centre. As he states, 'difficult' writers lead one to think that 'the learned and the subtle, like the primitive and the popular, tend toward a center of imaginative experience ... there *is* a center of the order of words' (117-18, his emphasis). On these terms, then, we can again speak of a world of the text. In the last analysis, we must choose between an endless labyrinth or a total form.

We cannot doubt that the whole of Northrop Frye's enterprise hangs on the thesis that the narrative order finally refers to this 'still center of the order of words.' This centre is 'what our whole literary experience has been about' (117). In any case, we would misconceive the whole point of archetypal criticism, and even more that of anagogical criticism, if we saw it as some kind of interest in mastery or domination, in the fashion of rational reconstructions of a phenomenon or a process. On the contrary, the schematisms arise from these two phases more than from some order whose cyclic composition we cannot master. We can hardly speak of the blossoming division of literary creations in terms of the myths of spring, summer, fall, and winter as taxonomy. Why? Because the imagery whose secret order we seek to discern is dominated from above by apocalyptic imagery that, through forms difficult to number, turns on reconciliation in a unity – the unity of a one yet triune God, the unity of humanity, the unity of the animal world in terms of the symbol of the lamb, of the vegetable world in terms of the symbol of the tree of life, and of the mineral world in terms of the heavenly city.

It is true that this symbolism has its demonic side, as expressed in such figures as Satan, the tyrant, the monster, the barren fig tree, and the 'primitive sea,' the symbol of 'chaos.' But this polar structure is itself unified by the strength of the desire that configures both the infinitely desirable and its contrary, the infinitely detestable, at the same time. From an archetypal and an anagogical perspective, then, all imagery is inadequate in relation to the apocalyptic imagery of fulfilment and yet at the same time in search of it. Consequently literature is to be characterized overall as a quest, whether we consider the romantic, the high mimetic, or the low mimetic modes, or the ironic one represented by satire. All of literature derives its movement and its amplitude from this structure. So while we should not really speak of process in apocalyptic/demonic imagery, all imagery, in that it does not measure up to this ideal, is nothing but process: the alternation of life and death, of labour and rest, of sorrow and joy. Within the cyclical character of these changes appears the reigning mark of the apocalyptic/demonic order. This is why we have to put the cycle of seasons, which plays such a large part in the fourth phase, under the sign of the Apocalypse. This reference to the Apocalypse divests this theory of seasonal myths of every naturalistic characteristic, not just, as I have said, because it is taken up into the hypothetical register of the poem or because of the non-reduplicating character of poetic mimesis, but still more because of the attraction that the apocalyptic/demonic imagery exercises on the verbal order. On the archetypal level, nature still contains man. On the anagogical level, man contains nature. Even his cities and his gardens are figures of a human universe configured by the infinitely desirable. In this sense, the Apocalypse is what draws the potent symbolism of nature, arising from the archetypal level, into the orbit of the mythical order of language.

For Northrop Frye, our whole literary experience stands in relation to this 'still center of the order of words.' It is 'what our whole literary experience has been about.' However, if we run through the four phases of the symbol in reverse, it seems as though it is this reasonable belief in the power of a centre to order and contain everything that, retroactively, confers its plausibility on the search for an archetypal order. It is this which, if we return to the earlier phase, allows us to expect to find those 'images' that are capable of being put into patterns. If we return to our starting-point it is this belief that allows us to say of each poem that it constitutes a hypothetical verbal structure. What is more, we must not fail to include the progressive movement from the literal sense to the anagogical one in this retrogressive move. The symbol can assume the mimetic, then the archetypal and the anagogical functions because it had from the beginning established the difference between the hypothetical and the actual. *The hypothetical is retained in the anagogical.* This explains the fine definition of literature in the anagogic phase as 'existing in its own universe, no longer a commentary on life or reality, but containing life and reality in a system of verbal relationships' (122).

We would completely misconceive the meaning of this assertion if we concluded that for Northrop Frye in the end literature and religion become identical. For Frye, religion remains on the realistic and, therefore, descriptive side of language, even if its language traverses phases comparable to those we have described. We must say instead that, within its hypothetical order, literature is driven by the same desire as is religion. And in this sense, nothing is closer to Blake's dream than Mallarmé's statement that 'Tout au monde existe pour aboutir à un livre' (cited, ibid.).

This analogy between literature and religion, an analogy which the hypothetical character of poetry prevents us from ever reducing to an identity, finds its highest expression in the symbol of the Apocalypse. In literature this symbol marks the internal limit, not the external boundary, of a desire that aims at wholeness by means of the imagination. Precisely because the bond with the natural cycle has been broken, it can only be imitated and becomes an immense reservoir of images. The Apocalypse reconstructs the cycle that on the level of nature has been lost on the successive levels of the hypothetical, the imaginative, the archetypal, and finally on the level of a universal gravitation of symbols around a centre. 'The conception of a total Word is the postulate that there is such a thing as an order of words' (126). Once again this formula sounds like a religious one, but religion for Northrop Frye is too devoted to what *is* and literature too devoted to what *may be* for them to be identified with each other. Culture 'interposes, between the ordinary and the religious life, a total vision of possibilities, and insists on its totality – for whatever is excluded from culture by religion or state will get its revenge somehow' (127). Culture thus establishes its autonomy precisely by developing itself fully in its imaginative mode. 'Between religion's "this is" and poetry's "but suppose *this* is," there must always be some kind of tension, until the possible and the actual meet at infinity' (127-8).

This aiming at totality through language in the mode of the imaginative and the hypothetical which is characteristic of literature cannot be fully appreciated, in my opinion, without reference to the dialectic of innovation and sedimentation by means of which above I tried to characterize the traditionality of the narrative schematism.

Two problems, the one the contrary of the other, then arise. On the one hand, we can ask to what extent the literary tradition, by virtue of its principle of sedimentation, allows us to discern a style of development, an order of paradigms. Such an order of paradigms, if it can be identified without doing violence to individual works, would make our tradition into a coherent heritage, in spite of the contingent appearance of individual works. However, we can also ask what amount of variation is authorized by the space of variation which tradition opens, before we have to talk of a 'schism,' that is, of a death of paradigms. Walter Benjamin, for example, in his essay 'The Storyteller,' seems to consider the extinction of the narrative function as a *fait accompli*: 'Familiar though his name may be to us, the storyteller, in his living immediacy, is by no means a present force. He has already become something remote from us and something that is getting more distant ... The act of storytelling is coming to an end ... It is as if something that seemed inalienable to us, the securest among our possessions, were taken from us: the ability to exchange experience' (*Illuminations*, 83).

Benjamin thus seems to pose a problem diametrically opposed to that of Northrop Frye, as does Frank Kermode when he refers to the passage from deviance to 'schism' in contemporary literature, and as do too the deconstructionists when they ferociously attack the very idea of a 'still center of the order of words.' For me, the most valuable question that Northrop Frye raises for us is this: whether the question of deviance or even of schism, of the death of paradigms, can receive an intelligible answer apart from the prior question of the order of paradigms. In relation to what, in effect, could there be deviance or schism or death, if not in relation to a style of development capable of being identified? What would there be to deconstruct if literature did not itself posit the postulate 'that there is such a thing as an order of words'?

*Anatomy of Criticism* attempts to answer this first, primary question. Its enterprise is plausible to the extent that the level where it occurs is not that of semiotic rationality but rather that of narrative understanding, and it does so in the first place by means of Northrop Frye's great familiarity with the works of which we are the inheritors, then in virtue of the twofold phenomenon of the schematism of traditionality which I described above. The order of paradigms that *Anatomy of Criticism* establishes is not atemporal inasmuch as it proceeds from the sedimentation that gives this schematism the unity of a style. Nor is it historical in the sense that it follows the chronology of the history of literature. Neither ahistorical nor historical, it is rather transhistorical, in the sense that it traverses history in a cumulative and not simply an additive mode. Even if this order includes breaks, these do not ignore what precedes them or that from which they separate themselves. They too are part of the phenomenon of tradition and its cumulative style.

The decisive test of Northrop Frye's conception of literary criticism would be to demonstrate that the phenomena of deviance, schism, and the death of paradigms constitute the inverse side of the problem posed by *Anatomy of Criticism* of an order of paradigms constituting the schematism of narrative understanding.

Translated by David Pellauer

**FRANCIS SPARSHOTT**

# The Riddle of Katharsis

'Let us speak of tragedy, recapitulating the definition of its nature that arises from what has been said. Tragedy, then, is imitation of a serious and complete action possessing magnitude ... accomplishing through pity and fear the *katharsis* of such passions.'[1] Ever since the Renaissance, Aristotle's claim that tragedy achieves a *katharsis* has attracted the attention of literary theorists and classical scholars, and when Sigmund Freud married the niece of Aristotle's most influential interpreter it was to be expected that the notion of *katharsis* would enter on a new career in speculative psychology.[2] Neither the amount of scholarly discussion of what Aristotle meant or should have meant or the prominence of the term *katharsis* in our less formal discourse bears any reasonable proportion to the part it plays in Aristotle's treatise: *katharsis* is invoked once, in a subordinate clause for which nothing prepares us, which is not explained, and which is not referred to in the rest of the *Poetics*. There is something absurd in devoting such reams of exegesis to what has almost the air of a passing comment. But once discussion has started it is hard to end it. It is the very brevity of the remark that tantalizes. Surely to Aristotle the meaning must have seemed too obvious to explain. We feel challenged to make the meaning equally obvious to ourselves and others. And we are tantalized because the power and appeal of tragedy do seem to need explaining.

At first it seems evident what Aristotle must have meant. We know from the *Nicomachean Ethics* what he thought about emotions. No emotion as such is good or bad. What is good is habitually to feel, and to act on, a given emotion to an extent and in a fashion appropriate to oneself and to the occasion of action. Consequently, if Aristotle thought tragedy had any good effect on any emotions, that effect must have been the promotion of such habituation – and in readers or spectators, rather than playwright and actors, for Aristotle assumes throughout that tragedy exists for the sake of its audience.[3] It is in this way that the *katharsis* clause was generally understood before the end of the eighteenth century.[4]

The difficulty with the apparently straightforward explanation just offered is that one cannot see how watching or reading plays could have such an effect, or how Aristotle could have thought it would. He insists that emotions are trained by appropriate action and in no other way (cf. *Nic. Eth.* 1105b2-18). And, if tragedy could after all provide a supplementary means of training, one does not see why Aristotle should not have said so in the language he uses elsewhere to discuss these issues, language in which the word *katharsis* plays no part. One must therefore look elsewhere for Aristotle's meaning, and a mountain of scholarly exegesis has arisen over his bones. The mountain has yielded some pretty mice, but the more scholars write the worse things get. Each scholar produces good arguments for his or her position and good arguments against preceding positions; what none of them manages to do is to demolish the good arguments in favour of the alternatives. The present article plans only to balance one small pebble on top of this monstrous cairn. Unfortunately, that cannot be done without recapitulating yet once more the vexed state of the question.[5]

The Greek word *katharsis* is the noun from the verb *kathairein*, meaning 'to clean': it means 'cleansing,' and more specifically 'purgation' or 'purification.' Plato in his *Sophist* (226c ff.) offers us something like a formal definition of the word: *katharsis* is a general term applied to all forms of discrimination in which the good (to be kept) is separated from the bad (to be discarded). In living things, he goes on, there are two main forms of *katharsis*: ridding the body of impurities and weaknesses, and ridding the soul of vices and ignorance. At this point, Plato is taking us out of philology into his own darling doctrines, but the initial point holds generally. Bernays, in urging what is still the standard interpretation of Aristotle's *katharsis* clause, argued that if one spoke of *katharsis* without qualification one could only be taken as referring to one of two things: the removal of waste matter from the body by medical means, and the removal of pollution from the person of a criminal by ritual means. That Aristotle had the former of these in mind rather than the latter was shown by a passage in his *Politics* (1341b32 ff.) that describes the 'healing and cathartic' use of music to rid the mind of disturbance, and refers the reader to some writing on poetry for further explanation of what *katharsis* means. Of course the single clause in the *Poetics* does not amount to that promised explanation, but it seems perverse to interpret the *Poetics* in a way that goes against the *Politics* passage, especially since that passage explicitly mentions 'pity and fear.' Bernays accordingly took Aristotle to mean that by inducing pity and fear tragedy rids the spectator's or reader's mind of pity and fear by a sort of homeopathic therapy. Bernays and his followers point out that genitives after the word *katharsis* indicate, as Plato's definition would lead us to expect, what is got rid of rather than what is cleansed: the emotions are to be eliminated rather than cleansed, whatever Aristotle may have said in the *Ethics*.[7]

Bernays' followers tend to take the medical metaphor rather crassly – one of them goes so far as to say that 'Theoretically the *katharsis* might equally well be provoked by a dose of medicine.'[8] But, as Schaper reminds us, since a dramatic performance is neither a religious ritual nor a therapy session, the reference to *katharsis* must be metaphorical; and, as Ničev observes, all Aristotle says is that those who experience relief are '*as if* they came to healing and *katharsis*' (*hôsper iatreias tuchontas kai katharseôs*, 1342a10-11).[9] One could go further: the *Politics* passage as a whole, though contorted to the point of incoherence, seems explicitly to repudiate the suggestion that those who experience the *katharsis* in question are in any way sick. This is easily brought out in translation by a well-placed parenthesis and a judicious use of italics.

Since we accept the classification of tunes that some philosophers make, into 'ethical,' 'practical,' and 'ecstatic' ... and since we affirm that music is to be employed not for one benefit only but for several (for education, and also for *katharsis* – what we mean by *katharsis* we will now state simply, but will state more clearly later in our works on poetry – and thirdly for recreation, for relaxation and relief from tension), it is evident that all modes are to be used, but not all used in the same way: for education the most ethical are to be used, but when listening to others play the practical and ecstatic are to be used as well. For what happens violently in some personalities takes place in all – the difference is a matter of degree – pity and fear, for instance (and ecstasy as well: some people are victims of this kind of disturbance too, and we observe that such people, when they use music that arouses the soul to enthusiasm, are brought by the sacred tunes to a condition in which it is as if they came by healing and *katharsis*). It must be that just the same thing happens to people subject to pity and fear, as well, and in general to people subject to emotions, *and everyone else* to the extent that they are subject to such things, and a sort of *katharsis* comes to them, and a pleasurable unburdening. Similarly, too, practical tunes provide people with harmless pleasure.[10]

What the passage seems to say is that some people are brought by ecstasy-inducing music to a condition resembling healing and *katharsis*; that a similar quasi-*katharsis* and a 'pleasurable unburdening' must be produced by unspecified means for people especially susceptible to pity and fear; and that this latter pleasure and benefit is available to everyone in so far as they are subject to pity and fear. And that everyone is subject to pity and fear we may gather, if we were inclined to doubt it, from the *Rhetoric*.[11]

Everything now seems clear enough. Aristotle ends his definition of tragedy with a clause that specifies the psychological (or social) benefit that tragedy brings: it makes the audience happier (or more stable) by relieving them of the demoralizing feelings of pity and fear.[12] But G.F. Else celebrated the centenary of Bernays' initial publication by arguing that this interpretation of the *katharsis* clause is untenable.[13] The definition which the clause ends is expressly said to sum up the preceding discussion. But nothing in that discussion fits the interpretation Bernays and his followers proposed. Moreover, a key point of that discussion had been that tragedy, as a form of 'imitation,' gives pleasure through recognition. That seems to be what tragedy is for, an impression confirmed when we read later that 'One must seek from tragedy not every kind of pleasure but the pleasure proper to it. And since the poet has to provide the pleasure that is derived from pity and fear by imitation, it is plain that this must be embodied in the events' (*Poetics*, ch. 14, 1453b10-14). There is nothing here or anywhere else in the *Poetics* to suggest that it is the function of tragedy to provide a therapeutic purgation.[14] That interpretation, as Else says (231, note), fits the *Politics* but not the *Poetics*. It is reasonable to suppose that what Aristotle meant by the *katharsis* clause is something in line with the earlier and later statements referred to above, if the words will bear such an interpretation. Else argues with great erudition and force that they will and, therefore, must. What the clause actually says is '*dia* pity and fear effecting the *katharsis* of *pathemata* of that kind.' Everyone translates *pathemata* by some word like 'passions,' but the word can also mean 'distressing experiences' or 'incidents' (228-9).[15] *Dia*, usually rendered 'through,' need mean no more than 'in the course of' (229). The incidents 'of that kind' need not be 'of the pitiful and fearful kind' but could be 'of the kind specified in our description of tragedy,' that is, intra-familial murders and the like (229). And the *katharsis*, the 'cleansing' of the incidents, should be appropriate to their nature. Aristotle emphasizes that such murders are 'foul,' the technical term for what requires ritual purification (1453b39, 1454a3), so that the *katharsis* achieved could be analogous to the ritual purification a murderer must undergo (430-2). When we put all this together, we see how the *katharsis* clause can be taken as giving a succinct preview of how a tragic plot works. The plot achieves the purification of what would otherwise be a foul crime, its machinery of reversal and revelation absolving the hero (438): 'The spectator or reader of the play is the judge in whose sight the tragic act must be "purified", so that he may pity instead of execrating the doer' (437). Else recognizes that this interpretation leaves the *Politics* passage unexplained, but thinks that unimportant. No doubt Aristotle when he wrote the *Politics* passage expected that a theory of the kind Bernays favours could be worked out, but when he came to do serious work on the art of poetry found it unworkable (442-3).[16]

The apparent mismatch between the *Politics* promise and the *Poetics* fulfilment suggests that the earlier passage was written (as indeed its incoherence suggests) in a fit of ill-judged enthusiasm. What led Aristotle to do it? We would not expect to know; but, oddly enough, we are in a position to guess. We happen to know that Aristotle's colleague Aristoxenus wrote somewhere that the Pythagoreans 'employed *katharsis* of the body by means of medicine, and *katharsis* of the soul by means of music' (fragment 26 Wehrli); and Aristoxenus is surely the person alluded to in the *Politics* passage as 'fellow-workers in philosophy and musicology' on whose authority Aristotle relies (1342a31-2). What more likely than that Aristotle picked up this notion from his friend and inserted the remarks about *katharsis* in a passage previously written, foreseeing a way of defending tragedy against the attack of the notoriously Pythagoreanizing Plato?[17] The idea is attractive; but, since Aristotle himself wrote works on the Pythagoreans about whose contents we know little, it is purely speculative.

The weakest single point in Else's interpretation is the idea that events are freed from pollution by being ascribed to misunderstanding and error rather than vice. To treat the spectator's mind as a sort of law court is rather a far-fetched metaphor, and it would be absurd of Aristotle to expect his readers to gather from his text that this is what he had in mind. He actually mentions 'foul' actions only to contrast them with 'tragic' actions; if he meant us to understand that the two were dynamically related, why did he not say so? This weakness is avoided in an interpretation by Leon Golden which otherwise follows the direction pointed out by Else.[18] The key to his position is the contention that the Greek word *katharsis* can mean 'clarification' as well as 'cleansing.' When all the evidence is reviewed with this in mind, 'There is good reason to believe that tragic catharsis will emerge, convincingly, as that moment of insight and clarification toward which it is the essential nature of art to strive.'[19] What a tragedy does is present a clarification of events – the pleasure of recognition that a tragedy affords is that of understanding the universal relationships that its incidents exemplify. Since the end is pleasure, pity and fear are indeed eliminated (though this is not what *katharsis* means), not simply because they are displaced by the pleasure of learning (though Aristotle's words do leave that possibility open), but because our understanding of the relation between the hero's error and his destiny releases us from pity for undeserved suffering and from fear of arbitrary misfortune.[20]

The trouble with Else's and Golden's interpretations, especially as the latter is presented by Harbison, is that they are too good. They expound what we may agree Aristotle ought to have meant if the *Poetics* were to form a coherent whole and if Aristotle had the training and sensibility of a modern literary theorist. But they do not expound what an unprejudiced reader can find in the text. It is useless to prove that a Greek word might mean this or that: the question is what it can be taken to mean in the context in which we find it. And then we have to insist that *katharsis* means 'clarification' rather than what Plato says it means only in the context of Epicurean philosophy, which in Aristotle's day did not exist.[21] And though *pathêmata* can mean 'unpleasant experiences' it more often means passions, and since pity and fear, which are mentioned in the same clause, are certainly passions, it is hard to see how any reader could take *toioutôn pathêmatôn* to mean anything other than 'such passions.'[22] And although it is grammatically possible for a genitive after *katharsis* to refer to that which is purified, its usual reference is to that which is purged away, and in the absence of a context demanding otherwise that is how it should be taken.[23] And really, though the *katharsis* clause is not the explanation promised in the *Politics*, it is absurd to suppose that the clause does not hark back to that passage, in which we are told of a *katharsis* of pity and fear and promised further information about *katharsis* in some work on poetry.[24]

It is not enough to say that the *katharsis* clause cannot naturally be read as Else or Golden would read it. We have somehow to explain what they found inexplicable: the apparent presence, at a strategic point in a general theory of tragedy as a means to a cognitive pleasure, of a clause that reduces the tragic effect to mere emotional dynamics. It is this challenge that Ničev attempts to meet. He starts by supposing that Aristotle, in his attempt to rebut Plato, adopts (if only for dialectical reasons) many of the latter's positions. It is assumed, for instance, that the good are never to be pitied and (since the gods are just) a good man has nothing to fear (28-32). Tragedy leads the spectator or reader from ignorance to knowledge and, in doing so, first arouses and then eliminates pity and fear. But the *katharsis* that has this effect on the passions is in itself intellectual – it is one of the kinds of psychic *katharsis* named in the *Sophist*, namely, the removal of error and ignorance (*Sophist* 230A-E, Ničev, 160). The erroneous belief that is removed is that the hero is unworthy to suffer, and it is this belief that makes the audience pity him and fear for themselves (50-57). What the poet does is first move the spectator to pity and terror by making him believe falsely that the hero is innocent, then relieve him of pity and fear by disabusing him of this error (68-9).

One feels of Ničev's argument, as one does of Else's and Golden's, that it is what Aristotle ought to have meant. It is harder to believe that it is what he did mean, and impossible to believe that such a meaning can be traced to the words in the text. And it shares with Else's and Golden's interpretations the defect of allowing no weight to the actual pity and fear. Aristotle does after all say that it is essential that readers as well as spectators should *phrittein kai eleein*, 'shudder and be sorry' (1453b5); and why should that be, if the passion is a mere concomitant of an intellectual exercise?

At this point, one may concede that no interpretation of the *katharsis* clause is free from objections, and decide that one or other of the proposals makes the best of a hopeless situation. If the *Poetics* is not fully unified and not always explicit, that will not make it unique among Aristotle's works. But, unless one rejects the clause altogether, one is left with the question why Aristotle should have felt called on to introduce and retain the idea of *katharsis* in his definition when he did not feel called on to explain what he meant.[25] What is really puzzling is not the difficulty of finding an acceptable explanation; it is the presence of the inexplicable term. It is to the solution of this residual riddle that this essay is to contribute a suggestion.

The initial question is why Aristotle should have written an *Art of Poetry* at all, and why, in doing so, he should have paid special attention to the already moribund genre of tragedy.[26] The only plausible answer is the one usually given, that he wished to rebut Plato's attack on tragedy in *Republic*, Book 10, an attack that formed part of Plato's critique of the moral and intellectual bases of Greek institutions. Such a rebuttal would be in line with Aristotle's general policy of subverting Platonism from within, preserving its values while demolishing its other-worldly bias and thereby discrediting its denunciation of existing Greek practice. In ethics, this meant retaining Plato's ideal of the good life while denying that morality depends on philosophic insight; in metaphysics, it meant retaining the centrality of substantial forms while denying their separate existence; in epistemology, it meant retaining the deductive structure of sciences while denying their dependence on a single first principle. And in this last connection it is significant that whereas Plato contrasted the love of sights and sounds with the love of truth (*Republic* 475D-E, 476B) Aristotle uses delight in the senses as evidence for the universality of human love of knowledge (*Metaphysics* A, 980a20-1).

Plato's main objection to tragedy was that it lacked contact with 'truth' – that is, as the context shows, with the clarification of moral concepts. The *Poetics* as a whole can be taken as a many-sided response to that objection from a thinker who does not believe that such clarification can effectively be achieved by talking.[27] But the *katharsis* clause, as usually understood, responds to a specific charge within Plato's general polemic: that by their vicarious grief at tragic performances the spectators get into the habit of indulging their emotions, so that the effect of being emotionally moved in the theatre is to make one a more emotional and therefore a less rational person (*Republic* 605B-606D). The claim that through pity tragic imitation purges or purifies pity gives the lie direct to Plato's thesis that 'If one nurtures and strengthens one's pitying tendency in the affairs of others, it is not easy to restrain it in one's own misfortunes' (606B). Ničev (12) makes it an objection to Bernays' 'medical' interpretation of *katharsis* that a mere description of psychological effects could not rebut Plato's critique, which was made on moral grounds; but, whatever force that objection may have in relation to the overall tendency of Plato's arguments, it overlooks the point that on this specific issue Aristotle would be using one causal speculation to rebut another. That the account of the mental processes involved is merely psychological speculation is given by Harbison as a reason for not attributing it to Aristotle, for 'It will bear repeating that Aristotle is writing about the art of poetry, not psychology.'[28] But if the aim of poetry is to give pleasure to an audience the theorist of that art cannot ignore psychological facts about what gives pleasure. And one must distinguish between a bad theory and a theory Aristotle is unlikely to have held. Harbison can hardly deny that Aristotle is no less given than Plato to psychological speculation: the *Nicomachean Ethics* no less than the *Republic* is full of confident conjecture about the dynamics of psychic processes.

If the argumentative context of the *Poetics* is the Platonic critique of tragedy, a beneficial or deleterious change in the dynamics of emotional life is certainly an issue in that context. A quasi-medical interpretation of *katharsis* is thus not out of the question. Of course it could not be literally medical; the audience are not invalids undergoing treatment, not even moral invalids.[29] But, just because no literal purgation or purification, either ritual or medical, is going on, something in the wording of the *katharsis* clause should strike us as very odd. We would expect Aristotle to say something like *perainousa katharsin tina* ('carrying out a sort of *katharsis*') or simply *kathairousa* ('cleansing'). The words he does use, 'effecting *the katharsis* of such *pathemata*,' clearly imply that the *katharsis* alluded to is one that is familiar, or to be expected, or already mentioned.[30] But no *katharsis* has been mentioned in the *Poetics*, and neither of the established sorts is in point. Aristotle must be referring to something else. But what? And we might wonder, more mildly, just why Aristotle speaks of 'such passions' rather than of 'these passions'; for pity and fear simply are passions, and no other passions are mentioned or relevant in this context.[31]

If the context of the whole discussion is Platonic, the familiar *katharsis* implied by that intrusive definite article in Aristotle's definition is no doubt one mentioned by Plato – not in the *Republic* this time but in the *Phaedo*.[32] The passage in question is chapter 13 (68B-69E), the general theme of which is highly relevant to Aristotle's concern. Socrates is speaking of the vulgar 'virtue' whereby people are rendered brave by a cowardly fear of disgrace, and are temperate in their desires so that their desires can be best gratified in the long run. Such a trading off of emotion against emotion achieves only a semblance of virtue, whereas the true virtue is based on wisdom. What is especially significant for us is that the very words in which this true virtue is described seem to be echoed in the *katharsis* clause of the *Poetics*: it is said to be *katharsis tis ton toiouton panton*, 'a sort of *katharsis* of all such things' (69B9-10 Burnet); recollection of the phrase *katharsis tôn toioutôn* may account for Aristotle's section of the phrase *perainousa ten katharsin* as well as his use of *toiouton* rather than *toutôn*. Socrates does not mention pity in the immediate context, but fear is included in the antecedent of our phrase: *hêdonôn kai phobôn kai tôn allôn pantôn toioutôn*, 'pleasures and fears and all the things of that sort' (69B5-6). If Aristotle's *katharsis* clause was written with this passage in mind, the implication is that it is not through intellectual attainments that *katharsis* is brought to fear and the like. Plato's condemnation of the internal dialectic that he discerns operating in the demotic virtues is misplaced. It is, indeed, only through emotion that emotion is purified, only through fear that the *katharsis* of fear is effected. And it is tragedy that does it. It is as if Aristotle were saying in his *katharsis* clause, 'So far from tragedy being baneful because of its emotional effects, as Plato urged, those effects bring about the very *katharsis* that Plato himself called for.' Aristotle regularly assumes that his readers are as saturated with Platonic philosophy as he is himself; they would immediately grasp that 'the *katharsis* of such passions,' not further specified, was the *katharsis* on whose desirability Plato had insisted.

The verbal resemblance between the *katharsis* clause and the phrase in the *Phaedo* has not been overlooked by scholars, but most of them have brushed it aside as an 'unconscious reminiscence' as Bywater does (156, note 2). After all, as Golden points out (1969, 150), the separation called for in the *Phaedo* is that between soul and body, and that separation is unthinkable in Aristotle's philosophy. So what Plato wants cannot be what Aristotle has in mind. But that is misleading. The '*katharsis* of all such things' as pleasure and fear is not, as such, a separation of soul and body, but a change in the quality of life, the value of which lies in experience and does not depend on the metaphysics of soul and body. The change is that described by the poet Sophocles in the *Republic* 329C-D) when he says that the 'peace and freedom' brought by the cessation of physical desires in old age is like release from bondage to a tyrannical master, and echoed later (588C ff.) when Socrates likens the mind's emancipation from uncontrolled desire to a man's release from servitude to a savage beast; and in neither of those passages is the separation of soul from body an issue.

It is clear enough that the *Phaedo* '*katharsis* of all such things' means replacing a behavioural and motivational system based on the animal aspects of our nature by a system reflecting a fully human spirituality, but it is less clear what this involves. Plato is not precise in specifying what is included in the 'all that sort of thing' that is to be subjected to *katharsis*, or what sort of *katharsis* it is to undergo – whether it is to be purified or purged away; for although there are indeed a pleasure and fear and such that should be got rid of, the highest intellect has essential pleasures and fears of its own. And in considering Aristotle's attitude to this Platonic *katharsis* one should bear in mind that for both philosophers the ideal life is one of sublimated emotion, in which all desires and fears are shaped by reason.[33] To be purged of crude, unreasoned feeling is to have one's emotional life purified. What the two philosophers differ about is the kind of reason involved and, consequently, the dynamics of the relation between reason and passion.[34] If, then, Aristotle is referring in his *katharsis* clause to a *katharsis* that Plato vaguely and ambiguously describes and subjects to a misleading anthropology, it is not surprising that his own language should take on a similarly vague and ambiguous quality. He has nothing to gain by precision, since his intention is polemic: *katharsis* is not a word he uses in expounding his own ethical system.[35]

Else's critique of traditional readings of the *katharsis* clause rests on the supposition that we know what we would have expected to find in the place where that clause now stands. We would have expected a grammatically suitable version of what we read at 1453b12-13, 'the poet must provide pleasure from pity and fear by means of imitation.' We are free to conjecture, if we wish, that just such a clause once stood in the place where Aristotle, alerted perhaps by Aristoxenus to the Pythagorean doctrines and practices of purification, later saw the possibility of substituting a phrase that would signal more clearly the relevance of his account to Plato's indictment. And we may guess, with Else, that when he wrote the *Politics* he thought that when he came to write about poetry he would find more to say about how those subject to pity and fear could be 'pleasurably unburdened' than he eventually did. In the end, no doubt, the fact that spectators and readers of tragedies 'shudder and feel sorry' but find the whole experience both pleasurable while it is going on and the occasion of a sort of serenity when it is over is more evident than is the truth of any explanation one might offer of just how and why this should be. We would gladly agree with those commentators who say it must be something to do with the lucid structure of the plots whereby playwrights achieve their effects, though we may resist their claims to know what, if any, specific mode of 'clarification' is being invoked. And we would be reluctant to agree that the clarification or enlightenment *is* the *katharsis* (let alone that that is what the word *katharsis* means), bearing in mind that in the *Politics* (1341a23) *katharsis* and *mathesis*, 'purification' and 'enlightenment,' are contrasted to each other.

Earlier in this paper it was suggested that by inserting a reference to the *katharsis* of the spectator's or reader's emotions Aristotle was moving out of a discussion of the art of poetry into the domain of psychology or politics, or at best that he was ceasing to describe or explain tragedy and starting to justify it. But one could argue that without something like the *katharsis* clause the explanation of tragedy would be incomplete. People often complain that Aristotle's account does not fit all tragedies, nor even all extant Greek tragedies. But that is part of its point. At the heart of Greek theatrical experience is a very special kind of play with a very special kind of plot. It is this privileged specialness that needs explaining. Aristotle's general account of how pleasure can be taken in the representation of unpleasant things makes that pleasure no different from the pleasure we take in the representation of pleasant or indifferent things (1448b10-19). That explains how tragic plays among others could be written and enjoyed, but it does not explain how a genre of tragedy could be established, much less how that genre could become one of the best entrenched and most highly esteemed cultural institutions of a great city. There must be something special about the specific pleasure we take in the representation of tragic events, and that specialness must have something to do with the pity and terror they are calculated to evoke. Tragedy, having the very peculiar structure and range of subject matter that is preferred for it, must exist and be cherished because it bears some beneficial relation to emotions felt to be weakening, or threatening, or degrading, to individuals or to society. And without the *katharsis* clause Aristotle's account of tragedy would have nothing to say about that at all.

That tragedy would not be cultivated if it did not afford some kind of *katharsis* is certain, but it is not at all obvious what kind of *katharsis* it would have to be. It is not even obvious whether civic support for the institution reflects a feeling that it raises the morale of the citizenry and hence potentially of the citizen army by making them more sanguine, or only the recognition that the quality of life is being enhanced. Nor does the probability that the *katharsis* clause refers more directly than is usually supposed to the concerns expressed in the *Phaedo* bring the riddle of *katharsis* much closer to a solution. That is partly because there is no riddle. The fact that Aristotle's words can be explained in so many ways, all illuminating and none free from objection, does not leave us with the task of either determining which is correct or finding an even better explanation; rather, it shows that the text Aristotle wrote is inherently vague. We cannot say precisely what he meant because what he said has no precise meaning. It evokes a number of contexts and experiences without specifying any one or any set of them. Nor can we provide ourselves with a solvable conundrum by asking what Aristotle had in mind when he wrote, instead of asking what he meant by what he did write. The vagueness of what he wrote shows that he had nothing precise in mind. To have entertained precisely one of the possibilities that scholars have canvassed would have been to exclude the others; since Aristotle says nothing to exclude them he cannot have meant to exclude them, and therefore cannot have had in mind one *as opposed to* or *as distinct from* the others. What is fruitful is not to impose on Aristotle a distinction he did not make but to do what in effect the collaboration of scholarly exegesis over the centuries has achieved: to explore all the kinds of *katharsis* a fourth-century mind could have envisaged, and all the ways they might be involved in the structure and experience of what Aristotle thought of as tragedy. In so doing we will have charted the domain towards which Aristotle has pointed us and within which he seems to suggest (but does not actually say) that the cultural value of tragedy is to be found. But we should not suppose that Aristotle meant to guide us to a specific location within that domain.[36] He has told us, at most, that tragedy does (no doubt temporarily and superficially, but for everyone) the sort of thing that Plato hoped would be done (permanently and fundamentally, but for a few people) by a lifetime devoted to philosophy. That is all he has told us, and we have no reason to think he had anything else to tell us.

As controversies age, it takes longer and longer to say less and less. One is embarrassed to have provided so little sack with such an intolerable deal of bread. But, since this is a birthday party, the ending of this paper must be further delayed while a candle is lit for Northrop Frye's cake. Like most such candles, this one will be short, thin, twisted, cheap, tasteless, and easily extinguished, however colourful, and it will not shed much light.

What have Aristotle's remark on *katharsis* and its various interpretations to do with Frye? According to Frye's general theory of literature, it seems, the literature of a civilization enshrines the most important of its fables, articulating the most pervasive of its structures and the deepest of its concerns.[37] But instead of voicing those concerns directly the literature as a whole reconstructs them in an imaginative order to which each work bears a determinate relation and by the totality of which the world of experience may be judged and, as it were, redeemed. A comedy, for instance, whatever incidents it may contain, neither promotes nor warns against marriage but adds to the meaning of marriage, a meaning in the light of which all actual marriages assume the depth of significance and the complexity of relatedness that enables them to be recognized as ceremony and sacrament. This function is a *katharsis*, as that has to be understood in the *Phaedo* context: it is the substitution of a liberated and rational emotional life for one of inarticulate sentiment. But how is this *katharsis* to be brought about? Frye leaves us in the same doubt as Aristotle did. Is the reader of a romantic novel to interpret it by relating it to the structures that Frye describes? Surely not. It is the task of scientific criticism to determine what those structures are, and readers of romantic novels are not, as such, scholarly or scientific critics. The reader must be making a proper use of the romance if he or she simply responds to its events imaginative-ly rather than practically – but what is an imaginative response, if not one that refers the incidents to the imaginative universe of literature, a universe of whose organization, and hence of its status as a universe, we have just said that the reader as such must be supposed ignorant? Alternatively, if it is enough for the reader to respond 'imaginatively' rather than practically, in some way that does *not* involve explicit reference to the total order of literature as the critic knows it, what is the literary status of that order? Is it not thereby shown to be an artifact of scholarly speculation rather than the core of literary reality? The reader of Frye confronts here the same problem that besets interpreters of the *katharsis* clause: the more adequate an explanation is to a deep analysis of tragic structure, the less plausible it is as an account of what the ordinary reader or play-goer goes through.

Surely the reader of a romance, agonizing vicariously with the hero or heroine, is acting appropriately. Why, if not to move the reader, did the author write movingly of moving incidents? The audience of a tragedy, we recall, are to 'shudder and be sorry,' and Euripides is the 'most tragic' of playwrights, not because his plots are the most lucid or clarifying, but because his incidents are the most affecting (*Poetics* 1453a29-30). But how exactly is this essential emotional response related to the purgation or purification that is postulated? Or, in Frye's case, what is the relation between one's specific response to the specific persons and incidents in the specific passage of the work one is reading and the general dynamics of the imagination? What grounds are there for claiming that what is really going on is an imaginative transformation or sublimation, or a spiritually or socially beneficial purification or purgation, rather than an immediate surrogate response whose significance and effects are as transitory as they are immediate? It is as hard to find a clear and cogent response to such sceptical questions in Frye as it is in Aristotle.

Let us suppose that the kathartic effect in Aristotle, or the imaginative transformation in Frye, whatever each of them may be, has been effected. How does this transformation affect the quality of our lives? It seems idle to claim that the imaginative world gives form to the world of social reality, the understanding of which must shape our actions. For the Aristotle of the *Ethics*, it is only by social behaviour that social behaviour can be modified, and the passions can be educated only within the world of social experience – he would not be surprised to hear of people who combined exquisite literary sensibility with social and professional callousness. And Frye leaves one with the question raised by Don Quixote. The imaginative world of literature can add resonance to social relationships only if it is on the same wavelength; otherwise what it articulates is an alternative or a merely fanciful world.[38] Frye's phrase 'myth of concern,' which appears to be designed to undercut the suspicion that social relationships might have a shape that does not depend on literature for its articulation, is (like Aristotle's *tên ton toioutôn pathêmatôn katharsin*) no more than a string of words until we are told clearly and unequivocally both what it means and how that meaning is earned.[39]

Aristotle, according to Bernays and his followers, sought to give his theory of the dynamics of literary experience an adventitious authority by invoking the speculative medicine of his day, which ascribed diseases and personality disorders as well as fits of passion to temporary excesses of this or that body fluid which accordingly needed to be purged away. Similarly, Frye's policy of referring literary forms to archetypal structures of which the reader is unaware seems to gain authority from the speculative psychology of the decades in which his theory was coming to fruition – specifically, the theories of Jung, still popular with literary folk though not with scientists. But in this respect Frye has been shrewder than Aristotle. He has repudiated the support of questionable science in the name of literary autonomy. So far from literature mirroring the structure of the 'collective unconscious,' the latter is a needless fiction devised to account for literary reality. In taking this step, however, Frye has taken an enormous risk, for without the support of Jung his theory has no support at all. A good theory, indeed, needs no support but is a support for others. But is Frye's theory good enough for that? Not without some very firm and persuasive answers to such questions as we have raised about the relationships between the structures Frye discerns and the particularities of the works that allegedly exemplify them, on the one hand, and the dynamics of social experience on the other.

The weakness of Frye's theory is its strength. It is that, like Aristotle's theory of *katharsis*, after raising directly and in a way that challenges by its tantalizing approximation to explicitness the most central and serious problems about our engagement with literature, it ends by frustrating every attempt to understand how it proposes to solve them. That is the strength of both theorists because a profound question cannot have a straightforward and satisfying answer.[40] The answer, like the moral *katharsis* Plato invoked in the *Phaedo*, must take the form of a transformation in the quality of our thinking and feeling. The best theories, in the long run, are those that by their well-placed vaguenesses and artful ambiguities lure us on to effect such a transformation.

NOTES

1 Aristotle, *Poetics*, ch. 6, 1449b22-8. All citations from Plato and Aristotle rely on editions in the Oxford Classical Texts and are translated by the author.

2 The uncle was Jacob Bernays, author of *Zwei Abhandlungen über die Aristotelische Theorie des Dramas* (Berlin, 1880). His influence on Freud is noted by Frank J. Sulloway, *Freud: Biologist of the Mind* (New York, 1979), 56-7.

3 According to Eduard Zeller, *Aristotle and the Earlier Peripatetics*, trans. B.F.C. Costelloe and J.H. Muirhead (London, 1897), II, 310, n. 3, Goethe thought it was the actors who were affected, but was alone in this view. One suspects that Zeller, here and in the following note, relies on the authority of Bernays, but in that case he is mistaken, for Bernays represents Goethe as protesting against saddling Aristotle with the foolish notion that tragedy has anything to do with the moral welfare of anyone (Bernays, 4).

4 Zeller (n. 4) says this view was universally held up to Lessing's time. But Ingram Bywater points out that Milton's preface to *Samson Agonistes* interprets the passage in the light of homeopathic medicine, and traces this 'medical' interpretation back to Italian scholarship of the early sixteenth century ('Milton and the Aristotelian Definition of Tragedy,'

*Journal of Philology*, 27 [1901], 267-75). Zeller and Bywater between them provide a useful survey of early interpretations of the *katharsis* clause.

5 No one source offers a full conspectus of the literature. Gerald F. Else, *Aristotle's Poetics: The Argument* (Cambridge, 1957), 225, n. 14, affords a bibliography of bibliographies. For reviews of the controversy, see Pedro Laín Entralgo, *The Therapy of the Word in Classical Antiquity*, trans. L.J. Rather and John M. Sharp (New Haven, 1970), 171-239; Alexandre Ničev, *L'Enigme de la catharsis tragique dans Aristote* (Sofia, 1970); and Leon Golden, 'The Clarification Theory of Catharsis,' *Hermes*, 104 (1976), 437-50. Each of these works invokes a rather different scholarly ancestry.

6 Laín Entralgo finds five meanings of the word *katharsis* in Plato: literal cleansing or purifying of dirty or adulterated things and substances; the religious purification of those who have incurred pollution or who are to enter upon some special status of enlightenment or redemption; medical purgation; the freeing of the mind from the body; and the complex ethical-medical-psychological '*katharsis* of mankind' such as is punningly attributed to the god Apollo at *Cratylus* 405A-B. But these are plainly not five different senses of the word to be set alongside that defined in the *Sophist*; they are different kinds or occasions of *katharsis* as the *Sophist* defines it.

7 Bernays. His essay on *katharsis* is translated by Jonathan and Jennifer Barnes as 'Aristotle on the Effect of Tragedy,' in *Articles on Aristotle*, 4: *Psychology and Aesthetics*, ed. Jonathan Barnes, Malcolm Schofield, and Richard Sorabji (London, 1979), 154-65. My citations are from this source, but use the 1880 pagination, which the translators give in the margin. Bernays' main contribution was to emphasize the *Politics* passage and to attend closely to the diction of the *katharsis* clause. Supporting evidence about the underlying theory of medicine was supplied by Ingram Bywater, *Aristotle on the Art of Poetry* (Oxford, 1909), and Hellmut Flashar, 'Die medizinischen Grundlagen der Lehre von der Wirkung der Dichtung in der griechischen Poetik,' *Hermes*, 84 (1956), 12-48. Flashar provides evidence for a psychophysical interpretation of pity and fear in Plato (18-26) as well as in Aristotle (36-47), and illustrates from the Hippocratic Corpus the practice of interpreting emotions as symptoms of physiological disorders.

8 D.W. Lucas, *Aristotle: Poetics* (Oxford, 1968), 285.

9 Eva Schaper, *Prelude to Aesthetics* (London, 1968), 103; Ničev, 7-8. But the metaphorical nature of the allusion to *katharsis* is essential to Bernays' original argument. It is because the word *hôsper* shows that *katharsis* is meant metaphorically that the latter has to be taken in a sense that is

both definite and concrete – otherwise there is no metaphor; and the only such senses available are those of religious purification and medical purgation. Of these two, it must be the latter that is meant, because it is familiar and well understood; religious purifications are too mysterious to explain anything (12-13). Bernays does, however, say that the standpoint of the *Politics*, and therefore of the *Poetics*, is 'neither moral nor purely hedonistic: it is a *pathological* standpoint' (10), and it is to this residual literalism that Schaper and Ničev demur.

10 Aristotle, *Politics* 8, ch. 7, 1341b32-1342a16. The reference to 'practical' tunes in the last sentence is Sauppe's conjectural emendation (accepted by Ross) of *praktika* for *kathartika*. This must be right, because the reference must go back to the threefold classification introduced at the beginning of the passage quoted, and the continuation goes on to speak of *anapausis*, 'relaxation' (1342a22), which was the benefit to be derived from 'practical' tunes according to that classification. This is important, because belief that the reference is to 'kathartic' tunes has encouraged interpreters to read the continuation as still concerned with the *katharsis* of pity and fear and hence with tragedy. Bernays, for instance, reading 'kathartic tunes,' continues his citation to 1342a27, and assumes that the passage about such tunes applies to drama. This is clearly mistaken; Aristotle is talking about musical performances given in public before large audiences.

11 Cf. *Rhetoric* 2, ch. 5, 1383a8-12: 'When it is better for one's audience to be frightened, one must put them in the frame of mind that they are the kind of people likely to suffer (for others better then they have suffered), and remind them of people like them who are suffering or have suffered, at the hands of the sort of people from whom they did not foresee it, things unforeseen at unforeseen times'; and compare ch. 8, 1386a1-3, on pity. These chapters on pity and fear are useful background for the *Poetics*. Note that Aristotle does not think of pity as primarily an other-directed emotion, as we tend to do and as Lessing did, who called it a 'philanthropic emotion' (cf. Bernays, 2): 'Let pity be a kind of distress at an evident evil of a destructive or distressful sort that overtakes someone who does not deserve it, such as one might expect oneself or someone related to one to suffer, when it is close at hand' (1385b13-16), the distress clearly being occasioned not by sorrow on the other's behalf but by the reminder of one's own vulnerability. What the Greek words for 'pity' and 'fear' (*eleos* and *phobos*) actually meant is exhaustively discussed by Wolfgang Schadewaldt, 'Furcht und Mitleid?' *Hermes*, 83 (1955), 129-71.

12 Lucas (273) says that 'When tragedy is defined in chapter 6, its end or

purpose is affirmed to be the *katharsis* of the emotions.' But Aristotle does not say that this is its function; he only says that it has this effect. Similarly, Golden argues that the *katharsis* clause must define the end of tragedy, because a definition of the nature of tragedy could not but reach a climax by specifying its end or function (443). But K.G. Srivastava points out that Aristotle says quite explicitly that 'The events and the story are the end of the tragedy, and the end is the most important of all (1450a22-3)' ('A New Look at the "Katharsis" Clause of Aristotle's Poetics,' *British Journal of Aesthetics*, 12 [1972], 258-75, p. 265). *Katharsis* cannot, then, be the end in a strict sense.

13 Else. Although Bernays' views on *katharsis* became notorious with their republication in 1880, his article had previously appeared as *Grundzüge der verlorenen Abhandlung des Aristoteles über die Wirkung der Tragödie* (Breslau, 1857).

14 Schaper argues that the *katharsis* clause is no part of the definition but is merely appended to it (70); but this strikes one as a mere evasion. And if one argues that the achievement of *katharsis* is not mentioned elsewhere in the *Poetics* because it is not an integral part of the art of tragedy but only the external reason why such an art should be fostered in cities, one is open to the objection that nothing in the text suggests that Aristotle had any such distinction in mind, and that, if he had, he was acting very strangely in adverting to such extraneous considerations in the context of his definition rather than in some appropriately peripheral part of his treatment. *Katharsis* may not be the 'end,' but Golden is right to insist that its place at the end of the definition gives it a central importance.

15 Else is able to cite Aristotle's own use of the word in this sense in the *Poetics* itself, at 1459b11 (and of *pathos* in the same sense at 1452b11; Aristotle seems to use *pathos* and *pathêma* as exact synonyms). Else says disarmingly that this shows that the *katharsis* clause is a later insertion in a text in which this passage already stood, for without this other use no one would ever have been able to guess that *pathêmatôn* in the *katharsis* clause meant anything other than 'passions.'

16 Else did not really need to make this concession. When one considers how little is explicitly stated about the *katharsis* of pity and fear in the *Politics* passage, it seems quite reasonable to take the whole description of tragic plots in the *Poetics* as the 'fuller statement' the *Politics* promised.

17 Willy Theiler, who makes this suggestion (*Untersuchungen zur antiken Literatur* [Berlin, 1970], 301), attributes it to G. Finsler, *Platon und aristotelische Poetik* (Leipzig, 1900), 120, but with excessive generosity; Finsler says nothing of the kind.

18 Leon Golden, 'Catharsis,' *Transactions of the American Philological As-sociation*, 93 (1962), 51-60, '"Mimesis" and "Katharsis,"' *Classical Philol-ogy*, 64 (1969), 145-53, 'The Purgation Theory of Catharsis,' *Journal of Aesthetics and Art Criticism*, 31 (1973), 473-9, and the *Hermes* article cited in n. 5; these will be cited hereafter by name and date. Golden's theory is also endorsed and expounded by Harbison in *Aristotle's Poetics: A Transla-tion and Commentary for Students of Literature*, trans. Leon Golden, comm. O.B. Harbison, Jr (Englewood Cliffs, 1968).

19 Golden 1973, 478. The reference to the striving of the essential nature of art is hardly Aristotelian in spirit; it represents an anachronistic high-minded-ness about Art that seriously detracts from the clarity and credibility of many interpretations of the *katharsis* clause, including that in J.G. War-ry's *Greek Aesthetic Theory* (London, 1962), ch. 7, which ends by saying that 'Our common experience, even where this is itself painful, must be elevated by association with other, more exalted elements. We are thus induced to accept tragic suffering for the sake of its dignity. In doing so we are temporarily reconciled to the worst that life can do to us, and this is the essence of poetic catharsis' (135).

20 Harbison, 116-19. This is the most explicit account of Golden's position, Golden's own articles being largely preoccupied with the scholarly evid-ence; but it is not clear whether Harbison has his mentor's authority for every detail of his exposition.

21 Golden's direct evidence that *katharsis* can mean 'clarification' is confined to two citations in Liddell and Scott's *Lexicon*, one from Epicurus and the other from the Epicurean Philodemus. Indirectly, he appeals to the general tendency of Plato's discussion in the *Phaedo* and the *Sophist*, and to the fact that the adverb *katharôs* means 'clearly' when used with verbs of knowledge (especially *gnônai* – Golden 1962, 56-7). But the idiomatic use of *katharôs* tells us nothing about the use of the noun *katharsis*, Plato's descriptions of this or that kind of *katharsis* do not prescribe a general meaning for the word *katharsis* itself, and Epicurus' oddities of usage are not binding on his predecessors.

In general, the method of interpreting a text by cobbling together dictionary entries for the words it contains is to be used with caution. One might, for instance, argue that because a 'piece' in English slang can be a young woman, and an 'eight' can be a racing shell, Long John Silver's parrot was taught to say 'pieces of eight' (note the nautical connection) by someone who lusted after female athletes.

22 Ničev is content to dismiss Else's thesis in a footnote, p. 36. Rage, pity, and fear are listed as paradigms of passions in the *Rhetoric*, 1378a21.

23 Ničev piles up the evidence for this point, 34-5. But there is something to be said for Schaper's contention that we can only be sure that the genitive is separative if we are already certain that *katharsis* is being construed as a sort of purgation rather than a purification (103). If we say, for instance, that when Plato speaks in the *Timaeus* (52E) of the *katharsis* of grain it is obvious from the context that he is not using the genitive separatively, that is only another way of saying that the *katharsis* in question is not a purgation.

24 Like many other scholars, Golden argues that it is a 'grave methodological error' to interpret the *Poetics* in the light of the *Politics* because the two works belong to different disciplines and must proceed from different first principles. 'There is every reason to believe that the two discussions of art have nothing to do with each other,' he says (1973, 474-5), invoking the authority of Richard McKeon. But Aristotle was not a Chicago Aristotelian; the *Politics* passage explicitly refers the reader to a work on poetry for further explanation of what is said about *katharsis*, and his works abound in cross-references from one work to another. His works are not, in fact, scientific treatises in the strict sense, and do not proceed from 'first principles,' at all: an axiomatized *Poetics* and an axiomatized *Politics* would no doubt be mutually unconnected, but that is not what Aristotle wrote.

25 Some scholars have, in fact, rejected the clause altogether. Antonio Freire, for instance, follows M.D. Petruševski in suggesting that the text originally read not *pathêmatôn katharsin*, 'purging of passions,' but *pragmatôn sustasin*, 'composition of events,' a phrase Aristotle uses at 1450a15 and elsewhere ('A catarse trágica em Aristoteles,' *Euphrosyne*, 3 [1969], 31-45). And so, of course, it may have done, but there is no reason to think it actually did. It is amusing, in this connection, to reflect that the manuscript which is our best authority for the Greek text actually read not *pathêmatôn* ('passions') but *mathêmatôn* ('items of knowledge'), but this reading has won little acceptance.

26 One can always argue that he did not, that he wrote or intended to write at equal length on comedy. Lane Cooper even thought he had found traces of this lost treatment in a wretched thing called *Tractatus Coislinianus* (*An Aristotelian Theory of Comedy* [New York, 1922]). That the *Poetics* as we have it is incomplete is not in doubt.

27 The very fact that the *Poetics* is announced as a comprehensive handbook on poetry (1447a11-12) may be taken as a rebuke to Plato's offhand separation of formal from substantive aspects of poetry (*Republic* 10, 601B and 607D), a separation that is crucial to Plato's refusal to consider whether poetry has any specific function.

28 P. 137. But Aristotle's promise to consider what *dunamis* ('power') each kind of poetry has might be construed as proposing to take psychological considerations into account. We cannot be certain a priori what a work on poetry should include or exclude; the *Rhetoric*, for instance, has to contain a lot of psychological material, because orators have to persuade people, and the *Poetics* certainly seems to have a lot to say about how plays affect audiences. Possibly Harbison is influenced by the idea, once current, that the *Poetics* belongs to an established genre, the *techne* or technical handbook, which had strict canons governing what could or could not be included. But there is no evidence that any such genre existed, much less that Aristotle was aware of such a genre, and the opening sentence of the *Poetics* announces a discussion that will be comprehensive rather than narrowly professional.

29 Modern protests against the crassness of an interpretation that would make the audience moral invalids may reflect the feeling that a disease is a recognizable, intrusive entity, rather than the difference between health and sickness being merely quantitative as Aristotle says. For this difference in attitudes to medicine see Michel Foucault, *Birth of the Clinic* (New York, 1973). We have seen (n. 4) that Milton did not feel that a 'medical' explanation was beneath the dignity of poetry.

On the issue of the moral 'health' of people in general, Aristotle was more of a Platonist than is commonly allowed. Although he did not share Plato's view that cities need philosopher-kings to maintain their moral equilibrium, he also did not think that equilibrium is sustained by the spontaneously self-perpetuating moral sense of the citizens: the neglected final chapter of the *Nicomachean Ethics* insists that the populace must be kept in line by the enforced rule of law. And the continuation of the *Politics* passage says of manual labourers, serfs, and similar unfree persons that 'their minds are, as it were, perverted from their natural condition' (1342a22-3). Presumably the majority of any city's population, and hence of potential theatre-goers, would fall into that category.

30 Aristotle's definition of tragedy is notably short of definite articles. There are only four. Two belong to the 'kinds' and 'parts' of tragedy, which have been mentioned before; a third belongs to the *pathêmata*, which have just been referred to. The only one that dangles is the one with *kartharsin*. It cannot just be shrugged off.

31 The wonder in this instance is mild, because one can easily think of explanations, most of them not very interesting. Bernays has a good one: 'The words *tôn toioutôn pathêmatôn* in our definition continue the sentence by picking up (and subjecting to adjectival transformation) the two preceding nouns *eleos kai phobos*; and they do absolutely nothing else. *Tôn*

*toioutôn pathêmatôn* simply means *eleêtikôn kai phobêtikôn pathêmatôn'* (29). He goes on to say that Aristotle says *toioutôn,* 'such,' rather
than *toutôn,* 'these,' because *eleos* and *phobos* are occurrent emotions
and not 'lasting affections,' which is what *pathêmata* are (30). But in fact
the distinction between *pathos* and *pathêma* seems not to be observed by
Aristotle – see the respective entries in Bonitz' *Index Aristotelicus.*

32 The *Phaedo* is one of the few dialogues Aristotle mentions by name (at
*Metaphysics* 991b3 and 1080a2 and at *Coming to Be and Passing Away*
335b10).

33 There is a sense in which fear is inevitably shaped by reason. It is defined as
'a sort of distress or disturbance arising from the imagination of an imminent evil that will be destructive or distressing' (*Rhetoric* 2, ch. 5,
1382a21-2), and such imagination depends on the judgment that whatever
it is is imminent, evil, and destructive or distressing. Judgment and feeling obviously determine each other (for an exploration of this theme see
W.W. Fortenbaugh, *Aristotle on Emotion* [London, 1975]). But reason
can be involved in a quite different way, by subjecting one's imagination to
more considered judgments about what is to be considered evil and destructive.

34 Although Plato's view of life depends on ascribing to the intellect pleasures and desires of its own, he regularly clouds the issue by speaking in
terms that contrast intellect with desire. It is because this leads to gross
confusion that Aristotle rejects out of hand the compartmentalizing of psychic functions into 'reason' and 'passions' (cf. *De Anima* 432b4-7).

35 Bernays thinks otherwise. 'Aristotle,' he says, 'we may safely say, intended
by catharsis some definite thing,' for the word 'is after all an aesthetic
term of his own invention' (5-6). But it is not clear in what sense the word
is 'an aesthetic term.' We can indeed be sure that Aristotle had something specific in mind, but that does not rule out a specific reference to a
vague discussion. Bernays says nothing of the Platonic antecedents of the
term.

36 Laín Entralgo argues that the tragic *katharsis* involves a threefold process
akin to that suggested in Plato's *Cratylus* (see n. 6 above): a psychophysical purgation of the humours induced by a workout of the passions, accompanied by an intellectual transformation, the whole amounting to a
pleasurable and complex 'existential transition – dianoetic, affective, and
physical at one and the same time – from confusion and disorder to
well-ordered enlightenment' (236). Something like this must indeed be
going on, but it is not clear that Aristotle had all of it in mind at any one
time, and he certainly never said anything from which it could be legiti-

mately inferred. (The word 'existential' is purely decorative, by the way –
Laín Entralgo uses it to show that he has read Heidegger, in the same
spirit that Winnebago drivers use bumper stickers to show that they have
visited Disneyland.)

37 I have stated how I understand Frye's theory of literature in 'Frye in Place,'
*Canadian Literature*, 83 (1979), 143-55, pp. 149-50. The present recapitula-
tion does not pretend to accuracy – let it fit where it may touch. If the recap
does not fit, it need not be worn.

38 Frye's deep conservatism in educational matters goes with his literary
theory. An adversary would say that ancient literatures are to be studied
not because what they imaginatively order is basic, but because it is
past.

39 It is only fair to point out that Frye has an effective way of rebutting such
objections. He simply identifies them as examples of this or that literary
trope, which he characterizes so tellingly that it is idle to protest that he
has invented the alleged trope for the occasion. Thus, in attempting to
argue that literature is after all contained within reality, one discovers that
one's argument is after all only a form of literature.

40 It is related that two philosophers, Elizabeth Anscombe and Geoffrey Warnock, were once engaged in public discussion. 'The question is,' said
Anscombe, and went on with much wringing of hands and searching of soul
to say what the question was. 'That's simple enough,' said Warnock, 'the
answer is – ' and he said what the answer was. 'Yes!' cried Anscombe in a
voice of agony; 'That's just the trouble: that *is* the *answer!!*'

PATRICIA
PARKER

# Anagogic Metaphor: Breaking Down the Wall of Partition

In the *Anatomy of Criticism*, Frye distinguishes five types or under-standings of metaphor: literal (simple juxtaposition: 'A;B'), descriptive (metaphor as implied simile: 'A is like B'), formal (metaphor as a condensed analogy: 'A is as B'), archetypal (the identity of an individual with its class), and finally anagogic, the radical or copular form ('A *is* B') which in sexual symbolism takes the form of the 'one flesh' of marriage, the 'metaphor of two bodies made into the same body by love,' and which in the Glossary is identified with 'apocalyptic' ('metaphor as pure and potentially total identification, without regard to plausibility or ordinary experience'). Both in the *Anatomy* and in *Fables of Identity*, Frye illustrates this copular or anagogic metaphor with reference to Shakespeare's *The Phoenix and the Turtle* and its anagogic world 'above time,' in which the lover and beloved are 'identified.'[1]

This poem's 'twain' made 'one' evokes both the 'one flesh' of the marriage ceremony and the mysterious joining of the Incarnation as the definitive 'Copula' (which Nicholas Udall calls 'The wonderful copula-cion of the sayd nature unto ours'). But it also evokes a joining which involves a breaking down – the removal of dividing walls through the Cross (Ephesians 2:14-15, 'For he is our peace, who hath made both one, and hath broken down the middle wall of partition between us ... for to make in himself of twain one new man').[2] In the passage from Ephesians, the architectural image of walls and their removal in the new house of the Lord is combined with the image of the body in which the two become one. 'Breaking down the wall of partition' between citizen Jew and 'alien' Gentile here (Eph. 2:12) joins the rending of the veil of the temple as a radical crossing or abolition of boundaries; and both link the Crucifixion to the anagogy it figures, the final apocalyptic removal of partition walls.[3] The discussion which follows, then, is an exploration of the connection between anagogic or copular metaphor and the breaking down of partition walls in four literary texts: first, by way of introduction, in *The Phoenix and the Turtle* itself; then, though in different ways, in two Shakespearean comedies – *The Comedy of Errors* and *A Midsummer Night's Dream* – in which an echo of Ephesians and its 'wall' appear; and finally in a crucial passage from Emily Brontë's *Wuthering Heights*.

In *The Phoenix and the Turtle*, Reason gives up when confronted with a radical joining or copula, the 'A equals not A' of metaphor which Frye insists is the basis of poetry, an aberrant coupling or twain-made-one which outrages the boundaries of both Reason and Property:

Property was thus appalled
That the self was not the same;
Single nature's double name
Neither two nor one was called.

Reason, in itself confounded,
Saw division grow together,
To themselves yet either neither,
Simple were so well compounded:

That it cried, How true a twain
Seemeth this concordant one!
Love hath reason, reason none,
If what parts, can so remain.[4]

The mysterious joining here recalls simultaneously the copula of the Incarnation and of the Cross, a sexual consummation which is also a death, the hermaphroditic 'one flesh' of both the Christian and the alchemical *coniunctio*, and the *mysterion* of the Trinity, a doctrine which, as Frye remarks (142), exemplifies 'a few of the difficulties in extending metaphor to logic.' The union which confounds 'division' (42,27) and 'property' – in the sense both of individual and of social enclosure – is presented from the perspective of what it transgresses, in lines whose puns pose the same outrage to property and place as the two-in-one of copular metaphor, defined classically as a crossing of boundary lines.[5]

The punning 'parts' in this poem ('If what parts can so remain') suggests both 'parting' and 'division into parts,' including the parts to be played by the procession of mourners summoned as Chorus to what, from Reason's perspective, is a 'tragic scene' (52). The form of the poem itself, however, is so elaborately processional that it begins to suggest that its own linear movement is one of the ordering structures of Reason and Property, a response to a radical union which has left them 'confounded' or 'appalled.' The poem's apocalyptic echoes suggest a union opposed to the purely sequential, to progression by neatly separable stages or stanzas from one part to the next. But the relentless staging of its 'scene' begins to give the opening summons a sense of theatricality or staginess and Reason's uncomprehending tragic Chorus more than a hint of the histrionic, of an understanding literally confounded by the effort to express in the syntax of logic a union which transgresses both logic and syntax. Reason's closing threnody arises indeed as a direct response to its earlier confounding ('*Whereupon* it made this Threne,' 49), a fact which suggests that its *threnos* is also a means of recuperation, a shifting from the threat of the death of Property and Number ('Number there in love was slain') to a conventional lament over the death of the lovers. The *threnos* is thus a 'closure device' not only because it closes off a sequence[6] but because it smooths out the earlier indigestible language of punning and paradox into the classical simplicity of a recognizable genre, with the finality and authority of an 'is' which now appears to be that of a definitive statement, a copular which Reason not only understands but habitually employs:

> Beauty, truth and rarity,
> Grace in all simplicity,
> Here enclos'd, in cinders lie.
>
> Death is now the Phoenix' nest,
> And the Turtle's loyal breast
> To eternity doth rest ...                    (53-8)

The union of Phoenix and Turtle is nowhere placeable within the processional structure of the poem and is everywhere in tension with it, exposing the structure itself as a structuring, as a means of retranslating a union which threatens boundaries back into the language of property and place. The processional 'requiem' (16) also suggests a liturgical event – the drama of the Cross which rends the veil of the temple and breaks down the partition wall; and this further resonance gives to the concluding *threnos* the ironic incompleteness of a Good Friday lament, a premature closure in which 'Death' appears as a definitive and final boundary line. Yet even this liturgical structure involves an accommodation of the simultaneous to the processional, to a temporal movement *from* Crucifixion *to* Resurrection – events which, in metaphor, might be one. Accommodation to the partitions of Reason and Property thus also reflects the accommodated time and space of Creation itself, which in Genesis takes the processional form of a hexameron, a spacing or *espacement* of the simultaneous which proceeds by the fiats of division and separation recalled in this poem's opening lines.

'Partition' and 'division' are in this respect part of the syntax of history, the sequential order before the anagogic end or 'period' of time, the apocalyptic 'point,' as in Augustine (*Confessions* IV.10), of God's sentence. But 'breaking down the wall of partition' in Ephesians and the anagogy its Cross and crossing anticipate are also connected elsewhere in Shakespeare with 'partition' in other senses – including the partition or division of a discourse into stages from beginning to end. 'Partition,' according to the OED, includes in its definition dividing a whole into its parts or separating into sides (*Cymbeline* I.vi.36-8, 'can we not / Partition make ... / 'Twixt fair, and foul?'); the dividing wall itself and each separate section, including the parts of a discourse and the stages of time; the division of real property; the scoring, in music, of 'parts'; and the division of a shield (an heraldic meaning precisely used in Helena's 'union in partition' speech in *A Midsummer Night's Dream*). The specifically rhetorical meaning of 'partition' which Demetrius puns on in this same play (calling 'Wall' the 'wittiest partition that ever I heard discourse') comes from the part of Cicero's *Topics* where a discussion of physical 'walls' is juxtaposed with a definition of oratorical 'partition,' the dividing of a discourse, like a body, into its parts or members. This definition is reflected, for example, in Burton's *Anatomy of Melancholy* with its multiplied 'Partitions' and 'Members' and its intellectualized dissection of a vast body of material – described with deadpan humour by Frye (311) as characteristic of the 'Anatomy' form both he and Burton share – and is exploited by Shakespeare in the comic partition of Falstaff's great body in *2 Henry IV*. 'Partition' in Quintilian is both a section stating the parts into which the discourse is to be divided – enumerating the parts ('first,' 'then,' 'finally') and seeking to avoid tedium by projecting the end from the beginning – and the sequential organization itself. But even more important, in the rhetorical tradition stretching from Cicero and Quintilian to the Renaissance handbooks and beyond, the 'partition' or 'division' of a discourse is a principal means of its dilation or amplification. John Hoskins in his influential *Direccions for Speech and Style* (1599) quotes the well-known rule that 'a way to amplify anything ... is to breake it & make an Anatomie of it into severall parts.' In the related art of preaching, the principal method of proceeding was to divide the scriptural text or theme into parts which could then be dilated upon so as to spread abroad (*dilatare*) the Word. Through 'partition' or 'division,' to quote Donne, the 'Word of God is made a Sermon, that is, a Text is dilated, diffused into a Sermon'; and this rhetorical dilation by division was to be used by preachers of the Word in the period of the 'dilation of the Kingdom' before Apocalypse, before the final anagogic end of 'partition' and of discourse.[7]

What follows, then, has a dual purpose. First, to suggest the tension between anagogic metaphor and a structuring which proceeds by partition, by division into separate parts. Second, to examine in detail three texts in which a specifically rhetorical 'partition' combines with an echo of Ephesians' 'partition wall': *A Comedy of Errors* and *A Midsummer Night's Dream*, in which the deferral (or, in Elizabethan usage, 'dilation') of ending entails the preservation of 'partition,' and *Wuthering Heights*, a text in which the 'one flesh' of radical, copular metaphor involves a simultaneity or joining as repugnant to reason and property as that of *The Phoenix and the Turtle* and in which the adoption of a linear or sequential form is also part of the recuperation of reason, a placing of partitions or walls against something which threatens to obliterate them.

The Epistle to the Ephesians, with its breaking down of the wall of partition, is itself in many respects the 'Joshua' book of the New Testament, all Recognition Scene. Yet though the wall is down between Gentile and Jew, the final anagogic removal of partition walls is deferred, leaving an interim or middle period which the rest of the Epistle treats in its counsels to 'patience' and 'forbearance' before the Master's return. If the hermaphroditic 'one flesh' of marriage (Eph. 5:31) echoes in its twain-made-one its sister passage in Galatians (3:28, 'There is neither Jew nor Greek, there is neither bond nor free, there is neither male nor female: for ye are all one in Christ Jesus'), its counsel to wives to submit to their husbands as the Church is 'subject unto Christ' (Eph. 5:22-4) and to servants to be obedient to their masters (6:5-9) preserves distinctions which in the meantime still involve an earthly sense of hierarchy. This dilated mean-time before Apocalypse is part of the mystery of the *nunc et nondum*, of an end both 'at hand' (1 Peter 4) and not yet come, of a hermaphroditic union ('neither male nor female') both accomplished and not yet achieved.

*The Comedy of Errors* – itself set in Ephesus – depends for both its structure and its errors on the combination of 'partition' and 'dilation,' a combination announced in the comedy's opening scene. Here Egeon, condemned to death for crossing the boundary between Syracusian and Ephesian, explains how he sought 'delays' (I.i.74) from an 'immediate death' (68) by the stratagem which led to the 'unjust divorce' (104) of his family's two halves and then, when he responds to the Duke's request that he 'dilate' his narrative 'at full' (122), gains the temporary reprieve from 'doom' (2) which becomes the space of the intervening play of Errors. Both parts come together at last at the appointed hour, at the place of death which turns out to be the place of recognition, a 'nativity' (v.i.404) for which the 'travail' (400) of the mother provides the punning twin or female completion of the father's 'travels' (I.i.139) in the opening scene.

The opening image of the two halves divided from one another gives to the play the tension implicit in the Platonic myth of the Hermaphrodite – of halves whose original partition or 'divorce' begins the dynamic of desire for reunion – and its reflection in the familiar Renaissance figure of the androgynous Adam, which makes the 'one flesh' of marriage not just a union but a reunion of divided parts and which gives to so many of Shakespeare's comedies the figure of the male-female, a hermaphroditic or 'phoenix riddle' (Donne, *The Canonization*) like the one posed by Viola and her violation of sexual boundaries in *Twelfth Night*. In *The Comedy of Errors*, this 'one flesh' appears as the central figure of the play's subplot – of Adriana's 'waiting,' 'fasting' and 'starving' for the return of her husband and counselled to 'patience' in scenes which directly recall both the counsel to wives in Ephesians and the 'patience' and 'forbearance' necessary in the period before the return of the 'Master' and 'Lord,' a 'tardy master' now 'at hand' (II.i.44) but not yet arrived, or, in the beaten servant Dromio's punning phrase, 'at two hands' (45), something too near and to be set at a distance. Adriana's long speech on the 'one flesh' of marriage in Act II (ii.110-46), with its 'undividable, incorporate,' its double-meaning 'estrangèd from thyself' (in a play whose two-in-one includes the 'one flesh' of marriage, the *double entendre* of puns, and the 'natural perspective' of twins bearing the same name), and its argument that her husband, as her 'flesh,' communicates his 'harlotry' to her, is a passage whose baroque variations are simply those present *in potentia* in the biblical figure itself.

The idea of 'divorce,' 'division,' or 'partition' is repeated at several stages of the play, from the original dividing line between cities and the law which forbids trespass, to the echo of the 'unjust divorce' of Egeon's family in the 'deep-divorcing' vow (ii.ii.138) of Adriana's speech, to the partition or non-coincidence which in the 'comedy of errors' proper becomes the series of missed encounters climaxing in the great failed recognition scene of the middle act (iii.i), where it is the wall between the twins which both keeps the 'tardy master' from returning to his house and keeps the brothers apart, preventing their recognition and allowing the 'alien' or impostor twin to usurp the master's place. The partition which keeps the twins on either side and defers the recognition of the delayed but proper 'master' must be removed before the play can proceed to its ending, an ending which includes an echo of Peter's deliverance from prison by an 'angel' who breaks down intervening 'doors' and 'gates' (Acts 12) in the punning 'angels' (iv.iii.38) sent to deliver the imprisoned Antipholus.

The intervening space of 'entertainment' (ii.ii.186) is the middle period of comedy described by Frye in *A Natural Perspective*, a space of enchantments and metamorphoses connected with Odyssean 'errors' and with the Ephesus of Paul's New Testament voyages. These enchantments or 'translations' (Dromio's 'I am transformèd' and 'I am an ass' anticipating the 'translation' of Bottom in *A Midsummer Night's Dream*) involve an *ec-stasis* shared by madmen, mystics, and twins ('I am ... besides myself,' iii.ii.76). But they might also be compared to the *translatio* of metaphor itself, frequently described as a trespass across boundary lines, a usurpation of the 'proper' by the 'alien' term, an impostor or 'guest' who displaces the 'host,' words whose relation is several times suggested in a play which ironically begins with a law setting an absolute dividing line between two places, between 'strangers' and those who properly belong.[8]

Before the final removal of the partition wall, the play which begins with this harsh and divisive law (i.i.25) provides an extraordinary concentration of biblical allusions to the space of waiting for 're-demption,' its own commercial metaphors nicely combining with the figure from Ephesians 1:14.[9] Typologically, 'breaking down the middle wall of partition' includes both the deliverance wrought by the Cross and its anagogic fulfilment. The concentration in the play's final scenes of New Testament allusions to the space before deliverance indirectly makes the structure of the play itself, from its opening reprieve from 'doom' (i.i.2) and its subsequent 'errors' to its end, an analogue of the dilated space before the final Judgment and apocalyptic end to Error.

The sense of a relation between the errors of this play and those of the time (2 Timothy 4) before the anagogic removal of the 'partition wall' is increased by the comic expansion of the figure of the 'kitchen wench' who in Act III keeps the door locked and the twins shut out from one another – that 'Luce' or 'Nell' who claims the wrong Dromio as her betrothed and who contains so much 'grease' (with a pun on 'grace,' III.ii.94) that 'If she lives till doomsday she'll burn a week longer than the whole world' (97-8). 'Swart' (100) like the Bride of Canticles and, like the New Jerusalem who gains her husband in Revelation, as broad as she is long (111) and decked with precious stones ('her nose, all o'er-embellished with rubies, carbuncles, sapphires,' 132-3), she seems to be both female versions of the world at once ('she is spherical, like a globe; I could find out countries in her,' says Dromio, as he proceeds to do just that), recalling both the Great Whore and the redeemed harlot or New Jerusalem, a figure who, if she were allowed to speak, might suggest something like Stevens' 'fluent mundo.'

Echoes of Ephesians and its breaking down of the partition wall are strengthened even in the play's closing lines, where the adopted Dromios question who is the 'elder' and who the 'younger.' Their exchange recalls the opening scene's reference to the mother's greater care for the younger and the father's for the elder twin (i.i.78-82), in what seems there a gratuitous echo of the story of Jacob and Esau, the twins on whose rivalry so much of biblical history depends; but it resolves it in a fashion which recalls Ephesians and its removal of the partition between Gentile and Jew, a division as absolute as that between Syracusian and Ephesian at the opening of the play. Miraculously, as Frye remarks of the harsh laws of Shakespearean comedy,[10] the law which condemns all trespassers to death is dropped in the final recognition scene, and the competition of elder and younger is corrected in a new partnership in which, in the language of Ephesians (1:5; 3:6), both are equally adopted 'sons' and 'heirs.' There is in the play's ending neither the original divorce and separation by a dividing wall, nor the organizing of this separation by hierarchy – a distinction in any case reduced to the absurd in the case of twins. The Comedy set in Ephesus ends as the reunited brothers walk 'hand in hand' together through the formerly locked door and into the same house.

In A Midsummer Night's Dream – a play which contains a character named Wall, puns on the crossing of 'wall' and 'partition' in discourse, and ends with the removal of the wall in the play of Pyramus and Thisbe ('the wall is down that parted their fathers,' v.i.337) – the idea of 'partition' is also linked to that of delay or dilation, to the deferral of consummation or ending. The opening scene establishes a link between the period of betrothal and its delaying of the 'nuptial hour' of Theseus and Hippolyta (with Theseus' 'how slow / This old moon wanes! She lingers my desires'), the period of reprieve ('Take time to pause,' 83) in which Hermia must come to a decision, and the projected period of 'patience' and 'trial' for the persecuted lovers (152-3), with its echo of Matthew 10. But whereas in *Romeo and Juliet*, with its forbidding 'walls,' what intervenes between betrothal and final consummation is death, here it is the mean-time in the wood. The metamorphosis effected here among the virtually indistinguishable lovers – the 'translation' (i.i.191) of Helena into Hermia – is the counterpart of the 'translation' (iii.i.114) of Bottom into an ass, a *translatio* which also may involve a distinction without a difference. The love which is blind (i.i.235) is like the darkness (iii.ii) which finally does cut off the lovers' vision, as the 'Wall' does in the play of Pyramus and Thisbe out of the *Metamorphoses*. At the end of this intervening period of 'amaze' (iii.ii.344), the lovers' longing for the night to end ('O long and tedious night, / Abate thy hours!' 431-2) links this middle space with the delaying of bed-time by the mechanicals' play, a 'tedious brief scene' (v.i.56) which draws from its audience complaints about how long it is taking, and with the space of 'lingering' time which keeps an impatient Theseus from consummation.

Theseus, however, also begins the play by commissioning a play, the 'interlude' (i.ii.5) which, when chosen on the wedding night to 'beguile / The lazy time' (v.i.40-42), delays the consummation much as *A Midsummer Night's Dream* itself does, thus becoming both a play within a play and a revealing metadrama, exposing the structures and strategies of the play which appears simply to contain it.[11] What is crucial for the relation between intervening walls and dilation, or delay, in both is the subtle and subterranean diffusion of the idea of partition throughout and not simply when the relation between 'wall' and 'partition in discourse' finally surfaces in Demetrius' witty pun. We see the mechanicals' play not just in the larger play's final act but in stages before its 'wall' is 'down,' from casting (i.ii) to rehearsal (iii.i) to hilarious performance (v.i). In the first, the division of both 'company' and play into 'parts' throughout recalls the language of 'partition,' of dividing or distributing a whole into its parts and the placing of each part in proper order. *Partitio* is distinguished in the handbooks from speaking 'generally' ('If in generality we said *hee hath consumed all his substance in ryot*: By distribution we might amplify thus ...').[12] When Quince the Carpenter opens the scene with 'Is *all* our company here?' (I.ii.i, italics mine), Bottom the Weaver, anxious to improve the level of organization, advises 'You were best to call them generally [i.e., individually] man by man, according to the scrip' (2-3) and goes on to lecture his friend on the proper 'partitioning,' in order, of a speech ('First, good Peter Quince, say what the play treats on; then read the names of the actors; and so grow to a point,' 8-10), in a scene which quickly becomes a comic version of workmen 'rightly dividing the word' (2 Timothy 2:15). The individual members then 'spread' themselves (15) and the company is divided into 'parts,' a word whose combination of 'partition,' 'part,' and 'parting' is finally made explicit in the 'part' played by the departing 'Wall' at the wedding ('Thus have I, Wall, my part dischargèd so; / And being done, thus Wall away doth go,' v.i.202-3).

Each of the three stages of the production, however, also provides a figure for the disruption of an order which proceeds by 'partition.' In the casting scene, Bottom himself wants to play all the parts at once and has to be called to order by a directorial Quince. In the rehearsal scene, where everyone is reminded to observe his 'cue' (III.i.72), Thisbe/Flute speaks 'all his part at once, cues and all' (94-5), as if it were a single continuous line or sentence, and is similarly called to order by Quince. Finally, in the performance, Quince himself, speaking as 'Prologue' ('the true beginning of our end,' v.i.111), misses the proper intermediate punctuation marks ('This fellow doth not stand upon points,' 118) and thus disorders the sequential and orderly 'chain' (124) of discourse. Bottom's counsel to proceed by proper parts is also contravened when, on awakening from his dream, he scrambles the echo of 1 Corinthians 2 and its own rhetorical divisions and amplifications of the 'word' ('The eye of man hath not heard, the ear of man hath not seen, man's hand is not able to taste, his tongue to conceive, nor his heart to report, what my dream was,' IV.i.209-12), in a passage which has to do with something beyond the ordered discourse of reason (v.i.6) and its neatly sequential chain, and then, after promising to relate the whole of his dream ('Masters, I am to discourse wonders,' IV.ii.28), gives up with a departing 'No more words. Away!' (42-3).

Bottom's 'so grow to a point' and Quince's not standing upon 'points' join another use of 'point' for arrival at an end or 'period' after a space of discourse or delay – Lysander's explanation of the 'tedious minutes' spent with Hermia before his 'reason' ripened to a 'point' (II.ii.111-19), a proclamation echoed when Demetrius protests that his pursuit of Hermia was simply a little *Odyssey* (III.i.171-2). Bottom's 'so grow to a point,' with its comic and subtle reference to the sequential partitions of a speech before its 'period,' clearly reflects in little the great 'point' or 'period' towards which the larger play proceeds, an amplification which also proceeds by division or partition before the 'wall' is finally 'down' (v.i.337). The connection between 'wall' and 'hymen' is clear not only from Theseus' impatience but also from the 'obscene' (I.ii.100) exchange between 'Pyramus' and 'Thisbe' before a 'Wall' whose obliging gesture of parting (v.i.175) creates the 'cranny' which is itself both a means of communication and yet another wall ('*Pyramus*. O kiss me through the hole of this vile wall ... / *Thisbe*. I kiss the wall's hole, not your lips at all,' 198-9). The exchange ends with Wall's departure, in lines which make the controversial Folio reading ('*Theseus*. Now is the *morall downe* between the two neighbours,' with Demetrius' rejoinder 'No remedy my lord, when walls are so wilful to hear without warning,' 204-5), if not the textually definitive reading, at least, in the continuing absence of one, a brilliant and structurally appropriate, multifaceted pun.

The play's own middle several times repeats the idea of 'part' and 'partition': Demetrius' *blason* of Helena depends on the conventional division of a body into 'parts' (III.ii.137-53); Hermia's insistence on sleeping apart opposes her betrothed's premature 'twain' made 'one' ('One heart, one bed, two bosoms, and one troth,' II.ii.40-60); Helena's appeal to her friendship with Hermia ('Like to a double cherry, seeming parted, / But yet an union in partition,' III.ii.200-10) echoes the 'one flesh' of Matthew 19 ('What therefore God hath joined together, let no man put asunder') but shifts the emphasis from generic 'man' to specific 'men' ('And will you rend our ancient love asunder / To join with men in scorning your poor friend?', 215-16), an emphasis which, though appropriate for a character who knows very well that 'man' does not necessarily embrace 'woman,' must in this play ultimately yield its one-sided union to the two-in-one of marriage. In the play of Pyramus and Thisbe, 'Wall' points to the 'cranny' which like it divides 'right' from 'sinister' (v.i.162); and this division into sides by a wall recalls the play's polarities or contrasted pairs – 'lover'/'tyrant,' 'reason'/'love,' 'night'/'day' and the others summed up in Hermia's image of the 'Antipodes' (III.ii.55). Theseus' response to the pairing of opposites in the 'merry and tragical,' 'tedious and brief' mechanicals' play ('How shall we find the concord of this discord?', v.i.60) reveals the play's underlying figure of a *concordia discors*, each 'part' playing its 'part,' while the world turns on its own poles or Antipodes, Creation itself before the apocalyptic end of all 'partition.'

In the middle scene of rehearsal in the wood – the scene in which Thisbe speaks all his part at once and must be taught proper spacing, Pyramus/Bottom makes the exit which will leads to his offstage 'translation':

*Pyramus*: But hark, a voice!, Stay thou but here awhile,
and by and by I will to thee appear. *Exit.*
*Puck*: A stranger Pyramus than e'er played here! [*Exit.*]

*Thisbe*: Must I speak now?
*Quince*: Ay, marry, must you; for you must understand he goes but to see a noise that he heard, and is to come again ... (III.i.81-7)

Both 'by and by I will to thee appear' and the Pyramus who 'is to come again' recall the disappearance and return of Christ ('most lovely Jew,' 90), whom Pyramus, killed for Thisbe (*anima humana*, wandering in search of the 'Spouse'), signifies in the tradition of the *Ovide moralisé* (IV), a resonance which may illumine retrospectively Flute's earlier 'What is Thisbe? A wandering knight?' (I.ii.41). The space between the disappearance and the return of this Pyramus is the interim in which 'the devil, as a roaring lion, walketh about seeking whom he may devour' (I Peter 5) – a 'lion' which the familiar moralizing of Ovid had no difficulty assimilating to the roaring lion of Pyramus and Thisbe and which is echoed twice in *A Midsummer Night's Dream*, in the comically roaring Lion who frightens Thisbe away and in the roaring hungry lion ('Now the hungry lion roars') of Puck's great 'time of night' speech (v.i.357-76) as the play itself looks forward to the 'break of day' (387). When the Pyramus who is Bottom does 'come again,' it is in a different kind of 'translated' form, as the 'ass' who frightens the others as effectively as the Lion played by 'Snug the Joiner,' but who is also traditionally a humble 'bearer of the Word' before the end.[13]

When the Wall or witty 'partition' of the mechanicals' play finally departs, there is an echo of Apocalypse ('*Thisbe*: 'Tide life, 'tide death, I come without delay,' v.i.201), the event which is to replace the 'morall' by the 'anagogical,' an echo which joins the intimations of anagogy in

Bottom's scrambling of 1 Corinthians 2. And when the wall between Pyramus and Thisbe is finally down, the much-awaited night of consummation comes. But the larger play ends with a 'night' looking forward once again to an anticipated dawn, a 'translation' (Colossians 2:3, 'who hath delivered us from the power of darkness, and hath translated us into the kingdom of his dear son') both accomplished and still to come. Puck's speech after the lovers go to bed includes another 'hungry lion,' the 'screech-owl' prophetic of death (*The Phoenix and the Turtle*, 7), and lines whose 'graves, all gaping wide' recall the earlier night of 'dreams' in the wood, a night whose anticipation of dawning becomes, in the Epilogue, that shared by the audience itself.

In both *The Comedy* and the *Dream*, the echo of Ephesians and its removed partition wall involves recognition and reunion; but both also defer the final anagogic joining, making a link between dramatic time and time itself, between the play which proceeds by division into 'parts,' delaying as well as moving towards an ending, and the 'partition' of all structures conceived as a sequence, including the movement of history. The plot of metaphor here is teleological, a principle of identity and of ending. But what metaphor would unite, discourse, including that of drama (*MND* v.i.150, 'At large discourse'), keeps apart, at least for the time being. In *The Phoenix and the Turtle*, with its metaphysical joining, an anagogy above time rather than at the end of time, the 'one flesh' of copular or anagogic metaphor is a threat, in the *midst* of linearity or sequence, to the ordering structures, and enclosures, of Property and Reason. In *Wuthering Heights*, copular metaphor also threatens reason and property and provokes an attempt at closure and containment. To move from Shakespearean comedy to Brontë's novel is to move from an Odyssean or comic plot of metaphor to a more unsettling and gothic one, in which the joining of anagogic metaphor becomes part of the uncanny or *unheimlich* and in which its union, as in *The Phoenix and the Turtle*, though in a different mode, threatens to collapse linearity and its careful spacing.

The anagogic union of Phoenix and Turtle is as foreign to Reason as the imagination of the 'lunatic, the lover and the poet' is to Theseus, the exponent of 'cool reason' (v.i.6-7) in *A Midsummer Night's Dream*. But wariness both of imagination and of metaphor, the agent of its transports, emerges even more strikingly in the subsequent Age of Reason (Dryden, 'Great wits are sure to madness near allied, / And thin partitions do their bounds divide'). In Book vi of Wordsworth's *Prelude*

(1805), in many ways an inheritor of this age, it is 'Imagination' which 'usurps' the 'light of sense' in that crucial passage whose intimations of 'apocalypse' follow immediately upon a 'translation' (523), the travellers' crossing of a boundary unawares, and in a poem whose own conflations of temporal boundaries suggest the kind of identity Frye cites (124) as the temporal aspect of anagogic metaphor – the grown man's feeling 'identical' with himself at a different stage in time – those 'awful' moments when the temporal partitions vanish and the intervening space of years drops away.

The 'translation' or 'transport' of metaphor involves, in its classical and neoclassical descriptions, a displacement or usurpation frequently inseparable from a sense of violation, or violence, an invasion of the 'proper' or familiar by the 'alien' or 'improper' term. Du Marsais' well-known metaphor for metaphor is that of its dwelling 'in a borrowed home' (*Des tropes* x), an image of domestication in which the guest becomes host, a conception as available for Gothic variation as the echo of Ephesians in the 'wall of flesh' of Young's *Night Thoughts* ('O, when will death / This mould'ring, old, partition-wall throw down?') and its vision of the ultimate removal of dividing walls 'when he who died returns' (IV). Anagogic metaphor's potential outrage to reason and property generates in this tradition a concern for its 'mastery' (Aristotle) or 'moderation' (Quintilian). But the very idea of its crossing of boundaries poses a threat to decorum, the possibility that it might be not only 'out of place' (*improprium*) but out of control, something beyond the 'master of metaphor' who attempts to stand outside and direct it.

Frye speaks in the *Anatomy* (123) of the 'descriptive phase,' of its tendency to see metaphor as a condensed simile – a conception more accommodated to plausibility and reason – and of its nervousness in the face of more radical forms. Hugh Blair begins his lecture on 'Metaphor' (1783) by defining it as nothing more than a 'Simile' expressed 'in an abridged form,' and proceeds with advice for its 'proper management.' But in his observation that metaphor 'insinuates itself even into familiar conversation; and, unsought, rises up of its own accord in the mind,' 'insinuation' begins to suggest something less under control, the appearance of the *unheimlich* even within the *heimlich*, or familiar, and its 'rising up, unsought' something more like the 'usurpation' which meets the traveller of *The Prelude*, a simultaneous crossing and obliteration of boundaries. Blair censures the impropriety and potential violence of 'far-fetched' or forced metaphor as contrary to the rule of Cicero ('Every Metaphor should be modest, so that it may carry the appearance of having been led, not of having forced itself into the place of that word whose room it occupies'). And Dr Johnson expresses uneasiness before a joining which takes too radical or copular a form, objecting that Gray's calling a 'Cat' a 'nymph' does 'violence both to language and sense' and exempting from censure only the lines in which the two are kept clearly divided. While radical or anagogic metaphor would unite separate entities through the copular 'is' – since, as Frye remarks (124), anything is possible in language, even 'black is white' – Johnson's concern is that the dividing lines be clear and in true Enlightenment fashion he praises only those poems which are 'at once poetical and rational.'[14]

Paul de Man has described the way in which such eighteenth-century discussions of the mastery of metaphor begin to sound, in the very effort of containment, more 'like the plot of a Gothic novel.'[15] Consideration of the following excerpt from *Wuthering Heights* may help to suggest why a nervousness about copular or anagogic metaphor should have a Gothic extension. The novel is remarkable for its emphasis both on proper place, or property, and on crossing or transgression, from the exchanges of characters between the two houses to the plot itself founded on a transfer, Heathcliff the alien brought into the Heights, regarded as a 'usurper' (ch. IV), and ultimately becoming its new master. It is also remarkable, however, for its narrative frame – the diary of Lockwood and, within it, the chronological history Lockwood asks the housekeeper to provide. The chapter that provokes his demand for sequence and chronology provides an extreme version of all sequential 'partition' – the sermon of Jabes Branderham divided into 'heads,' which is combined with an echo of Ephesians both earlier in 'Th'Helmet uh Salvation' rejected by 'Miss Cathy' and in the 'house with two rooms, threatening speedily to determine into one' in Lockwood's dream of the sermon on 'Seventy Times Seven, and the first of the Seventy-first':

We came to the chapel. I have passed it really in my walks, twice or thrice; it lies in a hollow, between two hills: an elevated hollow, near a swamp, whose peaty moisture is said to answer all the purposes of embalming on the few corpses deposited there. The roof has been kept whole hitherto; but as the clergyman's stipend is only twenty pounds per annum, and a house with two rooms, threatening speedily to determine into one, no clergyman will undertake the duties of pastor: especially as it is currently reported that his flock would rather let him starve than increase the living by one penny from their own pockets. However, in my dream, Jabes had a full and attentive congregation; and he preached – good God! what a sermon: divided into *four hundred and ninety* parts, each fully equal to an ordinary address from the pulpit, and each discussing a separate sin! Where he searched for them, I cannot tell. He had his private manner of interpreting the phrase, and it seemed necessary the brother should sin different sins on every occasion. They were of the most curious character: odd transgressions that I never imagined previously. O, how weary I grew! How I writhed, and yawned, and nodded, and revived! How I pinched and pricked myself, and rubbed my eyes, and stood up, and sat down again, and nudged Joseph to inform me if he would *ever* have done. I was condemned to hear all out: finally, he reached the '*First of the Seventy-first.*' At that crisis, a sudden inspiration descended on me; I was moved to rise and denounce Jabes Branderham as the sinner of the sin that no Christian need pardon.

'Sir,' I exclaimed, 'sitting here within these four walls, at one stretch, I have endured and forgiven the four hundred and ninety heads of your discourse. Seventy times seven times have I plucked up my hat and been about to depart – Seventy times seven times have you preposterously forced me to resume my seat. The four hundred and ninety-first is too much. Fellow-martyrs, have at him! Drag him down, and crush him to atoms that the place which knows him may know him no more!'[16]

The passage's juxtaposition of 'corpses' and 'roof,' or 'house,' gives to the juxtaposition of 'body' and 'house' already in Ephesians (2:14-16) a gothic turn, since it is this burial ground which will be recalled later in Heathcliff's plan to have his coffin and Catherine's opened to one another ('By the time Linton gets to us, he'll not know which is which,' XXIX, 319), a literalizing of 'one flesh,' or the twain-made-one, which would make Catherine's own radical copula – 'I *am* Heathcliff' (IX, 122) – a macabre fact. The sermon 'divided into *four hundred and ninety* parts' picks up the image of the divided house through its own 'partition,' what Blair, passing on the rhetorical tradition in his *Lectures*, calls the 'method of dividing a Sermon into heads,' the 'formal partitions' the art of preaching shares with all 'Discourse' (XXXI). But it also contravenes the traditional warning, echoed in Blair, against unnecessary 'multiplication into heads,' against dividing the subject into 'minute parts' and so fatiguing the listener. And there seems to be an uncanny mathematical logic at work in a dream in which a preacher with a name out of the genealogies of 1 Chronicles 4:9 preaches a sermon 'divided into *four hundred and ninety parts*' on the topic of the 'Seventy times seven.' The division into parts 'each discussing a separate sin,' together with the text from Matthew on the forgiveness of trespasses, links the very proliferation of partitions or dividing lines with the possibility of 'trespass.'

The 'crisis' reached at the 'First of the Seventy-first' involves a strangely literal reading of the partitioned text – the injunction of Matthew 18 to forgive 'until seventy times seven' – since this is precisely the point where pardon here ends and the 'First of the Seventy-first' becomes the sin for which there is no forgiveness (Matt. 12:31), a blasphemy against the Holy Ghost which also involves the image of a 'house divided against itself' (Matt. 12:25). Whatever the specific reason for the reference, the complex recall of a passage on Christ's trespass against the Law (which has to do both with the Holy Spirit and with a restless 'spirit' that returns to its 'house,' 12:44), may be related to the working of metaphor and its anagogic copula in this disturbing novel, and to an uncertainty about the spirit to which metaphor finally belongs. Arrival at the sermon's final partition leads in the dream to figures for biblical Endtime and for the upsetting of sequential order: Lockwood's 'preposterously,' with its sense both of 'outrageously' and of the reversal of proper sequence; echoes of the eschatalogical penulti-mate Psalm ('execute upon him the judgement written') in the 'concluding word' (III, 66) at which the assembly turns to violence; and a reminder of the Old Testament's penultimate book with its vision of coming judgment (Zech. 14:13) in 'every man's hand was against his neighbour,' in the final 'tumult,' and, curiously, in the 'branch' (Zech. 3) which both breaks into this first dream and leads to the unsettling 'return' of the next one.

Immediately after the quoted passage, Branderham's accusation of Lockwood ('Thou art the Man!', 66) recalls both the assault on Paul for a violation of the 'partition wall' (Acts 21:28) and Nathan's application of a parable to its hearer (2 Samuel 2:7), in a dream in which dreamer and preacher become increasingly similar. The Lockwood who objects in this first dream to the multiple partitions of Branderham's discourse erects, in the second, books as a partition wall to keep a wailing 'spirit' from returning to her house, an ironic extension of his own earlier quotation of Job 7 (9-10: 'he that goeth down to the grave shall come up no more. He shall return no more to his house, neither shall his place know him any more'). And, immediately after this disturbing night, he requests the story he will insist proceed chronologically or 'minutely' (VII, 102), a narrative spacing of this dream chapter's simultaneous 'Catherines' (III, 61) into a history in which the two characters who occupy the 'obtrusive name' (62) are distanced by a generation – a setting of partitions between individuals and times accommodated to the laws of 'property' and to the enlightened mind.

Lockwood loses his way in the chapter of his dreams, when the snow covers the 'line of upright stones' which had served as 'guides' and blots out the 'chart' in his mind (III, 73). Nelly Dean's explanatory history restores his sense of orientation, providing the chart of names and dates Lockwood has so far lacked and the figurative 'milestones' traditionally compared to the partitions of discourse (Quintilian IV.v.23; Blair, Lectures XXXI). But even in this reassuringly sequential narrative, the housekeeper herself tells of her unsettling vision of the grown man Hindley as a child (XI), an incident which collapses the intervening space of twenty years and sends her back in panic to the 'guide-post' (149). And this highly Wordsworthian conflation of times reinforces the sense elsewhere in the novel of something threatening the orderly divisions of that chronological history, even after the enigmatically juxtaposed names, the disturbing dreams, and the breaking down of a wall of partition in chapter III.

The juxtaposed names of the third chapter ('*Catherine Earnshaw, Catherine Heathcliff, Catherine Linton*') are themselves an instance of what Frye calls 'literal' metaphor ('A;B'), parataxis without predication, the 'ironic' counterpart of 'anagogic' metaphor and, like it, more repugnant to reason than the intermediate forms of implied analogy or simile. Catherine's defiant 'I am Heathcliff,' however, is metaphor in its radical or anagogic form, the kind of copula which Locke (whose name is recalled in Lockwood's), with others of his age, abhorred.[17] Its form suggests an hermaphroditic or incestuous coupling like that of Shelley's *Epipsychidion* – whose language of metaphysical union echoes that of *The Phoenix and the Turtle* – and its radical 'twain made one' involves ultimately, as in Shelley, the 'one annihilation' of death, a breaking through 'walls' which Catherine envisions before she dies (XV). Such a union, in its spatial as in its temporal form, would be a threat both to the structures based on 'property' (in all senses) and to the order of a narrative which proceeds by partition, both to the Linton society whose dogs rend trespassers (VI) and to the narrator residing in the Linton house, who rubs the hand of the ghostly Catherine against the broken glass of a partition which no longer divides (III). A sociological interest in this novel's preoccupation with property, a more formal concern with its narrative structures, and a fascination with its passionate couple and 'one flesh' would meet precisely at the question of boundaries or 'partitions.' The form of *Wuthering Heights* is so intimately connected with the perspective of its enlightened narrator that even its own forms of enclosure become open to question; and the echo of Job 7 and its boundary between life and death in the dream of Branderham's partitioned sermon raises the question of whether the novel's own ending, with Lockwood's visit to the graves of Catherine and Heathcliff, might itself be a defensive closure device, part of a desire to maintain the proper boundary lines.

Frye in the *Anatomy* speaks of anagogic metaphor as an apocalyptic principle of identity, and of narrative, by implication, as what has more recently been called 'spacing' – a term he indeed uses elsewhere in his description of the relentlessly sequential or processional form of Shakespeare's *Pericles*.[18] In *The Phoenix and the Turtle*, the poem's own processional structure suggests an ironic movement of accommodation as recovery – as recuperation in the midst of the outrage to Reason and Property, by a reinstitution of partitions and of 'parts.' In *Wuthering Heights*, the recourse to sequence also involves a recourse to partitions, a form of *espacement* accommodated both to rationality and to its dividing lines. But there remains in this novel, as in Shakespeare's poem, a sense of the revelation of its structures as themselves a form of structuring, as a movement of recuperation and as need. And there remains as well in Brontë's text a sense of something threatening to break down all such partitions, of the form of the novel itself as a house which cannot fully domesticate the alien, or *unheimlich*, presence of anagogic metaphor, or finally control its aberrant couplings.

NOTES

1 *Anatomy of Criticism* (1957; rpt. New York, 1966), 122-5, 365; *Fables of Identity* (New York, 1963), 102. Parenthetical references in the text are to *Anatomy* unless otherwise noted.

2 Biblical references are to the King James Version, unless otherwise noted. The 1585 Bishops' Bible translation of these verses is: 'For he is our peace, which hath made both one: and hath broken down the middle wall that was a stop between us ... for to make of twaine one newe man in himselfe.' The Geneva 1560 version gives 'hathe broken the stoppe of the particion wall.'

3 See, for example, the combination of the notion of a 'house' fallen into disrepair with the event which rent the veil of the temple, broke down the 'wall of partition' between Gentile and Jew, and abolished the 'cursed handwriting' (Col. 2:14) of the Law in Herbert's 'Church

Militant' ('King Solomon, / Finish't and fixt the old religion. / When it grew loose, the Jews did hope in vain / By nailing Christ to fasten it again. / But to the Gentiles he bore crosse and all, / Rending with earthquakes the partition-wall,' 21-6).

4 The texts of Shakespeare are from the following Arden editions: *The Poems*, ed. F.T. Prince (London, 1960); *The Comedy of Errors*, ed. R.A. Foakes (London, 1962); *A Midsummer Night's Dream*, ed. Harold F. Brooks (London, 1979).

5 See Cicero, *De Oratore* III.xxxix-xli; Quintilian, *Institutio Oratoria* VIII.vi. I have discussed this classical tradition of metaphor as boundary-crosser more fully in 'The Metaphorical Plot,' in *Metaphor: Problems and Perspectives*, ed. David S. Miall (Sussex, 1982), 133-7.

6 Angus Fletcher, *Allegory* (Ithaca, 1964), 175.

7 See T.W. Baldwin, *William Shakspere's Small Latine & Lesse Greeke* (Urbana, 1944), II, 109-12, 315-21; Sister Miriam Joseph, *Shakespeare's Use of the Arts of Language* (New York, 1966), 111-14, 314-16; *The Sermons of John Donne*, ed. G.R. Potter and E.M. Simpson (Berkeley, 1959), V, 56. For the relation of this rhetorical tradition of dilation through partition to the *ars praedicandi*, Lee W. Patterson, in 'Feminine Rhetoric, Masculine Reading and the Wife of Bath,' *Speculum*, 58 (1983), cites Simon Alcok, *De modo dividendi thema pro materia sermonis dilatanda*, ed. Mary J. Boynton, *Harvard Theological Review*, 34 (1941), 201-16. On rhetorical dilation, the etymological connection between dilation and deferral in *dilatio*, and patristic writing on the period of respite or dilation between First and Second Coming, see my *Inescapable Romance* (Princeton, 1979), 54-64.

8 See, in addition to Cicero and Quintilian, Isidore of Seville, *Etym.* I.xxxvii.2; Henry Peacham, *The Garden of Eloquence* (1593), 'Metaphora'; George Puttenham, *The Arte of English Poesie* (1589), xvi; Frye, *A Natural Perspective* (New York, 1965), 76-8; and the uses of 'host' and 'guest' in *The Comedy of Errors*, I.ii.9 and III.i.27.

9 See, among others, the allusion to the 'old Adam' of the Law waiting in 'Limbo' ('Not that Adam that kept the paradise, but that Adam that keeps the prison,' IV.iii.16-17); to Lucifer as 'angel of light' (2 Cor. 11:14), another impostor or usurping lookalike (Matt. 24:5, 'Many will come in my name'), to be exposed in an apocalyptic recognition scene; to the turning back of 'Time' at the sight of the Law (IV.ii.55-62); to the binding and loosing of Satan (IV.iii.72-3; Rev. 20:1-2); to the wanderings of the 'Prodigal' (IV.iii.18) from another story of a man who, like Egeon, 'had two sons' (Luke 15); to 'harlotry' (II.ii.136; IV.iii.50-65) in contexts

which suggest its use as a biblical figure for 'erring'; and to the defeat of Satan in the wilderness of Israel's wandering (IV.ii.48).

10 *A Natural Perspective*, 126.

11 I am adapting this term from James L. Calderwood's *Shakespearean Metadrama* (Minneapolis, 1971).

12 Angel Day, *The English Secretorie* (1592; London, 1635), 385. The example is virtually an English translation of the first example of Book II of Erasmus' *De copia*, which discusses the method of amplifying through the partition of a general statement with 'all' or 'whole' into its several particulars.

13 For a description of this symbolism, see James Nohrnberg, *The Analogy of 'The Faerie Queene'* (Princeton, 1976), 151-2.

14 Blair, *Lectures on Rhetoric and Belles Lettres* (1783), Lecture XV; Samuel Johnson, *Lives of the Poets* (1779-81), Life of Gray. I am indebted, for the connection between metaphor described as a 'usurper' and the 'usurpation' of *Prelude* VI, to my colleague Eleanor Cook.

15 'The Epistemology of Metaphor,' in *On Metaphor*, ed. Sheldon Sacks (Chicago, 1979), 21.

16 *Wuthering Heights*, ed. David Daiches (Harmondsworth, 1965), ch. III, p. 65. Parenthetical references in the text are to chapter and page number of this edition. On the relation between 'the proverbially long Puritan sermons,' with their multiple 'divisions,' and the plan of history between Creation and Apocalypse, see Frye, *The Return of Eden* (Toronto, 1965), 10, a work which ends with direct reference to the breaking down of all 'walls of partition.'

17 See in particular Locke's *Essay Concerning Human Understanding* (III.10) and de Man, 18-19; and, on *Epipsychidion*, Frye, *A Study of English Romanticism* (New York, 1968), 104, and J. Hillis Miller, 'The Critic as Host,' in *Deconstruction and Criticism*, ed.Harold Bloom et al. (New York, 1979), 238-47. A crucial irony of Shelley's poem, as of this tradition, is that a joining possible only in language is presented as impossible because of language.

18 See *A Natural Perspective*, 27-8, 154

**MICHAEL
DOLZANI**

# The Infernal Method:
# Northrop Frye and
# Contemporary Criticism

In 1942, a thirty-year-old Northrop Frye published what was, so far as I can see, his first full-length critical essay. It has never been and I imagine is not likely to be reprinted, not only because large sections of it went nearly verbatim, fifteen years later, into the *Anatomy of Criticism*, but because in several ways it shows itself to be an early article: the transitions are on occasion just a little abrupt, and the humour just short of dangerous. As a young man, Frye had a sense of humour at times nearly as irreverent as Blake's, an exuberantly tigerish wit barely held in check by urbanity and the horses of instruction, the latter represented in this case by a kind of heavy annotation with which in his later career he has mostly dispensed. For all that, the article is brilliant and immensely readable: its title is 'The Anatomy in Prose Fiction.'[1]

Both title and article may come as a surprise to some of Frye's readers: here is a demonstration of the form of the anatomy, in greater detail and with more examples, than has ever appeared subsequently. Nevertheless, its publication precedes even *Fearful Symmetry* by five years. Here, in fact, is the full theory of the four forms of prose fiction, eight years before the appearance of the article by that title,[2] which was itself incorporated in the *Anatomy* seven years later still.

Here is not so much a process of development as the presence of an informing structure of vision manifesting itself discontinuously, though steadily, throughout the total body of Frye's work. The question of Frye's development as a critic is quite an interesting one, which no one has explored very deeply yet to my knowledge. But it seems clear that simple-minded ideas about a linear development based, however implicitly, on a biographical concept of creation will not be adequate to any such study. There simply does not seem to be any point at which

Frye's informing vision or structure was not in some way present: present, that is (to postpone grappling for the moment with yet another problem of modern critical terminology), as a freely interpenetrating pattern and not as a grasping and graspable essence.

Frye's vision of interpenetration does not bog down in the presence-absence antithesis, this being what keeps the *Anatomy of Criticism* from becoming just an unusually elaborate sequence of classifications, an edifice resembling some gigantic purple-martin-house. The imaginative patterns of literature, like those of the other arts, are capable of rising beyond the culturally imperialist and the hierarchical: that is why they remain the models for civilization, and the works which re-create them the enduring classics. Only when archetypes decay into stereotypes do they become instruments of social mythology. Much leftward-leaning criticism of the last decade or two, with justifiable militancy, has concentrated upon this latter process, and especially upon the tendency for critical ideology to disguise itself as pure formalism, sometimes apparently managing to deceive even itself. But in the absence of a fully mature body of structural criticism to balance this kind of radical social criticism, a certain amount of confused demoralization has darkened the pages of literary journals for some time now. Without a theory of criticism strong enough to provide a healthy resistance to the political tendency to regard all literary patterns simply as ideological instruments (or, the other side of the coin, as individual strategies of repression), some critics seem to have begun losing interest in literature altogether except as a rhetorical weapon. Some of the more heated criticisms of Frye's work originate, I think, in the fact that it stands as a more massive obstacle to this tendency than almost anything else in sight.

At any rate, the introduction to *The Great Code: The Bible and Literature* reaffirms its author's fondness, exactly forty years later, for the prose genre known as the anatomy. A very central reason for this fondness is that the anatomy is able to make use of satire's subversiveness towards intellectual systems to become a very effectively 'deconstructive' vehicle, capable thereby of embodying such a vision of free interpenetration as lies at the heart of Frye's criticism. Frye is known most commonly as the rescuer of romance, but it is his affinity to satire to which I find myself returning whenever I attempt to relate his work to contemporary critical developments, and it is this connection which forms at least the broader subject of what follows.

Admittedly, Frye has himself observed in *A Natural Perspective* that he is an *Odyssey* critic, whose concerns revolve around comedy and romance, rather than an *Iliad* critic focusing upon tragedy and irony, and it is true that he has always had a great deal of fun being subversive of the recurrent tendency to identify irony with integrity. This detachment from judgments based exclusively on ironic values is one aspect of his general relativization of value judgments. Whether or not criticism could or should be called a science is not so important as the question of whether or not it is a genuine discipline, that is, whether it is sufficiently detached from social values, good ones or bad ones, to be trusted to look at its own data impartially. Frye has not exactly said that value judgments (though always subdued to the infinite vision of the arts) cannot emerge out of literary criticism, only that it may not start with them as its premises: when a scholar does so, he subordinates his quest for objective knowledge to his social values, and to the degree that he does so, what he will provide will be a polemical rhetoric rationalizing those values. It seems not always fully realized that the argument applies to radical social values as well as conservative ones, and is just as relevant when Barthes argues for French new fiction as it was when F.R. Leavis argued for English old fiction, partly because it is easy for radical critics to consider they are being detached when they are critical of the visible structure of social authority and the literature and scholarship which reflects it. What social assumptions such critics are detaching themselves from is indeed clear: what social assumptions they do accept often remain invisible except by implication. One thing which the Marxist critics have made certain is that no critic can escape having some social assumptions: even anarchists make their presuppositions. Literature and criticism both grow out of society, and do not exist in a vacuum.

We seem at first glance to have ended by denying the possibility of detachment which we set up first as a necessity. This is indeed one possible conclusion, and at least some of the implications of Jacques Derrida's work seem to converge upon it. According to Derrida, the mind perceives by delimiting the indefiniteness of space into a 'here' and freezing the fluidity of time in a 'now.' These are not exactly his terms, but they serve to indicate something about this normal mode of perception: that it is close to what Blake defined also as intellectual error, the kind of dualizing perception characteristic of the fallen Urizen. It becomes clear, however, that in a world in which we are alienated from our own bodies, there can be no true 'here'; there can be no true presence. In Chapter I of *Fearful Symmetry*, the first point that

Frye makes about Blake's theory of knowledge is that nothing can be real which is not present to perception. If there is no presence, there is no present either; anything we can point to is already moving into the past. Derrida's key terms evoke this alienation. There is never a presence, either in time or space, only a *trace*; there is no identity, only difference, and no true meaning, only a deferring of reference to something not really there; both these latter phenomena are fused into the pun word *differance*. As this *is* intellectual error, it dissolves into what Blake would call contradiction. Although any structure we perceive is a trace, it is a trace of something that never really could have been there in the first place. We perceive difference, but never the elements that differ; in other words, any structure we try to grasp as a *thing* turns into a set of conceptual relations, whose locus of reality is nowhere. Derrida calls this process an absence invoking a presence, Blake calls it a spectre pursuing an emanation.

This final dissolving of dualistic perception into the dead-end single vision of abstract reasoning is, in Blake, the inevitable entropic decay of passive perception from the world of Generation to the world of Ulro. One of the things that makes Derrida's exposition difficult is that he explores most of these ideas using the terminology of linguistic structuralism, where a parallel phenomenon in post-Saussurean scholarship is the vexed relation between signifier and signified. Here we return to our original topic of the detachment of scholarship. Our only approach to knowledge is through language, the only path to what is signified being through the signifiers. When Derrida drives a wedge through this dualism, it means that there is no way out; we become trapped in language, and in the culture created out of language. As language is founded upon error, the society growing out of it tends toward the corrupt; in particular, it tends to project a source of authority out of rhetoric, a central signified to dominate over all signifiers, which tend to become ranked in some sort of hierarchical relation to it. In short, it creates a class structure; or possibly, to avoid Marxist arguments about the superstructural chicken and the infra-structural egg, something like Nietzsche's will to power creates them both.

Frye's recognition of the subversive element in traditional humanist culture is linked both to his willingness to remain associated with the university as an institution, and to his profound conviction that, in a society obsessed with 'alternatives,' we have not begun really to tap the infinite transforming powers of the arts. The individual ego, or what

Blake would call the natural man, cannot live without illusion, and it is no good underestimating its real fear of culture's power of revelation. The voices shouting loudest that literature, criticism, or culture must be totally revolutionized or else scrapped are sometimes only voices of panic. Those who do not understand are sometimes the first to speak of failure or decline, and the compulsion to revolutionize literature and literary criticism is sometimes an evasion of being revolutionized *by* them. Perhaps this is the real form of the anxiety of influence, and it is what Frye in *Creation and Recreation* calls repression.

There must be a truly creative and liberating power to work in the opposite direction from repression, and it probably comes as no great surprise at this point to give this power its name as the Blakean 'human form divine,' the imagination. The word 'divine' is there because Blake meant something by it, not because he was merely being rhetorical. What he meant by it was something so simple that all the rhetorical, rationalizing powers of anxiety have to be hurled against it to keep us from thinking we understand it or believe it. When the mind-forged manacles of repression are unbound, the solipsistic ego opens out into a larger form of identity, no longer cramped into the categories of ordinary time, space, and causality. As this description suggests, it is something that could truly be called divine, though at the same time it is the only form of identity which is truly human. Any humanism founding itself on the natural man and his language of experience remains stuck with the terminal vision of a psychotic ape looking at himself in a mirror, as Frye puts it at the close of *Creation and Recreation*. The disestablishment of the 'subject' in structuralism – as well as the complementary disestablishment of the 'object' in deconstructive theories – ought eventually to lead along the same lines, as soon as literary criticism has established what the constructive power in human language really is: I think Frye is essentially leading up to this in one of his most brilliant essays, significantly titled (out of Blake) 'Expanding Eyes.'[3]

There are several ways of looking at this power and its effects. They seem to form a sort of spectrum, beginning with complete denial. Here, from Harold Bloom's *A Map of Misreading* (165), is a resounding example of complete denial:

Blake would have insisted that only the Spectre of Urthona and not the 'Real Man the Imagination' in him, experienced anxiety in reading Wordsworth or in reading their common father, Milton. Blakean critics, like Frye, too easily join Blake in this insistence. But this is not the critic's proper work, to take up the poet's stance. Perhaps there *is* a power or faculty of the Imagination, and certainly all poets *must* go on believing in its existence, but a critic makes a better start by agreeing with Hobbes that imagination is 'decaying sense' and that poetry is written by the same natural man or woman who suffers daily all the inescapable anxieties of competition.[4]

Yet even Bloom finds poetry valuable in the opening to *Figures of Capable Imagination* in so far as it can give us an image of our own crippling in the dark glass of ourselves. Surely even such a marginal capability of self-transcendence is not completely removed from a Blakean imagination, even down to the image employed in Frye's description of Blake's technique in the darker passages of *Jerusalem*, a technique he calls 'analogy.'

Likewise, Derrida leaves us with the vision of an unending series of deconstructions – each form of understanding, because it uses the language of presence, having to be undone by another, which itself will eventually be found out as blind at some particular point. If this were totally the case, however, the complaint would be valid which is voiced by Fredric Jameson in *The Prison-House of Language*[5] and by the translator's introduction to *Of Grammatology*: that Derrida's own set of linguistic and philosophic terms must be vulnerable at some crucial point, so that a science of writing, a grammatology, could not itself escape being merely one more interpretation added to the heap.[6] But what does seem to escape in Derrida is at least some consciousness of the limitations of consciousness, and some articulation of the limitations of language. When he speaks of taking joy in the play of signifiers, there is the same sense of an impersonal vision looking down upon an ironic cycle that we find in Blake, for example, or Yeats. Something gets liberated, in any event, even if it is not a 'subject' or consciousness in the ordinary sense.

This transpersonal vision is by no means confined to modern poets. Frye would have made this observation the centre of a book on Spenser, if he had not found himself distracted from writing it by a compulsion to write the *Anatomy of Criticism*. The insight survives at the end of *The Secular Scripture* in a description of Spenser's tremendous vision at the climax of the Mutability Cantos, a Sabbath vision of what the world would look like once the ego has disappeared. Spenser's vision is a Logos vision, which implies that language itself is capable of transfiguration. Frye's theory throws emphasis, not on the alienating principle of difference, but on the power of identification in language, the principle of metaphor.

Finally, there is a political aspect to the imagination, too. When the bolts are shot from the locks of the prison-house of language, a detached vision is liberated which is not only the foundation of criticism but the basis of any real social action. In the 'Conclusion' to his book *Beginnings*, Edward Said, speaking of the current debate on the 'politics of culture,' states, 'The net effect, and to an extent also the cause, of this debate in France and the United States has been to discourage "academic" or "scholarly" study. Each has come to seem a pedantic exercise, and most American scholars probably agree that even the idea evoked by scholarship lacks dignity.'[7] Frye's career makes an astonishing contrast with this depressing statement, and it is interesting to see why this came to be. In 1942, when Frye published 'The Anatomy in Prose Fiction,' there was a world war going on. Forty years later, the attitude is still present in *The Great Code* which seems to have come to focus under pressure of the crisis of World War II and the events leading up to it. Frye has written of those days:

I am, in cultural background, what is known as a WASP, and thus belong to the only group in society which it is entirely safe to ridicule. I expected that a good deal of contemporary literature would be devoted to attacking the alleged complacency of the values and standards I had been brought up in, and was not greatly disturbed when it did. But with the rise of Hitler in Germany, the agony of the Spanish Civil War, and the massacres and deportations of Stalinism, things began to get more serious. For Eliot to announce that he was Classical in literature, royalist in politics, and Anglo-Catholic in religion was all part of the game. But the feeling of personal outrage and betrayal that I felt when I opened *After Strange Gods* was something else again. And when Eliot was accompanied by Pound's admiration for Mussolini, Yeats' flirtations with the most irresponsible of the Irish leaders, Wyndham Lewis' interest in Hitler, and the callow Marxism of younger writers, I felt that I could hardly get interested in any poet who was not closer to being the opposite in all respects to what Eliot thought he was.[8]

For all Frye's urbanity and his detachment from any polemics limited by the egocentric implications of the word 'position,' it should not be forgotten that his attitude remains that of Blake's 'Mental Fight,' the moral and creative equivalent of that corporeal war in which it was forged: by contrast, Said suggests that it was the morale-crippling years of Vietnam which provided the context in America for the radical debate of which he is speaking. The reproach, then, that Frye's version of literary tradition is overidealized is often made by those who do not take its vision of social context into account. Most explanations of his theories sound more idealized, in fact, than he ever sounds himself, which brings me around full circle to the point about Frye's affinity for satire.

Frye published three full-length articles, by my count, before *Fearful Symmetry*: satire was the subject of two of these directly and of the third obliquely. In *Fearful Symmetry* itself, we get the extraordinarily direct statement: 'One may wonder, in fact, whether Blake's sense of the grotesque, of broad caricature and ribald parody, was really a minor quality, and good only for an occasional *tour de force*. One may wonder whether satire was not his real medium, whether in the long run he was not of the race of Rabelais and Apuleius, a metaphysical satirist inclined to fantasy rather than symbolism.'[9] After twenty-five years, it still seems that too much energy goes into attacking or defending the *Anatomy of Criticism* as a system, rather than regarding it as an effort like that of Blake's Los, who said 'I must create a System,' but only as part of 'striving with Systems, to deliver Individuals from those systems.' 'Satire on ideas,' according to the Third Essay of the *Anatomy*, 'is only the special kind of art that defends its own creative detachment. The demand for order in thought produces a supply of intellectual systems: some of these attract and convert artists, but as an equally great poet could defend any other system equally well, no one system can contain the arts as they stand.'[10] The elusive quality of all those exuberantly proliferating categories derives from an element of deliberate meta-phorical paradox, designed to turn the mind inside out by forcing it to contemplate literature in several different but valid contexts simultan-eously. Frye's wit, which in 1942 was sometimes sharp enough to cut glass, is probably an integral part of his perception: what he once called 'the low comedy of my style' is similar to the quality in Blake which the Appendix to *Fearful Symmetry* found startlingly close to the paradoxi-cal humour of Zen. Edward Said provides a description very suggestive of the *Anatomy* when he speaks of knowledge 'apprehensible in terms of *nomadic centers*, provisional structures that are never permanent, always straying from one set of information to another';[11] like Blake's 'Giant Forms,' one might add. In terms of the *Anatomy*, wherever we are in literature is potentially the centre of our literary experience. However, Said's next sentence is, 'When this position is compared with that of Frye's *Anatomy of Criticism*, the difference between them is seen to be dramatic.' This is because Said does see it as a systematization, 'premised upon structural principles for which Frye's analogies are tonal music and Platonic Christianity. The former gives him a well-tempered circle within which to enclose all literary discourse, the latter a *logos* by which to center all literary experience.'[12] Nevertheless, such a figure as a well-tempered circle is a descriptive metaphor, not a Platonic essence. Because it is descriptive, it must correspond to something about its object. But because it is a metaphor, it does not exhaust or contain that object, and so must interpenetrate with other metaphors which reveal its other aspects. The tension here between description and figuration, or construction, may not be logically resolvable, but it is unavoidable, and in fact gives the language of the humanities and social sciences a large part of its dynamism. Analysed by the intellect, it may eventually desiccate itself into a valley of the dry bones of intellectual paradox. But the metamorphosis which is death-by-division to the corporeal understanding is the resurrection and the life to the metaphorical imagination. As Frye has said, speaking of the figures of Blake's *mythos*, but in a passage evocative of the real nature of his own archetypes and the spirit of his own criticism:

And in Rabelais, where huge creatures rear up and tear themselves out of Paris and Touraine, bellowing for drink and women, combing cannon balls out of their hair, eating six pilgrims in a salad, excreting like dinosaurs and copulating like the ancient sons of God who made free with the daughters of men, we come perhaps closest of all to what Blake meant by the resurrection of the body. Rabelais' characters are what Blake called his, 'Giant Forms', and they are the horsemen who ride over the earth in the day of the trumpet and alarm, where we, in our sublunary world, see nothing but anguish and death.[13]

NOTES

1 'The Anatomy in Prose Fiction,' *Manitoba Arts Review*, 3.1 (Spring, 1942), 35-47.
2 'The Four Forms of Prose Fiction,' *Hudson Review*, 2 (1950), 582-95.
3 'Expanding Eyes,' *Spiritus Mundi* (Bloomington and London, 1976), 99-123.
4 Harold Bloom, *A Map of Misreading* (New York, 1975), 165.
5 Fredric Jameson, *The Prison-House of Language* (Princeton, 1972), see 182-6.
6 Gayatri Chakravorty Spivak, Translator's Preface to Jacques Derrida, *Of Grammatology* (Baltimore and London, 1974, 1976); see especially section v.
7 Edward Said, *Beginnings: Intention and Method* (Baltimore and London, 1975), 375.
8 'The Search for Acceptable Words,' *Spiritus Mundi*, 23.

9 *Fearful Symmetry: A Study of William Blake* (Princeton, 1947), 193.
10 *Anatomy of Criticism: Four Essays* (Princeton, 1957), 231.
11 *Beginnings*, 376.
12 Ibid.
13 *Fearful Symmetry*, 201.

**JOHN FRECCERO**

# Manfred's Wounds and the Poetics of the 'Purgatorio'

In the third canto of the *Purgatorio*, one of the excommunicants calls to Dante to ask if the pilgrim recognizes him:

> biondo era e bello e di gentile aspetto
> ma l'un de' cigli un colpo avea diviso.

> (Fair was he and beautiful and of gentle aspect, but one of his brows had been cleft by a blow.)

The mark is not enough to identify him, so that the spirit names himself:

> ... 'Or vedi';
> e mostrommi una piaga a sommo 'l petto.
> Poi sorridendo disse, 'Io son Manfredi,
>   nepote di Costanza imperadrice ...'

> ('Look here,' and he showed me a wound at the top of his chest. Then smiling he said, 'I am Manfred, the grandson of the Empress Constance ...')

The episode marks one of the most famous moments of the *Purgatorio*: a generic description of masculine beauty, slightly skewed by rhetorical distortion, is interrupted by the adversative 'but' that suffices to mar the ideal with what appears to be an accident of history. That cleft brow helped to make Manfred a romantic hero in the nineteenth century and serves as testimony today of Dante's prodigious power of representation.

At first glance, the representation might appear to be an example of what Erich Auerbach referred to as mimesis, especially since his classic

work on the subject began with a chapter entitled 'Odysseus' Scar.'
Manfred's wounds are equally unforgettable and perhaps for some of the
same reasons, but they serve a deeper purpose than Dante's desire to
hold up a mirror to reality. In fact, the wounds are an anomaly in the
representation, a flaw that seems to undermine the bases of Dante's
fiction: we learn, later on in the *Purgatorio*, that the souls wending
their way up the mountain have aerial bodies, fictive replicas of their
real bodies and exact reflections of the soul itself. Wounds are
inexplicable on such bodies, because they seem to be accidental
intrusions into the ideal corporeity of the afterlife. If Manfred's wounds
are reminiscent of Odysseus' scar, it cannot be at the level of descriptive
detail. Odysseus' scar, Auerbach tells us, is an example of Homeric
realism, described by the poet because it is *there*; Manfred's wounds, on
the other hand, demand an interpretation. They are *there*, on a body
made of thin air, and ought not to be.

The basis for associating the two texts is mythic, rather than mimetic,
and becomes clear when we challenge Auerbach's reading of Odysseus'
scar. The thesis of Auerbach's essay seems undermined by its title. The
purpose of the essay was to reveal 'the need of the Homeric style to leave
nothing which it mentions half in darkness and unexternalized.'[1] In the
style that 'knows only a foreground, only a uniformly illuminative,
uniformly objective present, ... never is there a form left fragmentary or
half-illuminated, never a lacuna, never a gap, never a glimpse of
unplumbed depths.'[2] Yet Odysseus' scar is itself precisely all of those
things: an indelible mark of the past within the present, an opaque sign
healed over a hidden depth. The scar is the mark of Odysseus' identity
and manhood, or there could be no recognition. In a passage whose
significance Auerbach does not discuss, Homer tells us that the hero,
when hunting as a boy, was gored in the thigh by a wild boar which he
then killed with his lance. Almost seventy lines are devoted to
describing the nobility of his lineage and his youthful courage, so that
the scar remaining from the hunting accident takes upon itself a
meaning never hinted at by Auerbach: it is a sign of Odysseus'
coming-of-age, almost a ritual scar, and it identifies him in the eyes of
his former nurse, not fortuitously, but rather as the sign at once relating
him to his ancestors and distinguishing him from them. In the
succession of fathers and sons, Odysseus' scar marks his place precisely,
bracketing him between his ancestors and Telemachus, his son, who is
about to undergo his own baptism of blood.

At some level, of course, Auerbach knew that the primordial drama of male identity was hidden beneath the apparently innocuous and realistic detail. When he turned for contrast in the same essay to an equally ancient epic in a totally different tradition, he chose the story of Abraham and Isaac, the foundation story for Israel and a foreshadowing of the circumcision. Odysseus' scar is also a kind of circumcision. It bears the same relationship to Adonis' fatal wound (in Northrop Frye's masterful reading of the myth)[3] that circumcision bears to castration. For all of the irreducible differences between the two epics, they are united by a common theme: the rites of violence that have traditionally been used by males to mark their identity and manhood.

Manfred's wounds hide a similar story, for they signify his relationship to his father, yet, by an ironic reversal of earthly values that is one of the functions of Dante's other-worldly perspective, they mark his passage away from patrilinear succession toward the mother. Critics have noticed that Manfred identifies himself only as the grandson of the Empress Constance; in fact, he was the son of Frederick II Hohenstaufen, known in Dante's day as *Stupor Mundi*.[4] This pointed reticence has been explained in various ways: psychologizing critics have suggested that Manfred, although Frederick's favourite, was a natural son and not the legitimate heir of the mighty emperor. It is indelicate, according to this line of reasoning, for a bastard to name his father. A slightly more sophisticated view, the thematic interpretation, insists that Frederick is in Hell, with the rest of the Epicureans, and thus is erased from the memory of his son. The contrast between Manfred's radiant smile and his ghastly wound serves as a contrast between the vicissitudes of history and the power of grace for the late repentant.

A more interesting thematic reading of the passage involves Dante's own political ideals. Frederick was the founder of the Ghibelline imperial dream, but was by Dante's time totally discredited as a heretic and an excommunicant. The fictive salvation of his son, mortally wounded at the battle of Benevento, might then represent a survival of the Ghibelline ideal, to which Dante clung against all the evidence of his senses. On this reading, Manfred's insistence on Grace, 'mentre che la speranza ha fior del verde,' might then mask a much more specific hope for Dante's own political dream. In the *Purgatorio*, Manfred remembers his daughter, 'la mia buona Costanza,' the honour of Sicily and Aragon, and asks the pilgrim to tell her that he has been saved, in spite of his excommunication. Manfred is therefore bracketed between the two Constances, his grandmother in Paradise and his daughter on earth. The ideal of Empire lives on, but in matrilinear succession, outside the city of man, and reconciled at last to *Mater Ecclesia*. Manfred's message to his daughter repeats, yet transforms, the popular oracle that was said to have kept Germany dreaming imperial ideals for centuries after the death of Frederick II: 'He lives not; yet he lives.'[5] The body of the father is entombed in porphyry, the monument to imperial aspirations in Palermo or, for that matter, in Paris, but Manfred's bones are scattered to the four winds:

> Or le bagna la pioggia e move il vento
> di fuor dal regno, quasi lungo 'l Verde,
> dov' e' le trasmutò a lume spento.

(Now they are drenched by the rain and the wind shifts them *outside of the realm*, along the course of the river Verde, to which the Bishop brought them, with extinguished candles).

The dispersion of Manfred's corpse suggests that, in so far as he is still a hero of a realm, the kingdom is not of this world.

Manfred's wounds are the scars of history, but his smile is a revisionist smile, belying the official versions of his fate. In spite of the fact that he was excommunicated by the Church, Dante places him among the late repentant, who will ultimately reach Paradise. Manfred tells us that the Bishop who had his body disinterred had misread that page in God's book; the implication seems to be that the poet, unlike the Church, has read God's book correctly. Manfred's salvation therefore represents an interpretation of the brute details of history, an allegorical reading of those wounds that belies the horror that they literally imply. As Manfred survived extinction, so Dante's political ideal survives historical contradiction by assimilation into the unity of his vision.

If Manfred's real body is dispersed, then it is clear that his fictive body is a representation, bearing symbolic wounds, diacritical marks slashed across the face of his father. Frederick's beauty won for him the title of *Sol invictus*: the adjectives *biondo, bello e di gentile aspetto* might have been taken from contemporary chronicles describing the Emperor.[6] At the same time, Frederick's *persona* is the mystical body of Empire, the head of state, as we still say, whose heart is the law. The dazzling incongruity of Manfred's smile serves to affirm the triumph of the ideal in spite of the apparently mortal wounds to both the head and heart. Like the scar of Odysseus, the adversative 'ma' serves to affirm sameness with a profound difference – that is to say, the syntax performs the function of ritual scarring. The wounds incurred in his father's name win for him his own: 'Io son Manfredi' – so that the mortal wounds are in fact a baptism, a rebirth into a new order, with what Saint Paul called 'a circumcision of the heart' (Romans 2:2).

For all of the apparently mimetic power of Dante's verses, there can be no doubt that corporeal representation in the poem is self-consciously symbolic. In this respect the *Purgatorio* does not differ greatly from the *Inferno*. The recognition of Manfred has its infernal counterpart in Mohammed among the schismatics, who bares his cloven chest as an emblem of theological schism and is introduced by similar syntax – 'vedi com'io mi dilacco.' In the same canto (XXVIII), Bertrand de Born's decapitated body suggests the schism in the political order. The clinical horror – Bertrand carrying his head like a lantern – lends horror to the more abstract political enormity. Bertrand is said to have set father against son:

Perch'io parti' così giunte persone,
  partito porto il mio cerebro, lasso!
  dal suo principio ch'è in questo troncone.
Così s'osserva in me lo contrapasso –

(Because I divided persons who were so conjoined I carry my brain separated from its source in this trunk. Thus is observed in me the counterpass –).

Applying the same figure, we may say that the marks on Manfred's fictive body also stand for his relationship to a wounded theological and political order which he has survived and, in a sense, redeemed.

The representation of Manfred is meant to bear witness of this redemption within the fiction of Dante's purgatorial journey. His wounds, apparently accidental, are in fact signs of his identity and distinction. They are like the marks of *history*, which cannot be accommodated by the abstract mimetic claim of a one-to-one correspondence between the aerial bodies of the Purgatory and the souls which produce them. At some level, the disfiguring marks of history mark the soul as well. Like writing itself, they deface in the name of significance. Their presence in the *Purgatorio* is at the same time the poet's mark, his intervention in the fiction that otherwise purports to be an unmediated representation of the other world. As wounds are inexplicable on an aerial body, so writing is inexplicable on what is claimed to be an exact representation of an other-worldly vision.

Paradoxically, the text 'mirrors' the other world only by virtue of its cracks.

Lest the parallel between Manfred's wounds and the text itself seem too ingenious for a medieval text, it should be pointed out that such an analogy is implied in what is probably the most famous and most solemn of recognition scenes. The newly risen Christ shows his wounds to Thomas so that he may believe what he has *seen*: 'Thomas, because thou hast seen me, thou hast believed: blessed are they that have not seen, and yet have believed.' Christ's wounds, made manifest to Thomas, bear witness to the Resurrection. The solemnity of that moment lends to the representation of Manfred a theological force that serves to underscore the strength of Dante's Imperial faith.

It is, however, the passage immediately following Thomas' recognition in the gospel of John that I wish especially to recall in this context. The narrative of Jesus' works ends with his remark to Thomas and, almost as if to end *his* work, John adds these words: 'And many other signs truly did Jesus in the presence of his disciples, which are not written in this book, but these are written, that ye might believe that Jesus is the Christ, the Son of God, and that believing, ye might have life through his name.' The writer of the gospel thereby establishes a parallel between the wounds of Christ's body and his own text, filled with signs that demand of the reader the same assent that is demanded of the doubting Thomas. As Christ's scarred body is *seen* by the disciples, so John's text is *read* by the faithful. That analogy is operative in Dante's poem. Manfred's wounds, slashed across a body made of thin air, stand for Dante's own intrusion into the course of history. They are, as it were, writing itself, Dante's own markings introduced across the page of history as testimony of a truth which otherwise might not be perceived. It is this parallelism between the text and the aerial body of the *Purgatorio* that establishes the fiction of the *Purgatorio*, the vision of the pilgrim translated by the writing of the poet, scars of history erased and assimilated into God's Book, where the Truth is finally conveyed, according to Saint Augustine, without letters and without words.

The analogy between the aerial body and the poem itself is consistently developed throughout the *Purgatorio*. It underlies the apparently gratuitous account that Dante gives us in canto xxv of the formation of the body in the afterlife. The question is how the souls in this circle can speak of nourishment or grow thinner in their askesis when there is no need of food. Virgil answers with generic theories of mimesis and poetic representation: the bodies of the *Purgatorio* are related to real bodies as the torch was related to the life span of Meleager in the eighth book of the *Metamorphoses* or as an image in a mirror is related to what it reflects. This statement of the relation of the aerial bodies to nature – like a mirror or like a lamp – establishes the context as unmistakably aesthetic, with ancient figures for doctrines of poetic inspiration that have become particularly familiar to us since they were studied by M.H. Abrams.[7] If the bodies of the Purgatory are related to nature as either mirror or lamp, then the poem itself is either a mimetic or metaphoric representation of nature. This is as far as Virgil will go in his explanation, asserting that a complete understanding of the process transcends human understanding. He then defers to Statius for a fuller explanation than he can provide.

At this point, Dante enters upon a digression that has been something of a scandal in the history of Dante criticism, not only because of its apparent irrelevance, but also because of its reputed technical aridity. In the midst of six cantos of the *Purgatorio* that deal more or less explicitly with poetry, Dante now embarks upon what amounts to a lesson in medieval embryology. This occurs when Statius chooses to answer the question about the fictive bodies of the Purgatory with a discussion of the general relationship of body and soul, on earth as well as in the afterlife. As we shall see, the lesson has at least as much to do with poetics as it has with embryology. Like an analogously technical discussion in the *Paradiso* on the nature of moon spots, this scientific disquisition can be skipped over by the general reader only at the risk of missing something essential about the nature of Dante's poetic theory.

To anticipate somewhat, I should like to suggest that Statius' discussion about conception and reproduction in canto xxv also serves as a gloss on canto xxiv, where the subject is *literary* creation and conception. More than that, it seems to suggest strongly an analogy between the act of writing and the act of procreation. Dante begins with the clinically obvious and proceeds to explain its metaphysical signific- ance. Sexuality is, for Dante, nature's expression of creativity, rather than the repressed subject matter of literary expression. This is one important sense in which it may be said that art imitates nature. As the soul is inspired in the foetus, so the inspiration of the poet comes from God. The body, however, is the work of parenthood. In the same way, the poetic corpus is sired by the poet, who provides the vehicle for God's message.

Statius begins by telling us how the seed is formed. A small portion of blood is stored and purified in the heart of the male and is eventually transformed into the male seed, which contains within it an informing power, *virtute informativa*, that will gradually mould the blood of the female into a human body, with all of its organs. When this power is released into the female, the two bloods unite and the foetus is formed. The foetus then naturally grows into a vegetative and then into a sensitive soul. As yet, there is no human life at all, strictly speaking; it is not until the brain is completely formed, in about the sixth month of pregnancy, that God directly inspires the intellective soul into the embryo:

> ... sì tosto come al feto
> l'articular del cerebro è perfetto,
> lo motor primo a lui si volge lieto
> *sovra tant' arte di natura, e spira*
> *spirito novo, di vertù repleto,*
> che ciò che trova attivo quivi, tira
> in sua sustanzia, e fassi un'alma sola,
> che vive e sente e sé in sé rigira.

(... as soon as the brain of the foetus is perfectly formed, the prime mover turns joyfully to such a work of nature's art and inspires in it a new spirit, filled with power, so that what it finds active there it draws into its substance and makes of itself a single soul, that grows and feels and reflects upon itself.)

Statius then moves directly to a discussion of the formation of the fictive body in the afterlife. At the moment of death, the soul falls to the shore to which it is destined and there the informing virtue which it possesses irradiates the surrounding air, as a ray of light irradiates moist air to form a rainbow, in order to form its aerial body. The soul *imprints*, 'suggella,' the surrounding air with its own form and so creates the ghostly body that the pilgrim sees.

Except for a passing reference in Hugh of Saint Victor, there does not seem to be a precedent in specifically Christian thought of the Middle Ages for the belief that the soul could unite with the air in order to form an aerial body, although that demons had such power was a commonplace of popular and learned belief. Neo-Platonic thought might well admit such a possibility, but the Christian emphasis on the indissoluble unity of the human composite and the Aristotelian theory of hylomorphism to which Dante subscribed rule out the possibility that Dante means us to take the fiction seriously as metaphysics.[8] It does not require a great deal of the reader's imagination to see in this fiction a disguised poetic claim. The seal of reality is stamped upon the dreamlike medium of the Purgatory as the seal of the soul is affixed to the wax of the body. Dante's poem seems to make a claim for a kind of mimetic essentialism – realism in the medieval sense of the word.

The 'realistic' quality of the *Purgatorio* is the central theme of this portion of the poem. It has often been remarked that the second realm of the poem is the most lifelike, the most modern part of the vision. Here souls are on the move, on pilgrimage as they were on earth, possessed of a temporality that is measured by the imagination of the pilgrim. His subjectivity is the stage of the action here. Unlike the claim of objective presence in the *Inferno* or the ethereal non-representation of the *Paradiso*, the surrounding world is here filtered through the pilgrim's *fantasia*, which is itself the power that creates images in the form of dreams, out of thin air. The action of *fantasia* is exactly analogous to the process of the afterlife as Dante imagines it. The bodies of the *Purgatorio* are of the same order of reality as the bodies of the imagination, quite literally the 'stuff that dreams are made on.' The pilgrim's initial question about the mode of existence of the bodies here amounts to a question about the relationship of his poem to the real world.

With this hypothesis in mind, Statius' discussion of conception takes upon itself a new dimension of meaning. There are echoes, in Statius' speech, of Dante's doctrine of poetic inspiration contained in the canto immediately preceding this. In canto xxiv, Bonagiunta da Lucca asks the pilgrim if he is the man who drew forth, 'trasse fore,' the new rhymes of the sweet new style. The verb unmistakably suggests childbirth and the adjective *new*, repeated several times, prepares the way for the discussion of the infusion of the intellective soul by God: 'spirito novo, di vertu repleto.' Most interesting, however, is the pilgrim's reply, which for centuries has been taken as Dante's definition of his own art:

> I' mi son un che, quando
> Amor mi spira, noto, e a quel modo
> ch'e' ditta dentro vo significando ...

> (As for me, I am one who, when love inspires me, take note, and in the manner that it is written within, I go signifying ...)

The moment of poetic inspiration exactly matches the moment of inspiration of the new soul: 'sovra tant' arte di natura ... spira spirito novo.' The work of art is not nature's art but that of the poet, although the source of inspiration, *spirito novo*, is the same. The forcefulness and syntactic isolation of the verb 'noto,' etymologically, 'I mark,' seems to highlight the moment of inscription; given the analogy with procreation, it would seem to correspond with the moment of conception, recalling Jean de Meung's playful references to 'nature's stylus' in the sexual act.[9] Dante's emphasis is however on the unitary source of spiritual inspiration, the soul of the foetus or the spirit of the text. At the same time, the gerund 'vo significando' suggests that literary creation is not a moment but a process, a constant approximation approaching but never quite reaching God's text within as its limit. The construction used in that sense has since been hallowed by literary tradition. When the Romantic Leopardi wrote his own lyric on the subject of literary inspiration, invoking the wind rather than God's spirit, he used a similar construction to describe his own effort: in 'L'Infinito,' the act of writing is rendered 'vo comparando' – 'I am comparing' – presumably the present text with Nature's own. For Dante, the gerund depicts the *process* of writing, the askesis that will bring the 'body' of the text closer and closer to the spirit which informs it. The words suggest that the poem, like the pilgrim, is still en route in the *Purgatorio*.

Manfred's wounds constitute the marks that must be expunged in order for history to be brought into conformity with God's will, just as sin must be purged in order for the soul to be made 'puro e disposto a salire alle stelle.' At the same time, the wounds have served a providential purpose, in much the same way that sin can prepare the way for conversion. In this respect, both history and sin are analogues for writing itself. As history *disfigures* the face of Manfred with apparently accidental marks that in fact give him his significance under the aspect of eternity, so writing progressively disfigures the page ('vo significando') in order paradoxically to make it clear. The process of interpretation, like the process of purgation, is an assimilation and a gradual *effacement* of the marks, like melting footprints in the snow: 'così la neve al sol si disigilla.' The phrase from the *Paradiso* signals the ending of the poet's work and the vision of God's Book, 'legato con Amore in un volume, ciò che per il mondo si squaderna.'

Readers of the *Purgatorio* will remember that its central action, for the pilgrim, is the *erasing* of his sins, sins that are at once *wounds* and *letters*. The instrument is not nature's stylus, nor that of the poet, but history's pen. The angel guardian of the Purgatory draws seven letter P's on the forehead of the pilgrim with his sword, as a representation of his history:

Sette P ne la fronte mi descrisse
   col punton della spada e 'Fa' che lavi
   quando se' dentro, queste piaghe' disse.

(He drew seven P's on my forehead with the point of his sword and 'see that when you are within, you wash these *wounds*,' he said.)

The penitential process for the pilgrim consists in the eradication of wounds inflicted by a sword. We may imagine this also to be the case with Manfred's wound, eternally there in the space of canto III, but effaced in the process of refinement toward the resurrected body. Later on, Statius describes the whole penetential process in this way: 'Con tal cura conviene e con tai pasti, / che la piaga da sezzo si ricucia.' (With such care and with such a cure will the wound be completely healed.) Underlying these images is the affirmation that the poem we read has its counterpart in Manfred's face.

In God's Book, Manfred's brow is clear. This is implied by a verse that has always presented a certain difficulty for commentators. Speaking of the Bishop who had his body disinterred and thrown into the river, Manfred says that had the pastor realized that Manfred was saved, he would have spared his body. The difficult sentence reads: 'Se 'l pastor di Cosenza ... avesse in Dio ben letta questa faccia,' and the difficulty resides in the translation of the word 'faccia,' which means either 'face' or, as Charles Singleton has translated it, 'page.' 'Had the pastor of Cosenze well *read* that page of God.' Our discussion thus far suggests, however, that one might equally well have translated the word 'faccia' as 'face,' thereby giving more force to the Bishop's misreading and more concreteness to the demonstrative adjective 'questa': 'Had the pastor of Cosenza well read *this face* in God.' God's Book has no marks that are subject to misinterpretation; Manfred's wounds, however, might have been taken as signs of his damnation when read from a purely human perspective, without benefit of that radiant smile.

Finally an additional nuance of meaning can be derived from comparing this passage with what is undoubtedly its source. There is a culminating moment at the end of Book VI of the *Aeneid* when Anchises points out to his son the shadow of a soul who might have been a hero of

Rome equal to Marcellus had he not died prematurely. Scholars tell us that he was the adopted son of the Emperor and Octavia is said to have fainted with grief when Virgil first recited his lines. They describe the handsome boy in terms that recall, if only by contrast, the description of Manfred, even to the adversative *sed*, which serves to indicate not a wound, but an enveloping darkness suggestive of premature death:

A man young, very handsome and clad in shining armour, *but* with face and eyes down cast and little joy on his brow ... What a noble presence he has, *but* the night flits black about his head and shadows him with gloom ... Alas his goodness, alas his ancient honour and right hand invincible in war! ... Ah poor boy! If thou mayest break the grim bar of fate, thou shall be Marcellus. Give me lilies in full hands ...           (*Aeneid* VI.860-85)

The foreboding darkness contrasts with the smile of Manfred in the same way that Virgilian pathos contrasts with the hope of the *Purgatorio*; even the eternity of Rome must bow before the death of this beautiful young man. He too is an emperor's son, but the success of Empire cannot mitigate individual grief. We are left with Anchises' futile funereal gesture.

From Dante's standpoint, of course, this is the Virgilian misreading of death; Manfred's smile, with an imperial dream in shambles, is in a sense a smile at Virgil's expense. It happens that this passage contains the only verse from the *Aeneid* literally quoted, in the original Latin, in the *Divine Comedy*: 'Manibus O date lilia plenis!' It occurs in a very different context, toward the end of the *cantica*, as Beatrice approaches for the first time. The angels sing out for the lilies of the Resurrection and Anchises' funereal gesture is turned into a note of triumph.

This deliberate misreading of Virgil brings me to the final point I want to make concerning the effacement of heterogeneity in Dante's text. I have said that Dante's doctrine of poetic inspiration cannot account for what may be called the 'body' of his text as opposed to its spirit. If the inspiration is claimed to be God-given, the poetic *corpus* is very much Dante's own. To extend the procreative image that Dante has established, we may say that the claim of inspiration does not account for the ancestry of the text, especially for the influence of Virgil, whom Dante refers to as his 'dolcissimo patre' at precisely the moment when he quotes the *Aeneid* verbatim, thereby acknowledging Virgil's part in the genesis of his own poem. Once more, heterogeneity is assimilated by an effacement before our eyes. The foreignness of the Virgilian sentiment here at the top of the mountain, underscored by the foreignness of the original language, is neutralized by the otherwise seamless context; death is transformed into resurrection, leaving behind the distinctive mark of the disappearing father, his text in Latin like a foreign element. Like Manfred's wound, the sign of the father is most in evidence at the moment of the son's triumph and, again like Manfred's wound, it is about to be effaced.

After that quotation from Virgil's text, the pilgrim trembles at the approach of Beatrice and turns to tell Virgil, 'Conosco i segni dell'antica fiamma,' – 'I recognize the signs of the ancient flame' – which is, not a direct quotation this time, but a literal translation of Dido's words of foreboding when she first sees Aeneas and recalls her passion for her dead husband while she anticipates the funeral pyre on which she will die: 'Agnosco veteris flammae vestigia' (*Aeneid* IV.23). Dante transforms those words as well, for he uses them to celebrate the return of his beloved and a love stronger than death. He turns to Virgil for support and finds him gone. Calling to him three times, the text evokes the merest allusion to a Virgilian text, the disappearance of Eurydice in the Fourth Georgic: 'Eurydice, Eurydice, Eurydice':

Ma Virgilio n'avea lasciati scemi
 di sé, Virgilio dolcissimo patre,
 Virgilio a cui per mia salute die'mi.

(But Virgil had left us bereft of himself, Virgil sweetest father, Virgil to whom I gave myself for my salvation.)

The calling out to Eurydice is the culmination of Virgilian pathos, lamenting death that is stronger than poetry, as it is stronger than love and even than Rome. Dante's adversative *ma* records the loss, yet transcends it with an affirmation. The progression from direct quotation to direct translation to merest allusion is an effacement, further and further away from the letter of Virgil's text, as Virgil fades away in the dramatic representation to make way for Beatrice. It is at that point, for the first time, that the poet is called by name: 'Dante!' The intrusion of Virgil's words into Dante's text is at that point the mark of poetic maturity.

NOTES

1 Erich Auerbach, *Mimesis*, trans. Willard Trask (Princeton, 1953), 3.
2 Ibid., 4-5.
3 Northrop Frye, *Anatomy of Criticism* (Princeton, 1957), 189.
4 On Frederick, see Ernst Kantorowicz, *Frederick the Second*, trans. W. Trask (Princeton, 1948).
5 Ibid., 421.
6 Ibid., 75.
7 Meyer H. Abrams, *The Mirror and the Lamp* (Cambridge, Mass., 1958).
8 Robert Klein, 'L'Enfers de Marsile Ficin,' in *L'umanesimo e esoterismo*, ed. E. Castelli (Roma, 1955), 264.
9 *Roman de la Rose*, XXXIV.72.

**JAMES
NOHRNBERG**

# 'Paradise Regained'
# by One Greater Man:
# Milton's Wisdom Epic as
# a 'Fable of Identity'

I

*Paradise Regained* makes an intense study of Christ's life as it can be divined and summarized upon the threshold of the ministry. At the same time, the poem takes a deeply retrospective view of Milton's own vocational history.[1] Milton's poetic canon closes with the canonization of Samson and the maturation of Christ, even as the Christological portion of that canon opened with the birth of Christ and the twenty-first birthday of Milton. Thus the ode 'On the Morning of Christ's Nativity' is also an ode 'Upon the Morn of Milton's Poetic Majority,' a Christian's accession to his legal majority being for Milton virtually identical with his birth.[2] Similarly, the second epic, 'Upon the Threshold of Christ's Vocational Maturity,' is also written 'Upon the Eve of the Poet's Retirement,' for Milton twice retired – to prepare to write poetry.

The Nativity Ode offered Milton the strongest evidence of his vocation: an authentication equivalent to that provided for a Hebrew prophet by his inaugural vision. The poem itself specified Milton's vocation to write poems about Christ's life, precisely at those points where the life was sacramentally aligned with the Christian year and Miltonic occasion. The Nativity Ode is cited as the precedent for beginning poems on the Passion and Circumcision, and Milton uses this manner of beginning – by referring to his own precedent – yet once more: for *Paradise Regained*, staged in the liturgical interval occupied by the Passion, at the end of Lent. Thus the poem completes the uncompletable 'Passion,' even while offering a prefatory parallel for the *patiens*-drama of *Samson Agonistes*.

In each of Milton's dramatically structured poems, a crisis of vocation is brought forward, enlarged upon protractedly, and climactically resolved. The Christ of *Paradise Regained* provides a ready summary of much of Milton's figuration of the vocational self: the oracle-silencing prodigy of the Nativity Ode; the active retirement ethos of *L'Allegro* and *Il Penseroso*; the untemptable virgin of *Comus*, delivered only belatedly to a quasi-Baptismal reparation of freshness; the absent and returning saviour-figure of the dying god myth of *Lycidas* (with the Petrine offices of pastor and fisher); and the newly decreed Son who defeats Satan on the third day of the contest of *Paradise Lost*. By the time of *Paradise Regained*, Milton was not choosing his subject; it was choosing him.

In this poem the emeritus epic poet reaffirms the wisdom of his choice of vocation and subject, by revisiting an archetypal scene of wise choice. But what comparable scene does Christ himself revisit? The Baptism and the returns to his Father's and mother's houses suggest the answer. So does the poem's first word, which is an 'I' announcing a subject thrown back upon the resources of his own ego. Prime among these resources will be the subject's consciousness of sonship. Thus both the youthful poet of the Nativity Ode and the justified poet of *Paradise Lost* have chosen the symbol of Christ, the adored infant and the man made perfect in the eyes of his Father. For the ego, the beloved Son is symbolic of the good effects of having chosen the right parents: of having chosen in their favour, and of having been chosen and sponsored by them. Thus the prior wilderness calling that Christ fulfils is the calling of the ego itself.

The original of Milton's double subject – the calling of the ego and the identification of one's calling – must be found in their template-relations: the prophet, after all, is called by name.[3] Christ is the symbol of the early ego, because he is in possession of the Messianic secret of his own future prevalence: that is what the infant is smiling about. The promotion of the ego from darkness is indeed an advancement to a new order of being, and a calling out of Egypt. The self's eventual ascendancy to maturity is a second such calling, regaining for the ego – in intentional form – that paradise and promised land of self-determination that the primary conferral of selfhood originally seemed to offer. In Milton's *De Doctrina* the first and most important of God's 'special decrees' is God's declaration of the Son, and every ego will feel the same about its own distinction.[4]

II

It might be thought that *Paradise Regained* is about temptation, but Christ is not tempted, only harrassed. By the time the temptations come from Satan, Christ has already faced and answered them. In effect, Satan arrives too late; his urgency pertains to his own supercession. Christ can treat the temptations almost retrospectively, because although the 'ego' of the poem dwells momentarily on past disappointments, it is not tempted by past mistakes. In rejecting some of the means and ends Satan offers on the second day, Christ sounds almost reminiscent.[5] Once Christ has refused, Satan sounds resigned too.

It is Samson who properly suffers temptation, because Samson continues to suffer his vulnerability. The case is quite otherwise with Christ, who has only the past of *other* men to atone for. But just as Samson contends with ghostly embassies from a past that is reluctant to release him, so Christ contends with demonic visitations from a future that comes out to meet him. Thus, in dealing with Satan, Christ must also deal with scheming Herod, an importunate Mary, faithless or opportunistic 'brethren,' Zealots among his followers, entrapping Pharisees, Jews murmuring over his claims upon the Father, Jews who would molest him and cast him from a cliff, the apostle Satanically inspired to tempt him to evade martyrdom, the armed men who arrest him, baffled Pilate, the scornful Bad Thief, the mockers at the Crucifixion, and Doubting Thomas. References to all of these are worked into Milton's text, in a *tour de force* of allusive virtuosity modelled on that of Christ in the gospel account itself.

Thus Christ is tried by the future. This orientation on the future explains the vocational placing of the temptation-stories in the Bible generally, near the heads of the various histories: antedeluvian (Adam), Patriarchal (Abraham), Mosaic (Israel), royal (David), and Christian (Peter). All express the trial and approval or disapproval of God's newly created subjects. What, then, do the temptations of *Paradise Regained* create; or rather, in the case of a being already as fully created morally as Christ is, what do they illustrate as 'good'? Here we would answer, the temptation-resistant ego itself: the temptations represent possible regressions from the ego's future, or delusionary presumptions on that future. Summoned by the future, the ego is formulated and reformulated as if it were the recipient of a series of callings. From the calling of hunger the base beginnings of the ego's separate existence can be deduced – from its continuity in the absence of food (bread temptation, first night's dream). The reflection of bodily well-being and whole-being in the cognate flesh of the mother calls the ego to the periphery of a diffuse romance pleasance; the outlines of the object call into being the coddled or self-boiled entity of the ego as body and subject. And need and its satisfaction call into being desire and wish (the dream of appetite, the banquet temptation). The imposition of training calls into being the will; the reproaching and forbidding of some desires calls into being the thirst for power and approval (wealth, power, and glory temptations). The sexualizing of the communion with the mother calls rivalry into being, and the thwarting of Oedipal love calls the virtue of 'longanimity' into being; Sonship now fosters a fantasy of eventual dominion over the fatherland – the mother in patriotic guise (the Kingdoms temptation). Christ is defined as fulfilling the vocation of 'one greater man,' and for the ego this enlarged personage is that of the parent. So even while Christ as post-Oedipal ego has resisted the vocational temptation to a vulgar greatness, which occupies the central place in Satan's offerings, he accepts the challenge to grow up and to express by matchless deeds his matchless sire.[6] Finally, knowledge (the Athens temptation) calls mortality into being (the 'ugly dreams' of the second night), through which the subject is perfected or recalled to non-being (pinnacle temptation).

The two great closures in life are the end of youthful maturation, with the advent of adulthood, and the end of full participation, which anticipates the concluding of existence. In so far as these two canonic points are valedictory and renunciatory, they call the identity into question, like a fast. In so far as these points summarize and recapitulate the identity, they express the self's objectification, or historical character, like a birthday or festival. Partly owing to Milton's late maturation and his early retirement (with his blindness), almost all of his major poems move towards these two poles. Two conspicuous ego-motifs of *Paradise Lost*, the undoing of precocity and the delaying of death, translate readily into the poet's life-scheme. For the great alignment in Milton's life occurs between the necessarily belated arrival of his vocational maturity as an epic poet (poets write only one great epic), and, with the onset of his blindness, the premature departure of an otherwise extended youthfulness. Because of the threat of regression implicit in his two great retreats to the privacy of home, Milton might well think of maturation as beset by dangers and tempters. Yet another alignment of this kind equates Milton's father's patronage of the Horton period (ages twenty-three to thirty) with the father's presence in Milton's house during the gradual failure of the poet's sight (the father died in his eighties – Milton was thirty-eight – with perfect sight). Both the poet's post-graduate retreat and his oncoming blindness would threaten to draw him back within the closed circle of an original dependency. The Lady of *Comus* (written in the Horton period) is glued to her chair much beyond the dispatching of the Tempter of Youth. The strongman of *Samson* is fettered at the mill after blindness has made him older than his nursing father. The fascinated virginal beauty of the Lady corresponds to the juvenile but unavailing strength of the Deliverer. In *Paradise Regained* these alignments are represented internally by the poem's two nights: that is, by the two secondary retirements of the poem's retiring subject.

The Temptation is bound up with the schedule of the elect life, because temptation is itself a time-bound phenomenon. Temptations are for a season, and seem to present an opportunity, while actually prompting the tempted subject to anticipate God's own time, and so to pre-empt God's plan of action towards that subject. Typically, then, the tempted subject is called upon to wait temptation out, and Christ at least must hear out the Tempter, who comes to him with a choice of lives. But Milton-as-Christ proves both prospectively and retrospectively untemptable. The younger Milton need owe nothing to some Mephistopheles for the vocational development of his great giftedness: his gifts, as symbolized by the presentation in and of the Nativity Ode, are present from the outset. The elder Milton also need ask nothing from the Tempter; he has already received his great gift from the Spirit. Nonetheless, Christ-as-Milton can be seen as having been subject to temptation, for the protraction of preparation necessary for the proper attempting of anything on the scale of *Paradise Lost* must entail an anxious period in the wilderness of an only mediately productive solitude. But Christ's quiescence here effectively displaces to Satan the frustration of action that resistance to temptation otherwise imposes upon subjects of such trials, Milton himself included.

Virtually any period of extended vocational preparation may be seen as a time during which missteps or wrong choices must be avoided, as it were, in advance: *Paradise Lost* constitutes an extended meditation upon the premeditated nature of the genuine or deliberate act, and its subject was 'long in choosing' (IX.26). The poem accordingly reconstructs the anteriority proper to the choice made in the Primal Choice, a story including the promotion of Christ, the fall of Satan, and the creation of the world. *Paradise Regained*, in its turn, re-creates the meditative anteriority necessary for the fulfilling of the poet's vocation in *Paradise Lost*. Within *Paradise Lost* itself, the creation of the world (in Book VII) follows upon the fall of Satan after his rebellion (in Book VI). The image of the poet as a fallen and blind Bellerophon, at the opening of Book VII, is the hinge between Fall and Creation. Similarly, the great creative act of Milton's life followed upon his blindness and the collapse of his hopes in politics. The fall of Satan in *Paradise Regained* similarly results in a renewal of the creation – again, out of waste, deluge, and debacle.

III

*Paradise Regained* is based on the archetypal 'fable of identity' as Christ would have known it. This is the wilderness experience he shares with Moses in the Midian and Israel in the desert.[7] Christ is moved to sequester himself in the same, enlarged threshold-space, being moved towards a deeper, more introspective possession of the mind's 'I,' as Israel in the wilderness was moved to articulate the patterns of its subsequent nationally-bound existence. Satan molests even the privacy of Christ's sleep, but his movement towards Christ can thereby be understood as the movement of Christ towards his own negative image in a mirror, or towards his silhouette, the space cut out of the world by the space one occupies in it. Satan finally tells Christ that he has been shadowing him all along, having been present on all the epiphanic occasions when the Son has come into public view. Satan is present at the Nativity not as the wise men, who are the future Gentiles, but as a witness who might have informed to the jealous Herod. Satan is also the negative image of Christ among the doctors, which is Satan among the groupies – seething to repossess the identity he has lost to his idol. Satan is Doubting Thomas as well, licensed or compelled to doubt, Thomas being the Twin. His filial identity is the birthright Satan as twin has deeded over to his other.

Both Christ and Satan consider themselves challenged to read the riddle of Christ's identity, both are engaged in making trial of it. The experimental impulse appears in Christ's fasting, a type of his 'emptying himself.'[8] But Christ is not committing suicide, for on the pinnacle he is not cast down. Satan's fall from eminence, on the other hand, is to be read as a precipitous rush to one's own place – the impulse of the thwarted Sphinx, Spenser's Impatience and Impotence, the Gadarene swine, perhaps Jocasta (being, like Antaeus, 'throttled ... in the air,' IV.568), Balaam, and Judas.[9] The young Christ 'could not lose himself'

(II.98), whereas Satan is 'Into thin air diffused' (I.499). Christ exhibits obvious ego-strengths: a sense of self, self-control, possession, assurance, knowledge, and perfect poise. Satan is a weak ego: quixotic, servile, importunate, whining, and overweening. The vanquished cavalier of *Paradise Lost* has become a nagging and parasitical degenerate. Recounting the Baptism, he finds it metrically expedient to omit the words 'I' and 'well' ('in him am pleased,' I.85): Satan's 'I' is not 'well,' or whole.

IV

The ego is first differentiated, then individualized. All earlier egos we can collect under the idea of a 'nameable' ego, one able to feel its difference from the objects that consciousness intends, and able to identify parts, sensations, and perceptions as its own. All later egos we can collect under the idea of a 'vocational' ego, one embarked upon the project of individuation, choosing or fulfilling the meaning of its name. The first ego is imposed upon by objects of cognition and desire. Less peripherally, the second ego is imposed upon by its own will. Its ethos is changed from voluptuary to activist. But when might the ego first impose on itself? Perhaps at the moment when, as it were, consciousness starts to entertain itself, i.e., during revery, when the infant temporarily assuages primal craving by means of imagery.[10] The hungry infant is momentarily summoned to perform a thaumaturgical act, to change unyielding blankness into a yield of imaginary sustenance, and to make the mind subject to the mind. The waking Christ refuses to turn stones into bread, but his imagination inclines this way in his subsequent dream.

Christ dreams of ravens that abstain from the food they brought Elijah. Like a diet pill, this food promises to enable Christ to do without more food. The minimally supplied appetite is reduced to a mere appetite for imagery. If the ravens do not eat what is in their mouths, they may be mother birds bringing food to their young: then Christ wishfully dreams of himself as the object of a maternal care from which he has separated himself at the outset. Thus a dream of self-feeding on food-images is almost a dream of weaning. Christ's response to Satan's subsequent banquet-temptation, 'with my hunger what hast thou to do?' (II.389), can also be read as signalling the termination of the child's direct dependency on his mother for feeding: it is at the wedding-feast of Cana that Christ rebuffs Mary with the divorce-formula, 'Woman, what have I to do with thee?' (John 2:4).

As Samson rejects the care of Dalilah, Christ rejects the creature

comforts of the banquet. The easy, tranquillized Nirvanah-conscious-
ness of the nursing child is presumably a paradise we lose early. But the
dispersal of the banquet-vision also reminds us that, in a world which
originally offers a perpetual feast for the eyes, a blind man is uniquely
condemned to a fast in a desert. For him a visual consumption of the
world is not more possible than for us a material consumption of the
verbal manna of Deuteronomy. 'Feed on Thoughts,' the blind poet
counselled himself in *Paradise Lost* (III.37), and Christ commends his
hunger to himself in about the same words.[11] If images themselves are
the 'far fet spoil' of the banquet – the sceptophilic 'spoil of beauty' found
in Spenser[12] – they may be snatched away by ravenous harpies, or kept
tantalizingly beyond real use.[13] The banquet disappears 'With sound of
harpies' wings' (II.403), like the stolen and polluted food of the blind
prophet Phineus: in Ariosto his descendant Senapo is tantalized and
punished precisely for attempting to regain a view of paradise.[14] Thus
the ego of the poem is deprived of a temptation to surrender its
autonomy to a reflexive object-world, even while it is tempted to
hallucinate the object-world in its absence. Satan, as the banquet's
presenter, has succumbed to this temptation.

The banquet represents something more than the mere efflorescence
of primal appetite; namely, the deceits of desire.[15] Not only does the
banquet represent the welter of impulse – desire described as myriad and
unappeasable – but also the polarized description of desire as fetishistic
or fixated, or as easily decoyed. Satan proposes to focus all appetites on
*haute cuisine*, whether a sensual appetite for luxury, a 'spiritual'
appetite for liberality, or an intellectual appetite for experience.
Furthermore, one discerns religious overtones of a profane sacrament,[16]
cultural overtones of an idolatrous theatre, and philosophic overtones
of the hedonist's answer to the problem of vocation. Nonetheless, the
first affinities of the banquet lie with the indulging of the wishful genius
of the ego as moveable pleasure-centre,[17] and with prolonging its
pampered and luxurious communion with a maternally controlled
environment. After the banquet, Satan offers to become a different sort
of parent. No longer pointing to Christ's healthy appetite, he points, as
sponsor, advocate, mentor, and patron, to Christ's potential for achievement. The new temptations imply a more strenuous conception of the
self, one defined by its appropriations of authority and anxieties about
the future.

V

In the first temptation Christ identifies himself especially by distinguishing himself from his other ('I discern thee ... the same I know ... Knowing who I am, as I know who thou art,' 1.348, 354, 356). And he allows the stones their constancy – refusing to invest them with the substance of a subject's wish – even while appropriating their obduracy for his own delineation. In the subsequent banquet temptation he 'divorces' his mother: the temptation is much more explicitly a seduction of the fixed ego by bodily arousals and love-objects and the stimulus of beauty. Disowning the pull of the object, Christ assumes a sovereignty that makes him the proposer of whatever proposals he is in the position of receiving. Similarly, the ego relinquishes a fantasy-life consciousness where it would permanently delay or decoy the forming of a more authentic and teleological volition.[18]

Purity of heart is to will one thing. The early type for this concentration of wish is the desire to possess the mother – a desire much more identifiable as 'my Father's will' than the desire to be fed. Where there is a will, there is a way; but where there is a wish, there is a wait: thus the banquet's subliminal appeal to a half-expressed, half-repressed erotic wish. For there are demons in woman's guise on the scene's edges – i.e., Woman, in the guise of women. But the banquet does not offer the vision of one woman, the proper object of Oedipal wishing, and the means whereby Eros economizes volition. For Christ, this woman would be an ideal Mary, a second Eve, or a faithful Church. Satan tells the devils there is no such perfect playmate, but he offers an army fit to besiege Albracca and recover 'The fairest of her sex Angelica' (III.341). He offers Rome, 'queen of the earth,' and Athens, 'mother of arts' (IV.45, 240). Rejecting Venus, Juno, and Athena, Christ also rejects the whore of chivalry, the whore of Babylon, and (so to speak) the whore of Mensa.

Between the bread and banquet temptations, Milton has interpolated both Christ's dream of hunger and Satan's repudiation of the suggestion of Belial – that Satan try the lure of woman's beauty. Satan's reaction to the suggestive demon, whose sensuality may be traced back through *Paradise Lost* to passages in *Comus*, might best be described as an 'ideological' reaction, for an ideological insistence on purity seems to be at the root of it. Thus the officious Satan might be speaking on Christ's behalf: one is reminded that certain speeches in Job which seem as if they ought to be assigned to Job's comforters are in fact given to Job. Here Satan himself rejects the argument Belial might have used, that the 'Sons of God' before the Flood enjoyed the 'daughters of men.' Thus Satan might be thought of as reacting to commonplace Renaissance arguments about love and marriage – that love is the desire to enjoy beauty and to reproduce it, and that one should marry and thus honour the institution to which one owed one's being. The Tempter, on the contrary, is not tempted to try unmanly temptations – Christ's virginity is apparently sacrosanct. Thus the Miltonic Christ, even as conceived by Satan, may be compared to the virginal and over-nice 'Lady of Christ's' (as Milton seems to have been called at college): Satan has insured that his charge will not become a Christ to the ladies, or even be given the chance to say no. Yet a dream of fair women, in effect, keeps coming back in this poem – and even afterwards, if we include the return of Dalilah. Belial himself is haunted by it: 'daughters of men, ... more like to goddesses / Than mortal creatures,' who possess a 'virgin majesty ... terrible to approach' (II.154ff.). But the first place in Milton that we meet such a figure is in *Comus*, where the virgin symbolizes the ideological purity of the adolescent ego, and reminds us of her author, the severe young man to whom any early sexual communion seems to have been denied. The repression of the lure of women might also be considered in the light of the paternally disavowed marriage choices of both Adam and Samson. Satan himself reprehends the carnal unions of the 'False titled Sons of God,' the 'false' implying that true Sons of God do not go whoring after strange women, however goddess-like their beauty. Beauty, Christ might say, is indifferently the whore or idol of Greek culture. Yet Christ's original, as the 'Son of David,' would be the Solomon who worshipped the idols of his wives: the father, psychoanalytically speaking, who worshipped or enjoyed the beauty of the mother. The Flood, in a way, consigns the resulting monstrosity to oblivion.

Milton's latency might be described a little differently. It seems to have been extended, as we have said, ideologically, beyond 'biology' and towards a cultivation verging on a cult: that of the sage and serious doctrine of virginity. Milton transforms Spenser's Guyon into his Britomart-as-Belphoebe, while Milton's father indulges the ephebe at the banquets and entertainments of Education and Culture. To judge by *Comus*, the son somewhat diffidently participated: by presenting as his heroine a Lady who rejects masques in general as more truly antimasques, and who cannot join the dance, however clearly she is at the centre of it. Not so dissimilarly, Satan designs to draw Christ only into 'Lawful desires ..., not beyond' (II.230), and thus seems to outlaw sex, even while hosting a party.

Transformed into a dutiful parental advocacy, Satan's subsequent urgings amount to a litany of 'gets' beginning with 'Get riches' and ending with Get an Advanced Degree: always it is Get Going. What intervenes between the *locus amoenus* of the banquet and the retirement of the Athens temptation is the development of the competitive ego. This means the competitive Renaissance ego, with its thirst for glory, self-display, and personal distinction: ultimately, the self-starting Satanic ego of *Paradise Lost*. But just as Christ sees the pleasance of youthful indulgence vanish, he also delays assuming the Solomonic perquisites of power. Yet this unaptness, Satan infers, is anticipation in disguise. Perhaps, then, Christ's desire may be further decoyed towards earthly rewards: Satan proposes Herodian usurpations of authority. Satan offered personal glory; Christ fervently opposes the glory of the Father. Satan encourages the aggressive fantasy of 'Zeal of thy Father's House';[19] to this zeal – or jealousy – Christ opposes submission to trial by the Father and the Son's sacrificial obedience. Jesus' mother has been similarly called: 'my very soul / A sword shall pierce, this my favoured lot, / My exaltation to afflictions high' (III.90ff.).[20] United by a common lot of 'piercing,' the scission of Christ and Mary inverts the misalliance of Oedipus and Jocasta: Sophocles' Oedipus threatens Jocasta's womb with the sword that Seneca's Jocasta herself uses to violate herself in the same place. The mortification of the desiring ego, and its redirection towards projects sponsored by the father, suggest a reconstructed Oedipal theme basic to all vocational striving. At this point we must step back to consider the possible comparability of Christ and Oedipus. For at virtually the end of *Paradise Regained* we learn that the whole poem, like the childish ego itself, is to be reconstituted under the aegis of this comparison.

VI

The two main allusions to classical fable in *Paradise Regained* follow directly upon Christ's final victory. Milton compares this victory to Hercules' defeating Antaeus – a wrestler who always won by falling to his mother earth.[21] And Milton compares the victory of Oedipus over the Sphinx – the riddle-solver went on to solve a mystery by incriminating himself in an original sin. Thus Christ is compared to a Herculean agonist whose antagonist must be defeated antithetically and dialectically; and to an ultimately self-sacrificing saviour-figure who, in the Sophoclean sequel – *Oedipus at Colonus* – is led on stage blind. Christ is thus compared to Samson as well, for Samson has enjoyed the gifts of a Herculean strength and an Oedipal insight into riddles; yet he has neither known himself, nor conquered his own antithetical weakness.

The Oedipal resemblance of Christ and Samson emerges when the latent doubleness of Christ and Satan has passed. Having defeated the lying and ambiguous oracles that Satan inspires and that helped ruin Oedipus, Christ is now free to return privately to his mother's house. In the wilderness and in Jerusalem, as on an earlier occasion, Christ has been about his Father's business. He will go on to expel Satan from 'demoniac holds' (IV.629): the inaugural act of the Johannine ministry, however, is the 'unarmed' purging of his Father's house. Christ has satisfied his Father's exercise of him in the wilderness. Oedipus, in contrast, is a fugitive from potential parricide who provokes his father to violence, returns to his parents' house, and pollutes his father's bed and his mother's womb.

Thus Satan is as much Oedipus as Christ. For Satan displays that contentious and discontented inquisition into a mystery of origins that is characteristically Oedipal. If directed towards himself, the inquiry would show that Satan had mortally offended his sire by an incestuous love of self. This Oedipal past is represented in *Paradise Lost* by the meeting of Satan, Sin, and Death, which is based on an Oedipal recasting of the family reunions of the *Odyssey* called the Telegonia.[22] As Oedipal father, Satan has committed incest with his paramour and daughter Sin; he is threatened with death by their Telegonic son Death, who has violated his Circean mother. As Oedipal son, Satan has 'known' a kind of mother-goddess, a sexualized fantasy-version of the Father's more Platonic filial consorts – Wisdom, Urania, and the Word.

Christ and Oedipus share the stigma of an absent father and an overdetermined relation with the mother. Thus Christ, since he knows the secret of his parentage, occupies the position of Tiresias, who first keeps and then darkly reveals Oedipus' secret. But at the outset it is Satan who enters as an old man, like Sophocles' prophet. Satan is also implicitly compared to the stick-gathering widow of Sarepta, who was met and relieved by Elijah of *Thebes* (so II.313 in the first edition).[23] Like either Oedipus or Tiresias, Christ is called upon to relieve the local distress. Like Tiresias, Satan is taunted into revealing his secret. Like Oedipus, Christ is moved to denounce the oracles and priestcraft of the other.

On the third day Satan catches Christ up and bears him off 'without wing / Of hippogrif' (IV.541-2) in a menacing echo of the Sphinx seizing on her prey. Christ, the action implies, has not solved the riddle of his identity to Satan's satisfaction. As Oedipus, Christ has read the riddle of the Messianic oracles in the Law and the Prophets: 'of whom they spake / I am' (I.262-3). Oedipus is more doubtful: 'I ask to be no other man than that I am, and I will know who I am.'[24] Satan also tries to complete or stabilize the typological equation of former and latter-day selves – he too is a son of the Father: 'I also am, or was, / And if I was, I am; Relation stands' (IV.518-19). Laius' child and his killer are the same man; Polybus' adopted son and Laius' rejected one are the same boy-child; Jocasta's baby and her second husband are the same male. Analogously in *Paradise Regained*, the heavenly begotten Son of God, the newly declared Son, and the future 'Son of David' are all the same Son: relation stands. He is the rider in the chariot of paternal deity who rode over the rebel-son in the fatal encounter in *Paradise Lost*; he inflicts the crushing blow on Satan's head, not only at the crossroads in the Oedipal past, but again on the Cross and in time to come.

The comparison extends to the life-cycles as a whole. (1) The oracles declare Oedipus will kill his father and marry his mother. Christ is announced to be the Son of God and Simeon prophesies that he will cause his mother pain. (2) Shepherds rescue the bound, pierced, and exposed in Oedipus; in Sophocles the piercing anticipates the blinding. Shepherds find Christ in a manger in swaddling clothes; in Milton the Circumcision anticipates the Crucifixion. (3) Having been adopted by the King, Oedipus is found at the court of Polybus. He is told by a drunken man that Polybus is not his father; when he asks his parents about this, they express chagrin. He seeks an oracle, which informs him he will kill his father. On the occasion of a religious feast, Christ is found in the temple by anxious parents; when he is asked about this, he says that he is about his Father's business. In Milton he is then told by his mother that he is the Son of God. (4) Self-exiled from Corinth, Oedipus comes to the crossroads and ignorantly kills an older man who offers violence; he does not know the man is his father. Christ comes to the Jordan where the Precursor acknowledges his successor and the Father acknowledges the Son. (5) Oedipus comes to Thebes, expounds the Sphinx's riddle, and causes her suicide. He is rewarded with marriage to the queen and the kingship. Christ enters the wilderness, quotes Scripture to Satan, and so repels temptations to receive kingdoms from him, or give him proofs of Sonship. In Milton Christ causes Satan's fall from the pinnacle, and returns to his mother's house. (6) Oedipus, on his father's throne, pollutes his parents' bed. Christ announces the advent of the Kingdom of his Father, beginning his ministry in John by 'divorcing' his mother at Cana and purging his Father's house in Jerusalem.

Being ignorant of much of his history Oedipus also recycles much of it.

He again inquires of oracles; Christ knows the 'Messianic secret.' Oedipus sentences 'the land's pollution' to exile, and discovers he is not Polybus' natural son; Christ discloses the secret to his own circle, and also announces the necessity of his dying a transgressor's death. Oedipus incriminates and blinds himself; Christ is tried and crucified for claiming to be the Son of God. Oedipus, accompanied by his daughters, dies in the grove at Colonus, and leaves no evidence of burial; Christ's tomb, visited by the women, is found empty. In the pinnacle temptation Christ is symbolically 'lifted up,' as in the Crucifixion. Milton frames Satan's two physical assaults on Christ – the storm and the abduction to the precipice – with the temptation of Athens and the refreshment of paradise. The Passion is framed with a typologically rich pair of gardens,[25] and while the olive grove in which Plato taught seems unrelated to the Mount of Olives on which Christ preached, Oedipus faced the Furies in the one, as Christ suffered the agony of Gesthemane at the other.

The analogy between Sophocles' and Milton's texts depends less on a story parallel than on a dramatic one: the connection, in each case, between the deep, oracular past, and the present crisis. A similar connection exists between the earlier and later texts themselves, and between Sophocles' two Oedipus texts, and Milton's two Paradise texts. The connections resist, even while demanding, reactivation and recognition: both *Oedipus the King* and *Paradise Regained* circumambulate about what is gradually revealed as an open secret. 'Think not but that I know these things, or think / I know them not' (IV.286-7), Christ says, apropros Athenian arts and sciences; but his words might as well apply to the interrogative impasse prevailing throughout Milton's poem. 'Why is it you question me and waste your labour?' Tiresias asks; 'Why do you ask this question?' Laius' herdsman echoes.[26] So Christ: 'Why art thou / Solicitous, what moves thy inquisition?' (III.199-200). Satan's pursuit of a ready equation allies him with the Oedipal kind of knowledge (e.g., 'One man cannot be the same as many').[27] Christ's perplexing of such an equation allies him with the Tiresian kind of mystery – the kind, as Tiresias says, 'establishing a grim equality between you and your children.'[28] Christ quotes his own birth-oracle as a warning to Satan (Luke 2:34, *PR* II.88), but something like Balaam who does not want to pronounce them, and Barak who does not want to acknowledge them, Satan repines at Messianic oracles.[29] 'The Father knows the Son; therefore secure / Ventures his filial virtue' (I.176-7), the angels affirm. 'Ye see our danger,' Satan says, 'on the utmost edge of hazard' (1.94-5). This 'utmost edge' anticipates the pinnacle from which Satan falls, but also echoes the vertigo of the Tiresian-minded herdsman as the crisis breaks in Sophocles: 'O God, I am on the brink of frightful speech.'[30] Oedipus is compelled to hear though it blind him, but Raphael's 'Solicit not thy thoughts with matters hid' (*PL* VIII.167) speaks for a whole class of Tiresian utterance in *Paradise Lost* directed against knowing too much.[31] Indeed, given what Raphael himself must know of the coming fall of Adam, the warning applies equally to the Tiresian speaker.

Oedipus' prophetic 'prosecutor' knows the secret of Oedipus' marriage. Satan's discerner Christ also knows a comparable marriage-secret: Milton says that the nature of the divine and human in the Son is a mystery about which we must be content to remain wisely ignorant.[32] Thus one kind of riddle-solving invoked in *Paradise Regained* is that traditionally associated with marriage-conditions. In the ballad *Riddles Wisely Expounded*, for example, the female riddle-solver alternatively exorcises the Devil or gets herself a husband.[33] Taken together, Milton's last works derive from Sophocles the retrospective proposing and expounding of marriage as an Oedipal riddle: Samson's marriage is a second one, Christ's a parental one.

The riddling mode permeates the entire discourse of *Paradise Regained*: we note the preponderance of the word 'what.' Riddles seem to have no answer to their 'what,' and Satan asks many rhetorical questions anticipating answers of 'none' or 'nothing.'[34] A quasi-algebraic language of unknown quantities is in fact diffused throughout the diction: 'they admire they know not what; / And know not whom' (III.52-3). Like marriages, riddles are properly proposed, and their pretentions meetly answered. Satan has 'proposed' a divine title for himself, 'What both from men and angels I receive' (IV.199-200), and he dares 'propound' the impious terms of worshipping him as a 'superior lord' (acknowledged as such by Herod-like 'Tetrarchs': IV.178, 167, 201).[35] So God once 'proposed / To draw proud Ahab into fraud' (1.371-2), Satan volunteering to be the lying means. The Theban monster similarly 'proposed / Her riddle' (IV.572-3; cf. also IV.370).

It is Christ who makes the poem's original proposal, when he comes among the learned in his Father's house 'to propose / What might improve my knowledge or their own' (1.212-13). Directly after this, his mother expounds to him his divine generation, and Christ promptly re-searches the Scriptures. 'Do you know who your parents are?' Tiresias asks Oedipus, and Oedipus is also thus embarked on solving a special case of the kind of identity-riddle that has the speaker or 'ego' as its answer, e.g., 'Brother, sister / Have I none, / But that man's father / Is my father's son.' Paradoxically, one of the strongest possible assertions we can make about a man's identity is that he is his father's son.

Marriage-riddles test eligibility, but identity-riddles test the special relation a thing bears to itself or kind. Satan seeks to learn 'In what degree or meaning' Christ is called Son of God: to know, he says, 'my adversary, who / And what he is' – 'what more thou art than man' (IV.516, 527-8, 539). *Man* was in fact the general answer to the riddle Oedipus solved, but Samson's Chorus is still exclaiming, 'God of our fathers, what is man!' (667). 'Many the wonders,' the Sophoclean chorus remarks, 'but nothing walks stranger than man.'[36] The key to the riddle was how man walks: thus its overdetermined relation to Samson (fettered, blind, and brutalized), and Oedipus (crippled and blind). The riddle's last clause – 'and what is weakest when its limbs are greatest' – admits of a sexual application as well.[37] Oedipus the Great is most vulnerable in tumescence, in the marriage-bed. Samson is emasculated as a strong man by his wife, when his wisdom is weakest and his locks most. Christ's feet and footing are also objects of interpretive scrutiny, for Satan is a Laius, consulting an oracle about the Son who will tread him underfoot. Satan has watched Christ's footsteps since his Baptism (IV.522) – 'Why move thy feet so slow?' he asks (III.224). Christ's particular guardian angels – 'They shall uplift thee, lest at any time / Thou chance to dash thy foot against a stone' (IV.558f) – must have a special significance for a blind man. Sophocles' fugitive from parricide 'had to fly ... nor set foot in [his] own country';[38] Satan 'never more hence forth will dare set foot / In Paradise' (IV.601-2). One reads the riddle of this regressive Oedipal son backwards: first he appears as a stooping old man in the dusk, then a sophisticated adult at noon. Finally, the morning after, he flies like the four-legged hippogriff, and falls like the Gadarene swine: his original rebellious forms as the fallen morning-star at the ends of Books II and VI of *Paradise Lost*.

VII

The allusion to Oedipus appertains to the total possible meanings of an archetypal *myth*: the wasting of the fertile place results from an original rebellion against the Father; the wasteland is redeemed by expounding the riddle of man's three 'ages.' But the extent of the myth – from the man ignorant of his father, to the exile who had killed his father – is mediated to Milton's poem by the Sophoclean *drama*: that of the saviour-king versus the pariah-criminal. For like the drama, the poem retails the story interrogatively. But being diffused and interiorized by the poem, the drama itself applies ambiguously: for the regent and isolated ego of the Sophoclean protagonist is redistributed between the rivalrous and filial halves of Milton's binary *dramatis personae*. The fact that we do not readily recognize the extent of the allusion points to the presence of the Oedipus *complex*; the poem might well recover 'deeds – though in secret done, / And unrecorded left through many an age' (1.14-15).

Tiresias tells Oedipus that he is living in sin; Christ divines approximately the same thing about Satan. But the Son is not living in sin: Christ 'Home to his mother's house private returned,' the poem having restored to its own last line the innocence that the Tiresian riddle-versions have lost in the Oedipus plays. Thus Christ's *first* line, 'Who brought me hither / Will bring me hence, no other guide I seek' (1.135-6), recasts Seneca's *last*: 'these guides it suits me to use.' Seneca's Oedipus accepts the guidance of the Furies driving him into exile. But in *Oedipus at Colonus* the Furies have become the Kindly Ones, and the hero, 'driven / By an insistent voice that comes from God,' guides his guides.[39] The entry of Milton's Samson 'quotes' Oedipus' entry in this play, and implies the same belated, psychoanalytic reconstruction of Oedipal conflict. Yet Milton – blind, gout-ridden, dependent on first his daughters and then his younger wife – anticipated 'the Abishag of age' from his first marriage. For he not only married a woman young enough to have been his mother when he was an infant (as most men do), he also married a woman young enough to have been his daughter, and hence young enough to some day be his nurse – an Antigone or Cordelia – in his old age. The same Oedipal indexing of spousal and filial-paternal equations is found in Adam's parental relation to 'the fairest of her daughters Eve,' and the immaturing of Samson by his youthful father.[40]

In the Oedipal phase of the child's development, the ego gains its second or 'spiritual' parent. In essence, the father announces to the ego, 'You are my son, today I have become your father.' That is what God says to Jesus at the Baptism in a textual variant of 'Thou art my beloved Son; in thee I am well pleased' (Luke 3:22). If Milton knows the variant, then both his epics originate from the same declaration. At the end of *Oedipus the King*, Oedipus is exhibited with his half-sister daughters. On the pinnacle, Satan invites Christ to *show his progeny* (IV.554). 'Progeny' means offspring, but Satan means 'pedigree,' relation to a progenitor. Milton means 'deeds,' and Christ is thus asked to appropriate for himself the initial deed of *Paradise Lost*: by exhibiting himself to the angels and provoking an epiphany of parental power, Christ duplicates the initial begetting of the Son.

In the Oedipus plays, the son does not so much gain a second parent as lose the same parents twice. Where the filial and vocational ego of *Paradise Regained* hears anew the call to Sonship and the Father's service, the rivalrous and insecure ego again hears its humiliation and exile. Hence Satan's compulsion to revisit the scene of Christ's differentiation, to find out how he lost to be a son of God. In defending his Sonship, the Johannine Christ vilifies the 'father' of his adversaries the Jews as the father of lies.[41] Thus a child might express his psychic need to be at one with one greater man; for 'who advance his glory, not their own / Them he himself to glory will advance' (III.143-4). Christ reproaches Satan with begrudging God his glory, but Satan might equally envy the new-begot his Father. In *Paradise Lost* the fervent Abdiel also identifies with the glory of the Father, and asserts that his Father can beat up the devils' father. The ego's fostering of this fostering relation is what makes possible the ego's vocational genesis, providing the ego with a missionary 'cause.' Who shall the ego say sent it? It cannot identify the 'I am' of its answer without further reference to the god of its Fathers.

Cast upon the wilderness like the bond-woman's son, or cast down from pre-eminence by his rival on the pinnacle from which he expected to eliminate him, Satan is not well served by any of his Oedipal identities. As pseudo-father, he presents the meddlesome patron, offering adoption and advice where they can find no acceptance; a proselytizer, on leave from the Limbo of disappointed fathers, he is doomed for a certain space of time to roam the earth, dragging his sad tale behind him. As pseudo-son he is the fatherless roamer who will never find himself. Despite his dreams of putting himself under Christ's wise tutelage, he is actually the derivative parasite who would only seek to serve his master by betraying him. His specious sonship appears in the first word with which he accosts Jesus, a servile 'Sir,' borrowed from his own previous appearances, in Milton's predecessors, as an 'aged Sire,' or father.[42]

'This day I have begot,' God declares in *Paradise Lost*, and Lucifer, pre-eminent among the sons of morn, begins to see himself degraded from a son to a servant. But Abdiel, by name the Servant of God, begins to see himself elevated to the status of son. Satan, who abode not in the truth of filial relations, sees the Son displacing him from heaven, for by committing sin he is made its servant, and the servant abideth not in the house forever – but the Son does (John 8:33-59). Intuiting from God's declaration that all things were gloriously begotten by God's word, the zealous Abdiel penetrates to the primal scene of his own creation, that is, his prophetic calling to serve God.[43] In the Son he is re-called, to Christian sonship, and he expresses his new-found 'filial freedom'[44] by the very *non serviam* he throws back at Satan. At the end of the glory temptation Christ replies as fervently as Abdiel did; he too invokes creation by the word, the Lord having acted in creation not for the sake of glory, but to impart his good (III.121-5).

What parentally bestowed 'good' was Satan unable to accept? Apparently, the knowledge that once upon a time the self was not. However self-taken, the self is not self-given, and not indigenous to any being but its own. Like eyesight or health, its essence may be taken away. Satan renounces a calling-into-being that means being contingent, deriving from a prior being. The declaration of the Son can only give him a gigantic castration complex. The hell into which he falls divides itself between the party madly seeking its own destruction, and the party sullenly refusing to rise to this challenge; Satan can only lead both camps up the path that widens the Satanic empire over death[45] – thereby colonizing the territory originally claimed by the Son in the name of the Father. Satan has denied his birthright, namely, God's paternity. The trauma is decidedly Oedipal: 'wounds of deadly hate have pierced so deep' (*PL* IV.99) that Satan cannot acknowledge God as his maker, only as punisher. In *Paradise Regained* Satan attempts to be the giver of all perfect gifts (James 1:17), to *be* the Father; he cannot submit to being *of* the father. As ego, Christ takes possession of himself in just this way, through the Father. The double genitive – the innocent form of the 'infamous double bond' of the Tiresian riddle-speech – figures critically in the diction: 'my Father's voice,' 'His Father's business,' 'my Father's will,' 'thy Father's house.'[46]

The wilderness fast represents a propitiatory sacrifice to the Father, that the Son may receive back from him the gift of being. The Father 'secure / Ventures' the Son 'for the purpose of exercising' his 'faith or patience, as in the case of Abraham.'[47] A corresponding 'filial obedience' appears in Christ's offering of himself in *Paradise Lost*, 'as a sacrifice / Glad to be offered' (III.269-70). The sacrificial son volunteers to die, but also wills to become a man. The ungrateful son shuns the burden of an interminable mortgaging of his being to the Father, but he also never outgrows his temptation of rebellion. Furthermore, he would impose his indebtedness for being on the Son, as his patron: 'For what can less so great a gift deserve?' (IV.169).

In Milton's *Ad Patrem* the exceptionally gifted and talented son of a money-lending father seems somewhat baffled by his indebtedness to the supporter of his studies ('even my greatest gifts could never repay yours').[48] The benefactor has provided an educational retreat analogous to retirement in the desert, thanks to which the poet has the opportunity to know virtually everything.[49] Christ also had the perfection of his wisdom from the Father.[50] Thus all such a one can return to his father is one's dedication to him – *Ad Patrem* itself. Such deity as the Son has is from the Father, and he does not need his own gifts,[51] ego-strength and manliness included. Milton does indeed seem to have lived with his father longer than other men. His decision to leave home may have been as momentous for his psychology as Christ's leaving heaven was for his theology. Only as he went blind, however, may Milton have found his father's renewed domestic presence emasculating. His loyalty to this parent might have returned upon him like the Philistines upon Samson, with the full force of an indictment of infantile weakness. Yet the post-Oedipal ego of *Paradise Regained* does not doubt its derivation from its father's side. In preferring the songs of Zion to the arts of Greece – the mother of arts – Christ invokes the patriotic Psalm 137, which affirms the vocation of the harpist even in his Babylonian captivity: 'If I forget thee, O Jerusalem, let my right hand forget her cunning.' The 'Hail, Holy Light' hymn of *Paradise Lost* ends 'Hail, Son of God, thy name / Shall be the copious matter of my song, / Henceforth, and never shall my harp thy praise / Forget, nor from thy Father's praise disjoin' (III.412-15). Milton, in the captivity of a Homeric blindness, vows his repeat hymnic performances not so much to a god, as to an unforgettable *relation*.

VII

Christ is *differentiated* by his nativity, by the declaration of him in heaven, by the acknowledgement at the Baptism (for other men the symbolic washing off of sin), and by forty days of fasting apart. He is *individuated* by volunteering in the Father's service and being glorified by him: in the war in heaven, in the Incarnation, and in the Temptation. Christ is haloed by a globe of light or angels on such occasions, because an integral with its centre derivable from any portion of its periphery can stand for the ego's identification with itself and its differentiation from what it excludes. Being luminous and glorious, the ensphered subject also stands for the ego's individuation: its affect, contentedness, sovereignty, and visibility to others.

Tempted by Satan to forfeit his differentiation, and to pre-empt his individuation, Christ is the once and future ego. Satan tempts Christ, as his rival, to be *like* something other than himself. Christ can let his ego be determined by the Parthia of rivalry, the Rome of presumption, or the Athens of pretension. Each is a source of ego-being that fathers the ego on something other than the Father. The Deity is one and omnipresent, omnipotent, and omniscient. Its gifts to the Son or the ego, 'the first-born of every creature' (Col. 1:15), are the enhancements of unity, capacity, and consciousness. But the competitive, imperial, and sophistical selves are not of this father, for the ideal father – present, powerful, and knowing – has no cause to be anxious about the son's vocation, or future.

Christ is 'fathered' by the Spirit of Truth, and therefore his three offices of prophet, king, and priest are charismatically conceived. Christ owes his anti-bureaucratic calling only to the prophetic word of God, the divine leadership of the Spirit, and the sacred priesthood of Conscience. Like the three offices, the three visionary kingdoms-temptations also address the problem of Christ's calling. They are proposed as a means for Christ to gain worldly experience – like the 'Grand Tour' Milton himself took at the age Christ was tempted. One goes out into the wilderness to meet with something, and a man who has met with the Diodati family, Grotius, Galileo, Tasso's noble patron, the Florentine literary-academic élite, and the Roman founders of modern opera, has not failed to do so. Milton visited, as it were, the 'Parthia' of Calvinist Geneva, the 'Rome' of the Worldly Church, and the 'Athens' of Late Renaissance Florence. Milton's Continental debut had a formative effect on his final conception of himself as an adult. Yet he came to reject not only prelatry and monarchy, but the Genevan model of government. He became Latin Secretary, but abandoned the Continental model of a literary career in the learned languages. Italian dramatic models for the great work were discarded, and the epic is not chivalric or military (Parthia),[52] statist (Rome), or mythological-Alexandrian (Athens). It is in his native tongue, on a Hebrew wisdom story.

Yet the Parthia, Rome, and Athens of Milton's travels came home to roost: in the 'Parthian' campaigns of the Grand Old Cause; in the Latin Secretaryship under the Protectorate; and in the academic labours of the pension period of semi-retirement. For the essence of the Parthian campaign is opportunist, strategic, and factionalist; that of the Roman establishment, ambassadorial and bureaucratic; and that of the Athenian institute, liberal and educational. Milton's pen was successively employed in sectarian controversy, state business, and classical studies. This tripartite reduction satisfies the criterion of the Oedipal riddle describing the morning, noon, and evening of man's career, for the visions pertain to endeavour in the field, ascendance to mastery, and retirement to leisure and the study.

The Athens temptation culminates the retirement-motif building throughout the poem: the wilderness-typology of Elijah, the Baptist, Moses, and Mosaic Israel; Judas Maccabee's desert-retreat to organize armed resistance; the Parthian strategy to overcome by flight (III.325); Tiberius' retirement from Rome to enjoy his state on Capri; Plato's retirement from Athens to the suburban 'recess' of academe – the grove into which Oedipus finally retired. The Parthians get linked to the quixotic quest for Angelica, and the ideal mistress is 'Skilled to retire, and in retiring' to entice her prey (II.161ff.). Of course every evening's retirement offers some measure of these enticements – privacy, recoupment, contemplative revery – and so Christ's dream-molested sleep itself contributes to the theme. The two nights therefore frame the voluptuary banquet and the contemplative Athens. These in turn frame the six activist offerings that intervene (getting money, power, glory; receiving Israel, Parthia, Rome). Thus the two nights correspond to the Horton period, followed by the subject's debut at the banquet (note Satan's new clothes), and the pension period, anticipated by blindness (Athens is 'the eye of Greece'), and interrupted and confirmed by the Restoration (the storm of adversity).

On the second day the concupiscent, ambitious, and curious appetites are addressed in an order that suggests the partying of youth, the power-games of adulthood, and the sagacity of seniority. Christ in turn has quieted the sensual cravings of the body, the impatient strivings of the spirit, and the curious restlessness of the mind. He has thereby accepted bodily pain, public humiliation, and the isolation and ultimate extinction of consciousness as the price of his chosen vocation. His individuation prepares, as it were, his martyrdom.

IX

It remains to say how the vocational ego of *Paradise Regained* is perfected, as Christ said he would be, on the third day (Luke 13:32 with

*PL* vi.669). The early Anonymous Life of Milton almost seems commissioned to tell us. Manoah's task of pure ablution, at the end of *Samson*, is in fact anticipated as early as the poem on the biographer-patron, father Manso, and the Life ends by interring the poet *with his father*.[53] The wilderness is the place in which the earlier generation perished, and thus Milton's last works do indeed stage the drama of the son's return to the father. All of the early lives imply the poet's final acceptance of life on those terms on which a father offers it: one's taking responsibility for it oneself, even while accepting indebtedness to another for it. Conscience has told Satan himself that to own this debt of gratitude is to have it instantly forgiven.[54] Yet perhaps only at the end of life can one fully satisfy one's Oedipal curiosity about what life holds, as the last words of *Oedipus the King* imply. Only in dying can one do all that the father has done. At the end of *Paradise Regained* Christ enjoys a gentle wafting by angels, which resembles the sleep-like death Michael predicts for Christians at the end of *Paradise Lost* (xii.435). Such a death is implied for Oedipus in Sophocles' last play, and death-by-translation is also implied by the phoenix image at the end of *Samson*. The deaths of Oedipus, Samson, and Jesus are alike in this, that they are considered and planned deaths, and so perfecting deaths: Oedipus dies outside of Athens on the holy site, Samson sacrifices his life in a temple on a feast-day. But even if one cannot die with Jesus outside of Jerusalem in the high season, one still owes God a death, and by this death the vocational ego might also expect to be perfected.

Milton's 'brief epic' perfects itself by perfecting a form for the wisdom element of *Paradise Lost*. Wisdom reduces the 'foundation epic' to the creation episode, the 'strife epic' to the rebellion or temptation episode, and the 'quest epic' to the research episode. Wisdom is a distillate, and the briefest episode of its own epic is also the most gnomic. On the pinnacle the 'moment of time' in which Satan showed Christ all the kingdoms of the world contracts back to its original gospel size. The temporal and spatial indications reconstitute the eschatological point of the Nativity Ode, 'When at the world's last session / The dreadful judge in middle air shall spread his throne': 'And then at last our bliss / Full and perfect is, / But now begins' (163-7). So the later poem: 'though that seat of earthly bliss be failed / A fairer Paradise is founded now' (iv.612-13).

Traditionally, Christ is tempted on the pinnacle to presume. In *Paradise Regained* a Christus Patiens triumphs over a Satanas Hybristes, and only Satan is tempted to compel a miracle proving the Father's paternity, or the Son's divinity. A model here is *The Bacchae*, in which

Dionysus the Inscrutable destroys Pentheus the Inquisitive epiphanic-
ally. The miracle-seeking of the last temptation aligns it with the first,
but the first is aligned with the miracle-temptation of the Crucifixion
itself: turn stones into bread – 'So shalt thou *save thyself and us* relieve'
(I.344, Luke 23:39). Thus if the Son were to precipitate his vocational
development in the Temptation, he would in effect elide his call to
martyrdom in the Passion. By not falling from the pinnacle, Christ
symbolically refuses the 'passion' of an Icarus – or Phaëton, Bellerophon, or Lucifer. These are the passions of prematurity and presump-
tuous initiative. We may compare Hamlet, called to revenge and
impelled towards the cliffs by a father who may be a demonic tempter.
Hamlet is as much called to delay, until it is *his* purgatorial story, and
not the ghost's, which the play's internal audiences are duty-bound to
unfold.

Nonetheless, a kind of soured perfectionism lurks in Hamlet's self-
abasement, a disease of the superego in which the counsels of perfection
merely inhibit and stultify.[55] The last temptation is terminated abruptly, as if Christ were uncomfortable on a pedestal of unapproachable
virtue where Satan should put God. Christ implicitly rejects a fruitless
desire to demonstrate moral perfection beyond any foreseeable use,
when he rejects the pretensions of 'A virtuous man, / Wise, perfect in
himself, and all possessing, / *Equal to God*' (IV.302-4): that is what the
Son is *not*.

Yet Christ also merely stands and waits – for the summons of the
Father. Thus he improves on Shakespeare's Gloucester, on 'the extreme
verge' which is the 'very verge' nature stands on in Lear.[56] Accompanied
by a devil-haunted wretch, the despairing, blind old man is air-borne to
the care of his invisible son. 'What thing was that / Which parted from
you?' Edgar asks – 'It was some fiend': having ended the temptation, the
devil departed from him.[57] Gloucester has fallen no further than his own
height, yet a blind man's every step harbours a potential precipice, and a
temptation to despair. What are the sources of Christ's Buddha-like
calm in the storm, and his gyroscopic poise on the pinnacle, when Satan
is having a temper-tantrum and throwing himself overboard? The
answer is, Christ 'Into himself descended.' For at the end of life, one
might find oneself 'perched upon an almost unmanageable summit, ...
as though men spend their lives perched upon living stilts which never
cease to grow until sometimes they become taller than church steeples,
making it in the end both difficult and perilous for them to walk and
raising them to an eminence from which suddenly they fall.' The words

are from the end of Proust,[58] where the perils of growing up modulate into those of growing old. We outgrow the various paradisal plateaux of development, yet their regaining is always development's private, Oedipus-like goal. 'It was into my own depths that I had to re-descend ... that moment ... still adhered to me and I could still find it again, could retrace my steps to it merely by descending to a great depth within myself.' Christ descends into himself to discover support for his vocation; Milton descends into himself to recover his vocation for support. 'All this length of time had not only ... been lived, experienced, secreted by me, but ... I was compelled ... to keep it attached to me, ... it supported me and ... perched on its giddy summit I could not myself make a movement without displacing it. A feeling of vertigo seized me as I looked down beneath me, yet within me, as though from a height, which was my own height, of many leagues, at the long series of the years.'

NOTES

1 The project of the present essay is suggested by the remarkable essay of Northrop Frye, 'The Typology of *Paradise Regained*,' *Modern Philology*, 53 (1956), 227-38, especially as revised for Frye's *Return of Eden: Five Essays on Milton's Epic* (Toronto, 1965), ch. 5, 'Revolt in the Desert,' 118-43. In terms of the following essay, Frye is not merely a father-figure to a genera- tion of literary critics; he has the place of honour in the genesis and articulation of the 'vocational ego' of a literary criticism that has been delivered from the parent body of humane letters. It is no surprise that the first version of his essay should have been published on the eve of the publication of *The Anatomy of Criticism* in 1957.

My second great debt in what follows is to William Kerrigan's wonderful articulation of ego-psychology in his essay 'Superego in Kierkegaard, Existence in Freud,' in *Kierkegaard's Truth: The Disclosure of the Self*, ed. Joseph Smith, vol. v of *Psychiatry and the Humanities* (New Haven and London, 1981), 119-65. Professor Kerrigan, not accidently, is a professional Miltonist, and some of the Miltonic implications of his work are suggested in his essay, 'The Articulation of the Ego in the English Renaissance,' in *The Literary Freud: Mechanism of Defense and the Poetic Will*, ed. Joseph Smith (New Haven and London, 1980), 261-308. Here the way is also pointed by James Holly Hanford, *John Milton, Englishman* (New York, 1949). Some of my own idea for the essay is suggested by Sir Max Beer- bohm's series of caricatures on the theme of the two selves, young and old, confronting each other. Compare especially the riposte of the provincial Young Self of Arnold Bennett to the self-satisfied observation of his Londoner Old Self:

*Old Self*: All gone according to plan, you see.
*Young Self*: *My* plan, you know.

One can imagine some other Young Self saying with equal pertinence, 'Not *my* plan, I'm afraid.' See S.N. Behrman, *Portrait of Max* (New York, 1960), 253-8.

Paradise Regained is quoted from *John Milton: Complete Shorter Poems*, ed. John Carey (London, 1971). The Bible is quoted from the King James Version.

I wish to thank Patricia Parker for her assistance in preparing this version of my essay.

2 Introducing his edition of Milton, *Paradise Lost and Selected Poetry and Prose* (New York, 1951), Frye writes: 'Not many of us can have much idea of what it would feel like to have such a poem as that tearing itself loose from one's brain at the age of twenty-one' (v). Frye's image implies the virgin-birth the poem celebrates, recast as the genesis of the ideate, as found in the birth of Athena as the Sin of the Satanic Son, or as the Wisdom of the new-made Father. Milton himself was born in his father's house, in Bread Street: Bethlehem means House of Bread.

3 See Gerhard von Rad, *Old Testament Theology*, vol. II: *The Theology of Israel's Prophetic Traditions*, trans. D.M.G. Stalker (New York, 1965), 76-8.

4 *The Christian Doctrine*, I.iii: 'Of his SPECIAL DECREES the first and most important is that which regards his SON, and from which he primarily derives his name of FATHER. Psal. ii. 7. *I will declare the decree: Jehovah hath said unto me, Thou art my Son, this day have I begotten thee*' (Sumner trans.; text from *John Milton: Complete Poems and Major Prose*, ed. Merritt Y. Hughes [New York, 1957], 916; hereinafter simply Hughes. Reference will also be made to Milton's *Complete Prose Works*, VI: *The Christian Doctrine*, ed. Maurice Kelley, trans. John Carey [New Haven and London, 1973]; hereinafter Yale *Prose Works*, VI. The above passage is found on 73 there [in Carey's translation].)

5 So Frye, on this aspect of the temptation of Parthia, in *Return of Eden*, 131-3.

6 This challenge is made to the twelve-year-old Christ by his mother, *PR* I.233.

7 'Fable of identity' echoes the title of the first of Frye's essay collections, and the theme of the concluding remarks of *Return of Eden*, 142-3. The Mosaic fable of identity is described in my essay 'Moses,' in *Images of Man and God: Old Testament Short Stories in Literary Focus*, ed. Burke O. Long (Sheffield, 1981), 35-57.

8 The modern trans. of Philippians 2:7 (RV, ASV, RSV), corresponding to Greek *ekenosen* and the Vulgate (cf. Rheims, 'he exinanited him self'), and to Milton, as in *Christian Doctrine*, I.v: '(literally, *he emptied himself*,) ... Nor can the infinite God be said to empty himself ... for infinity and emptiness are opposite terms' (Sumner trans in Hughes, 962; in Yale *Prose Works*, VI, 275.) Milton argues that the Father and Son cannot be 'relatives' if they are essentially one (and they are not), and cannot be 'equals' if the Son possesses the real contingency which his begetting and the mystery of the Incarnation with its attendant mortality both predicate.

9 The references are: *PR* IV.575 (the Sphinx 'Cast herself headlong from the Ismenian steep,'), *PR* IV.629-31 ('yelling they shall fly ... a herd of swine ... down into the deep') with Mark 5:13 (the swine 'rushed down the steep bank into the sea') and the fall of the angels in *Paradise Lost* VI.864-5 ('headlong themselves they threw / Down from the verge of Heav'n'); Spenser, *The Faerie Queene*, II.xi.47 ('yelling ... Hedlong'); *PR* I.39 (at the Baptism Satan 'Flies to his place' while the apostles retreat to a communion like the one in the post-Resurrection interval in the first chapter of Acts: *PR* II.36 echoes Acts 1:6); Acts 1:12 (in the same interval Judas 'by transgression fell, that he might go to his own place'); Numbers 24:11 (Balaam is warned by Barak, 'flee thou to thy place').

10 Both the question and its answer are suggested by William Kerrigan in 'Husserl's Epoché and the Genesis of Imagination in Psychoanalysis,' *Psychoanalysis and Contemporary Thought*, 3.1 (1980), 55-82.

11 *PL* III.37 with *PR* II.258-9, 'Nor mind it [hunger], fed with better thoughts that feed / Me more ...'

12 In Spenser beauty tempts the sense of the eyes (*FQ* II.xi.9) and characterizes the Bower of Bliss and its attractions (II.v.34: 'his fraile eye spoyle of beautie feeds,' and II.xii.78: 'Her snowy brest was bare to readie spoyle / Of hungry eies'). Cf. also the 'threasures' and princely 'spoiles' of the denuded Serena, with Castiglione, *The Courtier* IV.59: 'Beautie is the true monument and spoile of the victory of the soule' (Hoby trans.). Serena, of course, is about to be eaten (by cannibals, who spy on her sleep).

13 The snatcher or harpy demonology is invoked often enough in *Paradise Regained*: by the Apostles (II.55), in the hippogriff (IV.541), and in the

Sphinx (IV.573ff.). So also in the Spenserian prototypes in Mammon's Cave (*FQ* II.vii.23, 27, 34) and Acrasia's Bower (II.xii.36).

14 For Senapo see *Orlando Furioso*, xxxiii.101-xxxiv.4, and the allegories for his salvation cited in Nohrnberg, *The Analogy of 'The Faerie Queene'* (Princeton, 1976), 194. Phineus' sight was divinely snatched away according to the passage from Apollonius Rhodius quoted in Milton's autobiographical defence in his *Second Defense of the English People* (in Hughes, 824-5). Phineus is a type for the prophetic Milton in *Paradise Lost*, III.36.

15 Frye characterizes the table that proves merely a tableau in *The Tempest* (III.iii) as 'symbolic of deceitful desires,' in his introduction to the Penguin edition of the play (*William Shakespeare: The Complete Works*, gen. ed. Alfred Harbage [Baltimore, 1969], 1369). Satan is Prince of the Power of the Air, and hence is assisted by demonic Ariels.

16 The 'cup' of the banquet in II.385-6 is that of the Passion (cf. Luke 22:42, Mt. 26:39-54 with Mt. 4:11). Satan's 'sit and eat' suggests to the narrator the temptation of Eve (II.348-9). While Moses was forty days in the Mount (cf. II.15) the idolatrous Israelites sat down to eat and then rose up to play (Exod. 32:6), and Adam and Eve apostatize in the same way (cf. *PL* IX.1027, 'play').

17 Persius, *Sat.* V.151, 'Indulge the genius,' a Renaissance catch-phrase for a youthful hedonism; in context, a *carpe diem* counsel implying tomorrow one may die. The phrase might serve as the motto for the inviting genius whom Guyon refuses to indulge in the Bower of Bliss (*FQ* II.xii. 46-9); the Bower is a relative of various wandering islands, and its genius is an unnamed Comus.

18 This and the following paragraph echo Kerrigan, 'Superego in Kierkegaard,' esp. 152-3, but also his whole section on 'Will as the Reflexivity of the Postoedipal Ego,' 149-56.

19 The original for this characterizing of the expulsion of the money-changers from the Temple (John 2:17), is Phinehas' almost definitive pinning down of the primal scene of apostasy (fornication with an idolatress in the place of worship) in Numbers 25: Phinehas skewers both offenders.

20 Mary has been called by name: Heb. *marom*, 'high up,' and *marar*, 'bitter.' Carey's note on *PR* II.92, in his edition of Milton's *Complete Shorter Poems* (London, 1971), 454, cites Donne's derivation of the name from *exaltation*.

21 For Christ the Herculean wrestler, see Nohrnberg, *Analogy*, 300, esp. n. 25. But Satan may be 'Herculean' as well as Christ, for in the poem Eden and Christ are 'raised,' as it were, in the wilderness; Satan elevates Christ to the mountaintop and the airy pinnacle. Thus the Adamic hero,

as the son of Earth - that is, of an earthly mother - is 'lifted up,' or glorified, by his victory on the cross, or in the wilderness: by overcoming the world, or overcoming his dependency on it.

22 In the 'cyclic epic' of the Telegonia, Odysseus' natural son by Circe, Teleg-onus, comes to Ithaka seeking his father, and he unknowingly kills him in battle. Telegonus marries Penelope, while Telemachus marries Circe. So Proclus, *Chrestomathy* (in Loeb Classical Library, *Hesiod, The Homeric Hymns and Homerica*, trans. H.G. Evelyn White, 530ff.); Apollodorus, *Epitome* vii.34; and Hyginus, *Fab.* 127. The complexity of the parallel is beyond our present scope, but it includes even Death's dart: Telegonus' spear is armed with a sting-ray's spine.

23 1 Kings 17:9ff. and Luke 4:26. The widow of Sarepta appears in the liturgy for both the second Tuesday and third Sunday in Lent. The same kind of comparison also makes Satan a comic Sheba in wool clothing, coming to try a greater than Solomon with hard questions (1 Kings 10:1, Mt. 12:42, *PR* 1.481-2).

24 This is E.F. Watling's liberal translation of *OT* 1084-5, in *Sophocles: The Theban Plays* (Harmondsworth, 1947), 55. The Greek (*toisde d'ekphus ouk an edzelthoim eti / pot' allos, hostēmē 'kmathein toumon genos*) certainly includes 'nothing can make me other than I am,' and implies that the action of proving one's truth-to-self is seconded by finding the truth of one's origins, whatever they may prove.

25 For the typology of the scriptural gardens, see Nohrnberg, *Analogy*, 178, nn. 208-10.

26 *OT* 333-4 and 1143-4, in the trans. of David Grene, in *The Complete Greek Tragedies*, ed. David Grene and Richmond Lattimore, vol. II: *Sophocles* (Chicago, 1959), 24, 60.

27 *OT* 844-5, ibid., 47.

28 *OT* 424-5, ibid., 26.

29 Satan claims to put his hope for enlightenment in the example of 'Balaam reprobate' (1.490-1). Christ seems to quote this prophet's self-limitation, against Satan: 'thou canst not more' (1.495) echoes Balaam's 'I cannot go beyond the word of the Lord my God, to do less or more' (Numb. 22:18; cf. also 24:13).

30 *OT* 1169, trans. Grene, II, 62. Oedipus responds that he is on the brink of frightful hearing, but that he must hear. He subsequently says he would gladly have deafened as well as blinded himself (*OT* 1386ff.). Samson, in 'divorcing' Dalilah, similarly says that he has learned to deafen him-self (*SA* 936-7).

31 E.g., *PL* IV.774-5 ('happiest if ye seek / No happier state, and know to know no more'), IV.637-8 ('to know no more / Is woman's happiest know-

ledge'), VII.631-2 ('Thrice happy [men] if they know / Their happiness'),
VIII.72-4 ('The great architect / Did wisely to conceal, and not divulge /
His secrets'), VIII.172-3 ('heaven is for thee too high / To know what passes
there; be lowly wise'), VIII.281-2 ('From whom I ... feel that I am happier
than I know'), VIII.620-1 ('Let it suffice thee that thou know'st / Us happy').
This last, of course, responds to Adam's inquiry into heavenly sexuality.

32 *Christian Doctrine*, I.xiv, in Yale *Prose Works*, VI, 424, where Milton
reproves the theologian Zanchius' impertinences about what took place in
Mary's womb.

33 The first ballad in Francis J. Child's five-volume treasury (*The English
and Scottish Popular Ballads* [Boston, 1882-8]); see *The Viking Book of
Folk Ballads of the English-Speaking World*, ed. Albert B. Friedman
(New York, 1956), 3-7. For the spouse-getting riddle in *Samson*, cf. lines
1010-17. The solving of such riddles is a staple of Shakespearean marriage-
stories; the riddle on incest in the first scene of *Pericles* reveals the Oedipal
basis of the theme.

34 'What can be less in me than desire / To see thee' - Nothing can be more
(I.383-4). 'Where / Easily canst thou find one miserable, / And not enforced
... to lie?' - Nowhere (I.470-2). 'What wonder then if I delight to hear / Her
dictates from thy mouth?' - No wonder (I.481-2). 'What woman will you
find ... ?' - None (II.208). Christ takes up the form in discussing pagan
oracles: 'What confessed more true / Among the nations ... ?' (I.431-2);
'What have been thy answers, / ... what but dark / Ambiguous .. as good
not known?' (I.434); 'Who ever ... / Returned the wiser?' (I.438-9). He also
uses the form when discussing Job: 'What but thy malice moved thee to
misdeem / Of righteous Job?' (I.424-5); 'Who names not now ... patient Job? /
Who next more memorable?' (III.95-6). (So also in discussing glory: 'What is
glory but ... ?' [III.47]; the vulgar: 'What delight to be by such extolled?'
[III.54]; the mighty: 'What do these worthies, / But rob ... ?' [III.74-5].) In
Satan's mouth the mock-doubtful hearer to a pre-empted and so neces-
sitated choice: 'What doubts the Son of God to sit and eat?' (II.368). 'What
hope ... whence authority ... / What followers, what retinue ... / Longer
than thou canst feed them?' (II.417-19). 'What canst thou better do the
while?' (III.180).

35 Luke 3:19, 'Herod the Tetrarch,' with *PR* 201-2, 'Tetrarchs of fire, air, flood,
and on the earth / Nations besides from all the quartered winds.' The
emphasis is on Satan's rule of the air, with overtones of the quartering of
Christ's nation.

36 *Antigone* 332, trans. Elizabeth Wyckoff, in Chicago *Greek Tragedies*, II,
170.

37 One of the fullest versions is found in *The Greek Anthology*, XIV.64. This

version also describes man as changeable (Samson's Chorus seems to apply this to God's 'various' hand towards men - 'Or might I say contrarious' [668]). For the sexual theme, cf. Paul Fry's essay, '*Oedipus the King*,' in *Homer to Brecht: The European Epic and Dramatic Traditions*, ed. M. Seidel and E. Mendelson (New Haven and London 1977), 171-90.

38 *OT* 823-5, trans. Grene, in Chicago *Greek Tragedies*, II, 46.

39 *OC* 1541-3, trans. Robert Fitzgerald, ibid., 146.

40 *PL* IV.324, *SA* 1487-9 ('Sons [are] wont to nurse their parents in old age, / Thou in old age car'st how to nurse thy son, / Made older than thy age through eyesight lost' - the Chorus to Manoah). The survival of Manoah to Samson's sudden aging is of course strictly Miltonic, in that it contradicts the ending of Samson's story in Judges 16:31 - which is replaced with the ending of the story of Jepthah's daughter, in the preceding chapter. See sec. IX, first paragraph, for the biographical implication, with n. 53 below.

41 John 8:44, with *PR* I.407-8, 429.

42 Spenser, *FQ* I.i.29, 'An aged Sire' (Archimago's guise as a holy father), and Giles Fletcher, *Christ's Victory and Triumph*, ii.15, 'an aged Syre' (Satan's guise as the Tempter). As pseudo-father, Satan cannot correctly name the son Ishmael - he calls him Nebaioth (at II.309), Ishmael's own son.

43 The contest of Abdiel and Satan at the end of Book V of *Paradise Lost* restages the Messianic drama of the crucial Psalm 2, as decreed by the Father at *PL* V.603-6.

44 The words originally describe God's image in Adam, *PL* IV.294, with perhaps a play on Latin *liberi*, children, and *liber*, free. Cf. *Christian Doctrine*, I.xxvi: 'Christian liberty is that whereby we are loosed as it were by enfranchisment, through Christ ... to the intent that being made sons instead of servants, and perfect men instead of children, we may serve God ...' (Sumner trans. in Hughes, 1012; in Yale *Prose Works*, VI, 537).

45 Heb. 2:14 in the Vulgate.

46 *PR* I.282, II.99, II.252, IV.252.

47 *PR* I.176-7; *Christian Doctrine*, I.viii, on 'good' temptations (Sumner trans. in Hughes, 988; in Yale *Prose Works*, VI, 338); with *PR* I.155-6, 'I mean / To exercise him in the wilderness.'

48 *Ad Patrem* 8, trans. Carey, in *Complete Shorter Poems*, 153. Cf. *Christian Doctrine*, I.v: 'the Son himself professes to have received from the Father, not only the name of God and of Jehovah, but all that pertains to his being, that is to say, his individuality, his existence itself ...' (Sumner trans. in Hughes, 955; in Yale *Prose Works*, VI, 259).

49 *Ad Patrem* 73-6, 86-7, trans. Carey, 154.

50 *Christian Doctrine*, I.xiv: 'he could ... both *increase in wisdom*, Luke ii.52, after he had emptied himself, and *know everything*, John xii.17, that is, after the Father had instructed him, as he himself acknowledges' (Carey trans., in Yale *Prose Works*, VI, 425).

51 Sonnet XVI ('When I consider how my light is spent'), lines 9-10, with *Christian Doctrine*, I.v: 'What need was there for the union of divine and human nature in one person, if he himself, being equal to the Father, gave back again into his hands everything that he had received from him?' (Sumner trans. in Hughes, 942; in Yale *Prose Works*, VI, 229). This last passage includes references to the cup of the Passion and the defence of the Son by the Father's angels, as cited in n. 16 above (cf. Hughes, 941-2). Further on, Milton argues that the Father, unlike the Son, cannot be 'man' (in Yale *Prose Works*, VI, 264; cf. ibid., 424-5).

52 Cf. Frye, *Return of Eden*, 132-3.

53 'He had this elegy in common with the patriarchs and kings of Israel, that he was gathered to his people; for he happened to be buried in Cripple-gate, where about thirty years before he had by chance also interred his father' (text from Hughes, 1044). But compare the revisionary ending of *Samson* with Judges 16:31: 'Then his brethren and all the house of his father came down, and took him, and brought him up, and buried him ... in the burying place of Manoah his father.' The house in which Milton was born, his father's, burned in the Great Fire of London, a year before *Paradise Lost* was published, the final image of which is the judgment on Sodom impending over paradise. This house was called The Spread Eagle; the last comparison for Samson renews his fiery birth-portents with the image of the phoenix, or fiery eagle.

54 So Satan's first soliloquy in *Paradise Lost*, IV.50-7.

55 The argument is Karen Horney's, in *New Ways in Psychoanalysis* (New York, 1939), ch. 13, 207-31.

56 *King Lear*, IV.vi.27, II.iv.149-50.

57 Ibid., IV.vi.68-9, 73, with Luke 4:13.

58 This and the following quotations are from *The Past Recaptured*, trans. Andreas Mayor (New York, 1971; Vintage Books), 271-2. There is, of course, no 'fall' for the elevated Christ: Milton says that God in effect covenants with Adam that 'if you stand firm, you will stay; if you do not you will be cast out' - of Paradise (as Satan was *cast down* from heaven [*PR* IV.605]): so *Christian Doctrine*, I.iii (Sumner trans. in Hughes, 914; in Yale *Prose Works*, VI, 163).

## THOMAS
## WILLARD

# Alchemy and
# the Bible

The Bible has been quoted to many ends, providing everything from a code of behaviour to a code of art. Some uses of Scripture may strike us as being more productive than others; we may feel, for example, that Paul's warning about 'science falsely so called' is better used in a study of *gnosis* than at a school board hearing about evolution. But few applications seem farther fetched today than those which alchemists once made. They read the Bible allegorically, assuming that the prophets and apostles knew the secrets of transmutation, and they took the allegory literally as a formula for turning 'earth ... without form, and void, into pure gold, like unto clear glass.' In the process, they gave alchemy a reputation for the sort of inspired misreading that Harold Bloom finds in cabala. But their misreadings were readings all the same, based on definite principles of interpretation. These principles account for much of the continued interest in alchemy and remind us that hermeticism and hermeneutics have a common ancestor in Hermes.[1]

Alchemical interpretations of the Bible date back to the early Christian era and persist to this day, but grew most extravagant in the Renaissance. It was natural for Montaigne to think of alchemists when he wrote about the variety of interpretations, recalling a priest who showed him biblical grounds for this 'belle science,' or for Donne to compare them with other professional misreaders. After suggesting that politicians could learn statecraft from his own love story, Donne added: 'In this thy booke, such will their nothing see, / As in the Bible some can finde out Alchimy.' As a poet he exploited the biblical metaphors that delighted alchemists, and he likened himself to the metal in a refiner's fire, saying: 'Burne off my rusts.' But as a preacher and satirist he pointed out the dangers of conceited interpretations. He joked about Catholics who combed the Bible for evidence of Purgatory much as others looked for hints about metals. And he implied that Paracelsus, the great Renaissance alchemist, ruined men's souls with false readings of Scripture as cheerfully as he killed their bodies with false cures.[2]

What Donne said in jest others reiterated in deadly earnest, alarmed that Paracelsians recognized no boundary between religion and science. Bacon thought it 'extreme levity ... to found a system of natural philosophy on the first chapter of Genesis, on the book of Job, and other parts of sacred writings.' Thomas Sprat, a spokesman for the Baconians in the Royal Society and the Latitudinarians in the Church of England, regarded alchemists as 'downright *Enthusiasts*,' blinded by their own smoke. But although Renaissance thinkers questioned the alchemists' method of inquiry and conception of the world, they left the most interesting question for psychologists and critics in the present century: what were alchemists after when they struggled to join the outward reality of nature and the inward message of Scripture? The best answer so far is that they searched for a common archetype, and it confirms Donne's impression that alchemy is shot through with metaphor. We will return to the challenges and defences later on, but first we must see how alchemists drew on the Bible, taking the history and process of their art from biblical narrative and the structure of their world from biblical imagery.[3]

In using the Bible as a handbook, alchemists made two assumptions: their art concerned all sorts of transmutation, not just that of lead into gold, and it provided a key to any system aimed at change. These assumptions lie behind the two symbolic chains in alchemy, both likened to the golden chain in Book VIII of the *Iliad*. The first is the chain of being that reaches from heaven to earth and from man to the animals, vegetables, and minerals he has dominion over. The second is the chain of tradition that reaches from Adam or Moses to the alchemists and conveys the secrets of nature from generation to generation. Each chain relies on the other, and both came apart in the Renaissance. Copernicus took the lower links off the chain of being when he showed the earth did not hang below the sun and moon at the centre of creation, and Casaubon broke the chain of tradition when he dated the works of Hermes Trismegistus to the early Christian era, where they could no longer be said to connect Moses and Plato. Some alchemists and poets clung to the *Aurea Catena Homeri*, and Goethe praised an eighteenth-century work of that title when he dabbled in alchemy. But by Goethe's time alchemy was well removed from Christianity. Goethe's Faust rejects the traditional Logos when he concludes that the world did not begin with the Word, or even the thought or the power, but simply the act. At this point he becomes a modern chemist, as Northrop Frye remarks, studying nature as an object, not a revelation.[4]

The view of alchemy as a divinely ordained science began with the first Western texts. Written in Alexandria and reflecting the syncretism of Philo's time, they were often attributed to venerables. *The Chemistry of Moses* purported to contain directions to Bezaleel, who made the Ark of the Covenant, though several recipes came from earlier works by 'Democritus.' A treatise on stills by Maria the Jewess was said to be the work of Moses' sister Miriam, and a procedure called the labyrinth was ascribed to Solomon, who had Hiram make a 'molten sea' for the temple in Jerusalem. The first historical personage in Western alchemy, Zosimos of Panoplis, took special interest in the Book of Enoch, which explained what really happened when the sons of God came down to the daughters of men. The angels instructed their wives in all the crafts, but their offspring put chemistry and metalwork to the worst possible uses, making perfumes and swords. They were banished to a remote area, where the chief angel and smith was chained to a rock like Prometheus. But their crafts were rumoured to have spread among the children of Cain, their community being popularly identified with the city of Enoch which Cain 'the smith' founded, and somehow to have survived the Flood. This whole story went against the testimony of Baruch, who said the giants were too stupid to survive. But Enoch's book was quoted in the Epistle of Jude, and Zosimos cited a similar story in a book by 'Hermes.'[5]

The Book of Enoch gave alchemy a divine origin, but also a demonic cast. The Church Father Tertullian cited it to show the dangers of forbidden arts, especially in the hands of women, and alchemists were sometimes regarded as children of Cain. They countered with references to Bezaleel and Hiram, but increasingly they offered a counter-reading of Scripture. By the Middle Ages they studied the five books of Moses as the works of an adept who could produce *aurum potabile* by melting down the golden calf, and one reader took the dust-to-dust dictum of Genesis as evidence that Moses knew all about the *materia prima*. In the Renaissance the annals of alchemy swelled into lists of great men; a list attributed to Paracelsus included seven Hebrew adepts from Adam to Daniel and eight Greeks from Homer to Plato. Michael Maier, a Paracelsian with considerable literary gifts, claimed that Adam brought the philosophers' stone out of Paradise and used the elixir to prolong his life. Such claims fired the imagination of Jonson's Sir Epicure Mammon, who asks a sceptic:

Will you believe antiquity? Records?
I'll show you a book where Moses, and his sister,
And Solomon have written of the art;
Ay, and a treatise penn'd by Adam –

Like Mammon, many alchemists reached back along the chain of tradition in search of ever greater authorities. But others hoped to escape the endless regress by seeking instruction from the Holy Spirit, which taught the patriarchs and prophets, a spirit that would one day restore the Golden Age. Illuminated by this spirit, they could open what Shakespeare calls 'nature's infinite book of secrecy.'[6]

The metaphor of nature as a book, with God as the author, derived from a famous verse in Paul's letter to the Romans: 'the invisible things of him [God] from the creation of the world are clearly seen, being understood by the things that are made, even his eternal power and Godhead.' Tertullian quoted this verse to show that the world was not a place of deception, as Socrates told Phaedo, but the image of another world. The argument proved as important for alchemy as it did for Christianity. For it set up a chain of being, a Jacob's ladder stretching from visible objects to invisible truths. The student of nature could read God's works as he would read God's Word, and the analogy between nature and Scripture was often drawn. Hugh of Saint Victor referred to the world as a book written *digito dei* like the tablets from Mount Sinai and the whole Bible by extension. Bonaventura said the Bible became necessary only after man could no longer read the *liber creatorum* as Adam did when he named the beasts. Granted: Bonaventura had no use for alchemy, which he regarded as one more instance of man's efforts to build permanent models of an impermanent world. But alchemists replied, with the English Paracelsian Robert Fludd, that they studied a philosophy 'originally delineated by the finger of God.'[7]

The search for the Creator's marks on the creation, for types in the literal sense of prints from a pattern or blows from a mould, reached its extreme in the 'signatures' of Paracelsus and Boehme. The Rosicrucian manifestos explained: 'These Characters and Letters, as God hath here and there incorporated them in the holy Scripture the *Bible*, so hath he imprinted them most apparently into the Wonderful Creation of Heaven and Earth, yea in all beasts.' Interest in the Creative Word and its marks on the created world led Paracelsus to discuss the Creation story as an alchemical operation, a demonstration of what Fludd termed 'the high Chymical virtue of the Word.' It led Oswald Croll, another disciple, to treat the elixir as the visible counterpart of the invisible Word of God. Henry Pinnel, a translator of Paracelsus and Croll, prefaced their tracts with a praise of Wisdom as the philosophers' stone, packing seventeen biblical references into a single sentence. He then denied any wish to overthrow the Bible's authority: 'my desire rather is that both these Books of God (Nature and Scripture) might be better studied and more observed. Doe I seek to make voyd the Word of the Lord by his Works? God forbid; nay I establish the one by the other.' Contemporaries would have caught the echo of a verse much quoted in the Reformation: 'Do we then make void the law through faith? God forbid: yea, we establish the law.' Indeed, alchemists raised the same issue of faith in the Word as Luther, who said he liked alchemy 'very well.'[8]

What Luther liked best was not the work with metals, which he valued all the same: it was 'the allegory and secret signification, which is exceeding fine, touching the resurrection of the dead at the last day.' He liked the faith of alchemists, who said the philosophers' stone gave them a 'reassuring type' of Christ's resurrection. This faith resided in a personal vision, captured in the defiant motto of Paracelsus: Do not be another's man if you can be your own. Indeed, Luther and Paracelsus had a certain amount in common: both asserted the individual's right to shake off authority and pursue the spirit rather than the letter, Luther in the religious manifesto he nailed to a church door in Wittenberg, Paracelsus in the medical manifesto he posted outside a lecture hall in Basel. They both inspired radicals to prophesy the overthrow of authority, even to fight for it, and the aptly named Mary Rant predicted that Protestant alchemists would topple governments by making enough gold for everyone. She missed the point that authorities who coin money are alchemists and do turn the world upside down, a point that Marx would make two centuries later. But for many intelligent people of her time, alchemy became a symbol of threatening and irrational change, rather like the dynamo of Henry Adams. The alchemists' 'faith' began to look more like crazed 'enthusiasm,' which religious and scientific leaders tried to subdue.[9]

Religious opposition came mostly from Catholics, who thought alchemists denied the literal Church and clergy as they tried to become the 'lively stones' that Peter spoke of, 'a spiritual house, a holy priesthood.' Marin Mersenne, a Minorite, identified the first axiom of Fludd's philosophy: 'The whole of sacred Scripture refers to alchemy and alchemical principles. The mystical sense of Scripture is nothing else but explication through alchemy and the philosophers' stone. No matter what religion is professed, Roman, Lutheran, or another, he alone is catholic who believes in the catholic stone.' Mersenne's harangue extended to books and correspondence, arousing considerable support. Gabriel Naudé, the librarian of Cardinal Mazarin, planned to continue the assault and drew up a bill of grievances which began:

Our Alembick-Idolaters and Alcimists ... are a sort of people so strangely besotted with the Philosopher's stone that, having found out the secret Mysteries thereof under the *Metamorphoses*, the *AEneid*, and *Odissey*, the love of *Theagenes* and *Chariclea* [in Heliodorus], *Epitaphs, Pictures, Sculpture, Antick*, and *Fantastick* representations, and there being nothing but the *Scriptures* to make any further search in, they have been so prophane as to take the sacrifice of the *Masse*, and the miracle of the *Incarnation* for Emblems and figures of what they found to be literally express'd in *Genesis*, the last chapters of the Prophet *Esdras*, the *Canticles*, & the *Apocalypse* concerning that Soveraign transmutation.

He then listed other biblical alchemists, including Abraham, Job, and John of Patmos.[10]

Scientific opposition focused on the glibness of alchemists, who refuted Aristotle and other authorities by quoting Paul on the 'vain babblings' of Greeks or James on wisdom that is 'earthly, sensual, devilish.' In the preface to what may well be the first textbook of chemistry, Andreas Libavius complained that no real progress would occur until students stopped looking through the Song of Songs for what they could only find in the laboratory. He returned to this theme when he wrote the first attack on Rosicrucianism, giving rise to Fludd's first publication. Quoting the favourite verse from Paul, Libavius argued that two traditions existed side by side, the one concerned with visibles and reaching back to Greece, the other concerned with invisibles and reaching back to Israel. Whoever tried to replace the first with the second, he said, confused the light of nature with the light of grace. Libavius denied the existence of hidden analogies between the visible and invisible worlds, and he told the Rosicrucians: 'This magic and cabala of yours is nothing but rhetoric and poetic tropology, begotten of logical comparisons by similitudes of any kind, by means of which God can be transformed into a man and man into a god, with other changes more mirific than Ovidian metamorphoses can produce.' He used his terms precisely, being a former professor of rhetoric.[11]

Naudé and Libavius took the same tack: both accused alchemists of allegorizing the Bible, much as iconographers did the classics. Paracelsus and Fludd treated biblical symbols as figures of speech, and Maier found alchemical themes in classical myths, anticipating the 'fisica poetica' of Vico. By calling attention to the literary status of alchemical writings, adversaries discredited whatever these writings said about science or religion; and in doing so, they helped make religion and science less dependent on each other. The Bible was never meant to be a textbook of science, they argued; therefore, it should not hinder scientific discoveries, nor should discoveries threaten its authority. The vision of oneness in alchemy had little value for Libavius and Naudé, and none at all for Mersenne's associates Gassendi and Descartes. For it was a poetic vision.[12]

The same vision that made alchemy laughable or threatening three centuries ago has made it attractive in this century. Several thinkers have addressed the question that went unanswered on the eve of the Enlightenment: what needs did alchemy serve? Carl Jung devoted four decades to his answer, producing four large and learned volumes. He thought of alchemists as dreamers and studied the archetypal images in their dream, the images having a value in psychology quite independent of their value in religion or science. As scientists, the alchemists struck him as being deluded, for they projected ideas on to matter much as they hoped to project the philosophers' stone. As theologians, they seemed to be heretics, setting themselves up as saviours. But as dreamers, they engaged in a noble attempt to resolve basic tensions in Western culture, notably the split between matter and spirit, the powers of darkness and light. This view opened a fascinating door to alchemy, which became an analogue for the process of self-discovery, but it assumed that alchemists were dualists. Jung assumed that alchemists sought to free the spirit from matter rather than restore matter to its original perfection, as they often asserted. Consequently, he reached some of the same conclusions as Libavius and Naudé: alchemists confused nature with grace, he said, and the alchemical mass was in 'bad taste.' When he studied the parallel between the philosophers' stone and the Messiah, on which their mass was based, he emphasized the unorthodox elements in alchemy and did not deal with the analogy of nature and Scripture.[13]

In a penetrating review, Northrop Frye has suggested that Jung was misled on this last point by his lifelong preceptor, Goethe. Just as Faust denied the Logos, Jung questioned the Incarnation and the potential reconciliation of matter and spirit. As a result he paid little attention to the Incarnate Word and its cognates, the Word manifest in nature and Scripture. Blake offers a better guide to Paracelsus and Boehme, Frye has found, for Blake reminds us that their interest in the Word of God turned alchemy into a vision rather than a doctrine or ritual. Moreover, Frye notes, the same vision appears in poetry like Blake's, the Bible having provided both 'the definitive myth for alchemists' and 'the definitive grammar for allegorical poets.' Frye elaborates this grammar or myth in his 'Theory of Archetypal Meaning,' using many biblical images. And in a recent reassessment of Jung, he again notes that occultists and poets speak the same language: 'perhaps we cannot fully understand either one without some reference to the other.'[14]

By stressing the importance of archetypes, Jung and Frye have placed alchemy in an autonomous position, where it can withstand charges of being a false religion or pseudo-science. They have also explained the force of biblical symbols in alchemy. But perhaps we can gain further insight into the choice of these symbols, and the objections they aroused, if we recognize that they are sometimes antitypes as well. The antitype, of course, is a revelation of what has been concealed in the corresponding type; Paul considered Christ the antitype of the rock in the wilderness, for example, and alchemists regarded both as prefigurations of the philosophers' stone. Thus alchemy combined neo-Platonic archetypation with biblical typology. Its archetypes develped spatially through analogy and identity, while its antitypes functioned temporally through foreshadowing and fulfilment. And just as the archetypes crowned the chain of being, the archetypal standing above the heavenly and earthly in the three worlds of Hermes, the antitypes completed the chain of tradition. Alchemists found it equally irresistible to think archetypally and typologically: they would liken their stone to the stone with seven eyes in Zechariah, each eye governing a different planet and metal, or would compare their work in the alembic to God's work in the world from the Creation to the Last Judgment.[15]

The neo-Platonic chain of being seemed consistent with the biblical view. Indeed, Pico della Mirandola argued that Moses must have known about the three worlds that gave Hermes the name thrice great; otherwise Moses would not have divided the tabernacle into three parts. The chain extended through the three kingdoms: the animal, vegetable, and mineral. At the centre stood man, whom Pico regarded as a separate world and kingdom. All the links could be found in the Bible. For example, the first chapters of John offer this set of metaphors for the Messiah:

| | |
|---|---|
| archetypal world | Word |
| heavenly world | light |
| earthly world | life |
| human world/kingdom | bridegroom |
| animal kingdom | lamb |
| vegetable kingdom | bread |
| mineral kingdom | temple |

Looking over this table, we can see the theme of *Christus Recapitulatio Omnium*, beautifully expounded in William Alabaster's sonnet of that title. We can also appreciate the alchemists' fascination with the symbolism of the mass, the corner-stone of the temple being metaphorically identical with the bread and wine or body and blood. This fascination led to what is sometimes called Grail alchemy: the Grail became identified with the white stone in the Book of Revelation, and Wolfram von Eschenbach called it the *lapis ex caelis*. The philosophers' stone became known as 'the Food of Angels, *and* ... The Tree of Life.'[16]

Meanwhile, because the Word of God was transmitted by a chain of prophets, biblical images took on a historical and typological dimension. The 'mist from the earth' in Eden returned as the 'water of life' or 'living fountains of waters' in the New Jerusalem. The fiery furnace of Daniel harkened back to the 'iron furnace' of Egypt, a 'furnace of affliction' out of which God chose his people, but it also looked forward to the day of reckoning when God promised to save his people: 'I will bring the third part through the fire, and will refine them as silver is refined, and will try them as gold is tried.' Malachi predicted the Son of Righteousness would come as a 'refiner and purifier,' which led Paracelsians to think he would be a master alchemist. This refiner would 'fix' what Isaiah and the alchemists termed the 'flying serpent.' The precious stones of Eden could then be reproduced for the walls of the heavenly city. The covering cherub covered in gems, who guarded the gates of Paradise, would meet his match in the angels of the apocalypse, who would be clothed (as the earliest Vulgate manuscript said) in white stone.[17]

We can see both the archetypal and typological habits at work in Fludd's mind as he says of this passage in Job, 'A more excellent description of the materiall Elixir cannot be made by the wisest Alchimist or deepest philosopher':

Surely there is a vein for the silver, and a place for gold *where* they find *it*.

Iron is taken out of the earth, and brass *is* molten *out of* the stone.

He setteth an end to darkness, and searcheth out all perfection: the stones of darkness, and the shadow of death.

The flood breaketh out from the inhabitant; *even the waters* forgotten of the foot: they are dried up, they are gone away from men.

As *for* the earth, out of it cometh bread: and under it is turned up as it were fire.

The stones of it *are* the place of sapphires: and it hath dust of gold.

Here Fludd could see a stone reaching up the chain of being, through the bread it produced to the lions it nourished and onward along the 'path which no fowl knoweth' (the path of Wisdom, said one cabalist). He could also see in the stone that conquered darkness a 'type' or 'pattern' or 'image' of Christ, who would make all things new. Job's parable showed how the fire in the earth, the central sun of alchemy, drove the first matter through the round of elements until it became the philosophers' stone, a substance as transparent as sapphire. Similarly, man's body would become golden, the flesh in which he would see God. For this sort of speculation Fludd coined the term 'spiritual alchemy.'[18]

Fludd's comments on the Bible are ingenious, and we could certainly say he engaged in allegorical commentary. We would not be likely to call it criticism, unless we shared Swift's opinion that most critics distil 'the very Quintessence of what is bad' and are therefore alchemists themselves. But at least we can say that alchemists like Fludd followed certain critical principles as they studied the books of nature, Scripture, and their fellow practitioners. They assumed that knowledge was a whole, created and sustained by the Word of God, and they looked for analogies between different sorts of experience. Analogies were basic to the cosmology of the Middle Ages and Renaissance, so basic that it might be convenient to adapt Michel Foucault's distinction between commentary and criticism and say that allegorical commentary belongs amid the endless resemblances of the Renaissance, while modern criticism begins with the clear-cut representations of the neo-classical era. The distinction between commentary and criticism is not that sharp, yet the debate we have witnessed between alchemists and their adversaries in the seventeenth century was a clash between radically different world views.[19]

The alchemists lost, of course, and the Cartesian system became basic to the way we think and speak, as Chomsky has shown. But now that Chomsky and Descartes have been challenged by linguists suggesting that all thought is metaphoric, we are in a better position to appreciate the archetypal and typological thought in alchemy. Alchemy became a cosmic science precisely because it exploited the analogies in the chain of being: alchemists spoke of their art in terms of another world (as terrestrial astronomy, for example) or another kingdom (as a tillage of metals or hunting of the green lion) or man himself (as a chemical wedding). It became a key to all mythologies precisely because it pointed to the main biblical myth: alchemists said the first matter would pass through death to rebirth and go on to redeem the world, a process they could liken to the history of Israel or the life of Christ.[20]

A few alchemists like Armand Barbault have literally kept the fires burning, but the quest survives mostly in literature, as artists strive to become 'Full alchemiz'd' like Keats's Endymion or enter the 'golden city' with Yeats or even record the whole of history like Joyce's 'first till last alshemist.' To be sure, alchemy has produced such nightmares as the *alchimie du verbe* in Rimbaud, wrought by an infernal bridegroom or parody Christ, and the alembic town of Macondo in *One Hundred Years of Solitude*, where the experiment goes dreadfully wrong. The interplay of archetypal and demonic elements goes back to the Bible, metalcraft being both the invention of Tubal Cain and the spirit's gift to Bezaleel. It may provide a necessary tension in the alchemical process. The tension gets resolved, however, when the alchemical dream is over and we find, with Blake's awakened Albion, that the furnaces of affliction have become fountains of living waters.[21]

NOTES

1  1 Tim. 6:20, Gen. 1:2, Rev. 21:18 (Authorized Version); Bloom, *Kabbalah and Criticism* (New York, 1975).

2  Montaigne, *Essais* (Bordeaux, 1580), II, 363; Donne, *A Valediction: of the Booke; Good Friday, 1613; LXXX Sermons* (London, 1640), no. 78; *Ignatius his Conclaue* (London, 1611), 22-30.

3  Bacon, *Novum Organum*, trans. James Spedding, in *The Works of Francis Bacon* (London, 1858), Bk I, Aphorism LXV; Sprat, *The History of the Royal Society of London* (London, 1667), 38, 74-5.

4  Goethe, *Dichtung und Wahrheit*, II, 8; *Faust*, I, iii (1223-36); Frye, 'Forming Fours,' in *Northrop Frye on Culture and Criticism*, ed. Robert D. Denham (Chicago, 1978), 128-9.

5 *Collections des anciens alchimistes grecs*, ed. M. Berthelot (Paris, 1885), I.xx (see 1 Kings 7:23), IV.xii (see Exod. 31); *La Révélation d'Hermès Trismégiste*, ed. A.J. Festugière (Paris, 1949), I, 255; Gen. 4:17, Baruch 3:26-8, Jude 14-15 (see 1 Enoch 1:9).

6 Tertullian, *De Cultu Feminarum*, II, 10; Morienus, *A Testament of Alchemy*, trans. Lee Stavenhagen (Hanover, 1974), 13 (see Exod. 32, Gen. 3:19); Paracelsus, *Aurora Philosophorum* (London, 1659), chs. 1-3; Maier, *Verum Inventum* (Frankfurt, 1619), ch. 4; Jonson, *The Alchemist*, II.i.81-4; Adrian Mynsicht, *Aurum Seculum Redivivum* (n.p., 1623), Epilogus; Shakespeare, *Antony and Cleopatra*, I.ii.10.

7 Rom. 1:20; Tertullian, *De Anima*, XVIII, 12 (see *Phaedo* 65e-66a); Hugh of St Victor, *Eruditionis Didascalicae*, in *Patrologiae Latinae*, CLXXVI, 814 (see Exod. 31:18); Bonaventura, *Illuminationes in Hexaemeron*, Sermons 12, 13; Fludd, *Mosaicall Philosophy* (London, 1659), sig. A3r.

8 *The Fame and Confession of the Fraternity of R:C:* (London, 1652), 42; Fludd, 175; Pinnel, *Philosophy Reformed & Improved* (London, 1657), sig. A3r; Rom. 3:31; Luther, *Table Talk*, trans. William Hazlitt (London, 1857), item 805.

9 *Gloria Mundi*, in *The Hermetic Museum*, trans. A.E. Waite (London, 1893), I, 168; Eirenaeus Philalethes, *Secrets Reveal'd* (London, 1669), sig. A5v; Marx, 'The Power of Money in a Bourgeois Society,' in *Economic and Philosophic Manuscripts of 1844* (New York, 1964), 165-9 (see Acts 17:6).

10 1 Pet. 2:5; Mersenne, *Correspondance*, ed. Cornelius de Waard (Paris, 1945), item 156; Naudé, *The History of Magick*, trans. John Davies (London, 1657), 274.

11 2 Tim. 2:16, Jas. 3:15; Libavius, *Alchymia* (Frankfurt, 1606), sig. A2v; *Examen Philosophiae Novae* (Frankfurt, 1615), 18; see Owen Hannaway, *The Chemists and the Word* (Baltimore, 1975).

12 Vico, *La scienza nuova*, II, vii.

13 Jung, *Psychology and Alchemy*, 2nd ed. (Princeton, 1968), 22-5; *Alchemical Studies* (Princeton, 1967), 116, 158.

14 Frye, 'Forming Fours,' 126-9; *Fearful Symmetry* (Princeton, 1947), 150-61; *Anatomy of Criticism* (Princeton, 1957), 141-6; 'Expanding Eyes,' in *Spiritus Mundi* (Bloomington, 1976), 120.

15 Exod. 17:6, 1 Cor. 10:4, Zech. 3:9.

16 Pico, *Heptaplus*, Second Proem (see Exod. 26); John 1:1, 1:4, 2:19, 3:29, 6:35; Wolfram, *Parzival* IX, 469; Rev. 2:17; Elias Ashmole, ed., *Theatrum Chemicum Britannicum* (London, 1652), sig. B1v (see Rev. 22:2).

17 Gen. 2:6; Rev. 7:17, 22:1; Dan. 3; Deut. 4:20; Isa. 48:10; Zech. 13:9; A.E.

Waite, *The Brotherhood of the Rosy Cross* (London, 1924), 241-2; Isa. 14:29; Ezek. 28:13; Rev. 15:6, 21:19.

18 Job 28:1-8; 'Truths Golden Harrow,' ed. C.H. Josten, *Ambix*, 3 (1949), 84, 109 (see Rev. 21:5, Job 19:26); Christian Knorr von Rosenroth, *Kabbala Denudata*, I (Sulzbach, 1677), 602. For a similar but more recent interpretation see Mary Anne Atwood, *A Suggestive Inquiry into the Hermetic Mystery* (Belfast, 1920), 275-6.

19 Swift, *A Tale of a Tub*, Sec. III; Foucault, *Les mots et les choses* (Paris, 1966), chs. 2-3.

20 Chomsky, *Cartesian Linguistics* (New York, 1966); George Lakoff, *Metaphors We Live By* (Chicago, 1980).

21 Keats, *Endymion* I, 780; Yeats, *Byzantium*; Joyce, *Finnegans Wake* (London, 1939), 185; Rimbaud, *Une saison en enfer, Delerium II*; Blake, *Jerusalem*, pl. 96.

**JAMES
CARSCALLEN**

# Three Jokers:
# The Shape of
# Alice Munro's Stories

I

In Alice Munro's 'Marrakesh' a young woman named Jeanette tells how she was burgled: visiting the romantic city of the story's title, she discovered that her camper had been robbed of all her dresses and jewellery 'as well as my camera naturally.' Soon she found herself inside a different sort of camera, for when she accepted help from two young arabs she was promptly taken to 'a little bare room with a couch and a bright bulb'; and here, when the winning and blue-eyed first arab had gone to get food, his dark companion made advances to her at knife-point. But the first arab came back, apologized, offered a meal, and even asked Jeanette to marry him – though she said no, naturally.

Other cameras like the ones in this story meet us everywhere in Munro: in 'An Ounce of Cure' the baby-sitter learns about whisky in a quietly lit and sparsely furnished livingroom, 'an uncluttered setting for the development of the emotions'; Del Jordan in 'Heirs of the Living Body' is drawn into the stifling parlour at Jenkin's Bend, 'pierced with stray shafts of light,' to see her uncle exposed in his coffin; in 'Who Do You Think You Are?' it is in the Legion basement, illuminated by the last sunlight, that Rose meets Ralph Gillespie. If we take analogies further we soon have a sizeable collection of cameras, and a very strange one as well. Some of these cameras are as empty as the room in Marrakesh, some as junk-filled as Uncle Benny's house in 'The Flats Road.' They can be as sacred as a church or as profane as a dance-hall; as lofty as the Storeys' upper room or as humble as a basement; as central as the Union Station or as peripheral as Munro's many toilets, boarded-up lounges, and out-of-the-way farmhouses. However various, all these places are really the same place; and as we learn from bringing them together, this is a place of contraries. We will find the same thing if we link Marrakesh itself with another place. Jeanette has told an exotic tale – it is enough to make one listener cry 'How could you go to such a country?' – but when we consider all the other 'hot little boxes' of the enclosing story, we realize that the country is not so far away. Just as the travelling camper is oddly like the room at the heart of Marrakesh, so that fabled desert city is like an Ontario small town in a heat-wave, with several appropriate features. The distant shut-up room, moreover, is like the glassed-in porch next door where Jeanette makes love to the neighbour she has just met, and the police she suspects of watching the burglary are like the grandmother who watches the love-making. Marrakesh is both there and here: something, then, that is divided from itself.

This divided condition is what we might expect with a city that, in a more focused form, is the house of a sleeping mother – the house to which the blue-eyed arab takes Jeanette: for in its most general meaning this is the house of Nature, a maternal identity to which we are intimately bound but which is alien to us at the same time. Such a house is both this and that: both physical and mental, for instance. Marrakesh is famous as the city of red clay – the city, then, of Adam, the mortal human body – yet the glassed porch which is the same city is the camera of the eye, old Dorothy's schoolroom of consciousness. And when two lovers find their way both to this room and to each other, we have the conjunction of this and that not only as a situation but as an event: something penetrates a closed chamber in the same way that light enters a camera. The result of this mysterious entry is mysterious in turn, for it is an image, and an image both is and is not what generated it. An image reproduces but also reverses: in photographic terms, dark and light change places, and, as Munro reminds us elsewhere, people come out looking very unlike themselves – or perhaps more like themselves than they actually do. One way to deal with the mystery here – the strange meeting in a strange place, with its strange result – is to observe what 'Marrakesh' also suggests, that as this meeting is at the heart of all experience, so it is at the heart of any story. What I want to do in the present essay is show how meeting and story, the flash of picture-taking and the series of events the picture sums up, are the concentrated and distributed versions of the same thing.

II

Events like the dark arab's attack on Jeanette come at different points in various Munro stories; we also find them more than once in the same story. In the Garnet French episode of 'Baptizing,' for example, two great confrontations stand out. At the revival meeting in the town hall – another hot box, and with the low sun of a spring evening coming in – Del and Garnet experience their own kind of conversion, their operatic recognition of one another as lovers. They come together in a different way on an evening late in the summer: in yet another box, a seemingly still river that mirrors its opposite banks, they are suddenly turned into murderous enemies. Any human tragedy seems to begin with a baptism of water – a baptism of calling and promise – and then to move to an unexpected baptism of fire, or of what is now the water of death: and this means that events themselves reflect each other like the light and dark at the single point of a flash. This reflecting becomes more complex when we notice that Munro's world is haunted not only by two but by three: not only by such things as oxymoronic names and paired characters but by three gifts for Flo, three songs for Addie Morrison, three grandchildren of Mr and Mrs Carl Otis, three boys who rebuild a found boat. The Garnet French story can help us again here, since it shows clearly how a binary structure can be a ternary one as well. For one thing, its two baptisms are the beginning and end of something that also has a mid-point: in particular, the happiness of the supper with Garnet's family and of the lovers' first sexual intercourse afterwards. And two also become three in what at first seems a different way, by the mirroring of each other that we have seen. If the 'other place,' as Munro calls it in an early story, turns out to be not only other but like home as well, then the story is like a going out followed by a return to a starting-place (the story may of course be this in any case); and since in time you cannot be at the same point twice, we now have three points, and a cycle as well. In this way of seeing, the second of the two baptisms will make a centre, not an end – or, if we like, one aspect of it will be central and the other final. But this is not really inconsistent with our binary version of the story. If we consider how, in the ternary scheme, there must be a mirroring of the two ends as well as of the ends and the middle, we can arrive at the general formula that we need here: any two of the three points in the cycle make two baptisms in relation to each other (it helps to see them as making a triangle). Abstract as all this certainly is, the concreteness of Munro's ternary form can be found in any of her stories (to say nothing of other people's): like the anecdote Rose brings home from high school, they all seem to be stories about three jokers just as they are stories about two arabs – the first of whom, we should remember, comes back in a new role to make a third.

If we want to understand the pattern of Munro's 'tricycles' – to use a word slipped strategically into 'Walking on Water' – we can get some assistance from 'Princess Ida,' in which Addie Morrison, later Mrs Jordan, habitually tells and lives stories that go 'round and round and down to death.' Running away from a stern father, as she explains to Del, she first came to the world of Grandma Seeley, where she learned what it was to be treated kindly and put in the way of education. When this world collapsed she made her way to another, Owen Sound, and was briefly engaged there to a shadowy young man who unfortunately 'did not turn out to be the sort of person I had thought he was.' Then, disillusioned though not finished, she settled for the steady Mr Jordan and for Jubilee. Her later sales trips out from town and back go round in the same way, as does her brother's career in the United States and her daughter's short career as a prodigy. So, when we think of it, does 'Princess Ida' as a whole, and here again we can readily make out a pattern of three. First we find Mrs Jordan exciting Del with her Encyclopaedia and her stories, of which the most intriguing is the one about her ferocious brother Bill. Then Bill suddenly appears, metamorphosed now into a rich and indulgent uncle, but with another surprise about him: he is also a man dying of cancer. At the end, when he has left his sister with only a token bequest, there is a third point of concentration: 'a downflash like that of a wing or knife' when she feels the pain of her wound. Whether we see Munro's cycle in a tragic or comic aspect – as an ascent and fall or as some kind of underworld journey with a successful return – it always goes through the same stages as 'Princess Ida.' Expectation is aroused by a first revelation; there is a fulfilment with a surprising reversal to it; and lastly there is a return to normal that nevertheless brings some surprise of its own: a 'downflash' to match the reversal at the centre of the story.

It is this last flash especially that shows us what the cycle, like the binary scheme, amounts to. In Munro we often find a point of special clarity before or after some movement of arousal and subsidence. The girl in 'Images,' for example, having experienced the hermit Joe Phippen first as a demon with an axe and then as a harmless old man who gave her candy, finds herself 'falling asleep with my eyes open'; and this leads to a further eye-opening, for she wakes up to see, from an opposite direction, the house she left to follow the great curve of the Wawanash River. We find clarity in a more disturbing form when, in 'Baptizing,' a girl looks in a mirror to see herself as someone else; and in fact the closing recognitions in Munro's stories always have the power to disturb us, for they show both that we have attained a goal in spite of everything and that the goal is not what we had thought. At the end of 'Princess Ida,' when the embittered Mrs Jordan suggests spending her tiny inheritance on Bibles, not only does a new hurt revive an old one (the Bibles come from a childhood incident) but the gentleman's gift that was to deliver her from a hurt has turned out to be the hurt itself. In 'Age of Faith' Del discovers that the god she wanted is really in the world – as man's own need to kill; later she will find 'real life' as virtual death, and the 'truth' to conjure away 'reality' as reality itself. Although people may be more sleepy than open-eyed, what is there to be seen is always the same thing: you get what you bargained for, but in a form you thought you were not bargaining for.

III

The considering of cycles has brought us more than once to a question of scale: little cycles seem to crop up within bigger ones. The major reversal that we always find in the second phase of a story, for instance, tends to make that phase a 'tricycle' of its own, and the sighting of the house in 'Images' actually comes at the end of this second phase, though it corresponds to similar moments at the ends of whole stories. In fact any one of the three phases, when we can see enough of it, shows itself to be a little cycle in the same way. This is very clear in 'Executioners,' where three distinct phases all follow the same rhythm of approach and withdrawal: Helena's first dealings with Howard Troy (paralleled by those with Robina's family), the central crisis of the fire, with its mania and collapse, and the subsequent encounter, or encounters, with Robina. And if the central phase has a way of looming large, we also find that initial and final episodes tend to multiply in a way suggestive of ever-larger circles enclosing the smaller one of the main story. In 'Images,' for instance, it is mainly a matter of convenience whether we treat the father's invitation to go along on his trap-round as the beginning of the story proper or as introducing a central cycle within it, one that ends with the walk back to the house. The full story in the latter case might begin with the arrival of the formidable Mary McQuade and end with the girl's transformed thoughts about Mary at the very end. Pointless as it may seem, this notion of cycles within cycles leads us to an important further question: would we find a larger tricycle again if we examined a whole novel – which, after all, tells a story too?

The novel of Munro's that can enlighten us here is the one that clarifies its structure by implying an analogy with another story. *Lives of Girls and Women* – the story of a girl called Del Jordan, who lives in a town called Jubilee, is baptized by a boy from Jericho Valley, and in the end seeks an everlasting city – points us to the Bible: it is like Joyce's *Ulysses* in shadowing a model that is more established culturally and plainer in its shape. 'The Flats Road,' to describe this shadowing very briefly, is a book of genesis: Uncle Benny is a patriarch sustained by faith, and against uncertainties as giant as the Flood (which he mentions). The following chapter takes us to a much more incorporated world, a farm and a family as thriving as the 'living body' itself, with a serenely godlike overseer and scrivener flanked by two guardian sisters. This bountiful Egypt is equally a 'tiny sealed-off country' with no exit allowed along the 'river of blood,' so that its plenty only means bondage to a life that is death, or – the other Egyptian obsession, as all the mummifying shows – to a death that is a strange kind of life. In 'Princess Ida' people manage, by a desperate exertion of will, to make an exodus: Addie Morrison is able to escape from a farm that is want, not plenty, even if she must then spend her life on the 'Jericho Road,' forever repeating the same crossing. In the lonely wilderness of 'Age of Faith' her daughter is less independent, and, needing someone to protect her against the horror of seeing 'things,' invokes the powerful god of sheer being – although she finds that this god must necessarily be a thing himself, reflected by a no less jealous 'Mediterranean' god of mystery and suffering.

After this crisis we find Del in the more ordered world of school: a place troubled by outer and inner war but also one of agreed-upon law, where enemies – boys and girls, for instance – can start to play at friendship. 'Changes and Ceremonies' is thus a book of judges that is also a book of deliverers, with Frank Wales as a noble Gideon and Dale McLaughlin as a less noble Samson. The splendour of the kingdom arrives in the next chapter, 'Lives of Girls and Women,' with its civic institutions, its apes and peacocks, and above all its David: Art Chamberlain the warrior, vocalist, and adulterer. Art is even the divine consort Zion longs for, though as it turns out his parting of inner curtains brings no great revelation, and in the end Zion is left as a forsaken harlot. After all this adolescence both Naomi and Del move on toward womanhood, with the one going the way of legalism and ritual, like pharisaism and its Christian successors, while the other tries for love. Del's first serious attempt is with Jerry Storey, a lamblike boy who is too abstracted to touch the flesh he uncovers, although he forgives Del like the woman taken in adultery. With her other boyfriend, the mysterious and passionate Garnet French, Del reaches a more intimate baptism and, as she finds, a tragic one; but as the tragedy is nearing its end she is surprised to meet the simple Bobby Sherriff, and receives his blessing and calling, together with the taste of a banquet, before he makes his odd kind of ascension.

In its essentials this scheme – which does not have to come in exactly eight parts – seems to be that of Munro's other books as well: not only *Who Do You Think You Are?*, where the same course takes a woman through to middle age, but even, it may be, the two collections of short stories as they are arranged (although different aspects of a given story will stand out if we put it in different contexts). And this should not surprise us very much, since the same pattern is a general one in literature, including some other works that Munro may have specially in mind – it is intriguing, for example, to notice that both Lewis Carroll's books about another Alice have this pattern, and that in particular the eight squares of *Through the Looking Glass* parallel those of *Lives of Girls and Women* in substance as well as in number. Munro herself tends to give us the same pattern on the smallest scale as well as the largest, for we can discern something of it in enumerations like Miss Farris's cycle of operettas or the notes left by Rose's father – even in details like the kinds of lore in the Encyclopaedia or the street-names in Jubilee. What we have to ask here is whether this pattern has any structural relation to the pattern of three that we have been dealing with. The novels certainly show it to be cyclical – a Farris-wheel, so to speak – in that we find Del at the end of her story ready for the same compulsive junk-collecting or record-keeping with which it began, and Rose confirmed in the tale-telling and mimicry that she learned both from Ralph Gillespie and from Flo. And on further inspection, I think, this larger pattern will show itself to be a tricycle as well.

Like our other cycles the greater one can be fitted with threes of different sizes, but one specially useful fitting is suggested by Miss Farris's operettas. Since 'Changes and Ceremonies,' a 'Judges' chapter, concerns itself with the Pied Piper, we might expect the operetta of that name to come in the same place – about fifth, that is, in Miss Farris's list of titles. Actually it comes first, but we find that Munro's 'Judges' stories – stories about operettas of some kind, like 'Day of the Butterfly' or 'Forgiveness in Families' – are closely linked with her 'Wilderness' stories; and if this is so, the congruence of first and fifth begins to make sense. To use biblical terms again, the experience of Israel between the

Exodus and the Kingdom is the Book of Genesis repeated. The first of the Bible's inner cycles, in this reading, is that of the Chosen People before the special covenant of Sinai: a cycle that leads from an unsettled world into the established land of Egypt and, when Egypt proves to be a place of bondage, out again at the Exodus. At this point the Israelites are called, under a new leader, to be a people of the Law and receive a new home. Their second cycle reaches its height in the Davidic kingdom, which in turn is reversed into the Babylonian captivity that is really its own underside. The death of Jesus, in one perspective, completes this cycle, since it brings the end of what is only worldly in the anointed king. But Jesus also announces another exodus and a further kingdom; and so the new Israel of the Church – in the Bible's Christian version – sets out for its own city, with results we will have to consider later.

Now we have an important organizing principle, since for our purposes we can see in *Lives of Girls and Women* – and, I suggest, in all of Munro's books – a series of cycles like the biblical pattern I have described. And this means that we can now assemble a picture of Munro's three phases with many scales and correspondences to draw on: for brevity's sake I am going to shift among these without any special notification. It remains difficult, certainly, to see in various perspectives at once, and we must keep some possible sources of confusion in mind: the fact that all flashes are ultimately the same flash, and all cycles the same cycle; that any phase of a cycle must contain a cycle within it, just as a whole cycle must be part of a larger one; that an element which is central in one respect must be initiatory and final in others, since the present is not only a centre but the end of the past and the beginning of the future. But if we contrast phases rather than assimilate them to each other, and if, at this stage, we simplify matters by seeing Munro's containing cycle as tragic rather than comic, I think the pattern of this cycle will stand out clearly enough, for it is basically a very simple one.

IV

We begin in chaos or wilderness – a swamp, a snowstorm, or in 'Walker Brothers Cowboy' both lake and dry back country. Seen as a cycle of its own, the first phase will also take us to the refuges we find in chaos, such as the ark in the Flood or in the bulrushes, or the land of Egypt itself as contrasted with later worldly kingdoms. With its imagery of fawns and lilies and general whiteness – its magical grace and purity – this first kingdom may even seem a paradise before any chaos rather than a refuge; but within space and time Eden can only be like the 'Mock Hill' of 'Something I've Been Meaning to Tell You,' and another look at the first phase shows us what is already a world in collapse, a 'Charlie Buckle' place of sedentary or drifting losers in their crumbling mansions and improvised shelters. In this context of ruin Munro often sets a primitive culture of hunter-gatherers and nomads – Arabian knights – who in their dealings are something equally primitive: gamblers and tricksters (perhaps pedlars) who live by luck because they have nothing so structured as an order of law to rely on. Nor is there a reliable order of knowledge, for anything can happen here: a poltergeist, a miracle, a legend suddenly come true. In fact it is hard to tell reality from illusion, or sincerity from theatre, in a place where notions materialize and vanish like Rose's 'royal beatings' and 'Vancouvers,' and where people like her father play roles that are also their real selves. It is in such a shaman's world of illusions and theophanies that we find the initiatory adventures typical of the first phase: a temptation in a wilderness like Ben Jordan's visit to Nora Cronin, a perilous quest like Blaikie Noble's imagined search for a jewel under the ocean.

What draws the adventurer on is a light that shines in the darkness – or perhaps a bell, or Frank Wales' flute and flutelike voice. This is the story of Rose's first joker, the 'undertaker' who, in one of his senses, holds out an offer; and this offer is accepted by a man of faith who receives some kind of purification and enters into a covenant. The light that beckons us on is at the same time the gleam in a well that reflects something behind us. The instrument played by Frank Wales is actually a 'recorder'; Madeleine lures Uncle Benny toward sex by drawing him back to 'a lady with one child' – a mother and, equally important, an infant. The inhabitants of this first world are led to, and are, innocents, floating in a womb that precedes incarnation or birth or some other theshold, such as puberty. More adequately, since they are at an end as well as a beginning, they are both innocents and wizards, children and ancients, the latter including guardians as brutal as Tyde in 'Royal Beatings' and as indifferent as Mason Howey in 'The Flats Road.' If we add one more reversal we have the picture of stiff old Mr Lougheed and mischievous Eugene – Eros as an impish youngster – bound in a need and betrayal that are mutual.

This betrayal is the tragedy of the first world: an innocent is abused in his trust by a deceiver outside or a deceiver inside – a inner mistrust greater than any faith that is only a gamble – and so ends lost in chaos or, like Ben in 'Walker Brothers Cowboy,' trapped in the shelter he has covenanted for. We can call this the tragedy of the Pied Piper, since Miss Farris's operetta will give us all of its essentials. It is the tale of an outlandish wanderer who is cunning and simple at once, and in every other way as pied as the various motleys of this phase, all contained by the polarization of black and white. In one biblical form, for instance, this is the tale of Joseph, the youth of many colours who is both foolish and wise and who stands at the gate of an unknown world. Such a figure is not only a lure but a deliverer, even a creator who knows how to put down vermin; he is also of course a victim, for the Pied Piper is rejected by those he delivers and becomes a revenger in turn. His reward, like that of other sacrifices, is to become a story – to be 'set apart for legendary uses,' like Myra in 'Day of the Butterfly.'

Myra can also serve us as the Pied Piper's female reflex, since she is a child, and already an outcast, who is mysteriously struck down on accepting an invitation. And Myra is something more mysterious than that, for she has touches of seductiveness and power: she is in fact a cousin of Nora Cronin and Char Desmond, even of the tartar Madeleine – women who, for that matter, have their own kind of innocence. We can epitomize this perilous innocent – the woman at a door or beside a well – by an image that in one respect typifies the first phase, that of a thread: the cord of a blind, a rope-line in a blizzard, a white streak at a window, a red streak of lipstick or fire. This thread draws something in but also ensnares it; at the same time it guards a threshold against ever being crossed. What is even more mysterious is that images like the thread are also linked with figures who seem the opposite of perilous: women like the bustling and prudish Mrs Jordan, who shadow their more romantic sisters, trade blue for the latter's red, and, like Et Desmond, remain in control when the stricken Chars and Blaikie Nobles have faded back into myth.

The second world is a much firmer one, or the first one seen now for such firmness as it has. As a family this second world is a 'solid, intricate structure of lives.' It is equally a shining house or city, lifted above water and often set on a hill, for we have come to an Egypt of a more established kind or to a royal Jerusalem, the lady who stands on the mountain. The second world may also be like the biblical Babylon or Tyre: in 'Tell Me Yes or No' it is a glamorous city by the water with famous gardens, porthole windows, and a book-mart, and elsewhere we find a great deal of purple and blue among its colours, intense or bland depending on whether it is fullness or normality that is being expressed.

Here at the centre of the world we experience a comfortable sense of prosperity, unity, and sheer fleshly presence – one lady on a mountain, for instance, is the proud and sumptuous Cora of 'Privilege.' And Cora is not the only one who in a carnal way thinks she is somebody: the privileged of this second world all have the assurance and composure of Uncle Craig, or of Gabe in 'Material' and Clare MacQuarrie in 'Postcard' – or, in another key, they have the kind of 'self-respect' Mrs Jordan wants for women. Perhaps these self-regarding people can be summed up in 'Rex,' the central member of the 'trio' in 'Walking on Water,' a confident young man who rides the crescent of his moon-like girlfriend. Pharaoh and his god are one form of him; David and Solomon are another, and in the third biblical cycle the Christ who is transfigured or enthroned. Naturally there is a great deal of celebration in the courts of such a king: faith at this stage means 'having a good time' or 'taking your life' in the agreeable sense of enjoying something that is there to enjoy. For a great revelation and fulfilment are at hand, announced by all the media.

Yet this is also the phase of the 'contractor,' the second of the jokers: of a covenanted law, that is, which restricts any good time even in licensing it. Laurence in the recent 'Dulse,' a mature and successful contractor and the second of three workmen, would no doubt build you a shining house, but he would be sure to remind you of his terms, and he himself is vaguely weighed down by his own self-esteem. Not surprisingly some people hanker for a gipsy rather than Egyptian sort of good time, for we find a large amount of 'mischief' in this phase: furtive carryings-on with a Clifford, for instance, or with the unofficial version of Art Chamberlain. In fact, as Art Chamberlain shows, the faithful king is himself an adulterer, and his consort a Jezebel – the practised or brazen kind of harlot found in this phase. Their tragedy is thus one of overreaching or subversion leading to sudden downfall and shame, perhaps on the return of a law-enforcer or the death of a son.

More to our immediate purpose, in that it best shows the second phase as the high point of the three, is a comic resolution in which the great establishment is saved from collapse. The girl in 'Red Dress – 1946,' for instance, somehow accepts her mysterious obligation to be happy, and returns to normal like others who have defeated or beguiled some monster – a Mary Fortune or Joe Phippen without or a bout of rebelliousness within. But the arrangements which thus remain intact are only a diplomatic simulation of unity, a 'Peace of Utrecht.' In the story of that name this peace is the calculated and ambiguous good terms between the two sisters (with the self-possessed Helen subtly in control); it is equally the bond between Maddie and the inscrutable Fred Powell, a bond which may or may not be that of lovers, and has the same air of display, nervousness, and unmet need as other such liaisons in Munro. And we find this tenuous alliance within individuals as well: Art Chamberlain in his Davidic maturity is really an uneasy cross between a boy who must always have new Goliaths to knock down and an exhausted old man. The alliance, and the celebration of it, can be kept up for a time like the dogged exhilaration in 'Sunday Afternoon,' but it leaves an inescapable 'burden,' as does Mrs Jordan's self-respect; and beyond both pride and misbehaviour there remains a self like Mary's in 'The Shining Houses' that keeps its disaffected heart.

Before examining the third phase we should remind ourselves that it is the underside of the central experience projected outward in time, and that, in relation to one cycle or another, it occurs at various points in a story. In biblical terms it may come with the fall of Eden or Egypt or the Israelite kingdom, or with the Passion as the end of the Canaanite cycle, or, beyond that, with the destruction of the world as the end of a larger cycle. The best thing at this point is to treat all these endings as the same ending (though later we will have to make a distinction), and to treat this ending primarily as a tragedy after a comedy – the comedy of a kingdom in its days of glory. From an expansive world at the centre, then, we pass to something greatly shrunken on the fringe: in 'Simon's Luck' the last of the settings Rose can imagine fitting into is the modest if homey 'eating nook of a kitchen in a little stucco house by the bus stop.' Seen as a come-down this is a place in which to be 'tired and practical,' like Clive in 'Baptizing' after his spastic dancing, or from which to look back in chastened memory – for the third joker is only Runt Chesterton, the chartered accountant. And 'stucco' may remind us of Marrakesh, the city of flesh and hence of mortality: this is the place of age and death, the water or fire that waits for us at the end of things.

Yet a valley of fire or water can also be something to cross, as in a revivalist's sermon: the third phase contains, and may be from the beginning, a tale of attempted escape from a dying land. An important figure here is the failing provider of Munro's Exodus stories, who in the imagery of 'Princess Ida' and 'Half a Grapefruit' shows himself to be an Osiris, a slaughtered corn-god – in stories like 'Baptizing' we are reminded of the Christ who plays the same role. The dying God's consort and counterpart, the Isis of 'Princess Ida,' can best be divided into two forms like other female figures we have met (even if the relation between these is more complex than we can go into here) : at the Exodus there is both the lyrical Miriam and the priest's wife Elizabeth, and as we approach the Passion we find both a Mary who ponders and a Martha who decides to do something. The latter is like Addie Morrison or the Rose who says 'I'm not having any of it.' She bestirs herself, puts the past behind her, and also, like Ruby Carruthers in the story of the jokers, claims the right 'to know who I'm doing it with,' even though her disillusioned confronting of 'real life' must repress the deeper knowledge of desire, Mary's knowledge that goes underground.

If we consider the third phase as something in its own right – not only as a departure, that is, but as including an arrival somewhere – then we have a Promised Land after a wilderness: in other terms we have evening sun after rain, or Venus the evening star and planet of concord, or, as Munro also suggests, the Star of Bethlehem with its own promise of peace. Martha and Mary, when they choose this peace, choose different forms of it. For someone like Naomi it means the work and eventual domesticity – again the stucco house by the bus-stop – that she finds acceptable enough; and this practical or legal kind of resolution can take more festive shapes, even some as giddy as in the Brunswick Hotel or at Rose's party in Kingston, with its apocalyptic overtones. But the festivity remains as controlled as Naomi at the Brunswick: in other words it is only that of another second phase, even if seen in a more hectic light. It is thus an Egyptian vanity from which we find Mary keeping aloof, for in this perspective it is Martha who stays with something while Mary tries withdrawal, either at the same time or when the kingdom of the practical topples from its own weight. Mary's way is different: if there is pride in choosing a legal solution – as there clearly is, for instance, with the correctly genteel mother and daughter in 'The Ottawa Valley' – then Mary is a handmaiden, for she chooses grace. Mary gives herself like a child, and is free; with Mary, it seems, a seal is finally broken and something touched. It is Mary who receives the male opposite of the failing provider, the Messiah who comes as a lover. And so water and fire for her are the elements of life: they are like the gentle river in which Del imagines herself lying as she exchanges 'kisses, tongue touchings, suppliant and grateful noises' – gifts of the body as immediate as those of the spirit.

It is Mary's tragedy to see her lover dead, and herself the harlot-after-all of the third phase: someone who has given only in play and, like the grandmother in 'A Trip to the Coast,' has imposed herself even in surrendering. Mary's penance is to go back to the Egypt she seemed to have escaped, a world of loveless routine not unlike Martha's. Perhaps the divergence of the two sisters is only a symptom of disintegration, for the third phase in general is one in which things are coming apart, like a dying god or the accident-victims that Mrs French so enjoys describing. Mrs French may insist that 'We all used to be – we *are* – United'; there are even indications of world empires along with the various love-affairs and marriages. But there is something fantastic and baseless about all these: in other words, we have circled back to the shaky first world, and the coming of new life is only an illusion at the end of things like the gleam in the well at their beginning. The chief difference, when we want a difference, is that we now see this fringe world from a reversed perspective as well as the original one; and the result is the self-consciousness and syncretism of any 'turn-of-the-century' culture – in its manic aspect the born-again swinging of all Munro's Baptist Young People, hippies, liberated academics, and growth groups. All ages join the party, and for an emblem of their latter-day sameness-in-difference we can observe that the three boyfriends in 'Baptizing' make a kind of trinity – the fatherly, licensing Bert Matthews (shadowed by the revenging old man Del finds at Naomi's house), Jerry Storey the glorified son, and Garnet French the giver of life. The last of these brings us in a way to a high point; but his life, the life that remains within Nature, can only collapse into the death it strives against. As 'Spelling' shows, the inmates of an old people's home can take on a surprising new lease of life, but in this respect they are like Munro's various senile animals, which get shot.

V

Death sounds like the end of everything: at the same time, we have seen how the third phase can be a return to grey normality, or to a chaos that is as much beginning as end; and in fact the death which ends both this phase and the larger cycle is no end at all. We find the same thing with any of Munro's flashes, central or peripheral: in natural terms it is always less annihilating than we would expect. Perhaps it happens at the wrong time; perhaps it is not fully noticed or remembered, or, like Art Chamberlain's, seems not much of a flash anyway. And perhaps it does not quite happen at all: Jeanette and Dorothy both escape the strokes they fear, and Del escapes being killed by Garnet in the river – she gets away shaken but in command of herself, as she will later get away from Jubilee. As Dotty in 'Material' remarks, 'the things that don't happen to me, eh?' – after a crisis in which fire has not quite connected with water. So, as with Helena's lip in 'Executioners,' something is left nicked but intact: a mysterious hand has kept us in the Egypt of the natural cycle. From the world's point of view this makes the whole story like the 'Great Comic Scene' into which Del and Jerry turn their failure, with an apocalyptic triumph at the end – on terms that fix the world's discrimination of creatures into sheep and goats. But for a fulfilment the world cannot give we will need another exodus, and if this is not to be just a further step in an infinite regression it will somehow have to overcome the contradiction that made the regression in the first place.

There is another that sometimes looms beside Munro's three: a fourth like the dark and threatening bass in the gospel quartet, who is a member yet stands apart from the others and, unlike them, does not draw the listeners upward. Less formal groups of characters are often like this quartet. Del's mother, for instance, unexpectedly joins the aunts at Jenkin's Bend to complete her daughter's neutralization at the funeral – her views on the living body, after all, are only theirs in a more up-to-date form. In the same way the angry Garnet sums up the trinity of young men in 'Baptizing,' who amount to the same killer-god Del invoked by mistake in 'Age of Faith.' At the same time, Del's mother *is* different from the family she married into, and Garnet the killer – to distinguish him from the humble Garnet – is more unlike any of the trinity than they are unlike each other. The fourth – or the one more than whatever number we like, though three is a good number for cycles – may be an omnipotent god or he may be one of Munro's 'idiots,' but in some way he is always alone. He is, for instance, old Tyde in 'Royal Beatings,' left by three wastrels to die in the snow, and we find the same isolating in Munro whenever something is hidden inside or put outside – perhaps no more than a rag left to rot on a clothesline. If this wrathful and pitiful alien is to bring a new exodus, it is just his alienness that we will now have to deal with; and this will mean separating Munro's final elements considered as final from the same elements as parts of a continuing cycle. Among other things it will mean separating her Apocalypse stories from her Passion stories, and separating the Passion stories in the same way from themselves.

We should think again of the way alienness separates the fourth from the three with whom we find him. Del in 'Baptizing,' like Ruby Carruthers in the story of the jokers, is a fourth but not really an addition: rather, the three young men she encounters are grouped in opposition to her, so that in a way she is the outsider where Garnet is an insider. It is true that Garnet – the angry Garnet – feels himself to be an outsider as well, but this may serve to show us something further: how much these two proud youngsters have in common. If we go back to 'Heirs of the Living Body' we will find a similar situation; for not only does Uncle Craig make a fourth in our sense – he is the centre of his sisters' lives yet their victim as well, and one who at the point of death explodes in desperation – but Del has a special link with her uncle in that she too is both cosseted and driven to explosion. In the end all the characters we have dealt with reduce themselves to a pair of this kind, facing each other in a new dimension. While the pair endlessly trade roles, we will always find that one so to speak stands against, where the other stands for: one is alone, the other represents three, or many. One hangs on the cross while the other watches from a distance: one, that is, is at the centre and the other at the fringe, and one acts – in the sense of either doing or suffering – while the other is the spectator of whom we tend to become more aware toward the ends of Munro's stories. When Del in the river is confronted by her outraged lover, she realizes that she has been this spectator all along, controlling the cycle by the very fact of watching it: in this sense it is she who is a holy ghost, a spirit of aloof knowledge haunting the body of things.

But as a spectator Del has something of her own to give, for the camera in which a picture is taken is hers. Like a metaphor, the spectator's double recognition at the end of a Munro story – the recognition in what you come to of what you left behind – is a seeing of one thing in different things. As a tying together of the ends of the world it secures an Egyptian prison; but precisely in that final securing there will be a new opening if the spectator can tie things together in a different way. Earlier we saw the transformation of vision in 'Images' – a child passes through sleep from one clarity to a further one. And such a passage means liberation if, instead of leading back into a closed world, it leads to a greater world beyond detachment. We may, for instance, find a spectator who realizes not only that two figures on a screen are one, but that he himself is one with what he perceives: the screen is a mirror. When Rose learns of Simon's death she sees, however imperfectly, that she is not the only helpless person or the only one left to die alone. Her aloneness itself is what she shares with someone else, and it can become forgiveness and union if she can say 'yes' cordially to what her new understanding offers her.

Saying 'yes' in this way – with gratitude and self-giving – is what all Munro's changes and crossings point to: it is the genuine passage through the crack in a wall, or the turning around that Helena calls a gift. Beyond a first world of body-identity, when we are contained inside a parent, a second world of sexual or ego-identity, when a son glories in his separate potency, and a spectral third world of impotent reflection, there is a world of simple humanity, free of all such quarrels of opposites as that between parent and child. In other terms this world lies beyond the quarrel between 'truth' and 'reality' in Del's sense of the words – between the form we impose on things and things as they are imposed on us, subjective desire and objective law. This is because it is not 'real life' in an objective sense at all; for it is not something but something known, like the oneness in independence of an experiencer and his experience. Hence it is like a photograph, or a name – even as a child Del notices how her mother, naming the town to which she turns back, seems to create it. For this reason Munro's epilogue stories are all stories about play, and especially art: their central figure, a mad host or entertainer like Miss Marsalles or Ralph Gillespie or Bobby Sherriff, is generally a 'Milton Homer' of some kind. Bobby, for instance, in spite of studies at Trinity College, has not taken to the law. Rather, he is another kind of Pied Piper, damaged and lonely yet with a magic that draws Del to him, and can deliver her from an oppression if she will believe in it. In the same way Bobby is a photographer who, in a saving sense now, turns black to white. Del, as his successor, is to become a photographer in turn – a different sort of chartered accountant; and as his reflection she is to be the mother of what was conceived between them in a brief time of love and annunciation.

VI

All this is to make the passage into eternity sound simple and final: in a fallen world, however, we find it more entangled with the other last phase, the one that is part of an inescapable natural cycle. We have to remember that Bobby's calling is also that of a fool, and to a girl who responds only 'naturally, distractedly'; it is even the coming of a demon photographer to a hussy he arouses and abandons. The Del who longs for a radiant Jubilee is in this perspective only a vain girl who wants it all, like the frustrated narrator of 'The Ottawa Valley.' Even when we consider the calling positively, we must see that it stands out only by contrast with earlier ones: that is enough to give the story its shape, but it indicates the limitation we need to understand here. In 'A Trip to the Coast' the grandmother dreams of an unsettling vision at the 'Simmonses' gate' – the gate of Simeons. What she sees is a mask, a black bird shutting out the sun; moreover, the dream form of her vision is itself a mask, reversed in one way as a picture-negative is in another. Because the grandmother cannot fully understand, she cannot pass through the gate, and a similar obtuseness is necessary for anyone who has to go on living in the world. We notice it especially in Munro's sensible Ben Jordans and Roy Fowlers, who can see that frightening images are 'just nothing' without seeing that they are 'nothing but the truth' – ultimately a releasing truth; but in epiphanic stories like Munro's even the most clear-eyed perceivers see only in emblems: presentations in which two things, or things and their meaning, are driven together but can touch only at one uncertain point.

There is another way, however, of understanding the two figures who sum up Munro's world. At the climax of the great 'Executioners' Howard Troy suddenly runs through fire as a wall collapses; the watching Helena, at the same time, is struck dumb and blind. At this stage we can see the two as the fully human and the natural selves. It is the former that bursts out of the cycle of the world: for it a stroke does take place. The latter, seeing only in part, must go back to Egypt and its burden – must become what it has not recognized, and become it in a condemned and alienated form. Helena turns into a civil servant haunted by seemingly useless memories; Del at the end of her story is about to inherit the endless labour of her Uncle Craig. But there are two important qualifications to be made with this distinction between human and natural selves. On the one hand, we must not identify the human self with one of its fallen shadows: the merely controlling or thinking self or, as with Howard Troy, the merely passionate self. As an act of the natural will Howard's assault on the wall is as futile as Rose's attempt to get away from the parents who have given her a royal beating; and even Howard's wholeness of purpose is like lovers' sincerity elsewhere, what Eileen in 'Memorial' perceives as 'attention to realities, their own realities.' On the other hand, we should not identify Helena completely with the natural spirit of reserve, the mere reflex of this insincere sincerity. If humanity is a union of a giving and a receiving self, then the latter has its own worth, which it keeps even when the two have fallen into separation; and the giving self has recognized this worth by an invitation, for as the woman in 'Tell Me Yes or No' remembers, 'You told me that you loved me years ago.' Even the malice of the receiving self in holding the giving self to its contract is also a kindness. One fallen self reflects the other until it is reflected in turn, and both selves are redeemed – without such a circle of reflection there would be only being, single and unconceived.

The difference, and in this sense distance, between the giving and receiving selves is the same as that between central and peripheral events in a story – or between an event and a recognition, or an earlier and a later recognition: the one is a presence, the other memory and reflection. The malice of Munro's stories, and their kindness, is equally a matter of reflection. Her many jokers tease us into recognition, and stop only when we discover ourselves and so resolve the contradictions of what we see in the mirror. A Munro story – or any story – is thus like Caroline's stillborn baby or Del's stillborn novel: a 'hard yellow gourd' by itself but a life that can be the reader's if he will have mercy on it by acknowledging it. And this acknowledgment means both an end to cycles and a release for the jokers and arabs who live in them. Standoffish Jeanette, who insists that you never know what arabs are feeling, might consider that their feelings are her own. One of them 'said he loved me, naturally'; he even thought she could get him out of the country.[1]

NOTE

1 Northrop Frye's presence will be evident throughout this essay. Since bothering him in my first week as an undergraduate I have been indebted to him for more help, intellectual and personal, than I could ever reckon. It is a privilege to acknowledge that debt here, though not of course repay it.

**DAVID
STAINES**

# The Holistic Vision of
# Hugh of Saint Victor

Some critics ... stress the deficiencies of 'holism' as a critical theory; but we should distinguish between holism as a critical theory and as a heuristic principle.[1]

The reader of Northrop Frye's criticism will look in vain for any specific reference to Hugh of Saint Victor, yet the treatises of the twelfth-century theologian present an important perspective on Frye's work. As a student for the ministry at Emmanuel College, the United Church of Canada school of theology in the University of Toronto, Frye first encountered the writings of the Victorines, Augustinian canons who followed the community rule and lived at the Abbey of Saint Victor on the left bank of the Seine at Paris. Hugh was in charge of studies in the trivium and quadrivium and later served as master of the school, spending twenty-five years of his life at the Abbey.[2] In Hugh, Frye discovered a congenial mind, a theologian and a teacher who constantly sought underlying patterns of unity. At the beginning of the twelfth century, the great period of systematization, there was, as R.W. Southern asserts, 'one man of high distinction, himself a systematizer on a grand scale, who had the instincts of a historian and had not yet learned that these instincts were incompatible with those of a scholastic theologian. This was Hugh of St Victor, the dimmest of all the great figures of the twelfth century.'[3]

All of Frye's literary criticism, as he notes, 'beginning with a study of Blake published in 1947, and formulated ten years later in *Anatomy of Criticism*, has revolved around the Bible.'[4] As a literary critic, he sees the Bible 'as the major informing influence on literary symbolism.'[5] When he first read the writings of the Victorines, Frye recalls, 'they demonstrated to me the fact that my notions of typology were not based simply on a combination of Bible reading and my own personal reconstruction, but that there was a real tradition. I realized that the Victorine tradition is the landmark in the tradition of typology between Saint Augustine and the Renaissance.'[6]

It is not the purpose of this essay to enumerate parallels between Hugh's theological studies and Frye's literary criticism, for the singular importance of Hugh, as a theological influence on Frye, is the congenial thinker Frye discovered in Hugh's writings. By exploring one hitherto unnoted example of Hugh's patterning and its influence, we can discover an analogue to and a possible source of Frye's critical vision.

The scholastic movement of the twelfth century and Hugh's approach to history in particular had a profound and lasting effect upon the interpretation of the liturgical year or ecclesiastical calendar. In regulating the occasions and the content of the liturgy, the calendar determined the religious festivals and thereby influenced the art and the life of the Middle Ages. Until the twelfth century, commentaries on the liturgy were concerned with individual feasts of the year. During that century, however, commentators, following the contemporary trend of finding underlying patterns, discovered a unity to the annual liturgical celebrations. But before observing Hugh's influence on the understanding of the year, we need to follow its historical development.

The ecclesiastical calendar began with three distinct divisions of time: the daily cycle or divine office of prayers that occurs at fixed times throughout the night and day; the weekly cycle that culminates in the Lord's Day; and the yearly cycle that centres on the Easter commemoration of the Resurrection. All three cycles attempted to consecrate and sanctify time by imprinting on the rhythm of the movements of the sun and the moon the message of man's salvation through Christ's Resurrection.

In the earliest years of the Church, there were two annual liturgical feasts, Easter and Pentecost, destined to become the basis of the yearly cycle.[7] The fourth century's interest in the historicity of Christ's redemptive act led to an exploration of the events of redemption, not as a celebration of a single event, but as an historical drama of salvation; the drama itself, the events in Christ's life, became the focus of the patterns of worship. The Easter liturgy, for example, re-enacted the Resurrection so that worshippers might relive in their observances Christ's words and deeds. The historical orientation, therefore, is the efficient cause of the elaboration of an annual liturgical cycle. When this approach assumed increasing importance, the cycle grew outwards from Easter to encompass related events in Christ's life.

While Easter was the centre of a growing commemorative sequence that included the Passion and Death of Christ as well as His Resurrection and Ascension, Christ's Nativity became the centre of a secondary cycle of feasts related to His Birth. Of later origin and lesser importance than the redemptive cycle that constituted the Easter sequence,[8] the Christmas sequence or incarnational cycle began with the Nativity, included the Epiphany, and ended with the Presentation of Christ in the temple.[9]

By the end of the fourth century there is a defined sequence of six major feasts, the Nativity, Epiphany, Crucifixion, Resurrection, Ascension, and Pentecost, that comprise the basic structure of the liturgical year.[10] The events of Christ's ministry do not enter the original sequence of feasts, and future additions try to rectify this omission. Since the Nativity feasts occur at midwinter, while Easter, the Christian Passover, occurs at the spring equinox, the entire re-enactment of Christ's life is compressed into a period of less than four months. Despite this awkward time scheme, the structure is so fundamental to Christian worship that the compression is never altered. Later ages supplement the six feasts with an abundance of new observances, some only loosely related to Christ's life, yet they never question the propriety and importance of the nucleus of the liturgical cycle from the Nativity in midwinter to Pentecost in the spring.

With Christmas and Easter as the centres of the two constituent cycles that form the liturgical year, expansions develop directly from these feasts. Easter receives the preparatory Lenten season.[11] The Christmas cycle receives three fixed feasts, the Circumcision eight days after the Nativity, the Annunciation nine months before, and the nativity of John the Baptist six months before Christ's Nativity.[12] And Christmas has its own preparatory season of Advent, a kind of mitigated Lent.[13] The final stage in the development of the year as a commemorative cycle of the redemption is further unification of the major feasts by assigning particular masses to intervening Sundays, which become links in the overall cycle. Beginning in Advent and extending into a post-Pentecostal season, the liturgical year includes the most important events in the story of Christ's redemption of mankind.[14]

The earliest commentaries on the liturgy focus on individual feasts. Like the ecclesiastical calendar itself they follow the chronology of Christ's life. By the seventh century Isidore of Seville presents a succinct account of the nucleus of the Christological observances. After noting the daily hours of prayer and the importance of the Lord's Day, he devotes one chapter to the origin and significance of each of the following: the Nativity, Epiphany, Palm Sunday, Maundy Thursday, Good Friday, Holy Saturday, Easter, Ascension Day, and Pentecost; a one-chapter catalogue of martyrs' feasts concludes his survey of yearly rituals.[15] In enumerating the feasts he develops no relationship among them. 'We are accustomed to observe them,' he writes, 'during the circular revolution of one year,' yet he makes no effort to bring them into accord with the seasonal pattern or any other pattern that might presuppose an overarching unity. The feasts are investigated as independent commemorations occurring on specific days of the year.

Two centuries later Isidore's catalogue was still being respected, though studies of the calendar did include some new feasts. When Rabanus Maurus lists the church festivals, he devotes a chapter to Isidore's nine days as well as a chapter on the Lord's Day and one on martyrs' feasts; he adds a new chapter on the Purification and one on Septuagesima, Sexagesima, and Quinquagesima.[16] Like Isidore he follows the chronology of Christ's life, focusing on the significance of individual feasts rather than any overall structure or system. And in *De Ecclesiasticis Officiis* Amalarius of Metz introduces mystical symbolism into his account of the liturgical feasts. Despite the innovative importance of his allegorical explanations of many feasts, he follows earlier liturgists in accepting each feast as a separate area of investigation.[17]

The general literary decline that followed the Carolingian period parallels the diminished interest in liturgiology. Not until the second half of the eleventh century are there further studies of the church year. Here again, however, the focus falls on the individual feasts and their appropriate readings and ceremonies. Concerned only with the proper celebration of each day, the studies never notice any pattern uniting individual observances.[18]

The early twelfth century finds some commentators searching for possible patterns that unify the liturgical calendar. Rupert of Deutz' twelve-book *De Officiis Per Anni Circulum*, the most comprehensive analysis to date of the church year, follows the natural divisions of the church calendar, the Christmas cycle, the Lenten period, the Passion sequence, and the post-Easter period culminating in Pentecost and adding all the Sundays after Pentecost. The chronology of Christ's life that informs the sequence of feasts seemed sufficient for Rupert's detailed account of the ecclesiastical calendar. In *Gemma Animae de Divinis Officiis* Honorius adds symbolic meanings to the various periods of the calendar. The seventy days before Easter, for example, recall the deliverance out of Egypt, and they also symbolize man's enslavement to the devil before the coming of Christ. Easter is the deliverance both of the Jews from Egypt and mankind from Satan through Christ's redemption.[19] Such interpretations of sections of the year only develop the symbolic treatment introduced by Amalarius two centuries earlier. While adhering to the standard chronological sequence of Advent to Pentecost, Honorius pauses frequently to impose allegorical interpretations on sequences within the year without suggesting any comprehensive pattern that encompasses the entire year. *Gemma Animae de Divinis Officiis* is the last in a long series of liturgical treatises that survey the components of the calendar without positing any overarching structure to the year.

It was Hugh of Saint Victor who presented the pattern adopted by later liturgists in their discussions of the ecclesiastical calendar. Though Hugh himself never analysed the sequence of church feasts, his approach to theology through the use of history affected the understanding of the liturgical cycle. 'Almost alone among medieval theologians in the importance he attached to historical situations,'[20] Hugh did not write historical investigations, yet he brought an historical consciousness to his biblical and theological studies. And it was his sense of a unified whole to both theology and history that led to subsequent accounts of the church year as a unity of interdependent feasts.

For Hugh history has two fundamental meanings. It is, first of all, the literal content of the story as opposed to the allegorical and moral levels of interpretation. Every theologian must know first the fundamental story before constructing theological schemes and patterns.[21] Secondly, it is the method adopted to study the facts of a story.[22] History is, therefore, not only 'the recounting of actual deeds but also the first meaning of any narrative which uses words according to their proper nature.'[23]

When Hugh approached the articles of faith, he regarded Christianity as the history of salvation, an account of man's redemption by Christ, a series of events from creation to the Last Judgment. Sacred Scripture is the history of the redemptive process, written to illuminate one pre-eminent pattern, 'The Word was made flesh, God was made humble, man was made sublime.'[24] The study of Scripture necessitates an understanding of religion's centre, Christ, which permits the proper appreciation of surrounding events: 'Unless you know beforehand the nativity of Christ, his teaching, his suffering, his resurrection and ascension, and all the other things which he did in the flesh and through the flesh, you will not be able to penetrate the mysteries of the old figures.'[25] Only with the complete knowledge of Christ and His mission to the world can the student of Scripture comprehend the shape of church history, 'which began when the world began, and will last till the end of the age.'[26] Vehemently opposed to the Greek concept of cyclical time, Hugh regarded time as a linear progression from a beginning to an end. Any historical study, therefore, must begin at a beginning and follow a chronological sequence.

Study of the Bible persuaded Hugh to divide events into a series of epochs, and the pattern he observed in the sequence provided liturgists with a scheme to unify the feasts of the church year. Several possible divisions of history confronted him. The most common pattern, which the Middle Ages inherited primarily from Augustine, relates the six days of creation to the six ages of history, with the seventh day, when God took rest, corresponding to the realm of eternity beyond human history. Complementing this pattern is the superimposition of the seven ages of man. Like the life of an individual, mankind's history is linear and progressive: 'The true education of the human race, represented by the people of God as well as that of an individual, has advanced through certain stages of time or, as it were, ages that it might rise from temporalities to eternity and from things visible to the invisible.'[27]

Another division of history, much less common than the Augustinian pattern of the seven ages, originated with Saint Paul and made a tripartite division of human history according to man's progress towards spiritual salvation. Stretching from Adam to Moses, the first division, *ante legem*, is the time of the natural law before the written law was handed down to Moses. From Moses to Christ is the second period, *sub lege*, when the written law presented man with a set of commandments for human conduct. Explaining what is sinful, the written law did not, however, release man from sin. The third period, *sub gratia*, commencing with Christ and concluding at the end of the world, is the time of man's redemption from sin through God's grace. Augustine himself did reiterate this Pauline pattern and added a fourth division, *in pace plena atque perfecta*, the eternity beyond this life when men will know perfect fulfilment, 'first in the repose of the spirit, and afterwards also in the resurrection of the flesh.'[28] Yet the pattern of the seven ages permeated his writings, and the few references to the Pauline divisions had no effect upon subsequent historians and liturgists until the twelfth century.

In Hugh's writings the Pauline is more important than the Augustinian scheme.[29] Though Hugh did refer to the seven ages, he usually followed such references with an account of the Pauline triad. And when he came to write his major theological treatise *De Sacramentis*, he structured it according to Paul's divisions and made the history of the sacraments the chronological history of salvation:

There are three periods of time through which the space of the present world runs. The first is the period of the natural law, the second the period of the written law, the third the period of grace. The first is from Adam to Moses, the second from Moses to Christ, the third from Christ until the end of the world.

Similarly, there are three kinds of men, that is, men of the natural law, men of the written law, men of grace. Those can be called men of the natural law who lead their lives according to natural reasons alone, or rather those men are called men of the natural law who walk according to the desires in which they were born. Men of the written law are those instructed in living properly by external laws. Men of grace are those who, breathed upon by the inspiration of the Holy Spirit, are illumined to recognize the good that must be done and are inflamed as they love and strengthened to accomplish the good. And that we may designate these with a clearer distinction, men of the natural law are openly evil, men of the written law feignedly good, men of grace truly good.[30]

Divided into two books, the first ending with an analysis of the natural and the written laws, the second beginning with the Incarnation and God's grace, *De Sacramentis* chronicles mankind's continuous progression from the fall towards final union with God. The sacraments of the natural law, 'whether tithes or sacrifices or oblations, were so imposed on man from necessity that he who failed to do them incurred the guilt of transgression, just as he who faithfully cherished them found the reward of his devotion.'[31] In the second age God intervened more directly with a written law that focused more clearly on individual conduct. Yet the sacraments of both ages were only 'signs, as it were, and figures of those sacraments which now have been set forth under grace.'[32] The final age, the subject of the second book, examines the sacraments, rituals, and laws of the Church in order to show men of the age of grace the path to eternal salvation.

The theological content of Hugh's treatise parallels the historical content, for the sacramental trend of his thought is 'closely linked to the historical. Man's history is a history of the sacraments. God has ordered the "work of Restoration" through a series of sacraments, the natural, the

Mosaic, the Christian.'[33] Although *De Sacramentis* is a systematic treatise that accepted ideas and established texts, there is originality in the imposition of the Pauline scheme which offers a dynamic movement to human history. Giving an historical setting to the texts, Hugh arranges his most important work on an historical plan to show that every mystery holds a unique position in the grand scheme of salvation history.

Primarily a theologian, not an historian, Hugh emphasized the value of theological investigations existing within an historical framework. As long as the framework does not violate the materials but arises directly from them, it clarifies the subject by revealing the unity underlying seemingly disparate elements. In the twelfth century Hugh was the master of the traditional and ineradicable view of Christianity as 'an itinerary of man's journey toward the divine, a view which could not be reduced to a cyclical conception of the cosmos with neither commencement nor consummation.'[34] And it is this point of view, expressed in his constant reiteration of the Pauline scheme of salvation history, that gave him the pattern and context for his major treatise on the sacraments.

Since Hugh did not write explicitly about the liturgical calendar, it remained for his students to apply the Pauline movement to the annual feasts and thereby impose, for the first time, a pattern that seemed to reveal the unity of the church year.[35] The application of the scheme first appears in the Victorine treatise, *Speculum de Mysteriis Ecclesiae*, originally ascribed to Hugh himself, where the tripartite division, now expanded to four as Augustine had done, corresponds, though not chronologically, to the liturgical calendar:

From Septuagesima until Easter represents the time from Adam to Moses when death ruled. And therefore because the fall commemorated is contrary to justice, *Gloria in excelsis Deo* is silent. As an expression of peace there is heard, 'Fidelity springs up from earth and justice looks down from heaven' (Psalm 84). Because the punishment into which man fell through his fault is recalled by the scriptural readings, the *Alleluia*, the song of joy, is not heard. From Advent to Christmas is the time from Moses to Christ, when sin ruled, not because of ignorance as in the case of the first death, but because of the body's infirmity. Then *Alleluia* is sung, since the fathers were under the law, but *Gloria in excelsis Deo* is silent, since it is a sign of peace and justice, which the law could not bestow. The time from the first coming until the second coming is between Pentecost and the Advent of the Lord when the Church sings *Alleluia* in the hope of the resurrection and *Gloria in excelsis Deo* on behalf of the justice rendered ... The fourth time is between Easter and Pentecost and represents eternal happiness when *Gloria in excelsis Deo* and a double *Alleluia* are sung.[36]

Although the four divisions of the church calendar, Advent to Christmas, the seventy days before Easter, the fifty days afterwards, and the amorphous period between Pentecost and Advent, are awkwardly arranged to fit the Pauline pattern and the period from Christmas to Septuagesima is completely ignored, the Victorine author does attempt to adapt the church year to the same scheme Hugh found informing the history and the significance of the sacraments. Like Hugh he sees the history of salvation reflected directly in his subject: 'Therefore the state of the Church varies through the four seasons. The first introduced guilt, the second unmasks it, the third destroys it through justice but maintains the penalty, the fourth perfects justice and will absorb the penalty. The first was a state of guilt and punishment, the second one of punishment and prophecy, the third punishment and grace, the fourth grace and glory.'[37] Subsequent analyses of the liturgical calendar clarify and expand the correspondence first noted here between the feasts of the year and the Pauline pattern.

The most detailed description of the state of the liturgy in the twelfth century is found in the late twelfth-century study *Rationale Divinorum Officiorum* of Jean Beleth. A Professor of Theology and Rector of the University of Paris, Beleth embellished the Pauline parallel with the introduction of the four seasons as a further reflection of the Church's efforts to align her festal occasions and quadripartite divisions with the patterns of the solar year: 'Just as our solar year moves through the succession of the four seasons, that is, winter when seeds are sown in the earth, spring when the seeds come forth, summer when they are whitened in the harvest and fall to the sickle, and autumn when the grain separated by the wind is stored in the barn while the chaff is burned, so also the great year of the present life, which lasts from the beginning right to the end of the world, is measured by the variety of the four seasons.'[38]

With the exception of the Victorine author of the *Speculum de Mysteriis Ecclesiae*, no liturgist prior to Beleth studied the calendar in its entirety; only the individual sections and feasts were the object of scrutiny. Beleth's perspective is characteristic of the late twelfth century and analogous to Hugh's historical overview: 'Thus far we have spoken in general terms about the ecclesiastical offices. What remains is only to undertake more extensively an explanation of them in their complete yearly period.'[39] Without altering the Pauline pattern, he expands the significance of the complete structure and its progression:

There was a certain time of falling away among mankind, from Adam to Moses, when men turned aside from the worship of God to idolatry ... a time of blindness and ignorance. So too another was the time of recalling, from Moses to the Nativity of Christ, when men were instructed by the laws and prophecies about the coming of Christ, the avoidance of sin, and the love of one God ... The third was a time of return or reconciliation or justification which was from the Nativity of Christ to His Ascension, through which grace and the preaching of the gospel were given to men. Finally, the fourth was the time of pilgrimage, which was from the Ascension of the Lord and will last until the conclusion of the judgment at the end of the world.[40]

The time of falling away (winter) lasts from Septuagesima to Easter, recalling (spring) encompasses Advent, reconciliation (summer) extends from Easter to Pentecost, and pilgrimage (autumn) is the post-Pentecostal period until Advent.[41] The fact that the progressive movement of salvation history does not parallel the natural progression of the solar year is, for Beleth, a further indication of the Church's wisdom, for the Church 'makes a fine beginning of her soldierhood from the time of recalling, not from the time of falling away, lest she seem to begin from error. She observes that well, but she does not follow the order the evangelists often made. For if she seeks good health and wants to be cared for in the best way possible, it was necessary for her to begin with the physicians.'[42] Furthermore, the absence of the period from Christmas to Septuagesima in the calculations is now rectified. 'Someone may ask under which of the times the period from Christmas to Septuagesima is contained?' Beleth concludes. His response is the final example of the ingenious effort to fit the entire calendar into the Pauline pattern. Since the period from Christmas to the octave of the Epiphany is a time of joy, it belongs under the time of reconciliation; the octave of the Epiphany to Septuagesima, a time of pilgrimage, shares the features of the post-Pentecostal season.[43]

The ecclesiastical year as the embodiment of the Pauline scheme of salvation history became the accepted reading of the church calendar. Sicard of Cremona, who studied in Paris from about 1170 until 1180, reproduced much of Beleth's analysis of the four divisions.[44] By the thirteenth century the liturgical year was studied not only as a re-enactment of the major events of Christ's life but also as a representation of the entire history of the world based on Saint Paul's account of salvation history.[45]

The liturgical year is not the product of the late Middle Ages; it is the cumulative achievement of many centuries, and its structure is centralized in the event of the Resurrection, which gives form and meaning to the cycle as well as to the Christian faith. The liturgical year is the product of many centuries; its elaborate interpretation and underlying pattern are the products of the twelfth century and reflections of the importance and influence of Hugh of Saint Victor.

NOTES

1 Northrop Frye, 'The Road to Excess,' *The Stubborn Structure* (Ithaca, 1970), 165.

2 Few details are known about Hugh's life, though it is generally accepted that he died in 1140 or 1141. For a general introduction to Hugh and the Victorines, see Beryl Smalley, *The Study of the Bible in the Middle Ages* (Oxford, 1941), 58-155; Jerome Taylor, *The Origin and Early Life of Hugh of St. Victor: An Evaluation of the Tradition* (Notre Dame, 1957); Roger Baron, *Etudes sur Hugues de Saint-Victor* (Bruges, 1963). I am indebted to Jerome Taylor for reading an early version of this paper and offering helpful comments and suggestions.

3 R.W. Southern, 'Aspects of the European Tradition of Historical Writing: 2. Hugh of St. Victor and the Idea of Historical Development,' *Transactions of the Royal Historical Society*, ser. 5, 21 (1971), 163.

4 Northrop Frye, *The Great Code: The Bible and Literature* (Toronto, 1982), xiv.

5 Northrop Frye, *Anatomy of Criticism* (Princeton, 1957), 315-16.

6 Conversation with David Staines, 28 February 1982.

7 In the early third century Tertullian, the first ecclesiastical writer to enumerate the feasts of the Church, referred to the existence of only two annual observances, Passover, 'the day of great solemnity for baptism,' and Pentecost, 'which is, in a special sense, a festal day' (*De Baptismo*, 19, in *Patrologiae Cursus Completus, Series Latina* [hereafter *PL*], 1:1331). Unless otherwise stated, all translations from Latin texts are my own.

8 The earliest record of a Christmas feast appears in 354 in the *Depositio Martyrum*, though eastern churches were celebrating the birth on 6 January as early as the third century. Christmas has remained secondary in importance to Easter. In his fifty-fifth epistle Augustine regards the fixity of the date of Christmas as an indication of its lesser importance in

contrast to the mobility of the Easter feast (*PL*, 33:205). Leo the Great sees Christmas as a prelude to the mystery of the Resurrection (*Sermo* xlvii [*PL*, 54:294-5]).

9 Jewish law stipulated that the period of a mother's uncleanness lasted forty days after the birth of a male child. Consequently, the Presentation was celebrated forty days after the Nativity.

10 A list of annual feasts appeared for the first time in the third-century *Constutiones Apostolorum*, v, 13, ed. F.X. Funk (Paderbornae, 1905), I, 269-71, where the Nativity, Epiphany, Lent, Holy Week, Passover, the Appearance of Thomas, Ascension Day, and Pentecost constitute festal observances.

11 By the end of the second century pre-Easter fasting lasted in some places for one day, in others for two days or more. The earliest reference to the Quadragesima or Lenten fast of forty days occurs in the fifth canon of the Council of Nicea (325 AD). The fourth century favoured a fast of forty days as a parallel to Christ's fasting in the desert. The calculation of the forty days did not prove easy since Good Friday, Holy Saturday, and Easter Sunday were not originally part of the fast but rather part of the Easter festival and also since fasting was not required on Sundays. In the seventh century four days were added to Lent beginning with Ash Wednesday. About the same time a preparation for Lent was established in the three weeks preceding Ash Wednesday, the first of the forty days, and this addition consisted of Septuagesima, Sexagesima, and Quinquagesima, the seventieth, sixtieth, and fiftieth days before Easter. Extending nine weeks before the commemoration of the Resurrection, Lent and its preparatory season contrast with the joy and thanksgiving that characterize the fifty days after Easter.

12 According to Luke 1:36, the birth of John the Baptist took place six months before Christ's birth. The earliest reference to the feast occurs in Augustine, *Sermo* cxcvi (*PL*, 38:1021). The observance of the Annunciation dates back to the fifth century (Heinrich Kellner, *Heortology*, translated by a priest of the Diocese of Westminster [London, 1908], 231-4). The earliest reference to the feast of the Circumcision occurs in a lectionary from Capua for 546 (*Anecdota Maredsolana*, ed. Germain Morin [Maredsoli, 1893], I, 436-8).

13 Advent dates back to the fifth century. For its history in the liturgical year, see Benedict Steuart, *The Development of Christian Worship* (London, 1953), 242-5.

14 Developing alongside and gradually infringing upon the Advent-to-Pentecost sequence is the so-called sanctoral cycle, a collection of saints' feasts

that form an appendage to the major feasts of the liturgical year and usually fall in the post-Pentecostal period. Complementing the major feasts too is a series of Mariological feasts.

15 *De Ecclesiasticis Officiis*, I, 19-35 (*PL*, 83:757-71).

16 *De Clericorum Institutione*, II, 31-43 (*PL*, 107:343-57).

17 *De Ecclesiasticis Officiis* (*PL*, 105:985-1242). The opening book introduces the symbolism into an account of the Septuagesima-to-Pentecost observances; the third and fourth books investigate other feasts, especially those in the Advent-to-Pentecost sequence.

18 For example, Berno of Reichenau, *Dialogus de Jejuniis Quatuor Temporum*, 5 (*PL*, 142:1093), and *De Quibusdam Rebus ad Missae Officium Pertinentibus*, 3-4 (*PL*, 142:1061-6), and Jean d'Avranches, *De Officiis Ecclesiasticis* (*PL*, 147:27-62).

19 *Gemma Animae de Divinis Officiis*, IV, 42 (*PL*, 172:703-4).

20 'Aspects of the European Tradition,' 165.

21 'You have in history the means through which to admire God's deeds, in allegory the means through which to believe his mysteries, in morality the means through which to imitate his perfection' (*Didascalicon*, VI, 3, ed. Charles Henry Buttimer [Washington, 1939], 116). The translations from this work have been taken from the *Didascalicon of Hugh of St. Victor*, trans. from the Latin with an introduction and notes by Jerome Taylor (New York, 1961).

22 'First you learn history and diligently commit to memory the truth of the deeds that have been performed, reviewing from beginning to end what has been done, and by whom it has been done. For these are the four things which are especially to be sought for in history – the person, the business done, the time, and the place' (*Didascalicon*, VI, 3, ed. Buttimer, 113-14).

23 Ibid., 115-16.

24 *De Arca Noe Morali*, I, 2 (*PL*, 176:622). The translations from this work have been taken from *Hugh of Saint-Victor: Selected Spiritual Writings*, trans. by a Religious of CSMV, introd. Aelred Squire (London, 1962).

25 *Didascalicon*, VI, 6, ed. Buttimer, 125.

26 *De Arca Noe Morali*, I, 2 (*PL*, 176:625).

27 *De Civitate Dei*, X, 14 (*PL*, 41:292). For an account of the Jewish background to the pattern of the seven ages and versions preceding Augustine's formulation, see William M. Green, 'Augustine on the Teaching of History,' *University of California Publications in Classical Philology*, 12 (1944), 315-32.

28 *Enchiridion*, 118 (*PL*, 40:287). For Paul's own formulation of the scheme, see Epistle to the Romans 5-7.

29 In addition to the Pauline and Augustinian schemes, two other categor-
   izations were known in the twelfth century, though never employed by
   Hugh. There was the fourfold division of the ancient world according to
   the prophecies of Daniel. There was also the tripartite scheme based on the
   Trinity, where the age of the Father corresponds to the Old Testament,
   the age of the Son to the life and work of Christ, the age of the Spirit to the
   working out of Christ's promise. For a survey of the patterns, see M.-D.
   Chenu, 'Theology and the New Awareness of History,' in *Nature, Man, and
   Society in the Twelfth Century*, trans. Jerome Taylor and Lester K. Little
   (Chicago, 1968), 162-201.

30 *De Sacramentis*, 1.8.11 (*PL*, 176:312-13). In this treatise Hugh used the
   word *sacramentum* in an inclusive sense, meaning natural and supernatural mysteries as well as sacraments and sacramentals.

31 Ibid., 1.11.3 (*PL*, 176:344).

32 Ibid., 1.11.1 (*PL*, 176:343).

33 *The Study of the Bible in the Middle Ages*, 65.

34 'Theology and the New Awareness of History,' 199.

35 The influence of Hugh and his adoption of the Pauline scheme accounts, I
   believe, for the imposition of the scheme upon the church year. The
   Augustinian pattern, which might have been employed, was too cumber-
   some, since its six or seven divisions did not lend themselves easily to the
   natural divisions inherent in the established liturgical calendar. In addition, the Augustinian pattern had been employed in reference to specific
   sections of the year; for example, Amalarius introduced the idea of Advent
   as a representation of the first five ages, an idea adopted by all liturgists
   who used Amalarius as a source (*De Ecclesiasticis Officiis*, IV, 30 [*PL*,
   105:1218-21]).

36 *Speculum de Mysteriis Ecclesiae*, 4 (*PL*, 177:348-9). Its authorship remains
   uncertain. Originally ascribed to Hugh in many manuscripts, it is now
   regarded as a Victorine composition deeply indebted to Hugh's teaching.
   In the most comprehensive analysis of the text, 'Zur Einflussphäre der "Vor-
   lesungen" Hugos von St. Viktor,' *Mélanges Joseph de Ghellinck* (Gem-
   bloux, 1951), Heinrich Weisweiler concludes: 'Much in the *Speculum*
   remains as Hugh's own original property ... We have been able to show how
   Anonymous [the Victorine author of the treatise] in spite of all abbrevia-
   tion has yet taken over Hugh's fundamental thoughts into his own work
   and entered into the spirit of Hugh's range of ideas, particularly in the
   case of the fundamental expositions' (II, 569). The translation from the
   German is my own.

37 *Speculum de Mysteriis Ecclesiae*, 4 (*PL*, 177:349).

38 *Rationale Divinorum Officiorum*, 55 (*PL*, 202:60).

39 Ibid.

40 Ibid.

41 In connecting the four seasons to the church calendar, Beleth does not suggest they parallel the chronology of the calendar, but rather that their characteristics have significant parallels to the features of the church seasons.

42 *Rationale Divinorum Officiorum*, 55 (*PL*, 202:62).

43 Ibid., 56 (*PL*, 202:63).

44 *Mitrale, seu De Officiis Ecclesiasticis Summa*, 5, Prol. (*PL*, 213:191).

45 In the thirteenth century Durandus of Mende, the French canonist and liturgist, for example, did not omit any detail from Beleth in his exhaustive account of the church calendar and other quadripartite structures (*Pationale Divinorum Officiorum*, 6.1.1–12, ed. V. d'Avino [Naples, 1859], 381–4).

**JULIAN
PATRICK**

# 'The Tempest' as Supplement

The conspicuous dominance of middle states in narrative and dramatic romance (always after the before and usually before the after) tends to suppress what in other genres we recognize as the specific nature of beginnings and the finality of endings. Beginnings in romance are often resumptions, and endings are sometimes ironic or abrupt when they are not endless. Thus the true centre of romance cannot be in plot or character, as it must be in tragedy and realistic fiction, where the moment of the beginning is greatly emphasized, but rather in the retrospective and prospective movement of implication in the action. In romance, past and future are continually being woven together in the present space of narrative, or of dramatic re-presentation. In the *Odyssey*, for instance, the island of Scheria, land of the Phaiakians, is middled, as it were, by its complicated set of dual relations: between past and future, between the gods on serene Olympus and the suffering of shipwrecked Odysseus, between Poseidon's ship of stone and the craftsmanship of Athene. Scheria is also the place where Odysseus tells the story of his wanderings and where (through the meeting with Nausicaa, the repudiation of the haughty Phaiakian prince, and the show of strength with the massive discus) he prepares for the return to Penelope, his battle with the suitors, and the test of strength with the great bow. If we allow Calypso's isle to stand for all the islands that precede it in the chronology of the story (the island near the Cyclops' home, the island of Aeolus, Circe's island, the island of Thrinacia, etc.), then the *Odyssey* is a romance of islands, the middle space of wandering, being succeeded by the middle space of tale-telling, which gives way to the middle space of return. The ending is itself a middle, for Tiresias' prophecy to Odysseus of another journey inland to a place where the sea is unknown carries the imagination forward and beyond the abrupt ending that Athena's recalling of Odysseus to the seat of justice and political responsibility gives to the story.

Because the middle states of romances are both unstable and actively generative, works like the *Odyssey* and *The Tempest* have naturally attracted to themselves two different but related kinds of elaboration. As is well known, the reception of the *Odyssey* in classical times took the form either of relentless allegorizing of its many suggestive episodes, or of the continuation of its action by later romancers – as if the plot must mean more than it says, or, in order to mean at all, it must be made to say more. It is interesting that the same two procedures also characterize the reception of *The Tempest*: a brief examination of their characteristic strategies will help to define the subtle and complex relation between forms of supplementary elaboration and the structure of *The Tempest*.[1]

We can see what this structure is, and why it needs supplementary elaboration, at the moment when the structure begins to come apart in Prospero's conspicuous feeling of release, at the beginning of the fifth act, from the demands of dramatic production:

> Now does my project gather to a head
> My charms crack not; my spirits obey; and Time
> Goes upright with his carriage.       (v.i.1-3)[2]

Like the theatre-audience at the end of the play, Time can now begin to stand up straight because he has very little left to carry (to do). Unlike *The Winter's Tale*, which brought Time on stage to explain what the dramatic action has to leave out, *The Tempest* thinks of Time as supporting the entire action. And, of course, it does, in the literal sense that the theatre-audience has been in the theatre for the length of time that the court party has been on the island. But the personification also implies, less literally, that what time has supported has been a metaphor *for* time, that time in the play is to be understood *as* the various actions that the characters have undergone. Thus, it is at this moment, in the several meetings of the court party with Miranda and Ferdinand and with Caliban and his friends, that the various 'times' of the many subplot actions become the one, continuous and human time of Prospero's re-formed society. The final recognition, or meeting, takes place between Prospero and the theatre-audience, when Prospero implies that, in order to be released from his dramatic role, he needs the audience to understand the action he had built up for them. As Prospero has forgiven the court party, as Ferdinand and his father have mutually exchanged forgiveness, as Caliban has sought the same quality, so the audience, once they understand what they have seen (for the other acts of forgiveness were based on understanding, that is, on recognition) will also forgive, as Prospero has done, by responding. Understanding and mutual acknowledgment, then, gradually supplement and substitute for the bleaker knowledge of human nature embodied in Ariel's speech to the 'three men of sin' and in Prospero's disgusted repudiation of Caliban after the masque of Ceres. It is for this reason – to allow the time of human understanding to supplement the objectified and articulated structure of time that the audience has just witnessed in the main action of the play – that the shape of the fifth act is dominated by its incomplete, fragile, and perilous mergings and its delicate suspensions. The action cannot close definitively because its real closure lies in the imaginative capacity and commitment of the theatre-audience.

Yet it is very easy to imagine an audience who would lack such an understanding. For it, the action of The Tempest would close perilously only to open again as the romance imagination continued to wonder about the journey home to Milan and to the problems awaiting Prospero in his human, all-too-human, form. Thus, for F.G. Waldron in The Virgin Queen ... a Sequel to Shakespeare's 'Tempest' (1797), Shakespeare's ending is clearly a mistake.[3] On the voyage home, the spirit of Sycorax, inflamed by love for her darling Caliban, rises again and is only prevented from destroying Prospero's homecoming by the sudden arrival, in the very nick of time, of Ariel, who is carrying Prospero's once drowned book and his now carefully mended staff. The lessons Prospero learns this second time are those he should have learned the first: leave the bad characters behind on the island and keep your supernatural guns beside you.

Prospero's staff is also important to another form in which The Tempest begins to be rewritten by nineteenth-century men of letters. This is the interpretation of The Tempest as an autobiographical allegory, as an announcement to London theatre-goers that its author is abandoning the stage and returning to Stratford whence he came some twenty-four years before: 'Here Shakespeare himself is Prospero, or rather the superior genius who commands both Prospero and Ariel. But the time was approaching when the potent sorcerer was to break his staff, and to bury it fathoms in the ocean ... That staff has never been, and never will be, recovered.'[4] The implied contrast between the romancers and the allegorists is very interesting. Waldron's romantic impulse to rewrite the plot by continuing it past its point of closure is connected to a desire to free the action from the pressure of its informing ideas, recognition of which alone can make the ending satisfactory. The allegorists, in contrast, by fixing the significance of the action through its supposed autobiographical reference, ignore the play's constantly changing focus and turn its plot into pure repetition. Yet the play is as insistently allegorizable as its action is romantic. In what follows, the various manifest patterns of its structure, especially those which connect the dramatization of time with the play's many audiences, will be used to clarify the relation of the action of *The Tempest* to its systematic play of ideas.

I

Shakespeare begins both the narrated story of *The Tempest* and the dramatic action with an image of time. Antonio has usurped his brother Prospero's throne because he thought Prospero incapable of 'temporal royalties' (I.ii.110); and, in the opening shipwreck of the dramatic action, the terrible tempest is connected with the recovery of, among other things, temporal power, *tempestas* meaning both time and storm in Latin.[5] Usurpation and its consequences – the division of spiritual from temporal royalties – and the awareness of time itself are closely connected in Shakespeare's earlier dramatic practice. In many of his usurpation or substitution plays, time itself arises as a concept reflecting an interruption to the normal order of things. It is as if time would not exist were the rhythm of ordinary measurement not altered. The periodic and ceaseless rhythms of alternating phenomena, the sun setting and rising, the lunar cycle, the change of the seasons, the round of the year, and especially the systolic and diastolic motion of the heart felt in the pulse and the intake and expulsion of air in breathing, all these phenomena 'measure' time in its ordinary and 'timeless' appearances. Once these rhythms are interrupted, as in the eclipse of the sun-king by the storms of usurpation in *Richard II*, or, more subtly, by what Miranda calls the 'beating in [her] mind' of the pulse, which we associate with an extreme emotional identification, then the observer can become aware of time itself, as an idea that somehow reflects the interruption. In many of Shakespeare's substitution plays, usurpation and time are also connected with self-consciousness and theatrical representation. Thus, when Prospero's brother Antonio is described as a trusted substitute or supplement for Prospero (I.ii.103), when this metaphor is added to one drawn from music ('having both the key / Of officer and office, set all hearts i'th'state / To what tune pleased his ear, that now he was / The ivy which had hid my princely trunk' [I.ii.83-6]) and when, finally, Antonio's usurpation is described in a metaphor drawn from acting ('Hence his ambition growing – / ... / To have no screen between this part he played / And him he played it for' [I.ii.105-8]), it is clear that the play's concern with usurpation, time, representation, and self-consciousness links it with earlier plays and leads us to expect that Prospero's action will take a dramatic shape, by appealing to the imagination through the forms of time itself.

What the forms of time precisely are might seem hopelessly abstract or vague were it not for the almost unfathomable suggestiveness of *The Tempest* with regard to time. That *The Tempest*'s action is largely about time is suggested by the usually disregarded importance to the narrative frame of Claribel, the daughter of Alonzo, King of Naples. Antonio's power in Milan has been secured by taking momentary advantage of Prospero's secret studies. Milan is now a vassal state of Naples and must take its political direction, not from Prospero's knowledge of the liberal arts, but by following the purposeless lead of Alonzo. That Alonzo's leadership is without direction, even defeatist, is demonstrated by the fact that there is no good reason for the court party to be on the high seas at the moment the play opens. They are returning from the wedding of Alonzo's daughter, Claribel, to the king of Tunis; but this is a marriage no one has wanted, least of all Claribel, who has protested it bitterly. The marriage means that Claribel is as good as dead, being outside time as it is normally measured, and with the supposed death of Ferdinand in the shipwreck, the disinheriting of Naples appears to be complete: 'Claribel,' says Antonio when he tempts Sebastian to help with the murder of Alonzo,

> is Queen of Tunis; she that dwells
> Ten leagues beyond man's life; she that from Naples
> Can have no note, unless the sun were post –
> The Man i'th'Moon's too slow – till new born chins
> Be rough and razorable; she that from whom
> We all were sea-swallow'd, though some cast again
> (And by that destiny) to perform an act
> Whereof what's past is prologue, what to come
> In yours and my discharge. (II.i.246-54)

This deeply ironic description connects the machiavel-actor's dependency on momentary opportunities – the temporal illusion that now is the right moment, that the door is opening – with a consequent imprisonment within fate or destiny itself.[6] The passage makes us see the connection between political power *in* time, mere 'temporal royalties,' and the ideal possibilities *of* time, which it will be the task of Prospero's art to represent. When Gonzalo discovers that Ferdinand and Miranda are betrothed to be married, he expresses for the audience our sense that the action, in joining Ferdinand to Miranda, has reconnected temporal royalties with the larger royalties of art and thus has made sense, finally, of Claribel's marriage: 'In one voyage / Did Claribel her husband find at Tunis, / And Ferdinand, her brother, found a wife / Where he himself was lost; Prospero, his dukedom / In a poor isle; and all of us, ourselves, / When no man was his own.' (v.i.208-13)

This 'bountiful' conjunction of fortunes on the island suggests why the play's third scene, in which the court party talks desultorily about their luck in escaping from the shipwreck, takes the shape it does. The scene expounds symbolically the attitudes of mind that have underlain past events and, in this sense, it parallels Prospero's exposition of his own past to Miranda in the scene before. In precisely opposed attitudes to political time, Gonzalo dreams of establishing on the island a government 't'excell the Golden Age' while Antonio dreams of assassination. The attempt to escape from time in a fantasy of perfection is as useless as Antonio's ignoring of all but the most brutal of time's uses is self-regarding. The scene as a whole, with its desultory meandering dialogue, its mention of Widow Dido and Aeneas and Tunis and Carthage, is meant to be understood by us as a kind of temporizing, or playing for time, and to suggest that court life, without Prospero's knowledge of the liberal arts, could be only fantasy or plotting.

The opposite of this temporizing is Prospero's concentrated and at times agonized attention on every aspect of the island-stage, from getting the timing right for Ferdinand and Miranda's first meeting, to the slow-time of Alonzo's search for Ferdinand through the labyrinth of loss and guilt. Prospero's control over the rising action of the play can be understood as a combination of three analogies of ordinary temporal experience: events that follow one another in time, or succession; events that occur at the same time, or simultaneity; and events that recur, or permanence.[7] Succession is conveyed by the fact that each of the three dramatic subplots has its own sequence of events, each with its own temporal pace – very slow, for the court party; neither slow nor fast, for the comic subplot of Caliban (for whom the illusion is created that he is proceeding at his own sweet pace); and faster than the blink of an eye for the lovers. Each sequence leads to a climactic vision[8] and each of these visions disappears, to be replaced by a form of punishment, or, in the case of the lovers, by Prospero's 'revels' speech, which hastens to explain what could be regarded as a punishment, the loss of paradise.

If the experience of time as succession appears to divide the three groups from one another in the mind of the audience, the experience of time as simultaneity brings each group into significant association with the others. For the court party, Ferdinand is a lost heir, forever sunk beneath the seas. For Miranda, by contrast, he has been born from the seas and has found in Prospero a second father. Alonzo seeks Ferdinand in the muddy depths of the ocean; Ferdinand seeks to remain in paradise forever. Antonio's 'strong imagination' sees a crown dropping upon Sebastian's head, while Caliban tries to make Stephano king of the island. The final crown, as Gonzalo notes, belongs to the young lovers:

> Look down, you gods,
> And on this couple drop a blessed crown!
> For it is you that have chalk'd forth the way
> Which brought us hither. (v.ii.201-4)

These overlapping simultaneities reach their climax in the recognition scene, when the experience of the whole cast is defined in terms of degrees of conscious awareness, extending from the ship's crew, who have slept through the action, to Antonio and Sebastian, whose constant wakefulness is an index both of their scheming and of their blindness to imaginative experience. In between are the great dreamers of the action, Caliban, Gonzalo, the young lovers, and Prospero himself, whose own vision of paradise makes him forget the persistence of Caliban's foolish plot. Perhaps the most telling of simultaneities concerns the concept of plot. The plotting of Antonio, like that of Caliban, is defeated, but so is the 'plot' (iv.i.88) of Venus and Cupid against the chastity of the young lovers. In its place we find the 'grass-plot,' the 'very place' to which Ceres is invited 'to come and sport' (iv.i.73-4). Here the original meaning of 'plot' as a piece of land replaces its derived meaning, as a scheming in time, as a vision of paradise replaces an action in time, as a masque momentarily is substituted for a dramatic plot.

The experience of time as permanence is expressed in the masque of Ceres with its symbolic presentation of the *ver perpetuum* as a promise of fertility. The permanence of certain aspects of experience, in this case of earliest memories, is also suggested in the masque by a beautifully inobvious repetition. To her father's great surprise, Miranda is able to remember the four or five gentlewomen who tended her before in Milan (1.ii.44-7); this shadowy memory is given a permanent form in art by the goddesses Iris, Ceres, and Juno, who attend Miranda's betrothal.

II

To describe Prospero's art by means of these three analogies of time is to give some idea of how the complex temporal organization of the play is made to substitute for a more straightforward kind of dramatic action, but it cannot suggest the representational power of the three subplots – how they are related to conceptions of human time – nor how we are to understand Prospero's acute sense of crisis, his 'zenith' which 'depend[s] upon / A most auspicious star, whose influence / If now I court not, but omit, my fortunes / Will ever after droop' (1.ii.181-4). It has been noticed that the word 'now' is used more often in *The Tempest* than in any other play of Shakespeare. It is also significant that the longest stretch of dialogue in which the word is not used comes in the middle of the scene of temporizing action in which Gonzalo dreams and Antonio begins the temptation of Sebastian.[9] For Caliban, who, by contrast, shares Prospero's sense of crisis, the time for Prospero's murder is 'now,' because at this time, mid-afternoon, it is Prospero's custom to sleep. One way to kill Prospero, Caliban suggests, is to drive a nail through his head as he sleeps. He must have in mind the temple of the skull, the place where the skull is weakest and where the pulse, the chronometer of the body, can be seen most easily.[10]

We associate, however, the use of the word 'now,' together with the sense of crisis, of being burdened by time, with Prospero. It is this sense of time as crisis-time through which Prospero is most clearly related to Ariel and most clearly distinguished from him. Ariel's joy as Prospero's helper is to enact in spectacular dramatic form the thoughts of his master. Thus, we can understand Ariel as the spirit of instantaneous imaginative embodiment, as quick as thought itself,[11] the spirit that, in the famous terms of Theseus' speech in *A Midsummer Night's Dream*, makes 'apprehension' into 'comprehension' because 'such tricks hath strong imagination / That, if it would apprehend some joy / It comprehends some bringer of that joy' (v.i.18-20). Joy and freedom, those large apprehendable abstracts, are brought into the range of human comprehension and made temporal by words, the means by which air is given human, communicable shape. This is why Prospero, when he promises Ariel his freedom, says 'Thou shalt be as free as mountain winds: but then exactly do / All points of my command' and why Ariel replies, 'to the syllable' (i.ii.501-3). Northrop Frye remarks that although there are cyclical symbols deriving from the seasons, the round of the day, the evaporation and condensation of water, and the movement of the stars, 'there is no cycle of air: the wind bloweth where it listeth and images dealing with the movement of "spirit" are likely to be associated with the theme of unpredictability or sudden crisis.'[12] Surely, then, Ariel is that winged spirit of creation that comes in response to a moment of crisis or imagined failure, but because the spirit he represents is not cyclical, it is not really human either and is capable at any moment, and especially when the crisis has passed, of disappearing 'into air, into thin air' (iv.i.150).[13]

In a play so obsessed with the structures and phenomena of time, it is not surprising that Ariel's dispersal of the various groups from the ship 'in troops ... about the isle' (i.ii.220) should be precisely related to distinct aspects of time, that we should see in the very fact of the three subplots a division of human time itself into its constituent aspects, the past, present, and future. The action of the court party on the island reflects a progressive realization that their life especially is founded upon repetition. Thus, when Alonzo's labyrinthine search for his lost son Ferdinand is finally concluded by Prospero's description of him as a man of sin, Alonzo's response to this new knowledge suggests that Ferdinand has always been lost because born to such a father and that his drowning is for Alonzo a culmination:

> O, it is monstrous, monstrous!
> Methought the billows spoke, and told me of it;
> The winds did sing it to me, and the thunder,
> That deep and dreadful organ-pipe, pronounc'd
> The name of Prosper; it did bass my trespass.
> Therefore my son i' th' ooze is bedded; and
> I'll seek him deeper than e'er plummet sounded,
> And with him there lie mudded.                    (iii.iii.95-102)

The sounds of this remarkable passage together form an iconic duplication of the way in which Alonzo's linear, but maze-like and repetitive, search for Ferdinand keeps deepening, as it continues, into an image of the significance of the search. The apparently casual alliteration in the first two lines (the first, innocent indication of repetition) becomes progressively undergirded by the clustering towards the speech's end of words with double consonants or vowels ('Bass,' 'trespass,' 'ooze,' 'bedded,' 'seek,' 'deeper,' 'plummet,' 'mudded'), so that the principle of alliteration itself, as mere repetition of sound in time, becomes accused by a deeper sound.

If the activities of the court party on the island represent the falling back of what is only apparently a present moment into a representation of the past, making the provision of allegorical icons, like the disappearing banquet and the representation of Ariel as a harpy, psychologically appropriate to such a state, the dramatization of Caliban, Trinculo, and Stephano follows the opposite procedure. They are made by their actions to represent a present moment that will not become future despite Caliban's persistent attempts to organize Trinculo and Stephano into an assassination plot. For this reason we do not hear anything about Stephano's and Trinculo's arrival on the island until we see Trinculo discovering Caliban in the act of hiding from him. Because Shakespeare has not prepared the audience for this sudden encounter, the action of the comic figures tends to suggests a kind of pure present whose temporal relations to past and future become, despite Caliban's efforts, virtually irrelevant. Prospero is able to divert the assassination attempt by hanging theatrical costumes on the clothes-line for Stephano and Trinculo to dress up in, like adult-children unable to imagine anything more than present gratification. Hence, when Ariel comes to lead the comic characters to their punishment, he changes costume, appearing now as a piper playing on a drum and leading Stephano and Trinculo off stage as if at the head of a parade, the very index of present-centred activity.

If the first two subplots can be described, respectively, as a present that forfeits the quality of being present by repeating the past and as a present that remains present in its very obliviousness to other temporal modes, the love of Ferdinand and Miranda represents a present preserved so that it can ensure the arrival of a future. This is one of the functions of Prospero's irritable and alienating emphasis upon Miranda's virginity, as we can see by comparing once again the play's three conspiracies. The conspiracy of Antonio against Alonzo, by being prevented, is made to mirror the usurpation of Prospero twelve years before. The way Caliban's conspiracy is prevented makes it mirror his present frustration at what he thinks is Prospero's abuse. But the conspiracy, or 'plot,' of Venus against the young lovers fails and is replaced by a symbolic vision of married chastity and the fertility traditionally associated with it.

This suggests that the three subplots are being systematically related to one another. It is certainly clear that each is based on a different cluster of dramatic conventions – on allegorized narrative for the court party, on the *lazzi* and character conventions of the *commedia dell'arte* for the Caliban subplot, and on varieties of pastoral for the young lovers. But it is also true that the three subplots are based on distinct semiotic systems. C.S. Peirce's trichotomization of the linguistic sign into icon, index, and symbol is anticipated by the signs Shakespeare has chosen for his three subplots and perhaps explains why we feel, intuitively, that they go together so well. Iconic signs, as the word 'icon' suggests, are signs which contain within themselves actualizations of the object or referent to which they refer, or, in more neutral language, that possess by similarity or analogy the properties of the thing they denote. Thus, Ariel as a harpy is an iconic sign, an allegory of, or metaphor for, greedy desires which spoil what they touch. Indexal signs are not like their objects, as in the previous case; instead, they point dynamically to their objects because they are related to them metonymically. Thus Ariel as a drummer leading what amounts to a parade can be understood as pointing to the activity that best characterizes the comic subplot. The relation between the sign and its object is unmotivated for symbolic signs; there is nothing about a symbolic sign that necessarily connects it to its object. Symbolic signs are therefore culture-specific and their meaning has to be learned. Ariel as Iris presenting the masque of Ceres for Miranda and Ferdinand refers to the rainbow that comes after waters recede; but this association has to be learned (unlike harpies, who are, simply, harpyish, and drummers, who drum). Peirce himself recognized the different temporal registers of his division: 'an icon has such being as belongs to past experience. An index has the being of present experience. The being of a symbol is *esse in futuro*.'[14]

III

*The Tempest*, with its haunting repetitions and its totalizing picture of human time, has the capacity to remind us of our earliest needs and desires because its subject is the losses and gains of a whole lifetime seen from the perspective of Prospero, who is portrayed as alone having the power and wisdom to re-create the image of a whole society. Two extraordinary dramatic spectacles, the beginning shipwreck and the masque of Ceres, as they dissolve in front of our eyes, dissolve also in front of their principal spectators, Miranda and Prospero. Even after Prospero's explanation of their expulsion from Milan, Miranda does not understand the reason for raising the sea-storm (it is the beginning of time for her) and asks her father to explain it 'for still 'tis beating in my mind' (i.ii.176). By contrast, the masque of Ceres begins to vanish when Prospero remembers that the moment of Caliban's plot has almost arrived (it is a premonition of the end of time for him). Accordingly, he consoles Ferdinand and Miranda for their loss of paradise and tries to control his own emotions: 'a turn or two I'll walk, / To still my beating mind' (iv.i.161-2). In turn, this important echo reminds us of the extremely close relations in this play between the spectacle produced and the audience watching.

This is emphasized by the fact that, as has often been remarked, *The Tempest* keeps to the unity of time. We learn very quickly that the duration of the imagined action on the island will be identical to the time spent by the audience in the theatre. The care and wit with which this illusion is established makes us acutely conscious of the relation between the on-stage action and the theatre audience, since what is happening to the characters is, in temporal terms at least, the same as what is happening to us.

Thus, because *The Tempest* begins with a tempest, that is, with an event that actually appears to be happening right in front of us and is not mediated by a preparatory event of any kind, it is as if we were being hurried right into the centre of time itself as we see a whole society, from King to sailor, apparently being destroyed. But when Miranda and Prospero appear before us, suspending our sense of the inevitability of loss and death and replacing it with a complex action to rebuild the destroyed society according to ideal norms, the result is that the theatre audience is displaced from its privileged position as the central spectator of the action. It is not only displaced, it is made marginal by this movement from nature to art and from action to contemplation. From now on, until almost the very end of the play, what happens on stage happens to other audiences than us, as we watch others being watched.

By studying Miranda's response to the shipwreck, we can gain some understanding of the paradoxical position of the audience of *The*

*Tempest*, linked by time to the on-stage events but displaced by the apparent motive and direction of those events:

> If by your art, my dearest father, you have
> Put the wild waters in this roar, allay them.
> The sky it seems would pour down stinking pitch,
> But that the sea, mounting to th' welkin's cheek,
> Dashes the fire out. O! I have suffered
> With those that I saw suffer. A brave vessel
> (Who had, no doubt, some noble creature in her)
> Dash'd all to pieces! O, the cry did knock
> Against my very heart. Poor souls, they perish'd.
> Had I been any God of power, I would
> Have sunk the sea within the earth or ere
> It should the good ship so have swallow'd, and
> The fraughting souls within her. (I.ii.1-13)

What is striking about this speech is the division between father and daughter that threatens to open in Miranda's protest at the loss of the 'fraughting souls' and which is implied by her indirect identification of her father as a god of power who could have prevented the storm had he wished. To sink the sea within the earth, as Miranda suggests, is the opposite of what Antonio and Sebastian satirically suggest that Gonzalo would do with the island on which they have found themselves:

*Antonio*: What impossible matter will he make easy next?
*Sebastian*: I think he will carry this island home in his pocket, and give it his son for an apple.
*Antonio*: And sowing the kernels of it in the sea, bring forth more islands.

(II.i.89-94)

To fertilize the sea with islands is to expand the earth within the sea, to plant the sea and make it grow. Hence, both Miranda's response to the shipwreck and the implied response of Gonzalo to the island deny one half of the sea's essential nature, its separating and dividing force that causes loss and death. And each leads in the direction suggested by the whole structure of the play, towards the experience of the unexpected supplement to time that lies buried in the very nature of imaginative response. Miranda's response to the shipwreck is genuinely supplementary in the sense that her speech implicitly expresses a knowledge of something that we, the theatre audience, do not yet know. For the noble souls are not dead and Miranda's surmise of herself as a god of power is the imaginative form which that intuitive knowledge takes. There is, then, a sense in which Miranda's response precedes the shipwreck, and is a version of the cry and smile that preserved her father when they were expelled onto the sea twelve years before. The supplementary quality of Miranda's response is confirmed by the miraculous retention in her memory of the image of 'four or five women who once tended her' (1.ii.46-7). Her memory forges the first link with the past experience in Milan and is thus the first sign that there are indeed islands to be sown in the sea of time.

Prospero, of course, is not a god of power, as his troubled exposition of his past, his anger at Caliban's conspiracy, and his 'human' forgiveness of his enemies make very clear; only his 'art,' the art of constructing an image of time, makes him appear as one for most of the action. He is not a god of power because the action of *The Tempest* is not exclusively the re-creation of human society according to ideal models; it is also for Prospero his own re-entry into the stream of human experience. This becomes clear at the end of the masque of Ceres, when Prospero forgets the approach of Caliban's conspiracy because he is so involved in the spectacle he is producing for Ferdinand and Miranda. Caliban moves him to anger, not because the conspiracy poses any threat to Prospero – it is easily dealt with – but mainly because the movement from absorption in the spectacle of immortality, of a year without death, to confrontation with the stupid and vicious present, for which he is partly responsible, causes him to be reminded of time and therefore of his own mortality, a reminder perhaps always implicit in the movement of the emotions from any forgetting to any remembering.[15]

If Prospero is not a god of power and must continually be reminded of his human failures, time is not immortal either and the ideal vision of the masque of Ceres, though not questioned as art, is questioned in its relevance to what we have been calling the 'whole of Life.' The 'revels' speech consoles the lovers for the loss of their vision of perfection, but the form the consolation takes is to predict the final disappearance of time for the observer.[16] Thus the question is raised, what is left over from the vision, what could supplement the loss of such a perfect fusion of art and nature as the masque of Ceres has presented? A partial answer comes from watching how Shakespeare manages the gradual and beautiful disengagement from the dream world on the island. Whether we think of this disengagement as the image of the illusory spirits disappearing, or as Prospero's renunciation of rough magic, or as his goodbye to Ariel, or as his successive acknowledgments of Antonio, Sebastian, and Caliban, and finally the theatre audience itself, what is clear is that, in all these successive relinquishings, the dream world of the spirits is replaced within the frame of art by what had appeared before to be marginal and supplementary, that is, to have been merely an audience. That the audience gradually comes to fill up the frame of art as its perfect illusions disappear is made clearest by Prospero's last vanity, the display of Ferdinand and Miranda playing chess. It is significant that his 'high miracle,' as Sebastian calls it, has been managed without the aid of Ariel and that Ferdinand and Miranda had been the audience for the recent masque of Ceres.[17] Since the lovers are 'real' characters and not spirits, their appearance within the frame of art suggests both the dependence of dramatic art (as opposed to the art of the court masque) on images of the actual, and the reciprocal reliance on the forms of ideal art, if it is to be recognized, of the good in human nature.

So also with Caliban. From the perspective of Prospero's knowledge of his actions, Caliban is a born devil on whose nature nurture, or the merely supplementary, can never stick. But now at the close even Prospero must acknowledge what the audience has felt right along, that Caliban's status as a minor revolutionary and would-be rapist does not represent his true value. His desire, now, to 'be wise hereafter, / And seek for grace' (v.i.296-7) means that nurture has not been superfluous, or merely supplementary, but, by filling in an absence, has become necessary. Thus, beginning with the masque of Ceres, the audience in the theatre begins to sense that all the great correlative oppositions of the play, art and life, illusion and reality, contemplation and action, knowing and acknowledgment, draw strength from one another as interdependent concepts.[18]

This, at least, is one of the implications of the original form Shakespeare gives to *The Tempest*'s epilogue. Most dramatic epilogues, including all those in other plays of Shakespeare, form a kind of second, or supplementary, ending, in which the actor who has played one of the leading roles (Puck in *A Midsummer Night's Dream*, Rosalind in *As You Like It*, to name only the two most famous instances), steps out of character and approaches the audience as an actor (often referring to himself and the rest of the cast as actors, as Puck does). In this convention, the epilogue is a mere supplement to the main fiction, an addition or part conventionally tacked on after the action has been completed. Prospero, however, does not approach the audience as an actor but as Prospero without his magical powers; and he does not appeal wittily to the audience for their applause but seriously to the conscience and understanding of each person:

> Gentle breath of yours my sails
> Must fill, or else my project fails,
> Which was to please. Now I want
> Spirits to enforce, art to enchant,
> And my ending is despair,
> Unless I be reliev'd by prayer,
> Which pierces so, that it assaults
> Mercy itself, and frees all faults.
> As you from crimes would pardon'd be,
> Let your indulgence set me free.                (Epilogue, 11-20)

Now it is true that this epilogue follows convention in the sense that it makes an appeal to the audience to recognize that it has been well entertained by the skill of the actors. The 'breath' to which Prospero refers is the comment of the audience after the performance is over, and the 'prayer' the words of the epilogue. The break with convention comes within the convention itself in the seriousness of its appeal and the literalness with which it insists that only the audience's commitment to the meaning of what they have experienced will get the ship back to Naples and save Prospero from despair. Thus the epilogue is not a mere supplement to the play but its necessary conclusion, and because the epilogue has included the audience within the main action of the play, as its completion, the audience is suddenly revealed to be, not the marginal and displaced onlooker of the play, but its implied subject, its judge, and, in a way, its creator. Like death, this implied summons to the meaning of time comes from without (ends are always external to what they end); but again, like death (like the shipwreck), it has been there all along.

NOTES

1 For the allegorists, see Anne Bates Hersman, *Studies in Greek Allegorical Interpretation* (Chicago, 1906), 7-23, and Rudolf Pfeiffer, *History of Classical Scholarship from the Beginning to the End of the Hellenistic Age*

(Oxford, 1968). For the romancers, see the notes to *The Odyssey of Homer*, ed. W.B. Stanford (London, 1947). By using the term 'supplement' here and elsewhere in this paper, I mean to invoke what Jacques Derrida has called the 'logic of supplementarity,' the logic by means of which a concept or practice which was at first thought to be merely an external addition to something complete in itself, as education is to nature according to some theories, is revealed as being necessary to complete what it was first thought merely to 'supplement.' See Jacques Derrida, '... That Dangerous Supplement ... ,' in *Of Grammatology*, trans. Gayatri Chakrovorty Spivak (Baltimore, 1976), 141-64. See also the exposition of the concept in Jonathan Culler's essay on Derrida in *Structuralism and Since*, ed. John Sturrock (Oxford, 1979), esp. 167-8.

2 *The Riverside Shakespeare*, ed. G. Blakemore Evans, et al. (Boston, 1974).

3 See the synopsis in the New Variorum edition of *The Tempest*, ed. H.H. Furness (Philadelphia, 1892), 449-50.

4 Campbell, *Dramatic Works of Shakespeare* (London, 1838); cited from *The Tempest*, ed. Furness, 356.

5 '*Tempestas, atis* ... Time: a seasonable time and faire weather: a faire or good season: a tempest or storme ... a boisterous or troublous weather, be it winde, haile, or raine: commonly it signifieth a tempest, or storme of raine and haile together: also great trouble, business, or ruffling in a common weale: a storme or trouble of adversities' (Thomas Thomas, *Dictionarium Linguae Latinae et Anglicanae* [London, 1606]; cited by Gary Schmidgall, *Shakespeare and the Courtly Aesthetic* [Berkeley and Los Angeles, 1981], 160-1).

6 According to Richard Broxton Onians, the English word 'opportunity' expresses something like the Greek use of *kairos* to suggest the opening between the warp threads through which the shuttle passes with the woof. 'The opening in the warp lasts only a limited time, and the "shot" [of the shuttle] must be made while it is open. The belief in the weaving of fate with the length of the warp-threads representing length of time may have helped this use of *kairos*' (*The Origins of European Thought* [Cambridge, 1951], 346-7). Onians' entire section on 'Fate and Time' (303-466) is fascinating and full of suggestions for the literary representation of time.

7 Kant specifies permanence or duration, succession, and simultaneity or coexistence as the three analogies of experience which together determine the existence of appearances in time because 'taken together, the analogies declare that all appearances lie, in *one* nature, because without this *a priori* unity no unity of experience, and therefore no determination of objects in it, would be possible' (*Critique of Pure Rea-*

*son*, trans. Norman Kemp Smith [London, 1929], 237). The parallelism between Kant's three modes of time and the temporal organization of the subplot actions in *The Tempest* strengthens the claim that Prospero's art is presented as representing a total vision or imagination of human time.

8 This aspect of *The Tempest*'s structure was first clearly understood by Northrop Frye in his 'Introduction' to the Pelican Shakespeare edition of *The Tempest* (Baltimore, 1959).

9 'Now' is used seventy-nine times in *The Tempest*; it is not used at all between II.i.95 and II.i.255.

10 The word 'temple,' etymologically connected to Latin *tempus*, which translated many of the associations of the Greek word *kairos*, refers to the opening in the skull, the 'opportunity' or door into; Caliban would then be repeating the murder of Sisera by Jael (Judges 4:21). See Onians, *Origins*, 344n., and Frank Kermode's note in his Arden edition of *The Tempest* on III.ii.60.

11 Ariel's actions are probably to be understood as taking no time at all, as the following bit of dialogue suggests: 'I drink the air before me, and return / Or ere your pulse twice beat' (V.i.102-3).

12 Frye, *Anatomy of Criticism* (Princeton, 1957), 158-60.

13 Compare Shelley's profound extension of this imagery in another crisis poem, *Mont Blanc*, which also begins with a tempest 'in likeness of the Arve' and which ends with the following extraordinary passage on wind and the imagination:

> ... Winds contend
> Silently there, and heap the snow with breath
> Rapid and strong, but silently! Its home
> The voiceless lightning in these solitudes
> Keeps innocently, and like vapour broods
> Over the snow ...
> And what were thou, and earth, and stars, and sea,
> If to the human mind's imaginings
> Silence and solitude were vacancy?

14 C.S. Peirce, *Collected Papers*, ed. C. Hartshorne and P. Weiss (1933; rpt. Cambridge, Mass., 1960), IV, 447, and II, 148. See also the interesting extensions of Peirce's division in Patrice Pavis, *Problèmes de sémiologie théâtrale* (Québec, 1976). Peirce's own speculation about the origin of the concept of time is to be found in *Collected Papers*, IV, 642.

15 That Shakespeare is thinking along these lines is obvious from the 'Revels'

speech. Additional evidence is provided by Prospero's speech in which he abandons his magical powers (v.i.33-57), a speech Shakespeare imitates from Ovid's description of Medea's invocation of the spirits in *Metamorphoses*, VII, 197-209. The context in Ovid is Medea's successful attempt to prolong the life of Jason's father, Aeson. The context in Shakespeare is Prospero's abandonment of analogous powers.

16 The contrast between the image of time that Prospero constructs out of the shipwreck and the disappearance of time for the observer is analogous to the philosophical distinction between objective time and subjective time. In *The Tempest*, value resides in the passage from one to the other.

17 There is an interesting treatment of the final scene of *The Tempest*, to which I am indebted, in Mary Chan, *Music in the Theatre of Ben Jonson* (Oxford, 1980), 318-31. Her major subject is Jonson's masques and especially the increasingly impossible position of the audience in them, as the masque evolved. She reads *The Tempest* as being aware of and adroitly avoiding the major structural problems of the masque form.

18 The logic of supplementarity pervades *The Tempest*; it is perhaps most obvious in the case of Caliban. Made marginal by the failure of Prospero's efforts to educate him ('a devil, a born devil, on whose nature / Nurture can never stick' [IV.i.188–9]), the persistence of his attempts to murder Prospero sharply limit the range of application of Prospero's art and bring on the recognition of the eventual disappearance of time for the observer. It is traditional for audiences to feel a great deal of sympathy for Caliban and to see more in him than Prospero sees; the foundation for this sympathy lies in the logic of the supplement, in the fact that the action of *The Tempest* makes the audience and Caliban both marginal and necessary.

**HELEN VENDLER**

# The Golden Theme: Keats's Ode 'To Autumn'

> Apollo is once more the golden theme.
> *Hyperion* III.28

Most critics of my generation must have discovered, in turning to write on a poem, that Northrop Frye has anticipated their own insights. Those of us who heard, in the fall of 1956 at Harvard, his two revelatory courses (one on Criticism, one on Myth) found there a poetic full of confidence and power. To hear the *Anatomy of Criticism* spoken before its publication was to be exhilarated for a whole term; and to be taught Blake by Frye was to have a baffled hunger satisfied by daily bread. I do not recall Frye's then mentioning Keats; but I found him before me, as always, on the Keatsian path.

Keats's ode *To Autumn* is the quintessential poem in our literature of what Frye has called 'revealed Nature.' Though the ode needs to be seen in the light of Keats's earlier odes, even when it is taken up alone some of its powers appear. Among those powers is a religious one – in Frye's words, the 'intense feeling of communion ... in the sacramental corn-and-wine images of the great Keats odes.' Frye invokes the earlier odes in his brilliant summary remark, 'The corn-goddess in Keats's *To Autumn*, the parallel figure identified with Ruth in the *Ode to a Nightingale*, the still unravished bride of the Grecian Urn, Psyche, even the veiled Melancholy, are all emblems of a revealed Nature.'[1] What I wish to argue in this essay is that Keats's great ode reveals Nature (and man) as much by its structures as by those central symbolic and allegorical images remarked by Frye; and that Frye's remark on the 'sacramental' nature of the imagery requires some qualification.

The Autumn ode, unlike its predecessors, exhibits several great organizing motions, some already noticed by commentators, engaged in mute interplay.

The first great motion is the temporal one. We see as the poem opens the ripening fruits of the earth, next (in a flashback) the flowers that preceded them, and then the proto-harvest of nectar from the flowers, accomplished by the bees, the first harvesters. In the second stanza we view the second harvest of corn and fruit (the apple-pressing is the last step in the fruit harvest); and finally in the third stanza we come to the stubble-plains. From budding flowers to denuded fields we go in one motion, but with incidental oddities to which we shall return.

The second great organizing motion of the ode occurs in space. The poem rises in a wide haze of mists and maturing sun, an overview not to be returned to until the final stanza of the ode. Within the body of the ode, there is a remarkably meticulous geography, beginning with the human dwelling, the thatched cottage and the grapevines encircling its eaves, the first and closest of many concentric plottings of space. Beyond the cottage we pass to the apple-orchard, the kitchen-garden with its gourds and nut tree, and the beehives (placed by convention near the orchard) – all the immediate surroundings of the central house. In the next stanza we go 'abroad' – to the outbuildings, the granary, the threshing floor, the building housing the cider-press, and to the cornfields full of wheat and poppies. (We also learn that the gleaner must cross a brook to get from cornfield to granary.) In the third stanza we see or conjecture spaces farther afield. We may look to the horizon where we see barred clouds, and we may reach in thought beyond the stubble-plains (and their incorporated tributary brook) to the river (one natural perimeter of the farm), to the hilly bourn of sheep pasturage (another natural boundary), to the hedgerows (planted usually where river or hill did not demarcate one farm from another) and finally to a croft (perhaps a far corner of the farm leased to a crofter). Finally, after this careful situating of perimeters on a plane, the space of the poem becomes in the last line three-dimensional; and, in a remarkable freeing of vision, we lift our eyes up to the skies, the upper 'boundary' of the farm.

Besides the temporal passage from flowering and fruition to last oozings and stubble-fields, besides the spatial expansion of perspective from the cottage to the perimeter of the farm and its upper boundary by the sky, the poem seems to sketch, though lightly, a passage through a season-spanning 'day' – from the mists of dawn, through the noon heat in which the reaper drowses, to a sunset.

There is also a movement in the field of imagery. Though descriptions of what sort of imagery animates the first two stanzas have differed (with emphasis given to kinaesthetic imagery in the first, and visual imagery in the second) everyone agrees that in the last stanza it is the ear, and not the eye, which is the chief receptive agent.

Finally, and most interestingly, it has also been noticed that the figure of Autumn, shadowy at best in the first and third stanzas, rises to a visible presence in the second stanza. This rising and subsequent effacement, probably the most beautiful motion in the poem, has inevitably asked for explanation.

The orchestration of these five large effects – the successive harvests, the spatial expansion, the sequence of the 'day,' the change in field of imagery, and the appearance and disappearance of the personified figure of the season – is itself accomplished with remarkably little strain, and with no announcement. Imperceptibly, the poem moves on in time, space, imagery, hour, and 'population' – for if the second stanza is 'inhabited' by the allegorical female figure, the first is equally 'inhabited' by fruits and the third by creatures (to speak in approximations). Within each of these large movements, there are puzzling sub-motions, which we must mention before proposing any 'reading' of the ode.

In the first stanza, the puzzling sub-motion is the (chronologically late) appearance of the bees' proto-harvest from the flowers. In this earliest of harvests, the landscape remains undespoiled: the bees do not pluck the flowers but rather extract from them their nectar, which in the form of honey is stored in the bees' granaries, the 'clammy cells' (the adjective comes from Dryden's *Georgics*) of their hives. This is an Edenic harvest, a harvest belonging to summer, where not only is there no visible damage to the landscape, but rather, in the manner proper to paradisal fruitfulness, the earth continues to produce of its own volition more and more offerings. The bees, our surrogates, live in a prelapsarian dream, thinking that 'warm days will never cease.' (We may notice in passing that the birds of the earthly paradise, who sing their spring songs of true love, are missing in Keats's adaptation of the *topos* in the first stanza, but are later remembered in the backward glance to the 'song of spring.') In this appearance, out of sequence (since it is mentioned after the appearance of fruit) of the flower-harvest, we can see the undertow of nostalgia at work in the ode, an undertow which, while the ode moves forward in time, itself moves in reverse, till it brings us to the Shakespearean backward glance to the sweet birds of spring at the beginning of the last stanza, and to the equal backward glance to spring lambs in speaking of the autumnal full-grown sheep. This counter-current represents the last expression of Keats's wistful hope that art, or harvest, could coexist painlessly with nature, that poetry could come as naturally as the nightingale's song, or leaves to the tree. For the moment, we can leave this counter-current remarked, and pass on.

A competing sub-motion in the first stanza, however, reveals why it is necessary that the bees and their early flower-harvest be placed last, after the appearance of fruits. Many of Keats's verbs representing the actions of autumn are verbs having, if allowed to progress, a natural terminus: loading ends in overloading, bending ends in breaking, filling ends in overflowing, swelling ends in bursting, plumping ends in splitting. If the fruits of the earth are not harvested when they are ripe, natural process dictates a continuing into overripeness, bursting of skins, rottenness, and death. More than one poet has let the first stanza of Keats's ode continue uninterrupted in his imagination – has let the apples fall from the trees 'and bruise themselves an exit from themselves' (Lawrence), or has let the gourds swell to streaking and bursting:

> We hang like warty squashes, streaked and rayed,
> The laughing sky will see the two of us
> Washed into rinds by rotting winter rains.                   (Stevens)

In deciding to make his ode not a poem about nature alone, but rather a poem emphasizing man's *intervention* in natural process, Keats has to warn us of the mortal termini which nature, left to herself, without harvest, would attain. Strained as we are by his verbs of loading, bending, filling, swelling, and plumping, we need to be relieved by one action brought to its natural end – Summer has 'o'er-brimmed' the honeycombs. The cup that runs over is not only a hallowed image of harvest, but is also the only agreeable choice among the Keatsian termini. One long trajectory of ripening, then, comes to an end in the bursting-of-bounds symbolized by the overflowing honey; the other trajectories are not allowed their natural termini in rotting or splitting because they are interrupted by the harvest of full-ripened apples, grapes, nuts, and gourds. There is no seed here left to fall back to the ground, no implication of the cyclical process which would, left to its own devices, produce the fruits of a following spring. Nor is there any ripened fruit which falls to earth and dies. The interpenetration of agricultural harvest and natural process – not natural process alone – is the central topic of the poem.

It is time to glance at the opening of the first stanza, where the mythological framework of the poem is introduced. The myth invoked is that of the sky-god impregnating the earth so that she may bear fruit; Apollo and Gaea embrace, 'and forth the particulars of rapture come' (to quote Stevens). In Keats's version, the sky-god is not classicized as Apollo but naturalized as the sun, the earth-goddess is Autumn, and their relation is euphemized as one between 'bosom-friends.' She, all mists and mellow fruitfulness, and he, the maturing agent, conspire together, he breathing warmth, she moisture. In this allowing of the 'lower sense' of sexuality into his poem, Keats gives full credence to the sexual origins of all 'teemings' – those of art as well as those of nature. After the brief appearance of the sun, Keats removes him from the landscape, and the activities we see, though logically governed by the verb phrase 'conspiring with him how to x,' seem in fact to be activities of the season alone as, once impregnated, like Shakespeare's widowed wombs, she brings forth fruits. The sun's participation in the action of the first stanza seems to extend chiefly to blessing, as the first verbs after the conspiring of season and sun are a pair combining practical and spiritual activity – 'load and bless' – whereas after this pair, the verbs, occurring singly, are only practical ones, as the season goes about her work of bending, filling, and so on. We are perhaps justified, then, in seeing the 'blessing' as the work of the sky-god Apollo – that 'sweet fire the sire of Muse' in Hopkins' words – who, having bestowed his blessings, can withdraw his active presence, leaving 'the mind the mother of immortal song.'

Some of the pathos of the ode arises, in fact, from the unaccompanied nature of the divine season as she appears in the second stanza, though that pathos is not fully evident until the vigil at the close. As Geoffrey Hartman has remarked, the goddess in this poem is not chary of her appearance. On the contrary, she is generously present to all beholders: 'Who hath not seen thee oft ... ? / Sometimes whoever seeks abroad may find / Thee.' The strenuous infinitives of Autumn the sponsor of fruitfulness in the first stanza are replaced by the habitual present tense of the second stanza, and Autumn the harvester is seen in any number of characteristic dispositions in the landscape.

The second stanza is divided into two unequal portions, the first concerned with the corn harvest, the second with the apple harvest. We recognize the underlying convention of the two autumn harvests of corn and grapes, normally resulting in bread and wine, but we must explain (especially since grapevines are present in the first stanza) the choice of apple-juice rather than wine as the harvest-product of this ode. (Though

England is not a wine-making country, the ode could easily accommodate wine in its unspecified geography.) We recall of course Keats's characteristic sobriety, inherited from Milton's *L'Allegro*:

> I will fly to thee,
> Not charioted by Bacchus and his pards,
> But on the viewless wings of Poesy.

It is inconceivable that the Autumn ode, which originated in Keats's praise of temperate air, chaste weather, and Dian skies, could admit wine and intoxication to its harvest scene – though we see the return of the repressed in the 'fume of poppies' (a phrase derived from Silenus' drunkenness in Dryden's *Virgilian Pastorals*).

We must still inquire why the harvest scenes take the form they do, a question that has been frequently put. We see in this poem a thresher who does not thresh, a reaper who does not reap, a gleaner who does not glean, a cider-maker who does not turn her press. Though determined on his interruptive harvest, rather than on inertial natural process, Keats forbears to show us the season undoing her own activities of fruition: instead, he shows her insensibly matured and then depleted through the harvest. She sits careless first, like a girl caressed by the wind; next, she is seen drowsy, fulfilled, in an involuntary intoxication of crimson poppies, in a maturer sensuality; thirdly, she takes care in the bearing of a gleaned burden on her laden head; and finally, she sits patient in a long vigil, watching 'the last oozings hours by hours.' In this harvest stanza, the flowers of the proto-harvest reappear, inextricably twined with the grain in an image of total sexual maturity, masculine and feminine. But the verbal intimations of a staying-of-harvest do not themselves explain Keats's rearranging of the normal order of the grain harvest. Where we would expect reaping, then gleaning, then threshing, we find instead first threshing, then reaping, then gleaning – a sequence invented, I believe, to show the difficulties of presenting an inactive harvest, and one imbued with pathos. Though the archetypal and Shakespearean image of harvest is that of reaping, the most energetic single image is that of threshing. When 'the stars shall be threshed, and the souls threshed from their husks,' as Yeats and Blake knew, then would come the trampling out of the vintage where the grapes of wrath are stored. Keats (as I would argue against Bloom) wishes to avoid any appearance of apocalypse; and so the season, far from herself wielding the flail, becomes in the threshing scene entirely passive, and is herself, in the metamorphosis of her hair into grain, 'winnowed' by the soft wind. Gleaning must occur last in this series of harvest scenes because it is by definition the most pathetic of the phases of harvest, associated as it is in Keats's mind with the image of Ruth 'amid the alien corn' listening, 'sick for home,' to the song of the nightingale. And yet, refusing to succumb entirely to the pathos possible in the image of gleaning, Keats permits us to see the gleaner only as a careful tributary presence on her way to the granary. In the arrested motion of this stanza, the thresher sits, the reaper drowses, the gleaner balances her laden head, and the cider-maker watches the last drops ooze from the press. 'Store' yields gradually to store undone: the soft-lifted hair of the intact wheat gives way to the half-reaped furrow of poppies and corn, which in turn is replaced, imaginatively, by the last cullings in the basket burdening the gleaner, and all disappear in favour of the crushed and no longer recognizable apples, obliterated into oozing drops.

At this progressive diminution and extirpation, the mind rebels, and yields to nostalgia for its spring time. The natural question for it to voice in its nostalgia, given the consistent imagery of fruits and flowers hitherto marking the season, would be 'Where are the flowers of Spring?' The illogicality of 'Where are the *songs* of Spring?' can be explained, however, if we remember Shakespeare's autumnal tree with its ruined choirs, and if we assume that the image of the gleaner, by its association with Ruth and the recently composed *Ode to a Nightingale*, also helped to summon up the backward glance to the heard melodies of Spring, those bird-songs of love not mentioned in the first stanza of the ode, though belonging by decorum to any picture of the earthly paradise. In the antiphonal question-and-echo (reminiscent of the questions put to the Urn) opening the last stanza, the season herself seems to be re-voicing the question of her poet: he asks 'Where are the songs of Spring?' and 'Aye, where are they?' she sighs back (if only in his conjecture). Touched by her grief, which he has unwittingly caused, he bends to reassure her and comfort her lack, rather than his own: 'Think not of them, thou hast thy music too.' In this, the central debate-exchange of the ode, the poem becomes most self-reflexive; and we shall return to that meditation on itself (in which most great poems somehow engage) later on. But here, we must pass to the main intent of this closing stanza which, like the two preceding it, is divided into two apparent parts. As we saw the fruits chiefly in the first stanza (but with a brief glimpse of the bees and the later flowers), and as we saw the corn harvest chiefly in the second stanza (but with a closing tableau of the apple harvest), so here we meet chiefly the music of the creatures (but with some brief attention to the landscape).

It is, in fact, the landscape that we see first in the grand syntactic balance: '*While* this, *then* that; *and now* the other.' The landscape is delineated in terms of agent and effect: the 'barrèd clouds bloom the soft-dying day, / And touch the stubble-plains with rosy hue.' But of course the barred clouds are not the actual agent of this rosy light: the Apollonian setting sun, obscured by the level clouds on the horizon, is the real agent, and the 'bloom' of the sun's present work echoes, phonetically, the 'bless' of his first appearance. The sun, creator of life, here is no longer able to work his maturing inward power; now he can be only a painter, capable simply of external effect, setting a bloom on the day like the flush of a dying face, and touching the denuded plains with a rosy hue. Keats borrows his image of the sun as painter from his original association of the autumn scene with the 'way that some pictures look warm,' and (as the manuscripts show) from Shakespeare's line about the morning sun 'gilding pale streams.' The sun keeps to the end the same mystery: veiled by mists at the beginning, by cloud at the end, he remains remote from the visible landscape.

During this brief moment, while the sun's transient hue washes the stubble-fields with colour, gnats, sheep, and crickets utter their sounds. In the oddly following period, introduced by the fateful 'and now,' the whistle of the robin and the twitter of swallows conclude the poem. In this stanza of the creatures, the element most noticeably contrasting with earlier stanzas is the unmoving centre from which all is seen and heard. The listener stands rooted to one spot, noting the directions from which the sounds come to him. The listener hears the gnats mourning *among* the river sallows, the full-grown lambs bleating *from* hilly bourn, the crickets singing *in* the hedges, the redbreast whistling *from* a croft, and swallows twittering *in* the skies. The listener does not himself wander from river to hill to hedge to croft; rather, the sounds converge toward him, creating a centripetal sub-motion opposing the powerful centrifugal motion of the stanza which is concerned to establish the outlying boundaries – river, hill, hedge, and croft – of the farm.

In the description of the creatures, Keats engages in a testing of his own feelings towards his closing scene. At first, in the passage on the gnats, all is pure pathos: the 'small' gnats, those ephemeral insects, are assembled in a 'wailful' choir, singing an infantine dirge as they 'mourn': in their helplessness they are wholly in the erratic power of the air, 'borne aloft / Or sinking as the light wind lives or dies.' The next passage, too, yields to pathos, as sheep are represented as 'full-grown lambs' (the equivalent of calling men in some context 'full-grown infants'), who, in a parallel construction of rapid diminution, 'loud bleat.' (Since we associate bleating, when predicated of lambs, with the young seeking their mothers, this is rather like calling men's speech 'loud babytalk.') In each case the stoic modifiers ('full-grown' and 'loud') raise to 'adult' status the central noun and verb ('lambs ... bleat') which nonetheless are the essential descriptive words, and retain their infantile connotations.

However, after these two descriptions, of the gnats and the lambs, Keats pulls himself up short with an enormous effort of will, refusing childlike pathos. In a chastened realization that music, even if not that of the nightingale, is nonetheless music, he announces that crickets – plain crickets, unmodified by adjective or adverb of pathos – 'sing.' After this second stiffening of courage, retrospect ends, and the speaker and his utterance converge in the present: 'and now' redbreast and swallow join the choir. The final verbs are not pathetic, but rather are acoustically exact: the redbreast whistles, the swallows twitter. However, to banish pathos entirely would be as untrue as to yield to it utterly, and so the modifiers of these two admirably neutral verbs are allowed some fleeting measure, introduced more by reader than by writer, of pathos. The redbreast is said to whistle 'with treble soft,' and though this can be taken simply as a musical notation, still the context urges us to associate the modifier (as in the phrase 'childish treble') with that soft high voice we associate with child singers; and the swallows (in the most gently touched of these phrases) are 'gathering,' in a mutual cluster – whether for their night-wheeling or for migration is deliberately left unspecified, but once again, the inexorable progress of the season in the sonnet urges us to think of Winter.

If, now, having observed the chief motions of the poem, we attempt to arrive at a reading of the whole, we must pass to more spacious questions of sequence, disposition, myth, tone, and logic. Since I see no reason to ignore information when we possess it, I would begin with the originating image of the entire poem, the stubble-plains. The whole poem, to my mind, is uttered from the stubble-plains, and its tones, even of greatest celebration, are, I think, intelligible only when they are heard as notes issuing from deprivation. It would seem that in spite of his somewhat forced approval of the stubble-fields, as it is voiced in his letter ('Aye better than the chilly green of the spring'), Keats's first imaginative act, on seeing the bare plains, was a reparatory one, comparable to the act which prompted the *Ode to Psyche*. He wished to avert his eyes from sacrifice, to return to an anterior plenitude, to fill up the empty canvas, to replenish its denuded volume, to repopulate its boundaries. And so, like his own Autumn, he begins to 'load' the bare autumn landscape with a thatched cottage, grapevines, an apple-orchard, a kitchen-garden, a nut tree, beehives, and flowering mead-ows. The espousal of earth and sun fills the scene, too, with a golden pair, even if they are felt rather than seen. This reparatory effort is a literal evisceration of self. The autumn bounty that pours onto the page represents a fantasy of recreating the depleted landscape out of one's own fevered art-conspiring.

If Keats cannot, in restitutive fantasy, resurrect 'the teeming autumn, big with rich increase,' his imagination will, in a second attempt, rise to another response to the stubble-fields. The human fantasy embodied in the second stanza of the ode is a providential one: a figure of care, enhancement, and concern can hover in the landscape, even if the fruits of the earth prove fugitive. The 'Dian skies' of the letter perhaps suggested the incorporation of a goddess into the panorama, and, as we know from the sonnet to Homer, Keats thought of Diana as 'triple Hecate,' 'Queen of Earth, of Heaven, and Hell,' a goddess possessed of triple sight. The female goddess also brings to mind Ceres and Pomona and Lucina; even Proserpina seems present in Keats's imagination. The girl sitting careless on a granary floor or asleep amid the poppies is like Milton's Proserpina before her abduction, when she becomes 'herself a gathered flower.' The more burdened and careworn figures of the gleaner and the watcher by the cider-press resemble the sadder figure of Ceres after Proserpina's disappearance. Whatever the exact correspon-dence, we see in the shape-changing female figure in the landscape unmistakable resemblances to classical goddesses. On the other hand, goddesses do not reap furrows or carry burdens or press apples. In spite of the arrested motion here, it is certainly the figure in the landscape who has reaped the half-furrow, and it is her hook, as she sleeps, that spares the next swath. At most, goddesses of the harvest hold a symbolic scythe or bear a basket-cornucopia; they do not do work, or sleep in the midst of work, or walk with laden head. This female in the landscape is, then, a human figure who also looks divine, or a divine figure who has taken on the creations and labours of the earth; we recognize her provenance from Milton's Eve.

If Keats's poem is not about natural process, but about harvest, we touch, in the appearance of this figure, Keats's most intimate conviction that nature herself would assent, if with reluctance, to the harvesting of her beauties and her amplitudes rather than their abandonment to the wind and the weather. But her will to harvest meets her knowledge (expressed in the scene in the granary) that it is she herself who is winnowed; and so her scythe stops in mid-motion. By awakening his figure, by returning her, laden, across the brook, by stationing her, in her own passion, next to the last drops of harvest pressing, Keats makes her the participant in, and witness to, her own willed and sacrificial death. Her life – her grain and fruit – is, by her own action, transmuted into that 'store' which should fill her rich garners and her urns.

In the most ascetic choice of the poet we are now forbidden any view of the usual harvest-counterpoise – those 'rich garners' full of grain, and the overflowing cup. Keats's two initial reparatory motions of replenishing the landscape, whether with fruit or with figure, have exhausted themselves, the one in the o'er-brimming of the clammy cells (a proto-image of 'rich garners,' but not a beautiful one), the other in the sacrificial vigil over the oozings of the cider-press. His third effort, at this point in the poem, since he will refuse both conventional harvest celebration and magical return to spring, must be to find something to write about in the bare landscape from which he has now twice averted his eyes – that landscape left after life's self-immolation into art.

The loss of the female figure from the landscape precludes any celebration of the ingathered harvest. When she is gone, there is nothing left remarkable. The eyes see only a *nachschein*, external, not indwelling. The desolation of the visible scene, once the female presence vanishes, is the desolation of the little town robbed by the urn of its inhabitants; the absence at the heart of things is the shrine of Melancholy in the very temple of Delight. The goddess dwindles in direct proportion to the stored harvest, as motive is transformed into product, energy into representation, life into art. The *consolatio* following on the synecdoche 'Where are the songs of Spring?' must of course itself be musical; but Keats suggests, by his deliberate invoking of gnats (small and wailful and helpless in the wind, however light), and by his infantilizing of sheep (as bleating lambs), as well as by his attributing a 'treble soft' to the redbreast, that the post-sacrificial autumnal music issues from a choir of orphans. He borrows this symbol, as we recall, from Shakespeare: 'Yet this abundant issue seem'd to me / But hope of orphans, and un-fathered fruit.' If Keats's creatures in the last stanza are orphans, they are in mourning for a dead mother. The figurative clinging together of the orphan-choir, as they converge in centripetal sound toward the listener, illustrates their precariousness and insecurity. In Keats's final lines, we hear the weak voices of orphaned children, blown helplessly by the winds of circumstance, but yet, 'spite of despondence, of [an] inhuman dearth,' uttering their sounds of life into the twilight.

If we pause, now, to ask the largest questions, those prompted by the totality of the ode, we are inevitably drawn into some comparisons. Elsewhere Keats has been prompted to other responses when he discovers an absence at the centre of the world. When 'the harvest's done' in *La Belle Dame Sans Merci*, Keats's surrogates, speaker and knight, remain in the void without feeling the stir of any compensatory energies, helplessly enthralled and disenthralled, their will powerless in the outcome. In the *Ode to Psyche*, to cite the opposite extreme, Keats engages solely in a reparatory fiction, and ends his poem once the point-for-point construction of the reparatory shrine is complete. In *Nightingale*, art once again fills the void, but is rudely insufficient as a device to fill the vacuum of death. The *Urn* had for the first time acquiesced in the deathliness of art by admitting that the folk on the Urn could not return to the town, but could not reconcile the livingness and deathliness of art, choosing to see them alternately rather than simultaneously. But *To Autumn*, once its reparatory effort at vegetable plenitude is abandoned, subsides at first into an attempt at balance. While the nostalgic note of rosy light over the land is sounded *sostenuto* in the syntax, the creatures are allowed their independent possession of the air. Had the nostalgic memorial gleam been allowed to remain fixed on the fields for the entire duration of the last stanza – had the syntactic frame, that is, been simply 'While this, then that' – we might say that the sense of loss remained unobliterated, for all the poet's best efforts at objectivity. But such is not the case. In the last moment of the ode, both loss and its compensatory projections (whether in ripening fruit, in peopled landscape, or in rosy bloom) are forgotten in an annihilation of subjectivity and a pure immersion in the actual:

> ... and now with treble soft
> The red-breast whistles from a garden-croft;
> And gathering swallows twitter in the skies.

These sounds are detached, syntactically, from the sunset glow bathing the earlier orphaned songs. The glance that rises to the skies in the last line (the swallows twitter 'in,' not 'from,' the skies) has lifted itself away from the panorama of the stubble-fields, and is purged of self-referential pathos and nostalgia for the past. The ode has floated free from the deprivation which occasioned it, and ends poised in the air, sufficient unto itself.

The restorative hopes of the first two stanzas have been abandoned. The extraordinary mimetic power of representation, its gift of *trompe l'oeil*, however consoling a fiction, is a fiction nonetheless. A poem is not a 'picture,' it cannot 'reproduce' either the stubble-fields it contemplates or the richer produce of an earlier season. And a poem is not a conjuration; it cannot reincarnate an unravished bride, a dead mother, or a dead goddess hypostasized from the life of the fertile earth. A completed poem – so Keats seems to be insisting in leaving his pictures behind and in choosing sound as his last figure – is nothing but a thin thread of sound, rising and falling in obedience to its governing breath. Though a poem possesses, seemingly, all the expressive power of human speech, it is in fact not ordinary speech but rather sound lifted and sinking as the metrical law governing it rises and falls. Faced with the stubble-plains, the poet can only, after his first denials of fact in his representational illusionist effects, subside into his own oscillatory utterance, shrinking, in its smallest dimension, to phrases like 'to swell the gourd' or 'hedge-crickets sing,' and swelling, in its widest expansion, to the small incorporated narratives of the bees, the sleeping goddess, and the gnats. It is for this reason that Keats's 'perfected' verb, for which he had been seeking throughout the last stanza, is 'twitter,' a verb which preserves the association of a fluttering sound, rising and falling, though within the smallest of compasses.

We find, I think, an ampler solace than that offered by a fictive reparatory fullness in this return, by Keats, to visual poverty, a return in which expansive gestures of denial are stilled in favour of the sobriety of a truer aesthetic. Still, the poem as a whole has other dimensions besides this self-reflexive one affirming that a poet has no recourse – in the face of all he knows of creation, flowering, fruition, of disappearance, denudation, and extinction – except to utter a tenuous stream of sound.

In mythological terms, the poem retells the story of the death of the mother, which, otherwise considered, is the story of the attainment of adulthood. The poem remembers, with perfect fidelity, every phase of the mother's presence, from her active energy in animating all created things to her relaxation and fatigue in her accomplished maternity, followed by her gradual decline into patient vigil. This poem spares us the vision of the mother's face 'bright-blanch'd / By an immortal sickness which kills not,' but the mother's deathwards progress is both intimated in the second stanza and confirmed in the third as she, the soft-dying day, is attended by her grieving children just as she herself attended the last drops from the cider-press. The love which Keats has shown for the season through the first two stanzas threatens, in his deathbed watch, to turn into pity and grief alone, though it is only by her death that he has been prompted to call her back to life in verse. For a moment, resolve and art falter, and, forgetting his independent energy, Keats feels like a helpless gnat blown hither and thither, like a far-off lamb, however full-grown, bleating for the ewe. The poem, in this mythological construct, gives full credence to the child who remains within every adult, and to the infant crying in the night at the mother's death. The great effort of will required to convert grief into something that can legitimately be called not wailing or mourning or bleating, but song, is at once the effort to rise from childhood to adulthood, and the effort to assume the objectivity of the Orphic voice. To leave a group converging downward to the deathbed and join a group in the skies is to make that same growth in stature and expansion of view.

One is not exempt, however, while lifting one's vision to the skies, and lifting one's voice in song absolved of grief, from conveying some metaphysical sense of the lived import of existence and death. At the end of the ode, Keats abandons his personification of Autumn, seen in her benevolent action in the first stanza, and in her harvest postures in the second. In letting the singing creatures (who seem, since Autumn here is exclusively a vegetation goddess, to be independent of her agency) possess the final stanza, Keats shows the season expiring without causation, dying simply out of its own intrinsic allegorical definition as a span of time. Keats learned from the Shakespearean 'Consum'd with that which it was nourished by' to make his poem one not of natural process alone, nor one of a vegetative season alone, but rather one in which harvest, the human consumption of fruit, is necessarily linked with nourishment, the earth's fruition. And once the great Shakespearean autumnal paradox has been played out, with all inevitable reluctance, Keats can find a music worthy of 'the death bed whereon it must expire.'

The leisureliness and spaciousness with which the paradox is enacted, in Keats's first two stanzas and in their formal epilogue in song, gives, however, a very different sense of life from that conveyed by Shakes-

peare's fiercely concentrated epigram in Sonnet 73. Keats's sense of
suspended time and expanded space, above all, forbids all conception of
life as cramped, hurried, cut short, or incomplete. On the contrary, it
thins out into gleanings, oozings, and twitterings before it finally
becomes invisible, but it has all followed a rhythm at once so seasonal
and so human that the nearly invisible last choir seems to suggest the
participation of life in the rhythms of a third, aesthetic, realm – more
elusive than the natural vegetative one or the human agricultural one,
standing over them in a vibration of the ether, a polyphony in the skies.

Just as the human figure in the second stanza rises almost imperceptibly from among the fruits of the earth, so the voices of the last stanza rise
invisibly above the extent of the stubble-plain, and form that suspira-
tion of life paralleled by the light wind, itself the symbolic respiration of
the world. If there is an 'ideology' (as Hartman would say) expressed by
this ode, it is one which perceives a harmony among the varied rhythms
which have evolved in man's long life in nature. Vegetative growth and
human harvest combine to form a new sort of goddess, one who is
available to all of us because she is ourself in our labour, as well as being
the goddess of all that grows. Perhaps without the Christian doctrine of
the Incarnation and Milton's conception of Eve, Keats's goddess, so
clearly human, engaged in the work of cultivation and patient in vigil,
could not have been imagined. But this goddess embodies a reproof to
Christian incarnational myth. She arises from no external necessity –
Keats's universe has no offended God exacting atonement. She incar-
nates herself, in fruition, habitation, and harvest, simply out of that
divine affinity for the earth of which Keats was so sure, that mutual
greeting of the spirit between the sublime and the senses. The rhythm of
incarnation, growth, and self-sacrifice which permeates the poem is
wholly self-generated, prompted by no debt, demanded by no doctrine.
The poem represents a radical secularization of the Christian myth of
the divine incarnating itself in the human, a secularization prompted in
part by Wordsworth, but reaching to a union of the natural, the human,
and the divine envisaged but not, I think, accomplished in *The Prelude*.
In Keats's ode, that union of the gods, the earth, and human agricultural
and aesthetic labour has become, as Wordsworth had hoped it would, 'a
simple produce of the common day.'

The constitutive trope of the ode is enumeration – the trope of
plenitude – and in Keats's lists of flowers and fruit, of visions of the
goddess, and of autumn songs, we see that each phase of life is rich in its
own plural being. Keats needs the whole of the natural world for his

final metaphor. The poet's medium is language – an ethereal medium able to be the song of any season, the song of autumn as well as the song of spring, a nightingale here, a cricket there. Like his sun-inspired season, the poet touches everything into life, but his wand is the wand of Fancy; he too in creative energy loads and blesses the bareness of the world with his working brain. Just as surely, in sacrificial self-immolation, he gleans with his pen what his fertile brain has conceived; as life is transubstantiated into art, it loses its 'natural' shape and turns from 'drooping oats' to winnowed grain, from apples to oozing drops, without, however, losing its truthful origin in life. The transubstantiated beauty of poetry does not mimetically represent the beauty of life – how could it, consisting as it does of a poor thread of sound? Verisimilitude is dismissed as an aesthetic criterion; 'appropriateness' is substituted, as the songs of the gnats and crickets are appropriate to autumn just as the song of the nightingale was appropriate to spring. Keats, at the end, is the listener to his own music. He does not use it to distract him from death, as he had in *Nightingale*; he now listens intently while gazing at the full spectacle of a bare world, in a soft-dying day. Beauty now includes as intrinsic components dissonance (bleats and twitters and whistles) and death, just as creation entails disappearance. Apollo appears no less as the Presider, as Keats knew:

> The dying tones that fill the air,
> And charm the ear of evening fair,
> From thee, Great God of Bards, receive their heavenly birth.
>
> (*Ode to Apollo*)

The many roles Keats adopts in the ode – he is successively creator, harvester, singer, and listener to his own song – permit him to exhibit the grand movements of profusion, decline, expansion of view, sadness, and equanimity which combine in the poem. Life, with its human seasons, and art, with its teeming, its gleaning, and its garners, seem coterminous and even indistinguishable here, in Keats's richest ode.

NOTE

1 Northrop Frye, 'The Drunken Boat: The Revolutionary Element in Romanticism,' in *Romanticism Reconsidered*, ed. Northrop Frye (New York, 1963), 15, 21.

**MILTON
WILSON**

# Bodies in Motion: Wordsworth's Myths of Natural Philosophy

At the end of a richly suggestive essay on the scientific context of English eighteenth-century literature, G.S. Rousseau concludes that out of the relations of various branches of natural philosophy a new, synthetic science of man gradually emerged during the period.

Willis's brain and nerve theory, Locke's psychology, Newton's optical ideas: all seemed isolated terrains until they converged early in the eighteenth century and produced a revolution in knowledge ... 'The science of man' – and as time progressed, from the 1750s to the 1780s, the scientific portion grew more significant than the humanistic – was ultimately the totally new product of a hitherto unprecedented coalescence ... Suddenly – so it must have seemed to Burke writing in the *Enquiry* – suddenly all the sciences were converging into a radically new synthesis, not 'expiring' and causing the return of Chaos and Night, as Pope prophesied in the *New Dunciad* of 1743 ... Now analyses of the mere prismatic hue of Newton's wave of light, or the tiny wonders of the insect world were not enough. A certain irrevocable act of integration had occurred.[1]

Professor Rousseau's thesis provides an apt introduction to the concerns of this essay, but with a few modifications. Whereas he emphasizes Newton's *Optics* almost to the exclusion of the *Principia*, I shall find the physics of bodies in motion almost as hard as physiology to separate from psychology. Whereas he sees literature and natural philosophy as sharing a newly convergent subject matter, I see them as sharing words which have been given newly convergent roles. Whereas he is dealing with authors who are in the vanguard of a radical 'act of integration' (self-consciously so, as he argues in his discussion of Burke), I am dealing with an author for whom the act has fully occurred and who takes it for granted. Because in Wordsworth the ingredients have become absorbed into 'constructive elements' and virtually nothing is left of the obtrusive subject matter, or 'descriptive elements,' of 'versified science' (to use Northrop Frye's distinction and phrasing),[2] we can easily fail to notice the presence of what has so successfully converged in the immediate scientific past, as his first readers are unlikely to have failed. I say 'his readers' partly in order to prevent from the start any assumption that this essay is a study of direct influence from particular natural philosophers to one particular poet. I am not concerned with what, if anything, Wordsworth took from Newton or Hartley or Burke, only with things in Wordsworth's language which someone from the reign of George the Third might be sensitive to, who was both fond of poetry and also aware of the language traditions accumulated and integrated in natural philosophy during the Restoration and eighteenth century.

In order to set in relief what is distinctive about Wordsworth's sort of convergence, consider an example of psychological physics from an author who shares with him an unselfconscious taking for granted of the revolution which Professor Rousseau has posited. The hero of one of Scott's novels (like many of his other heroes) is naturally inert, or at least slow to start moving, but once impelled to act, his movement progresses faster than the initial cause would seem to justify. It is easy to imagine suitable imagery from post-Renaissance physics as analogy to this psychological condition. The mind can be seen as a stone lodged at the top of an inclined plane. A force is needed to dislodge it, but that force's nature – the hand of a boy or of a giant – is irrelevant; once it has been dislodged the gravitational acceleration will take over as it progresses. The novelist's chosen language can underline the overlap in language between him and a natural philosopher: by including, say, 'put in motion,' 'forcible progression,' 'proportioned,' 'speed,' 'motive of impulse,' and perhaps (finally) 'put in motion' again. Here is the passage as actually written.

His was a mind unwillingly aroused from contemplative inactivity, but which, when once put into motion, acquired a spirit of forcible and violent progression. Neither was his eagerness proportioned in all cases to the motive of impulse, but might be compared to the speed of a stone, which rushes with like fury down the hill, whether it was first put in motion by the arm of a giant or the hand of a boy.[3]

This hero is Ravenswood in *The Bride of Lammermoor*. Without my tendentious introduction few modern readers of that passage would assume that they were reading an image from physics at all. In context, the give-away diction is so fully absorbed or taken for granted as to refuse to be disengaged, even for the sake of natural philosophy. Still, once disengaged, it is difficult not to notice, and it is easy for a reader who is already thinking of Wordsworth to remember that 'impulse from a vernal wood,' that mind 'by one soft impulse saved from vacancy,' or even perhaps that 'motion and spirit ... that impels.' But what is to some degree still analogy in Scott ('might be compared' stands out, despite all the language overlap) seems literal in Wordsworth. His bodies in motion are an integral part of his science of man. His myths of natural philosophy are inseparable from the facts of his psychology, so that there is no split between the language of poetry and the language of science. Each is what Wordsworth calls 'a dear and genuine inmate of the household of man.'

> No motion has she now, no force,
> She neither hears nor sees,
> Rolled round in earth's diurnal course,
> With rocks, and stones, and trees.

The reader sensitive to Wordsworthian diction will be poised between taking the physical first line and the physiological second either as separate negatives or (think of 'those hallowed and pure motions of the sense' in *The Prelude*, of the eye that 'moves' over the 'shining water' in Book I or 'binds' with 'unrelenting agency' in Book III) as negatives in apposition. And, after the shared diction of the first two lines, even 'diurnal' seems somehow to belong to the linguistic household of man.

As evidence for the nature of this convergence between physics, physiology, and psychology in Wordsworth, I shall examine four of his most famous passages: the boating, birdsnesting and skating scenes from Book I of *The Prelude* and the second paragraph of *Tintern Abbey*, culminating in the 'aspect more sublime' passage where 'we see into the life of things.' Each of the four derives much of its power from the distinctive way in which it conceives of body in motion, or, rather, in the case of *Tintern Abbey*, motion suspended. The physics of that 'motion and spirit' which both 'rolls' and 'impels' (and also 'interfuses') in the other 'sublime' passage in *Tintern Abbey* I must perforce omit. The passage would need an essay all to itself if the poetic and natural-philosophic context of its diction and syntax were to be properly explored.

According to emblematic tradition, rowing a boat can be seen as a pretty dubious activity. In Dekker's *News from Hell* Charon is depicted as 'looking before him, ... that's to say, behind him,' and the image of the waterman, whose eyes point one way while he moves in another, is a recurrent emblem in the Renaissance and after for the hypocrisy of courtiers, women, preachers, and others. Thomas Howell, in his *New Sayings* of 1663, writes: 'the Politician like a sculler, he looketh one way, and roweth another.' I take these two examples from Tilley's *Dictionary of Proverbs*, but one which Tilley misses and which has stuck in my mind since the first time I read *Pilgrim's Progress* is of course Mr. By-Ends, who got his estate by following the directional ambiguity of his great-grandfather the waterman. Professor Sheldon Zitner has also reminded me of the figure of June in the *Mutabilitie Cantos*, who by riding on a zodiacal crab behaves like a bargeman, with, in Spenser's compressed phrase, 'force contrary to face.'

The Wordsworthian passage is about how, as a boy, he stole and rowed a boat, and about the consequences of that theft and that rowing. So the moral dubiousness is built into the episode before the rowing even begins, and all that the face-vs-force situation does is to make the boy aware of it. The realignment of background and foreground incited by the rear-view moving perspective arouses in him a primitive sense of the taboo he has broken by untethering that shepherd's boat from within that cave beside that willow tree. Wordsworth gives us a terrifying optical illusion, a kind of Gothic physics. To secure his direction straight backwards, the boy, like a skilled oarsman, fixes his view 'Upon the summit of a craggy ridge, / The horizon's utmost boundary.' This fixed gaze before the moment of optical illusion reminds one of the fixing (the same word is used) before the precisely opposite situation of relative movement in *Strange Fits of Passion*, where Lucy's moon drops behind the cottage as the poet approaches.

> My horse moved on: hoof after hoof
> He raised, and never stopped:
> When down behind the cottage roof,
> At once, the bright moon dropped.

There (in Wordsworth's strange psychic fit) it is the inertia of the forward movement of the horse and its failure to stop which causes the planet to drop. Here (in the boating scene) the background rises from behind the foreground as the boy recedes with equally relentless thrusts of movement. The main difference is between the striking abruptness which climaxes the one and the terrifying persistence in the other. I quote the central lines of the latter.

>                                 ... lustily
> I dipped my oars into the silent lake,
> And, as I rose upon the stroke, my boat
> Went heaving through the water like a swan;
> When, from behind that craggy steep, till then
> The horizon's bound, a huge peak, black and huge,
> As if with voluntary power instinct
> Upreared its head. I struck and struck again,
> And growing still in stature the grim shape
> Towered up between me and the stars, and still,
> For so it seemed, with purpose of its own,
> And measured motion like a living thing,
> Strode after me.

The extraordinary physiological energy of this passage makes it impossible to separate the bodily pressure on the oars from the striding of the cliff. Stroke, stroke; stride, stride. The boy seems to be both fleeing that grim shape and pulling it after him. The shape's motion is measured (and how to measure motion was the triumph of Newtonian fluxions and Leibnizian calculus), but here it is measured because so are the stroke-by-stroke efforts of the living thing it pursues. My earlier phrase about Gothic physics may have seemed a bit strained. But for a revealing contrast recall that most Gothic stanza of *The Ancient Mariner*, about the fearful one who walks 'on a lonesome road,'

> And having once turned round walks on,
> And turns no more his head;
> Because he knows, a frightful fiend
> Doth close behind him tread.

And note how that fearful one turns and looks once and then never turns again. The boy Wordsworth, because he is rowing, is permanently turned; he flees and faces his pursuer at the same time, an unarmed Parthian with no way of escape. No way, that is, unless he makes a genuine, complete turn. The turning point of the passage, the reversal of both boat and theft ('I turned ... and stole ... back') replaces the troubling prize within its covert and beside its tree. But even here no escape is to be found. The boy can return the boat, but the rear-viewing rower, as such, can never see the grim shape shrink back into its lair. There remains in the boy's mind a kind of abstract or dehumanized set of moving forms, primary masses of extension drained of life and colour, and yet somehow moving within him.

> No familiar shapes
> Remained, no pleasant images of trees,
> Of sea or sky, no colours of green fields;
> But huge and mighty forms, that do not live
> As living men, moved slowly through the mind
> By day, and were a trouble to my dreams.

It can be said of few poets that the words which stick in their readers' sensibility as most fully charged with meaning from their poetic context are words like 'motion' and 'thing.' I think of Lucy: 'She seemed a thing.' One asks oneself: how does Wordsworth produce the energy which presses from within the superficially almost contentless double use of the word 'motion' in a climactic clause like 'and with what motion moved the clouds!'

> Oh! when I have hung
> Above the raven's nest, by knots of grass
> And half-inch fissures in the slippery rock
> But ill sustained, and almost (so it seemed)
> Suspended by the blast that blew amain,
> Shouldering the naked crag, oh, at that time
> While on the perilous ridge I hung alone,
> With what strange utterance did the loud dry wind
> Blow through my ear! the sky seemed not a sky
> Of earth – and with what motion moved the clouds!

Out of four forces – the pressure of his body, the resistance of the rock, the pull of gravity and the impact of the wind – Wordsworth produces that energy which he transfers to the motions of the sights and sounds of his environment. He also produces it partly out of the force-at-a-distance power of his memory, which gives the experience a coherence and meaning which could not have been part of it originally. Who could distinguish the strange tone and transverse motion of that 'loud dry wind' which blew 'through my ear' while expecting to be himself blown into space at any moment, or observe the way in which, from the body's lost earthly security, the sky itself ceases to be a 'sky of earth'? But most striking is how the fingers which seize those 'half-inch fissures in the slippery rock,' that shoulder which presses against 'the naked crag' and that body hanging from the ridge ('hung' is used twice, and I need hardly remind anyone of Wordsworth's self-admitted fascination with the word, as in that great synaesthetic phrase from *Tintern Abbey*, 'hung upon the beatings of the heart'), how such things are so fully assumed to be a part of the transformation of the motions of visual sensation as to make any definition of how the clouds are seen to move somehow unnecessary, and the key pair of words is allowed its own pure tautological impact: 'and with what motion moved the clouds!'

*The Prelude*'s skating scene exists in a rich variety of contexts. I shall concentrate, however, exclusively on its motion and hope that the result will at least seem an illuminating distortion. Skating, as motion with the bare minimum of earthly friction, in which, as Wordsworth puts it, we give 'our bodies to the wind,' allows us the sense of that 'everlasting motion' invoked twenty lines earlier. That the skater is competing with the motion of the heavenly bodies emerges most vividly when he tries 'to cut across the reflex of a star / That fled, and, flying still before me, gleamed / Upon the grassy plain.' (Note that in the 1850 version which I am quoting the impression that he is pursuing the star has been intensified, indeed, introduced, by gradual post-1805 revision, and the word 'image' – 'shadow' in 1798 – has been changed to the more technical-sounding 'reflex,' which Wordsworth never uses elsewhere.) But surrounding this more or less rectilinear pursuit which cuts across the icy surface of the field is a sequence of images which establishes a circumference and a pattern of spinning or concentric motion. First of all, long before the boy is depicted as leaving the throng of skaters and pursuing his star-reflex, their boisterous clamour is heard echoing with different sounds off one medium after another from near to far until the combined ringing and tinkling reaches and includes a melancholy diapason from distant hills, while, beyond that horizon, and on both sides of its circumference, 'the stars / Eastward were sparkling clear, and in the West / The orange sky of evening died away.' It's a beautiful transition from sounds and echoes to image and reflex (the pursuit of the star-reflex immediately follows), characteristic of Wordsworth, as anyone who thinks of the echo-reflection transition in *There Was a Boy* will agree, and I hope I'm not being too fanciful when I say that for this reader the last sounds that reach the boy at the centre of his echo-chamber seem to come from that last sparkling and fading horizon itself.

But it is in the concluding lines of the passage, and in the darkness, that the spinning motion takes over in earnest.

> ... and oftentimes,
> When we had given our bodies to the wind,
> And all the shadowy banks on either side
> Came sweeping through the dark, spinning still
> The rapid line of motion, then at once
> Have I, reclining back upon my heels,
> Stopped short; yet still the solitary cliffs
> Wheeled by me – even as if the earth had rolled
> With visible motion her diurnal round!

My comments on this pasage are confessedly insecure, because I really don't know whether my physical response to it is eccentric (shall I say) or shared. The echo passage has already established a series of sound-boards stretching out to the horizon, but now in the darkness there are only two that can be visually sensed, the banks spinning in the foreground and the cliffs wheeling in the background. As anyone who has stared out of a train window at telegraph poles knows, the optical illusion of relative motion makes the foreground move backwards while the background moves forward. You and the horizon are both travelling in the same direction. So the sequence of motions in these lines is: first the spinning of the banks back past the skater, then the abrupt halting of the skater's motion, and then the strange sense that the cliffs on the horizon are still wheeling forward with him, even if he himself has stopped moving. To this optical illusion is added the effect of vertigo, a 'dizziness ... true to our own experience'[4] as Professor Jackson points out in his recent book. Thus, the whole world spins around the head of a boy who somehow seems to be at its centre.

Professor Jackson (not in print) has also suggested to me that the difficult phrase 'spinning still / The rapid line of motion' might possibly refer to a rotating line of skaters engaged in the sort of game which is today called 'crack the whip.' Such rotation would certainly produce vertigo, particularly for the skater at the end of the line. But for me the syntax of the passage insists that it is the 'shadowy banks' which are (in the first place anyway) doing the 'sweeping' and 'spinning.' The cryptic phrase can best be read as a compressed version of 'spinning *along* the rapid line of motion.' And it is worth noting that in Erasmus Darwin's *Zoonomia* (1794), skating pure and simple serves as one illustration of the sort of rapid motion which incites vertigo. 'A second difficulty we have to encounter,' writes Darwin in the section 'On Vertigo,' 'is to distinguish our own real movements from the apparent movements of objects. [It takes practice] to ascribe the apparent motions of the ambient objects to ourselves ... Unusual movements of our bodies [can make us] vertiginous ..., as riding backwards in a coach, swinging on a rope, turning around swiftly on one leg, skating on the ice, and a thousand others.'[5]

One last point about skating. Wordsworth does not stop by turning at right angles to the line of motion, as any modern skater would (such a halt would break the forward motion of his spinning illusion). He stops face forward in the direction of impetus, 'reclining back upon my heels.' In so doing, he was being technically old-fashioned, but the method no doubt suited his practice as well as his poem. The late eighteenth century was a time of transition between the straight-on and the transverse technique of stopping. As Nigel Brown points out, in his historical study of skating, the first English treatise on the art was published by Robert Jones in 1772, and Jones insists on the virtues of the new transverse technique against its rival. Brown's description of that soon-to-be-superseded rival fits Wordsworth's action admirably. 'The skater leant well back on his heels bringing his entire weight upon the back of his skates, while the toes pointed into the air.'[6]

When we read Burke's *Enquiry into ... the Sublime and the Beautiful* (and its aesthetic fellows in the eighteenth century) for aid with Wordsworth's 'aspect more sublime' and 'sense sublime' of *Tintern Abbey*, we tend to skim some of the most germinal (physiological) parts, perhaps supposing them outmoded for us and therefore irrelevant to the Romantics. By so doing we are destroying the sort of convergence emphasized by Professor Rousseau. 'Beauty acts by relaxing the solids of the whole system,'[7] says Burke, and for him it is the contracting and tensing of muscles that gives the sublime its physiological reality. He spends a good deal of time insisting that in darkness the relaxed dilation of the pupil is accompanied by the muscular tension of the radial fibres of the iris, not by their relaxation. He has to make this point; otherwise how could darkness be a cause of the sublime? And without repeated, similar vibrations of the membranes of the ear, how (according to Burke) could we get that aural sense of a potentially unending series, without which our sublime conception of infinitely continual sound would be non-existent?[8] Samuel Monk, in *The Sublime*, has demonstrated that Burke's physiological emphasis leaves its mark on Webb, Gerard, and Kames, even when they seem theoretically opposed to it. He quotes as evidence a remarkable passage from Kames: 'A great object dilates the breast, and makes the spectator endeavour to enlarge his bulk ... In describing a great object [unreserved persons] naturally expand themselves by drawing in air with all their force. An elevated object ... makes the spectator stretch upward and stand on tiptoe.'[9] One immediately thinks of how, according to Charles Cowden Clarke, Keats 'hoisted himself up and looked burly and dominant' when he praised Spenser's phrase 'sea-shouldering whales' and how, according to Severn, he leaned his body forward when gazing at a field of barley in a high wind.[10] He also stood tiptoe at the beginning of a prospect poem. It is important not to see in the physiological sublime an inconsequential and detachable part of Burke's system. It's worse than leaving the fibres and vibrations out of Hartley.

But my immediate subject is the 'material sublime' in the second paragraph of *Tintern Abbey*, including some of what precedes its 'aspect more sublime' climax. Characteristically, the medical basis of the imagery is very eclectic – both archaic and up-to-date. The paragraph begins with

> sensations sweet,
> Felt in the blood, and felt along the heart,
> And passing even into my purer mind,
> With tranquil restoration.

The last two lines seem to be a relic of the Galenic-Arabian tradition of the various spirits carried by the blood, of which the most purified in substance – the animal spirits – mount to the fibres of the brain. The eighteenth century was an important period in the discovery of the components of the blood, but during much of it the old doctrine of the spirits managed temporarily to combine with new discoveries taken from under the microscope. We are still, at least partly, in the physiological world of Milton's Satan, trying to taint Eve's dream through 'th'animal spirits that from pure blood arise' or even of a sixteenth-century treatise like Woolston's on the reasonable soul, which tells us that the vital spirit 'ascendeth up into the brayne, by whose vertue it is made more cleare.'[11] Hence, in part, the 'purer mind' and 'tranquil restoration.' Like his 'old man travelling,' but in a different way, Wordsworth achieves 'animal tranquillity' and ultimately 'moves with thought.'

Less archaic and certainly more striking are the sensations of the previous two lines: 'Felt in the blood and felt along the heart.' For most readers today that pair of phrases is an impressive and even witty example of what one might call the prepositional concrete: from 'in' to 'along,' from containment to extension, with just a trace of reversed expectations, since we recall unconsciously that it is depth or inwardness that belongs to conventional heart imagery (Sidney's muse advised looking in your heart, not along it) and movement or alongness that belongs to the blood. The unusual immediacy of 'along the heart' comes from the reader's sense of surface, length, and tangibility, from his sense of renewed physical fact. The renewal has its eighteenth-century context. We have noticed in Burke his desire to associate the sublime with muscular contraction and the beautiful with muscular relaxation. In Harvey's seventeenth-century discussion of the systolic-diastolic alternation in the beating of the heart, he mistakenly supposed (as commentators regularly note) that the contracted heart was longer and the relaxed one shorter. 'Every fibre that is circularly disposed,' he explains, 'tends to become straight when it contracts.'[12] Despite their respect for Harvey, his eighteenth-century successors had to correct this notable error. Haller, for example, in his *First Lines of Physiology*, denies systolic elongation and asserts diastolic elongation.[13] The organ stretches as it relaxes. One might almost say that it is in compensation for Harvey's error that the works of eighteenth-century physiologists are so full of attempts to define the processes by which the length of the heart is changed during the muscular impulses of its beat. For an arbitrarily chosen pair of examples, I quote from Cullen's late-eighteenth-century translation of Haller how 'motions of different kinds appear to be propagated along its surface'[14] or refer you to the elaborate discussion of elongation and different kinds of elongators in John Hunter's *Treatise on the Blood*[15] at the very end of the century. Anatomists were fond of feeling directly the very process of the heartbeat in dissected creatures by running their finger along the surface of the organ itself or its arteries as they dilated or shrank.[16] One does not have to read much in the eighteenth-century *Philosophical Transactions of the Royal Society* to gain a lively sense of the heart as physical object, or, for that matter, in Coleridge's *Notebooks*: 'that one Feeling at my Heart / felt like a faint Pain / a spot which it seems I could lay my finger on.' 'My poor Heart (& truly this seems to be something more than a phrase or metaphor with me, so local is the feeling, so apparently co-present in the same [...] identical place with the gnawing, & palpitation – strange sense of Stopping.'[17] 'And yet I had a terror,' writes Keats when he sees the veiled face of Moneta, 'that made my heart too small to hold its blood.'

Wordsworth's very different 'strange sense of Stopping' comes at the end of his paragraph, which leaves behind those 'sensations sweet, felt along ... the heart,' and culminates in an 'aspect more sublime' whereby we 'see into the life of things.' Here the bodily self-consciousness consists of a process through which the feeling of physical and meaningless weight seems gradually to be lifted. That process of growing weightlessness reaches its climax when

> the breath of this corporeal frame
> And even the motion of our human blood
> Almost suspended, we are laid asleep
> In body and become a living soul.

There is a fine passage in David Perkins' *Wordsworth and the Poetry of Sincerity* in which he analyses the postponed completions of this entire two-sentence paragraph, its stretched predicates, its accumulation of appositions and parentheses, its whole technique of static syntax.[18] Indeed, one feels persuaded to try to read the last fifteen lines with held breath and suspended animation akin to the state of body and soul being presented to us. Burke himself relates the passion caused by the sublime to astonishment; 'and astonishment,' he tells us, 'is that state of the soul, in which all its motions are suspended.'[19] Maybe, as Professor Durrant seems to suggest, Wordsworth's eye was still on the object when he gazed at the arterial stasis of London from Westminster Bridge and responded: 'all that mighty heart is lying still!'[20] In *Tintern Abbey* Wordsworth's sublime state exists balanced between the sort of suspension of natural process traditionally ascribed to the mystical experience (although his weightlessness is not exactly levitation) and the sort of physiological suspension observed by medical scientists. Dr. Hunter concludes his discussion of one case of stoppage and resumption of pulmonary and cardiac motion: 'this shows that breathing depends on the actions of the heart; and it also shows that under certain circumstances the actions of both may be suspended, and yet death not be the consequence.'[21] The period of Wordsworth's youth is of course the period in which the work of Priestley and Lavoisier aroused a new understanding of the relations between respiration and the circulation of the blood. Wordsworth's account of this 'aspect more sublime' causes the reader to be intensely aware of the weights and motions within the body dissolving and slowing down into a waking sleep in which one feels the body's presence and its absence at the same time. The living soul in its new state of power and joy sees into 'the *life* of things.' Or should it be 'the life of *things*'? I never know quite how to read that phrase. As we reach the conclusion of the paragraph we experience the material sublime as it loses its materiality. The phrase 'corporeal frame' has strayed out of an anatomical textbook and 'become a living soul.'

NOTES

1 G.S. Rousseau, 'Science,' in *The Eighteenth Century*, ed. Pat Rogers (London, 1978), 200-1.

2 Northrop Frye, 'New Directions from Old,' *Fables of Identity* (New York, 1963), 56.

3 Sir Walter Scott, *Waverley Novels*, xiv (London, 1830), 8.

4 J.R. deJ. Jackson, *Poetry of the Romantic Period* (London, 1980), 121.

5 Erasmus Darwin, *Zoonomia*, 1 (London, 1794), 229-30.

6 Nigel Brown, *Ice-Skating: A History* (London, 1959), 44.

7 Edmund Burke, *A Philosophical Enquiry into the Origin of Our Ideas of the Sublime and the Beautiful*, ed. J.T. Boulton (London, 1958), 149-50.

8 Ibid., 145-6, 140.

9 Samuel Monk, *The Sublime* (Ann Arbor, 1960), 114.

10 See W.J. Bate, *John Keats* (Cambridge, Mass., 1963), 33, 195.

11 James Winny, ed., *The Frame of Order* (London, 1957), 84.

12 William Harvey, *Works*, trans. Robert Willis (rpt. New York, 1965), 23.

13 Albrecht von Haller, *First Lines of Physiology*, trans. William Cullen (rpt. New York, 1966), 1, 60.

14 Ibid., 1, 59.

15 John Hunter, *A Treatise on the Blood* (London, 1794), 106-9.

16 Ibid., 120.

17 Samuel Taylor Coleridge, *Notebooks*, ii, ed. Kathleen Coburn (New York, 1961), Notes 2036, 2046.

18 David Perkins, *Wordsworth and the Poetry of Sincerity* (Cambridge, Mass., 1964), 208-9.

19 Burke, 57.

20 Geoffrey Durrant, *William Wordsworth* (Cambridge, 1969), 155.

21 Hunter, 150.

**GEOFFREY H. HARTMAN**

# Reading Aright: Keats's 'Ode to Psyche'

> As once, if not with light regard
> I read aright that ancient Bard ...
> Collins, *Ode on the Poetical Character*

I

Pascal's dictum is well known, that 'The heart has reasons which the reason does not know of.' Since Richard Hurd's *Letters on Chivalry and Romance* (1762) we have become aware of a trend in English poetry that seems to have its major epoch from Spenser to Keats, and which Ezra Pound, referring to its medieval and non-English exemplars, summed up as the 'Spirit of Romance.' It has been the task of Northrop Frye to disclose that Romance has reasons which the reason does not know of. Rationalizing Romance is a tricky business, however, like reasoning upon ritual: Romance rejects a knowledge which is only sorrow, or – like Keats's Grecian Urn – the ravishments of truth. Keats's imaginative sallies seek to penetrate, empathically, the scenes depicted on the urn, but the scenes, though bacchic, remain inanimate ('Cold Pastoral!'), betraying only the heat of the inquirer, his *libido sciendi*. It is not difficult to pass from the special case of Romance to Keats's 'poesy': a form, that is, close to 'posy' because it is made up of flowery, pictorial, emblematic words. Such lyrics often naturalize their 'poetic diction' or 'art-diction,' yet we wonder if ordinary language can translate what is being said.

If it cannot, if every reading of such poetry is a weak translation or entropic paraphrase, then there is danger of losing poetic language altogether. Keats, it is known, sought a natural language with a force equivalent to that of art-diction while Blake inflated the poetic clichés of his time to recover their visionary potential. Both poets suggest that Romance is the field in which two orders of language, the vernacular and art-diction (or other forms of hieratic speech) competed; and that there is a continuity between the apparently technical or doctrinaire issue of diction and the larger issue of the justification of Romance in terms of its perplexing design, its laxity of unity, its wonder-wanderings.

Frye attempts a contemporary justification of Romance. (In the intellectual milieu of a Georg Lukács, *Fearful Symmetry* might have been subtitled 'The Theory of Romance.') Starting from Blake, he denies that the obliquity of romance promotes obliquity of meaning. The confusing allegorical mass of Blake's epics is reduced to a grammar of archetypes, as Frye neglects the question of diction and cuts through the unity of the separate poems to emphasize the 'total form' of Blake. There is an argument in Blake, there is exact meaning, but only if his poems are seen as a total form; and precisely this total form is the real burden.

For it wakens in the sophisticated reader a new receptiveness for Romance. The very method of critical decoding has visionary implications. It is as if Frye's were a Quest Criticism, and descended from modern Quest Romances that refuse to purchase knowledge by loss of vision. What is desired is not so much the grail of meaning as the reader's capacity to engage questionable forms, and so to rekindle his spirit toward them.

Like Blake himself in his Epics and Canvases, Frye strives for Public Works. The aim is monumental. Yet Frye continues to write criticism, which is a highly accommodated form of prose. A contradiction remains between his wit and urbanity and the giant humours or characters of a poetry like Blake's – which tries, in fact, to reject accommodation. (Blake's disparaging remarks on clarity and on 'fitting' are well known.) This contradiction is a fruitful one: not only does it remind us of how daring Frye's project is but it puts the problem back where that belongs: in *language*, in the resistance of complex words to a totality ('total form') which always tends to be over-reconciling.

To reinforce the public reception of Romance, of its 'visionary forms dramatic,' we should therefore turn back to language. This sets up a paradox I would like to explore: not to lose Romance means to lose ourselves in the language of Romance. That is the road not taken by Frye.

II

As soon as we take this road, we understand why Frye passed it by. For now the question of obliquity moves to the centre again: the obloquy of obliquity in an era (still ours) which regards indirectness as privatistic and self-indulgent. Because of these charges, readers interested in the slippery yet productive nature of language (like a Blakean Giant Form it seems to engender an endless series of symmetrical differences) must find a theory. To have a theory, such as semiotics, would join them once more to a corporate enterprise. It would rebuff the suspicion that they are fanciful interpreters, mere virtuosi; and it substitutes for the lack of immediate public relevance. Instead of turning to theory I wish to stay within the realm of impression, taking each word or phrase as it passes. I will use concepts, of course, often linked to this or that theory; but they remain unstable, deprived of 'total form.'

To begin with Collins. It is easy to lose oneself in his diction. Led by a natural slippage of the ear (Keats's 'soft-conched ear') from 'As once,' the first words of his *Ode on the Poetical Character*, to 'One only one' (line 5), and finally to the 'One alone' of the closing lines, we ponder, half-rejecting, the possibility that this 'One' (index of Collins's despair) may contain the echo of its homonym, 'Won.' The same ear cannot but select the word 'read,' appreciating its twofold meaning, already in Spenser, of 'unriddling' as well as 'reading.' The slight archaism 'aright' also points back to Spenser who had used the phrase several times in *The Faerie Queene*; while the combination of soundshapes formed by *regard, read, aright, gird* evoke a girdle-riddle of their own, which erects the ear perhaps, but does not right it.

These seem to be the semantics of the 'evening ear' (*OPC*, 64).[1] It is an ear that fades into a purely textual gauze, of 'brede ethereal wove' (*OE*, 7). The flare of visionary or primary symbols – as archetypal or absurd as Fancy's girdle – remains only in this nuanced, vestigial form. We are far from the sun of sound. Air is hushed, and to its enfeebling of the ear (how strong a feebleness, however!) is added a doubtful seeing like that of the 'weak-eyed Bat' (*OE*, 9). Perhaps the central, though partly hidden, figure is that of 'stealing': the *Ode on the Poetical Character* uses with stylized trepidation the story of Florimel's girdle, misappropriating or even stealing it in quest of a lost poetic if not Promethean fire (*OPC*, 22); while in the *Ode to Evening* the poet's uncertain numbers 'steal' along the dusky vale (*OE*, 12). This stealing is now without an object except inspiration – or composition – itself, for there is no beloved who motivates the ode's elaborate variation on Classical addresses to the evening star. Here the shadow is the prey. Perhaps the simplifying passion for silhouettes and the interest in clear outlines (Flaxman) which emerges later in the century is in reaction to the darkly inwrought – yet still classicist – nature of verses such as these.

III

The invocation of the *Ode to Evening* delays its own closure for some twenty lines. It begins, moreover, with an apologetic 'if' and continues with a muted or stuttering O. 'If aught of oaten stop, or pastoral song, / May hope ...' The syntax of Keats's *Ode to Psyche* is straightforward in comparison, and the invocation immediate. 'O Goddess! hear these tuneless numbers, wrung ...' The theme of hearing, of getting to the goddess through her 'modest ear' (*OE*, 2) is stated outright.

This directness is relative, however. The meaning of Keats's lines, like those of Collins's, is shadowy. Who is the goddess called Psyche? Is she, though specifically named, really different from 'buds, and bells, and stars without a name' (*OP*, 61)? What does it mean to *hear* 'tuneless numbers'? Goddess, Psyche, bowers, flowers, gardener Fancy, schmancy language ... what is going on? what is being represented?

One can claim, of course, that it is the conventions or *topoi* that matter, and they are clear enough; or that what matters is the general impression left by these tendrils of words. Psyche, for example, can be looked up in Lemprière, Keats's mythological dictionary. 'Tuneless numbers' can be construed as the modesty *topos* of a Collinsian poet-votary, hardly fit to touch the hem of the inspiring vision. Please enjoy these flowers of language: they are not obscure to the initiate, the careful student of this mode. They do not distract the devotee of artifice from what is subtly represented.

From one point of view, then, no problem of meaning exists. All right readers see that Keats's poem brings love insidiously close to what the *Nightingale Ode* calls easeful death: 'I have been half in love with easeful Death / Call'd him soft names in many a mused rhyme' (*ON*, 53). Our sole problem is one of judgment: shall we enjoy these perfumed words, these soft names, or should we purge them as euphemisms – pierce through the flowery poesy till we come to a 'desolation of reality'? Keats himself, from the beginning of his career, tried to go beyond the pleasure principle in language, to leave the realm of 'Flora and old Pan,' or of 'Romance.' Is his 'fine spell of words' an antidote to 'the sable chain

/ And dumb enchantment' (*Fall of Hyperion* 1.9-11) or does it simply affirm the liaison between love poem and death poem?

The convergence of love and death has always perplexed the intellect: we describe rather than understand it. But it has not always seduced the intellect, as in this quasi-classical ode full of art-diction and belated myth-making. While the ode's formulas are direct, and derive from an ecstatic or theophanic tradition, the theme remains oblique, retarded by the ode's very richness of diction. Matthew Arnold considered surfeit of verbal detail as Keats's sweet vice, weakening his poetry's structural design. Yet this kind of conspicuously digressive form has been the hallmark of Romance.

IV

Can we find its reason? A close-up of the ode's first lines is almost more than enough. 'Tuneless numbers,' though a modesty *topos*, can also be a reminder that lyric poetry is no longer chanted to an accompanying instrument. This introduces a sense of loss, however slight, as Keats creates the purely formal paradox of *hearing* something close to silence. 'Tuneless numbers' may then recall the 'ditties of no tone' of the Grecian Urn. In this context, however, 'tuneless' is not a negative at all but evokes a quieter, more natural poetry than Wordsworth's. Despite Wordsworth's claim to simplicity or naturalness his lyrics continue to be, according to Keats, marred by 'palpable design' or 'ugly clubs' of themes. 'Man should not dispute or assert but whisper results to his neighbour,' Keats wrote to his friend Reynolds in lines that anticipate Thoreau. The ideal, then, is that of 'wide quietness' (*OP*, 58), and it comes remarkably close to the neo-Hellenic sensibility of Winckelmann: grandeur in repose, 'might half slumb'ring on its own right arm' (*Sleep and Poetry*, 237). The ideal poetry remains, like the Grecian Urn, a 'bride of quietness.'

The opening of another ode, 'No, no, go not to Lethe' (*Ode on Melancholy*) shows explicitly a 'lethal' drift that, being resisted, fills out the poem. The drift toward quietness in the *Ode to Psyche* also brings with it a fulsome feature: Keats's art-diction in the form of a 'language of flowers.' Where we now read 'O brightest' (*OP*, 36) there was originally 'O bloomiest.' Psyche's brightness is associated more with Flora than with Apollo: it is not that of Collins's 'Youth of Morn' but of Spenser's Clarion (*Muiopotmos*), an aurelian flower-fly that merges with her bowery realm. A sense of violating that bower is present, of course – if

Psyche's offence is not alluded to, the poet is nevertheless anxious not to offend the goddess's 'ear' or 'secret' – but it is far less acute than in Collins. The poet's aspiration toward a liberty or enlightenment like that of the gods is retarded by this language of flowers, the equivalent to Collins's 'honeyed paste of poetic diction ... the candied coat of the auricula' (Hazlitt). Though Keats disenchants his language of flowers by giving it the hyperbolic force of a soft boomerang, one must first acknowledge its euphemistic quality.

That euphemistic strain is so effective that it would be impossible to find a Mrs Barbault – who denounced Collins's *Ode on the Poetical Character* as 'neither decent nor luminous' – objecting to what allegory there is. Think how gleefully we ridicule Kenneth Burke when he joyces the 'Beauty is Truth, Truth Beauty' equation in the *Ode on the Grecian Urn* as 'Body is Turd, Turd Body.' Keats's ravishment cannot be ravished this way: 'twould make him a sod to his high requiem. Yet a sense of requiem, of covering up (in flowers, in leaves) a feverish imagination, this surely remains; and Burke's ugly club is only a symptom of analytic impotence.

Deconstruction as an analytic mode means disturbing the poem according to its own fault-lines. It examines how the language of flowers – the euphemistic phrasing – is betrayed by 'flowers of language': figures of speech that insist on their figural status, or the fact that they are rich nothings. This may be called reading against the grain; but we actually remain in the grain of the poem. Yet now the negative appears once more as a substantial and barely containable factor. When to the morphemic negative of 'less' in 'tuneless' we add the pseudo-morphemic 'numb' in 'numbers' – recalling also the closeness of 'numbness' in the first line of the *Nightingale Ode* ('My heart aches, and a drowsy numbness pains / My sense') – then Keats's quietistic lyricism declines toward a deadly slumber evoking the opiates he repeatedly rejects. The chime of 'numbers' and 'numbness' revives a sleeping negativity associating poetry with emptiness rather than fullness – and in the *Nightingale Ode* with a self-emptying brought on by passion.

More exactly, with a state described countless times in the older Petrarchan mode of paradox when the lover is so drunk with the haunting absence (that is, imagined presence) of the beloved that he feels he has no self within him but only in her. He is ecstatic, too happy in the other's happiness; not envious but overidentifying. Keats's poetry turns around this Other, but who is she, even when explicitly named?

> But who wast thou, O happy, happy, dove?
> His Psyche true! (*OP*, 23)

Dove, nightingale, winged boy: glimpsed here yet in the *Nightingale Ode* only heard, and in the *Ode on a Grecian Urn* not even heard, though the subject of wild surmises – Keats's perspective recedes into 'silence and slow time' as he attempts a positive identification.

V

I have not managed to read aright even the first verse of our ode; and I now stumble over its last word, 'wrung.' Together with 'enforcement' (in the last line) it heightens the *topos* of hesitation that suggests a trespass or a necessary ravishing. Is 'O Goddess! hear' a petition, or is it a manly command? Why does the poet want Psyche to hear her own story: why that closed circuit? One poetic impulse moves toward rousing the goddess, a second toward not rousing her. 'Wrung': the very word is like a bell, but does it signal waking or sleeping, revelation (what must be seen) or requiem (what must be laid to rest)?

The line introduced by 'wrung' is indeed peculiar. 'By sweet enforcement and remembrance dear' places a noun adjective phrase against an adjective noun phrase to create a chiasmus. Flanked by the semantic overlap of 'sweet' and 'dear' this chiasmus reduces the gap in meaning between 'enforcement' and 'remembrance.' They are pushed together not only as words but as meanings. Yet they are far from agreeing with each other – unless both refer to the same thing: poetry. Are they a hendyadis, one idea expressed through two words joined by a conjunction? Hear my poetry, Keats may be saying, a poetry that is forced from me through the experience of poetry. By understanding his verses in this way we have not righted or solved anything. On the contrary, we have somewhat increased the scandal of the poem's redundancy, or its oblique and mannered mode.

It is not explicitly stated, but the numbers must be 'wrung' from the poet himself. To remember what he has seen (especially since it was dreamlike), or to speak about it, needs a force applied to a memory that retains its inwardness. The poet qualifies this force as 'sweet' and is at pains to make it agree with what is remembered, as if that too contained something forceful. Yet his euphemistic phrasing veils the identity of what makes the memory forceful. We can best infer it from the experience described in the first stanza or the Psyche-myth as a whole, and say that they impress Keats so strongly that he must tell what he knows. But a hint remains that memory itself is the 'dear' or 'dire' force. Memory makes both the goddess and the poet hearers: they are reminded of something ravishing, and their response is not unambiguous. There is a resistance involved.

Is Keats being forced by memory into 'remembrance'? And can that memory be particularized, or must we take the Psyche story as its true content? The more we lose ourselves in the words, or the more we ponder their euphemistic and figurative mode, the less the narrative or thematic content of this poem moves us boldly on. This retardation is characteristic of lyric romances that will not give up myth or story-line. The myth remains forceful, a power; but the myth comes mediated by its own literary aura. The story of Psyche is particularly interesting as a model instance because it is so belated that something in it remains unfulfilled; and Keats, while compelled into remembrance, is also tempted toward a self-forcing: toward a poetry more purely his own, neither derivative nor transumptive, but as 'natural' as 'branched thoughts' (*OP*, 52).

There is an impasse, then. To adapt Keats on Wordsworth: 'We are in a Mist – *We* are now in that state – We feel the "burden of the Mystery".' The readerly dimension is so enriched that we cannot 'read aright' or emerge from that 'mist-Mystery.' It will come as no surprise that on the writerly level a similar impasse is discernible, since the pressure of reading aright affects the poet as well.

For 'remembrance dear' is quite literally the remembrance of a prior text. It echoes, in a softer tone, the opening of Milton's *Lycidas*. Milton says that 'Bitter constraint, and sad occasion dear' prompt his poem. That verse is harsh rather than comforting. But the mnemonic force it exerted on Keats, as well as the counterforce in him – by which he transforms it into a verse of his own – these are, wishfully or not, represented as 'sweet' and 'dear.' Milton, moreover, had himself initiated the topic of force in those opening lines by talking of his poem as an untimely enterprise. His 'forc'd fingers rude' pluck something still unseasoned, not fully mature. He doubts his calling even as he tests it – so Psyche too seems unable to tolerate the unknown, and Keats is unsure of having glimpsed his goddess. The quest for identity, or leaving the state of 'negative capability,' implies a prematurely forceful and perhaps disastrous issue.

Yet the euphemistic strain is so deep in Keats that he evokes not the force that leads to disaster – Psyche's or the Poet's overreaching wish for clarity and identity – but a *beautiful* truth, in the form of a persuasive consonance between hand and ear, poetic speech and imaginative hearing. 'Wrung / By sweet enforcement and remembrance dear' shadows forth Milton's hand as it traces a prior and classic moment of stylized trepidation. This hand, now Keats's own, does not wish to be as *forcible* as Milton's, only – by finer repetition – as *great*. The pastoral element should remain, despite Keats's empathic (sexual or writerly) impetuousness. The quality of the verse is so tender, so involuted, that it already binds up 'with garlands of her own' (*On the Sonnet*, 14) the very consciousness it would rouse.[2]

VI

So equivocal is this double movement, which tends at once toward a hardcore knowledge and a dreamy consciousness, toward truth and beauty, toward a traumatic caesura and its rhythmic internalization (cf. *To Autumn*'s 'Sometimes whoever seeks abroad may find / Thee ...'), that when disclosure comes it is in the form of a questioning surmise: 'Surely I dreamt today, or did I see / The winged Psyche with awaken'd eyes?' As a statement, moreover, the surmise is opaque from the point of view of syntax. That the seeing is unsure, all can agree: yet the query not generally put is to whom the 'awaken'd eyes' belong.

They are the poet's surprised eyes, yet in the myth they were Psyche's eyes. She discovers Cupid's identity by looking at him with the torch perhaps alluded to in the ode's penultimate lines – and so loses him. And, hasn't she just made love, and is awakened in that sense? Or, is the poet, who comes upon this primal scene, awakened by being granted a visionary truth? Or, did he see her in dream, and was woken by that seeing, as when the content of a dream startles you awake and you see – a blank, or the very thing you dreamed about? 'The Imagination is like Adam's dream,' wrote Keats, thinking of Adam's first encounter of Eve in *Paradise Lost*, 'He awoke and found it truth.' Dream and truth converge, they cross a temporal gap – as they precisely do not in *La Belle Dame sans Merci* where the unfortunate lover wakes up in a desolate landscape, 'And no birds sing.'

Here Psyche and Cupid are the birds: while the textured music of Keats's branched thoughts, the 'fane' ('feign') of his poem, is their internalized song. Our ears are no more startled into guilty knowledge than our eyes, which remain fragrant rather than flagrant in this milieu

(*OP*, 10-15). Such lyricism wins for us a region of 'wide quietness,' of thoughts removed from ocularity, from the look! see!, the I spy or I psy (sigh) kind of verse. The romance mode of poetry is neither a confessional nor an overconscious 'egotistical sublime.'

But am I, having said this, reading or allegorizing? My remarks suggest that *To Psyche* is an Ode to the Nymphal State, or to some magical post-nymphal recreation of it. 'Organized Innocence' Blake would have called this state, and assigned Psyche's bower to Beulah, the lower Paradise of harmony, where all disagreeables evaporate. Mostly Mozart, and no lovers' quarrels. Yet Paradise proper, according to Blake, has only interludes of peace, being engaged in a Mental Strife that forges, like a blacksmith, fiery not flowery conception. This Blakean insight is not entirely out of place. Despite the intricacy of the ode's euphemistic structuring, something naively ecstatic remains that allows us to caricature it. There is an archaic skeleton of oriental fantasies, as in Collins: and that is not wholly absorbed by the evening ear or the textured diction. This skeleton, moreover, is a static one, unlike Blake's metamorphoses, his pop-art inflation of the personification allegory of his time, his reanimation, ludic or ludicrous, of stellar junk. In Keats the apostrophic sequence of O, O, O, Yes, intimates an erotic fantasy reinforced by such images as 'delicious moan / Upon the midnight hours' and 'Heat of pale-mouthed prophet dreaming.' (What heat did you say?) Byron, too worldly-wise, accused Keats of 'viciously soliciting his own imagination.'

Also true is that in statues of Psyche, like those by Canova, the butterfly emblem which mythographers claim denotes the immortal soul is shaped like a delicate physical organ freely exhibited. It compensates Psyche for not having what Cupid has. Cupid is the 'winged boy'; the butterfly too is winged, but in such a way that a convergence of male and female is adumbrated by the merging, in one shape, of clitoris and penis, the labia appearing as embryonic wings, 'lucent fans.'

May it not be, then, that just as Keats does not confine the 'awaken'd eyes' to Psyche or Poet, so his poetry also remains sexually indeterminate or double: a daring, inventive mimicry of feminine feelings, of what Erich Neumann, the Jungian analyst, calls the quest for the feminine, in his commentary on Apuleius's Psyche story? Keats begins with the happy ending, with Psyche and Cupid reunited; and the labours or trials Psyche had to undergo seem now to be the poet's. It is he who has to build her temple, institute her worship. Psyche's labours are, as it

were, elided into the diction of this very poem. In building Psyche's fane
Keats labours to produce a new kind of poetry: an art-diction that is not
only Miltonic-male but also feminine – as if Milton had a sister, or one of
his daughters had reindited him. Though Keats's idiom is far from
natural it is in search of naturalization, and its special obliquity is
characterized by its unembarrassed use of the language of flowers. This,
then, is what Keats undertakes on behalf of Psyche. It is the temple he
builds, for our psyche too:

> Yes, I will be thy priest, and build a fane
>   In some untrodden region of my mind,
> Where branchèd thoughts, new grown with pleasant pain,
>   Instead of pines shall murmur in the wind:
> Far, far around shall those dark-clustered trees
>   Fledge the wild-ridged mountains steep by steep;
>                   ...
> And in the midst of this wide quietness
>   A rosy sanctuary will I dress.               (*OP*, 50-59)

VII

The *Ode to Psyche* is a revision of the Poetical Character. The latter is no
longer imaged as a Youth of Morn, however richly mothered and
endowed with a halo of hair. The recuperation of the feminine is more
thorough and more sensuous. It produces a remarkably bisexual poetic
diction, which affected many nineteenth-century readers as too feminine. It also produces a remarkable idea, that of 'Negative Capability,'
closely joined to Keats's revised conception of the Poetical Character. In
one definition he uses enough sexual innuendo to show what is on his
mind. Thinking of Shakespeare and Wordsworth, and finding it hard to
bring the two together, he writes: 'the poetical character itself, (I mean
that sort of which, if I am anything, I am a Member; that sort
distinguished from the wordsworthian or egotistical sublime; which is a
thing per se and stands alone) ... is not itself – it has no self – it is
everything and nothing – It has no character ...'

Once we see Keats's ode as a redress of the feminine in the Poetical
Character – as the very thing ('vale' and 'veil') Collins sensitively
described but could not value in itself – could value only, despite his
exaltation of Fancy, as the afterglow of an era of literary creativity –
once we understand the *Psyche Ode* in this context, then it becomes a

language-event that projects its own historical importance. Psyche is post-Augustan, as Lemprière said; but for Keats this meant more than that her myth came into prominence after the reign of Augustus. His psyche-language modifies the Augustan era in *England*. Psyche does not institute a new mystery (Keats, like Wordsworth, always wished to 'ease the Burden of the Mystery' by a 'widening Speculation'); rather, Psyche disqualifies naive concepts of progress or Enlightenment. No wonder we lose ourselves in the diction and cannot get past the opening lines. The manner of proceeding in this Romance lyric is devious, not obvious.

What are these naive myths of progress or Enlightenment? They have to do with the 'grand march of intellect' or similar beliefs that there was a providential forward movement in history, that the Reformation, for example, produced real benefits and dispelled real sufferings. Keats remained haunted by 'something real' not only in the world generally but also in history; and all his poems attempt a career-leap forward, out of a less real, enchanted or superstitious, stage. The idea of enlightenment, of seeing like a god sees, of Apollonian vision, always hovers before him. 'Though no great minist'ring reason,' he writes in *Sleep and Poetry,*

> sorts
> Out the dark mysteries of human souls
> To clear conceiving: yet there ever rolls
> A vast idea before me, and I glean
> Therefrom my liberty; thence too I've seen
> The end and aim of Poesy.

Yet even as he yields to these projects for the sun, his striving for *positive* knowledge is displaced by *negative* capability: the 'libido sciendi' or truth-drive, honoured by him with the name of Philosophy, is subdued to a more empathic and chameleon imagination, unconcerned with the maleness or the solidarity of the ego. Relaxed moments of visionariness ensue – I have called them moments of surmise – that lead to such darkling passage as 'I cannot see what flowers are at my feet' (*ON*, 41). This non-seeing is always a fragrant-eyed, imaginative fullness and the obverse of the enlightenment depicted in Genesis 3, verses 4-5: 'But the serpent said to the woman, You will not die. For God knows that when you eat of it your eyes will be opened, and you will be like God, knowing good and evil. So ... she took of its fruit and ate ... and he ate. Then the eyes of both were opened, and they knew they were naked.'

The *Hyperions* too are projects for the sun. Yet the sun never rises: something holds Hyperion back and prevents Apollo, his metamorphic double, from moulting into the 'rich-haired Youth of Morn.' In the final lines of *To Psyche* there is the same drag against progress of a possibly traumatic kind. As at the ode's beginning, a sense of threshold replaces that of trespass, and time remains arrested between *one minute past* (that glimpse of Psyche and Cupid) and *one minute before* ('A bright torch, and a casement ope at night, / To let the warm Love in'). Love is about to cross that threshold, yet there is no leap of the imagination ('Already with thee!'), no 'Let the warm Love in.' Only, 'To let the warm Love in.' Instead of an imperative we have an infinitive, a stationing moment as at the end of the *Nightingale Ode*'s seventh stanza: 'Charm'd magic casements opening on the foam / Of perilous seas, in faery lands forlorn.' In *To Psyche* we do not even reach the perilous event, which the received myth gives as Psyche's lust of the eyes, her use of that torch to discover the identity of her lover. A next, fatal step is omitted, as if lyric were opposed to narrative, which can lead too far, which goes *beyond*, to spoil everything.

Despite the bright torch, then, we remain suspended, we hang there, in that 'bright ... night.' The next step might bring the knowledge which is sorrow: open eyes, separation, exile. Thus Keats, in this counter-enlightenment poem, extends the liminal movement and deepens our sense of negative capability. When we appose the *Nightingale Ode*, we see that the latter too almost ends at casement or threshold. Yet it then comes upon a word, 'forlorn,' that designates the very state Psyche must indeed traverse. But it is only a *word* that is found, and a word that depicts what is *not* represented in the *Psyche Ode* (except through the anticipatory and richly converted negatives of stanza 3). The echoing turn of 'Forlorn! the very word is like a bell / To toll me back from thee to my sole self!' (rather than soul-self or Psyche?) reinserts the elided motif of death, time and 'thing per se.' Feigned happiness becomes faint once more.

VIII

'The faint Olympians' (*OP*, 42). The beginning of *Hyperion: A Fragment* gives their picture. Psyche is not there; she is yet to be conceived, perhaps; and the poet who admits 'I see, and sing, by my own eyes inspired' (*OP*, 43), merging psyche with Psyche, is also not there. The vision seems to stand in itself, or on someone emptied into it. These are numb-ers, however eloquent. We are denied a more than imputed sense of their matrix, even as the poem anticipates a coming generation and breaks off with a scene that depicts a great birth.

This absence of a matrix, together with the climactic suggestion of Apollo's labour pains, should not be too quickly understood as a gnostic usurpation of the maternal element, the imaging of a second birth that is 'of the father.' On the contrary: that impressively impersonal opening suggests the need for as well as absence of a psyche. We are shown the image of a *dead bower*: a bower without wind to wing anything ('No stir of air was there ...'). Nothing here to bear up the fans of Psyche. This is a negative induction, a landscape whose soul or authoring hand is so submerged that the very absence recalls the fact that epics begin with invocations to some inspiring, in-breathing source. Wordsworth too begins *The Prelude* with a landscape, but it becomes, in hope, renovating and inspiring. 'I cannot miss my way. I breathe again.'

Even as we follow the way indicated by the footmarks of line 15, we come only upon a 'nerveless, listless' hand. A hand without poetic nerve, a hand without the 'list' or epic catalogue that is a sign of sublime inspiration through Mnemosyne's agency, a hand at best potentially 'list'ning' (line 20) like Saturn's bowed head. Not only does the ensuing narrative barely progress, trapped within an unmoving movement between one minute past (Saturn's stroke) and one minute before (Hyperion's dawn, or Apollo's new-birth). Not only does the sun fail to rise as, meanwhile, this sublime, ambrosial language leads nowhere. But we are forced to guess what the relation might be between listless hand or 'cold finger' (14) and a head listening to the 'tuneless numbers' of a 'voiceless' stream (11) as if it sought comfort from the earth, its 'ancient mother' (20-21). 'O Goddess! hear ...' There is a mute petition in these opening lines. It specifically concerns Saturn's ebbing power, but the diction in which it is cast is so monumental that it blocks off the maternal language that might stir the archaic form.

Thea's advent, of course, and other suasions, do rouse the god. Yet the dead bower does not turn into a living one until Book III, which soon breaks off. As Apollo, still an ephebe, is described, the language of the gods becomes once more a language of flowers, or is reconciled with it:

[He] in the morning twilight wandered forth
Beside the osiers of a rivulet,
Full ankle-deep in lilies of the vale.
The nightingale had ceas'd, and a few stars
Were lingering in the heavens, while the thrush
Began calm-throated.                                        (33-8)

But almost immediately a new flaring movement beyond the realm of
Flora and the Romance of nature begins.

The same 'beyond' characterizes in more stylized fashion the second
*Hyperion*. Its setting is a grove of trees and blossoms of all sorts, liquorish
delights; and by the patently ritual device of a magic potion which the
poet drinks he is transported into a higher world, symmetrical to that
found at the start of the first *Hyperion*, though now explicitly marbled,
a pseudo-Hellenic Stonehenge. Yet the poem does not really begin in the
pleasant grove among the language of flowers: there is, first, an
induction or formal opening which this time explicitly evokes the poet
as writer: 'this warm scribe, my hand.' What Keats asks us to infer is that
his identity – whether or not he is a poet – is decided by two things: his
hand or the poetry he may still write, and the relation of that hand to
Providence, the language of the gods. But just as the opening of the first
*Hyperion* leads beyond the image of a listless hand to the fallen giant's
bowed head that seems to listen to his ancient mother, so within the
second *Hyperion* we also come upon a *mater nutrix* (14-15).[3] The poet is
capable of speaking his visions 'if he had lov'd / And been well nurtured
in his mother tongue.' Love, nurture, and the mother-tongue join as a
rich compound. And thinking back to the opening lines of *Hyperion: A
Fragment*, we realize what is wrong with the dejected Saturn. He is a
god and yet an infant: he lies near 'his ancient mother,' near the
feeding-source, unable to take nourishment. He is not, or no longer,
'nurtured': he has gone back to the nursing position. Whether he can
take no food because he is dejected or is dejected because he finds the
source dried up and voiceless, it is not necessary to decide.

It becomes clear in the second *Hyperion* that the poet's hand is listless
because it is not linked to the mother-tongue. The split between poetry
as language of the gods and poetry as human speech, between (to
simplify) Milton and Wordsworth, is now, in Keats's time, so pronoun-
ced that poetry tends to fall mute.[4] In *The Fall of Hyperion*, therefore,
the language of flowers tries to naturalize art-diction and to create a
new romance language: English, Northern, 'posterior to the Augustan

age' (Lemprière). The first-person form breaks through again, a revision of the Wordsworthian egotistical sublime in the light of Dante's illustrious vernacular epic.

Yet the language of flowers or the psyche-language cannot bear the old burden: it gives way once more to a marbled diction before breaking off. The poet does not find the voice of poetry for his time – though this non-finding, this losing himself in words, may be his achievement. Perhaps he was deceived by the ideal of a language of flowers, that is, a 'natural' language, a mother-tongue strong enough to displace the language of the gods. After all, there is no language of flowers but only figuration, or flowers of language, and nothing can make them unartificial. Keats fails in his project: not that of fathering but rather of mothering language. No wonder that the *Autumn Ode*, written as he gives up the *Hyperions*, evokes a stored stillness of foods: it is a 'full draught' (*Fall of Hyperion* 1.46), a nurturing and natural, rather than magical, potion of native words. In that ode, hand and mother-tongue are no longer *disjecta membra*.

IX

The discourse of poetry, then, what Keats lived as *poesy* and kept questioning, goes past Collins's evening ear and past the nostalgia for a homebred 'eastern voice' or archetypal language of the gods (*Endymion* IV.1-20). It does and does not go past Psyche as the lost nature – the lost womanly nature – of speech. Keats acts out once more that dream of a common language or illustrious vernacular that has haunted Western literature since Dante. When we call Keats a Romantic, we evoke not a moon-eyed, mawkish attitude, or sentiments to be purged; we evoke, rather, a literary tradition that is deliberately post-Augustan and seeks to draw its inspiration from the developing vernaculars, the *Romance languages*, in order to enrich and illumine each mother-tongue. But once Psyche is found, once the Romance element is redressed, she must be lost again, in accordance with her nature. The losing of psyche to poetry means the discovery not of a new myth or matrona (though adumbrations of these appear, from Collins's Fancy and Eve to Keats's Mnemosyne and Moneta) but a poetic texture that cannot be 'righted.' 'If I am a Poet,' Keats declared in a letter about the Poetical Character from which I have already quoted, 'where is the Wonder that I should say I would right no more?' (He then cancels 'right' and puts 'write' above it.) The structure of Romance, its wonder-wanderings, its 'error,' cannot be separated from that rich impasse which proves to be Keats's strength and limit: losing oneself in the very texture of words that wish to be more than marble, that aspire to be genuinely musaic. Keats does not find a pure mother-tongue, which he perhaps overestimated as 'sweet sooth.' But with him the cult-ode becomes so wayward and inwrought that psyche is indeed like a text.

NOTES

1  I use the following abbreviations. For Collins: *EO, Ode to Evening; OPC, Ode on the Poetical Character.* For Keats: *OP, Ode to Psyche; ON, Ode to a Nightingale.*
2  The late fragment, 'This living hand,' comes close, however, to an arousal of consciousness that is unforgiving, unappeasable, beyond pastoral or euphemistic remedy, despite its conciliatory if still minatory 'I hold it towards you.'
3  Cf. Leo Spitzer, 'Muttersprache und Muttererziehung,' *Essays in Historical Semantics* (New York, 1948).
4  Even this generalization I continue to question because the conflict is by no means limited to the antagonistic genius of *two* poets, or the mark they put on poetic language. Keats never quite gives up his aspiration toward 'light' verse – light-hearted, perhaps, but certainly light on its feet, in the manner of Hermes, say (cf. *Lamia*), whether the message is momentous or erotic and ambiguous. There is, in short, another language of the gods, close to the neo-Hellenic ideal, and with the advantage of being socially accepted. Christopher Ricks has written perceptively about Keats's sense of the 'rediculous,' also in its relation to the class gulf, in *Keats and Embarrassment* (Oxford, 1974), esp. ch. 4, 'Keats, Byron, and "Slippery Blisses."'

**ELEANOR
COOK**

# Riddles, Charms, and Fictions in Wallace Stevens

No man though never so willing or so well enabl'd to instruct, but if he discerne his willingnesse and candor made use of to intrapp him, will suddainly draw in himselfe, and laying aside the facile vein of perspicuity, will know his time to utter clouds and riddles.
Milton, *Tetrachordon*

But not yet have we solved the incantation of this whiteness, and learned why it appeals with such power to the soul.
Melville, *Moby-Dick*, XLII

Among the many riddling poems Wallace Stevens has given us are some that are riddles structurally. That is, they cannot be read with much beyond pleasurable puzzlement until we have found the questions for which the poem provides answers. One example, published in the last year of Stevens' life, is *Solitaire under the Oaks* (1955):[1]

In the oblivion of cards
One exists among pure principles.

Neither the cards nor the trees nor the air
Persist as facts. This is an escape

To principium, to meditation.
One knows at last what to think about

And thinks about it, without consciousness,
Under the oak trees, completely released.

The key to this compact little poem is Descartes: René Descartes and *des cartes*, the cards with which we play card games. The wit lies in the questions and answers implicit in the poem. What card game would a Cartesian, would M. Cards himself play? Why, solitaire, of course. We all know that our problems as *solitaires* – isolating self-consciousness, separation of nature into thinking self and outer object – stem from Descartes' principle, *cogito ergo sum*. Solitaire is the quintessential Cartesian card game. But what has M. Descartes forgotten? (He has forgotten something: 'In the oblivion of cards ...') Answer: trees and air and indeed the cards themselves (which is to say, himself) as facts rather than as principles. Yet the card-game of solitaire does offer compensating escape to principium, to meditation, as in Descartes' *Principia philosophiae* and *Les Méditations*. One escapes the burden of consciousness as long as one exists within this card-game, thinking according to its rules.

I am not interested here in Stevens' view of Descartes. (It has more to do with the Descartes of Coleridge and of Valéry, I think, than with the seventeenth-century Descartes.) I am interested in the function of the riddle-poem. Itself a game, this little riddle simultaneously enacts a game and comments on other games, both small and large – solitaire and Cartesian philosophy and poetry too. In its play with paradoxes of outside and inside, it suggests that there are multiple ways to think of a player and a game, or of a reader and a text. Poetry comes closest to game in riddle-poems, those 'generic seeds and kernels, possibilities of expression sprouting and exfoliating into new literary phenomena,' as Northrop Frye says of both riddles and charm poems.[2] And 'those who want to study the relation between form and function in a contemporary setting' may well 'turn ... to the rigid context of games.'[3] The topography of riddles and charms has been finely mapped by Frye in his 1976 essay, 'Charms and Riddles'; my exploration here proposes to extend that map only a little farther.

Games in riddle-poems may be multiple in less logical ways, as my second example is meant to demonstrate. What question do we ask to bridge the gap between title and couplets[4] in the opaque poem of 1950, *The Desire To Make Love in a Pagoda* (OP 91)?

Among the second selves, sailor, observe
The rioter that appears when things are changed,

Asserting itself in an element that is free,
In the alien freedom that such selves degustate:

In the first inch of night, the stellar summering
At three-quarters gone, the morning's prescience,

As if, alone on a mountain, it saw far-off
An innocence approaching toward its peak.

We begin by noting the double sense of the title: the desire (felt by a human) to make love in a pagoda, and the desire felt by a pagoda to make love. We note also the different senses of 'peak,' and reflect that the act of making love has a peak physiologically and emotionally, and that pagodas are 'strange buildings which come to a point at the end,' as Ruskin says. We recall the old trope of the body as the temple of the Lord, and remember that a pagoda is for most of Stevens' readers a foreign or 'alien' temple. Finally, we read the second line as if the noun clause were written by Lewis Carroll. 'Rioter,' 'when things are changed,' is anagrammatically a near-complete 'erotic,' which we might expect in a poem about a desire to make love. These preparations are sufficient for a reading of the poem as the gently witty, erotic, multi-layered verse that it is: on desires of the body and of feelings; on primal desires for morning, which a temple might desire, as in love; on the desire to make riots or anagrams of letters, and to trope. The riddle takes the following form. Query: Is the body a temple? A temple of the Lord? Answer: Sometimes it is a pagoda. We begin with a sailor and a rioter and an anagram, but by the time the word-play culminates in 'peak,' only six lines later, Stevens has left behind the mode of Lewis Carroll. This is a riddle-poem whose games can touch as well as amuse the reader.

These two examples are built as riddle-poems. More often, Stevens will include a riddle as part of the larger argument of a poem. For example, why does Jerome beget the tubas in *Notes toward a Supreme Fiction* (III.i)?

To sing jubilas at exact, accustomed times,
To be crested and wear the mane of a multitude
And so, as part, to exult with its great throat,

To speak of joy and to sing of it, borne on
The shoulders of joyous men, to feel the heart
That is the common, the bravest fundament,

This is a facile exercise. Jerome
Begat the tubas and the fire-wind strings,
The golden fingers picking dark-blue air ...

In his letters, Stevens' answer to my question is carefully and courteously straightforward and also carefully limited: 'Jerome is St. Jerome who "begat the tubas" by translating the Bible. I suppose this would have been clearer if I had spoken of harps' (L 435, 12 Jan. 1943). But why tubas and not simply harps? It is true that through his translation of the Bible into Latin Jerome begat sundry *tubae*; that he begat the 'jubilas' of line 1 as in the best-known plural 'jubilas,' *Jubilate Deo*; that he begat the association of 'exult' and 'jubilas' though his several pairings of forms of *exultare* and *jubilare*. It is also true that he gave us the sound-association of *tuba-jubilate* in the Vulgate, to say nothing of Jubal and Tubalcain, which we also know from the English Bible.[5] (Joyce exploited the sound-association three years before Stevens: 'jubalent tubalence,' 'tubular jurbulence.')[6] But there is another reason. Stevens owned a Lewis and Short Latin dictionary, whose use gave him 'delight,' as he testified to Robert Frost when making Frost a present of one.[7] There he would have found two meanings for the word *juba*: 'the flowing hair on the neck of an animal, the mane,' and 'crest.' These are precisely the tropes of Stevens' second line, in a happy mingling of nonsense-echo and metaphor, the metaphor being, 'A multitude is a lion.' Stevens' huge Christian lion – not so much the Church triumphant as the Church rampant – is related to an earlier lion in *Notes* (I.v) and also to the lion that iconography commonly places beside Saint Jerome. After all this, how could Jerome beget only harps? He begat the tubas not only through orthodox biblical association, but also for the good poetic reason that they rhyme with *jubas* (in a proper Latin feminine accusative plural ending too), and together the two words offer heterodox associations for the word 'jubilas,' whose power we might otherwise reverence unduly.

I offer these examples partly as cautionary tales, for I think that sometimes Stevens' seeming obscurity and nonsense are in fact examples of wit we have not yet come to appreciate, riddles whose sibylline ideas of order we have not yet pieced together. To christen a questing, mountain-climbing lady Mrs Uruguay has a good deal more point when we recall that the capital of Uruguay is Montevideo, as Frye once noted. To marry her to a Mr Alfred Uruguay also has a certain point when we recall that the most famed Alfred in modern poetry has as a surname Prufrock, and begins his poem thus:

Let us go then, you and I,
When the evening is spread out against the sky
Like a patient etherised upon a table;

To which famous simile, Stevens' opening line to *Mrs. Alfred Uruguay* mischievously replies in an Eliot ragtime rhythm:

So what said the others and the sun went down ...

It does not do to underestimate the capacities for riddling and general word-play of a poet who can pun on the words 'artichoke' and 'inarticulate': ... 'a dream they never had, / Like a word in the mind that sticks at artichoke / And remains inarticulate' (*OP* 47) – 'rather an heroic pun,' as its inventor endearingly remarked (*L* 366, 27 Aug. 1940).

If all Stevens' riddles worked as these and many others do, we would be dealing with a fine, formidable wit,

Logos and logic, crystal hypothesis,
Incipit and a form to speak the word
And every latent double in the word,

Beau linguist. (*Notes* I.viii)

Our problems as readers come when Stevens' hypotheses are clouded, when the latent doubles in the word refuse to become patent and remain half-shadowed, figurae without fulfilment. I have offered readings of some of Stevens' riddles using as means of interpretation puns, logic, well-known tropes, Latin equivalents, nonsense-rhymes, iconography, literary antecedents. Though these riddles stand in varying relations to the arguments of their poems, and though their effects differ, they may all be read coherently. The interpretive devices I have mentioned satisfy our desire as readers that consistent if multiple answers be possible for riddles in texts.

But Stevens sometimes moves toward more problematic kinds of riddle. I am not thinking so much of impenetrable lines, which await a wise reader, as of lines where the riddles appear only partly soluble, and the problem becomes not only how to answer the riddle but also how to read the answer. Such lines include sinister-metamorphosis or horrid-metamorphosis poems like *Oak Leaves Are Hands*; 'metamorphorid' is Stevens' fine portmanteau word for the process. They also include lines in which Stevens engages in intertextual word-play. For example, in *Esthétique du Mal*, part v, what are the 'obscurer selvages'? 'For this ... we forego / Lament, willing forfeit the ai-ai / Of parades in the obscurer selvages.' We can answer this question only so far. Selvages are edges, of course, and so belong in this canto of limits and bars. They may be more precisely placed, however, by reading them against the first five lines of the opening canto of Dante's *Inferno*. There Dante finds himself in a dark wood, *una selva oscura*, and the noun *selva* is repeated in line 5, where its sounds at once expand into *selvaggia* – *esta selva selvaggia*: *selva oscura ... selva selvaggia*, *oscura ... selvaggia*, obscure selvage. *Selvaggia*, however, is cognate with our word savage and not with the word selvage. Eliot makes use of correct etymology in *The Dry Salvages*, third of the *Four Quartets*, published three years before Stevens' poem. The Dry Salvages are a small group of rocks off Cape Ann, Massachusetts, as Eliot tells us; the name, he says, was originally *les trois sauvages*. By anglicizing this name, New Englanders have brought it somewhat closer to its Latin root (*silvaticus*, from *silva*) and much closer to its Italian cognate, *selvaggia*. In Eliot's poem, there is an implicit play on salvages (the rocks), savage, salvage (flotsam and jetsam), and I think salvation (which has the same Latin root as salvage) – play that includes the metaphor of the rock of salvation and allegories of travelling. I read Eliot's title as interwoven in this word-play, and as echoing the *selva ... selva selvaggia* of the beginning of Dante's journey.

Stevens echoes sound but dislocates denotative meaning, as he summons the ghost of a Dantean *topos* only to de-centre it. For Dante's *selva oscura* is not in the middle of life's way for Stevens – neither as doctrinal allegory nor as personal allegory nor as a place for poetry. As allegory, it is on the edge of things, peripheral to Stevens' earthly vision. Even more on the edge – and thus the 'obscur*er* selvage*s*' – is Eliot's poem, *The Dry Salvages*. Yet, having answered this riddle, we find problems in reading the answer. Is this simply ironic distancing? If so, what is the angle of difference between Stevens' troping and Dante's, Stevens' troping and Eliot's? Or is this perhaps what John Hollander calls metaleptic echoing?[8]

Another example of a problematic riddle is the passage about the Arabian in *Notes toward a Supreme Fiction* I.iii. Here the relation of the reader to the text, even of the interior 'we' to his own text, shifts as we read and reread the canto. I should like to pause over these lines and to look at the different relations of reader and text, for I think they may tell us something about the functions of riddles, and of charms as well. Here is the entire canto:

> The poem refreshes life so that we share,
> For a moment, the first idea ... It satisfies
> Belief in an immaculate beginning

And sends us, winged by an unconscious will,
To an immaculate end. We move between these points:
From that ever-early candor to its late plural

And the candor of them is the strong exhilaration
Of what we feel from what we think, of thought
Beating in the heart, as if blood newly came,

An elixir, an excitation, a pure power.
The poem, through candor, brings back a power again
That gives a candid kind to everything.

We say: At night an Arabian in my room,
With his damned hoobla-hoobla-hoobla-how,
Inscribes a primitive astronomy,

Across the unscrawled fores the future casts
And throws his stars around the floor. By day
The wood-dove used to chant his hoobla-hoo

And still the grossest iridescence of ocean
Howls hoo and rises and howls hoo and falls.
Life's nonsense pierces us with strange relation.

We are not surprised to find a 'Coleridgean idealization of poetry'[9] (lines 1-12) in a meditation upon a supreme fiction, but the presence of what appears to be nonsense-verse in such a meditation is startling, and its relation to lines 1 to 12 a problem for commentators. If lines 13 to 20 are pure nonsense[10] with no affective function,[11] why does Stevens say in line 21 that life's nonsense pierces us? We can hardly exclude nonsense-verse from life's nonsense when we have just been given several lines of it. And whether lines 13 or 20 are read affectively or not,[12] what connection is there with the canto's first part? And what does the movement from the Coleridgean lines into the 'hoobla' lines have to do with a supreme fiction?

At least two different types of word-play run through this canto. The first is word-play which makes sense; the second is closer to the uses of nonsense-verse. One proliferates from the English word 'candid' and the Latin word *candidus* and dominates the first part. The other plays with Coleridgean echoes, which are submerged in the first part and surface in the second. *Candidus* in Latin, like 'candid' in English, means white, but a dazzling white as against a lustreless white (*albus*). It has been used in Latin of the moon, the stars, day; of swans and snow; of Dido's beauty; of gods and persons transformed to gods. It also means 'spotless' and is thus synonymous with 'immaculate' in Stevens' canto. Figuratively, of discourse, it means clear, open, perspicuous, and therefore the opposite to riddle or *aenigma*, which is in rhetorical tradition an 'obscure allegory'[13] and into which Stevens moves in line 13. Until then, he weaves an entrancing web out of multiple meanings and associations of 'candid' and *candidus*.[14]

Simultaneously, we may hear an uncanny echoing of Coleridge when we read this canto as a type of riddle poem. Thus: Stevens has transposed the dove's conventional English-language sound of 'coo' to 'hoo.' If we similarly transpose the Arabian's sounds, we hear 'coobla-coobla-coobla-cow.' Then we don't. We hear 'coobla-can,' and we begin to hear a nonsense refrain, much like something out of James Joyce: Kubla Khan but hoobla how? This refrain suggests that lines 13 to 20 function at least in part as a riddle whose answer is Coleridge's *Kubla Khan*. Once we have begun to hear this echo, other Coleridgean echoes proliferate. We ask ourselves if it is nonsense to hear subliminal assertions of power in the homonyms for 'do' and 'can' in the opening line of *Kubla Khan*: 'In Xanadu did Kubla Khan.' And to read in Stevens' canto that the poem brings back a power again that gives a can-did kind to everything. Of course it is. But in the realm of nonsense riddle, this is how we read.

Outside this realm, back in the realm of rational discourse, we recall that *Kubla Khan* came to Coleridge 'without any sensation or consciousness of effort,' to quote his phrase, and comes as close as any poem to showing the 'pure power' of the imagination. We recall also that the Khan could simply decree a stately pleasure-dome, while Stevens must work toward a supreme fiction which 'must give pleasure.' *Kubla Khan* in this reading is at least one of the poems, and I think the prototypical poem, which refreshes life in the ways suggested in lines 1 to 12 of Stevens' canto.

Lest this riddle-reading appear too arbitrary, I should observe that Stevens engaged in word-play with *Kubla Khan* elsewhere. In 1923, in *Academic Discourse at Havana*, he invented a 'mythy goober khan,' which is a peanut stand. ('Khan' as 'building' we are most likely to know from *The Arabian Nights*.) But the phrase 'goober khan' functions chiefly as a parody – 'a peanut parody / For peanut people' – through its unmistakable echo of 'Kubla Khan.' (I read the entire poem as a forerunner of *Notes* I.iii, for it ends with sleepers awakening and watching moonlight on their floors, and comments of itself that it 'may ... be / An incantation that the moon defines.') In 1942, the year of *Notes*, Stevens opened his weird and haunting *Oak Leaves Are Hands* with a parody of the opening lines of *Kubla Khan*, as Helen Vendler has noted:[15] 'In Hydaspia, by Howzen, / Lived a lady, Lady Lowzen ...' Coleridge is present in other ways in the work of Stevens at this time. Among Stevens' essays, he appears only in a quotation in a 1942 essay, and in the 1943 essay, *The Figure of the Youth as Virile Poet*, where Stevens calls Coleridge 'one of the great figures.'[16] In a letter of 1942, Stevens makes use of Coleridge's phrase, 'willing suspension of disbelief,' along with William James's 'will to believe,' in a discussion crucial to an understanding of *Notes* (*L* 430, 8 Dec. 1942). In *Notes* itself, he echoes part of Coleridge's definition of the primary imagination (III.viii).[17] Coleridge is pretty clearly one of the ancestral voices with whom Stevens does battle, or records past battles, in *Notes toward a Supreme Fiction*. A *Kubla Khan* riddle, given other parodies of the great Khan's name and poem, and given Coleridge's place in *Notes*, does not seem to me an overly arbitrary reading.

How do lines 13 to 20 function in Stevens' debate with Coleridge? They work, I think, as a reversal of lines 1 to 12, and their first function is to demonstrate how disabling such a reversal may be. 'Hoobla how?' sings or plays or challenges the Arabian, and the phrase is 'damned' because one answer is: Kubla Khan but you cannot. The voice of this canto's first part talks about a power in which the reader feels invited to share as part of a communal 'we.' To give a 'kind to everything' is to bring about unity and kinship, a process quite unlike 'strange relation.' Power in the second part is exercised by the Arabian certainly, but it is a power that excludes the reader in the sense that we cannot agree on even an approximate common stance for reading lines 13 to 20. If the first part shows us the power of the human imagination, just as *Kubla Khan* does, the second part shows us the helplessness of that same imagination, just as the longer *Kubla Khan* we do not have also and most painfully does. (Coleridge's preface to *Kubla Khan* makes a useful gloss on this canto; the return to 'his room' and to a dissipated, fragmented vision is, I think, one source for Stevens' Arabian lines. Yet one hardly likes to bring a hoobla-how-Kubla-Khan riddle too close to the memory of Coleridge, even in fancy.)

We can work out the reversal: suggestions of white magic to suggestions of black; radiance to night, with eerie moonlight and broken constellations; openness to riddle; the future as immaculate end to the future as something cast – a context of fate rather than destiny. The visual becomes vague or erratic; the oral reduces itself to the same limited series of sounds as if the Arabian made the memory of the wood-dove chant to his own tune and allied himself with the ancient continuing hooing of the ocean. Language, once glowing with power and moving outward in its ex-prefixes, becomes fitful and nothing to read by or into. The Arabian splits fores and casts, and into the split he throws the future. By line 20, the salt ocean has prevailed over the freshening of line 1. Incantatory multilingual echoes cry through this line, with its monosyllabic equivalent of a Latinate ululate-undulate word-play, and an implicit French-English pun on *houle* (sea-swell) and 'howl.'[18] 'Oh! Blessed rage for order ... The maker's rage to order words of the sea.' But the Arabian with his damned words is master now, the moon at its most unpropitious (the connection is presumably through the figure of the crescent).[19] Against the human 'will' and 'can' of lines 1 to 12, another voice says 'how?' The puns move away from vanished chant and down toward incantation:[20] adnominatio to parnomasia to monotonous echo. How, hoo, who, indeed.

The movement to wood-dove and then to ocean is toward losses other than the loss of poetic power, one of love and the other (I think) in death. A sequence of 'gross, grosser, grossest' is implied in the superlative form of the adjective at the end; iridescences may also be of the moon and of doves,[21] and if we use the word 'gross' in the sense of 'material,' we may see here a logical sequence of downward imagery (moonlight, bird, ocean) and of loss (of poetic power as the least fleshly, then of love, finally of the body itself). I think also that the memory of the erotic dove merges with some memory of the poetic dove who broods creatively over the abyss – descendant of the biblical and Miltonic bird of the Holy Ghost through Wordsworth's 'brooding mind' to Joyce's 'Coo' and Stevens' chanter of hoobla-hoo. The poetic voice has now lost the voice of the dove; the operative forces are the Arabian and the howling, hooing sea. The three realms here (moon, woods, ocean) are those of the triform goddess (Luna, Diana, Hecate) if we accept the ocean as Stevens' form of the underworld. The chanting of hooblas and how and hoos, a circle woven thrice as in the charm-poems of Theocritus and Virgil, resounds like some mage's spell to undo the white and shining enchantment of the first part.

Stevens' riddling here verges on the type of poetry Frye calls charms, poetry whose rhetoric 'is dissociative and incantatory,' uses repetitive devices ('refrain, rhyme, alliteration, assonance, pun, antithesis'), and seeks to 'break down and confuse the conscious will.'[22] Charms and riddles are two different kinds of play with language; 'Magic would disrupt Nonsense,' Elizabeth Sewell argues. But the two may converge: 'the game or the dream, logic or irrationality, may lead us to the same point in the end.'[23] For 'charms and riddles ... are psychologically very close together, as the unguessed or unguessable riddle is or may be a charm.'[24] That is what I think we have here: a riddle-and-charm poem with two contrasting parts. 'Like primitive astronomers, we are free to note recurrences, cherish symmetries, and seek if we can means of placating the hidden power: more for our comfort than for theirs.'[25] But there is minimal comfort, if any, in the dwindling symmetries which the reader can ascertain in Stevens' nonsense-lines. The moon has come down from heaven and brought a most uncandid charm, one potentially damning and disabling.

What Stevens accomplishes here is a systematic undoing of his first world, and with it all such 'immaculate,' idealized first worlds – childhood or erotic or religious paradises – and perforce all idealized theories of poetry. The strategies of undoing dominate the first cantos of *Notes*, and *Kubla Khan*, with its magical transformations of biblical and Miltonic paradises[26] and with its yearning poet, serves Stevens' purposes wonderfully well. Such an undoing may be disabling, as it is, for example, in a lunar sequence in *The Man with the Blue Guitar* which moves from 'immaculate' (vii) through 'unspotted' (xiii) to 'the spot on the floor' (xv). But for Stevens such an undoing may also be a defence. I have read 'we say' as 'we find ourselves saying' and so have followed the voice of the poem into the power of the fiction of the Arabian. But Stevens' cryptic 'we say' also bears the sense of 'it is we who say.' As soon as we read not 'an Arabian ... with his damned hoobla-hoobla-hoobla-how,' but 'it is we who say an Arabian ... with his damned hoobla-hoobla-hoobla-how,' another response to his riddle becomes possible: not the accuser saying Kubla Khan but you cannot, but rather the self saying Kubla Khan and I cannot. This is to acknowledge poverty but not helplessness. It is a defensive strategy against the authority of words, including the words of supreme fictions, say 'candid' or *candidus*. Riddles and charms do not merely assert that we are makers of our own words, but demonstrate this by showing how words may be reversed and fictions undone. Stevens' nonsense-lines read to me like an archetypal riddle-and-charm poem, the precise opposite of the archetypal 'original spell to keep chaos away,'[27] the Word of God or Logos.

'To indulge the power of fictions and send imagination out upon the wing is often the sport of those who delight too much in silent speculation,' Imlac says in *Rasselas* (XLIV). 'Then fictions begin to operate as realities ...' He is speaking of an astronomer, who is persuaded he has the power to control the weather, the sun and even the planets, and so could if he wished do just what Stevens' astronomer does. The astronomer is for Imlac an admonitory example of the hazards of taking fictions for realities. Imlac's idea of what constitutes a fiction differs from Stevens', of course; his religious beliefs are not to him fictions. For Stevens, they are, and Stevens was sensitive to the hazards as well as the benefits of all belief, including poetic belief: 'Suppose the poet discovered and had the power thereafter at will and by intelligence to reconstruct us by his transformations. He would also have the power to destroy us' (*NA* 45, 1943). This would be to make art, including sacred art, into magic, and the poet, including the writer of scripture, into an arch-magician and arch-riddler. For Stevens, it is a necessary knowledge that we say and therefore can unsay all our fictions, including our most august stories. Riddles and charms, which by definition are distanced from referential discourse, can make this point very clearly. We not only can unsay all our fictions, but must, for this is how one part of the imagination works, as Stevens says in 1947 in what I read as comment on canto I.iii of *Notes*:

> It must change from destiny to slight caprice ...
>                                  ... move to find
> What must unmake it and, at last, what can,
> Say, a flippant communication under the moon.                    (*CP* 417-18)

We are by now so familiar with the ways of deconstruction that my argument thus far appears to claim simply that Stevens is a modern poet. For example, my first reading of *Notes* i.iii.13-20 would be seen by Derrida as an example of non-radical 'illegibility,' that 'non-sense' (*le non-sens*) which is still 'interior to the book, to reason or to logos.' My second reading would open the possibility of 'radical illegibility' (*l'illisibilité radicale*) or the deconstruction of the traditional doctrine of logos, reason, and the book.[28] Yet the implications of these readings may be disquieting for the reader and lover of fictions. If we deconstruct the old, unifying Coleridgean theories of the imagination, as it seems we must, do we lose the power of illusions, the ability to suspend disbelief? Do all our fictions become Arabian fictions of nonsense, powerful within themselves but without much power over us? Or mirrors of another imagination, Coleridge's perhaps, as the sea mirrors the moon and the moon mirrors a greater light? We seem to be caught. When we are knowledgeable enough and defensive enough about the ways language works, how far can it then affect us? This is a question that John Bayley raises in another context,[29] and it lies behind speculation about the end of narrative. For Stevens, there is the further question: how can we then create or hear a supreme fiction?

Riddles and charms can show us in a nutshell three relations of reader to text. The reader may enter and share the assumed power of the text, answering riddles and feeling exquisite enchantments (in other terms, playing the game or dreaming happily). He may enter the assumed power of the text, unable to answer riddles and feeling sinister enchantments (in other terms, becoming the played-with or experiencing nightmare). Or, he may step outside the blessing and damning power of words, observing that we make the rules of the games and (as we now say) 'privilege' the text. But in so far as we still use words, or they us, what power do they then retain?

It takes the whole of *Notes toward a Supreme Fiction* to answer that question fully. Two parts of the answer are pertinent here. The first is suggested in Stevens' final line to *Notes* I.iii: 'Life's nonsense pierces us with strange relation.' Not 'relations,' as we might expect, but 'relation,' which includes more pointedly than the plural noun a relation that is a fiction. The word 'pierce' is unexpected too. It is a powerful word in Stevens:[30] one use makes it a function of speech ('the acutest end / Of speech: to pierce the heart's residuum' [*CP* 259]); another use makes it an effect of illusion, and here we need to remember that there is benign as well as harmful illusion for Stevens[31] '... the laborious human [of *Notes* II.v] who lives in illusions and who, after all the great illusions have left him, still clings to one that pierces him' [*L* 435, 12 Jan. 1943]). In *Notes* I.iii, for all the possible defence in the clause 'we say,' Stevens does not end defensively. He ends with a piercing or wounding, even by nonsense-language, even by the 'hoo' we hear the ocean saying, even in the full knowledge that we say these things ourselves. If we read the poem's last line as in part Stevens' gloss on his own nonsense-lines, then he is putting before us the possibility of words as not only a power to bless and damn, a power against which we must defend ourselves, but also a power to pierce and to which we cling because (not although) it pierces us. In *Notes* III.viii, Stevens asks: 'Am I that imagine this angel less satisfied?' Are we who say the riddle and charm of the Arabian less pierced? Only if we defend ourselves completely against the power of all fictions. And a self that cannot be pierced by words cannot be healed or refreshed by them either.

How words 'wound' has been explored by Jacques Derrida and more recently by Geoffrey Hartman.[32] This canto suggests another pattern for such speculation through its echoing of religious diction, including the language of grace in line 1 and the language of sacrifice in line 21. Stevens may be said to prefigure here the only version of the incarnate Word which he could accept: the human imagination re-entering and being wounded by a world of language that it has itself created. This is, in effect, what happens in Poe's story, The Power of Words, a story which Stevens admired.

A further answer to my question is suggested by Notes III.viii, a companion-piece to canto I.iii and part of the beautiful climactic development of the whole poem. Here the assertive statement that the poem 'satisfies / Belief' becomes interrogative: 'What am I to believe?' Satisfaction is implied but limited: 'Am I that imagine this angel less satisfied?' 'Is it I then that ... am satisfied.' All the sentences are interrogative, though one modulates through its clauses into a sufficiently assertive mood to drop the question-mark. This canto does not send us 'winged by an unconscious will.' 'I' both sees as spectator and experiences as angel, and sees his experience, of a movement downward 'on his spredden wings,' a movement protracted and without landing, a suspension. The time of fulfilment is not in terms of undefined beginning and end, but is specifically limited: an hour, a day, a month, a year, a time. Ex- words here (expressible, external) are limited in comparison with the outward movement – the ex-ness, so to speak – of such words in I.iii (exhilaration, excitation). We might suppose that a movement from first-person plural to first-person singular, from assertive to interrogative mood, from winging our way from immaculate beginnings to immaculate ends to seeing and being a falling angel, from extended to modified adjectives, from excited participation in power to a multiple stance where power is questioned – that all these limitations would make for a lesser canto. But this is not what happens. Stevens' enchanting first world is presented anew here in strength. His canto both enacts and comments on 'that willing suspension of disbelief for the moment, which constitutes poetic faith.' Coleridge's definition and Stevens' canto are powerful and live for us not in spite of their careful limiting but because of it. Stevens' 'I am' claims no more than he can sustain: 'I have not but I am and as I am, I am.'

At the end of this canto, the Cinderella story reverses the angelic moment, as the Arabian's story reverses the world of 'candid' and *candidus*, the two reversals being very different. It also reverses the Miltonic and biblical world of the aspiring Canon Aspirin in the three preceding cantos (v-vii). 'Candid' is used only once elsewhere in Stevens' poetry ('candor' never again) in a way that associates it with 'canon' and 'canonical.'[33] When we note that a candidate may also be an Aspirant (*OED*, 'candidate,' 2.a), the candid-Canon-canonical association appears firm. In 1909, age twenty-nine, Stevens noted the Cinderella story in his journal in a one-word entry: 'pumpkin-coach.'[34] The entry follows immediately on these lines:

What I aspired to be,
And was not, comforts me –

The lines, unidentified, are from Browning's *Rabbi Ben Ezra*, so that Browning's rabbi must take his place as another of the aspirers who make up that compound ghost, Canon Aspirin. For all Stevens' love for the white worlds and aspiring figures of a biblical, Miltonic, Coleridgean, and Browning heritage – rather, because of his love – their power has to be undone, whether by riddle or by charm or by fairy tale. Only then can Stevens lead us toward the exquisite fiction of his fat girl in the final canto of *Notes*. Only then can he write at all, can he 'patch together' (Stevens' revisionary version of the word 'compose'). For *Notes* ends with a Stevensian poet who

Patches the moon together in his room
To his Virgilian cadences, up down,
Up down. It is a war that never ends.

NOTES

1 *Opus Posthumous: Poems, Plays, Prose by Wallace Stevens*, ed. Samuel French Morse (New York, 1957), 111, hereafter cited as *OP*. Other abbreviations in the text are: *CP*, *The Collected Poems of Wallace Stevens* (New York, 1954); *L*, *Letters of Wallace Stevens*, ed. Holly Stevens (New York, 1972); *NA*, *The Necessary Angel: Essays on Reality and the Imagination* (New York, 1951).
2 'Charms and Riddles,' in *Spiritus Mundi: Essays on Literature, Myth, and Society* (Bloomington, 1976), 123.

3 E.H. Gombrich, *Art and Illusion: A Study in the Psychology of Pictorial Representation*, 2nd ed. (Princeton, 1969; pbk.), 119-20.

4 Cf. John Hollander: 'Wallace Stevens ... has frequently been cited as a writer whose titles function with indirection, apparent perversity, or some symbol-making quality that is characteristic of the fundamental methods of his poetry. If they direct a particular kind of attention to the poems that they head, it is much more an analytic or interpretive role that they play than more properly a genre- or type-defining one' (*Vision and Resonance* [New York, 1975], 218).

5 *Biblia Sacra Latina*, Psalmus c:1 (*Jubilate Deo*); Psalmus LXXXI:1 (*Exultate ... jubilate*), Psalmus XCVIII:4 (*Jubilate ... cantate, et exultate, et psallit*), Zacharia IX:9 (*exulta ... jubila*), Psalmus XCVIII:6 (*In tubis ... et voce tubae ... Jubilate*) and Genesis 4:21, 22. This numbering varies slightly from the Vulgate.

6 *Finnegans Wake* (New York, 1958), 338, 84.

7 Letter of 16 July 1935, Dartmouth College Library; quoted by permission of Holly Stevens and Dartmouth College Library. Cf. L 275, 4 March 1935.

8 'Echo Metaleptic,' in *The Figure of Echo: A Mode of Allusion in Milton and After* (Berkeley, 1981), 113-32. *The Figure of Echo* is essential reading for anyone who talks about echoing, as I do in this essay. It came into my hands after this essay had gone out of them.

9 Harold Bloom, *Wallace Stevens: The Poems of Our Climate* (Ithaca, 1976), 182.

10 I use the term 'pure nonsense,' that is, self-contained nonsense with no apparent affective function, where others use simply 'nonsense.' Cf. John M. Munro, 'Nonsense Verse,' in *The Princeton Encyclopedia of Poetry and Poetics*, ed. Alex Preminger (Princeton, 1974); Elizabeth Sewell, *The Field of Nonsense* (London, 1952); and Michael Holquist, 'What Is a Boojum? Nonsense and Modernism,' *Yale French Studies*, 43 (1969), 145-64.

11 Cf. Hugh Kenner, 'Seraphic Glitter: Stevens' Nonsense,' *Parnassus: Poetry in Review*, 5 (1976), 153-9, and Irvin Ehrenpreis, 'Strange Relation: Stevens' Nonsense,' in *Wallace Stevens: A Celebration*, ed. Frank Doggett and Robert Buttel (Princeton, 1980), 233-4.

12 For an affective reading, see Bloom, *Wallace Stevens*, 181-3.

13 Cicero, *De Or.* III.xlii; Quintilian, *Inst. Or.* VIII.vi.52. On *aenigma* in relation to the structure of allegory, see Angus Fletcher, *Allegory: The Theory of a Symbolic Mode* (Ithaca and London, 1964), under *aenigma*, passim.

14 Cf. William Empson on the word 'candid,' in *The Structure of Complex Words*, 3rd ed. (London, 1977), 307-10.

15 Helen Vendler, *On Extended Wings: Wallace Stevens' Longer Poems* (Cambridge, Mass., 1969), 151.

16 After quoting at length an anecdote from *Biographia Literaria*, Stevens goes on: 'As poetry goes, as the imagination goes, as the approach to truth, or, say, to being by way of the imagination goes, Coleridge is one of the great figures.' Coleridge's definitions of poetry are for Stevens 'valid enough,' though these definitions 'no longer impress us primarily by their validity' (*NA* 40, 41).

17 Cf. Bloom, *Wallace Stevens*, 169.

18 Exploited by Eliot in *Dans le Restaurant* ('Oubliait les cris des mouettes et la houle de Cornouaille'), but lost, or much submerged, in the revised English version (*Waste Land* iv), where Eliot alters the acoustical effect to a whisper. For nightmare associations of 'hoo,' cf. Eliot, *Sweeney Agonistes*: 'You've had a cream of a nightmare dream and you've got the hoo-ha's coming to you. / Hoo hoo hoo.' Stevens' associations with the word 'hoo-ing' in *The Man with the Blue Guitar* are pejorative (*L* 789, 12 July 1953).

19 'There are several things in the NOTES that would stand a little annotating. For instance, the fact that the Arabian is the moon is something that the reader could not possibly know. However, I did not think that it was necessary for him to know' (*L* 434, 12 Jan. 1943).

20 Cf. Frye: 'There is a perilous balance in paronomasia between verbal wit and hypnotic incantation' (*Anatomy of Criticism* [Princeton, 1957], 276).

21 Cf. 'the moon ... with its dove-winged blendings' (*CP* 119), and 'she ... bathed the dove in iridescence' (Ruskin, *Love's Meinie* ii).

22 'Charms and Riddles,' 126.

23 Sewell, *Field of Nonsense*, 40, 43.

24 'Charms and Riddles,' 137-8.

25 Hugh Kenner, not of Stevens but of Samuel Beckett, in *Samuel Beckett: A Critical Study* (New York, 1961), 10.

26 Cf. Thomas McFarland, in *New Perspectives on Coleridge and Wordsworth*, ed. Geoffrey Hartman (New York, 1972), 203. On *Kubla Khan* as a model for other nonsense-verse, see Kenner, 'Seraphic Glitter,' and James Rother, 'Wallace Stevens as a Nonsense Poet,' *Tennessee Studies in Literature*, 21 (1976), 86-7.

27 'Charms and Riddles,' 129.

28 Jacques Derrida, *Writing and Difference*, trans. Alan Bass (Chicago, 1978), 77.

29 John Bayley, 'Tropes and Blocks,' *Modern Language Review*, 73 (1978), 748-54.

30 Cf. Bloom, *Wallace Stevens*, 194.

31 'Poetry as a narcotic is escapism in the pejorative sense. But there is a benign escapism in every illusion ... Of course, I believe in benign illu-

sion. To my way of thinking, the idea of God is an instance of benign illusion' (*L* 402, 18 Feb. 1942).

32 Jacques Derrida, 'Edmund Jabès and the Question of the Book,' in *Writing and Difference*, 64-78, and Geoffrey H. Hartman, 'Words and Wounds,' in *Saving the Text: Literature/Derrida/Philosophy* (Baltimore and London, 1981), 118-57.

33 *From the Journal of Crispin*, in *Wallace Stevens: A Celebration*, 43: 'His town exhales its mother breath for him / And this he breathes, a candid bellows-boy, / According to canon.'

34 *Souvenirs and Prophecies: The Young Wallace Stevens*, ed. Holly Stevens (New York, 197), 220.

**W. DAVID
SHAW**

# Poetic Truth in a Scientific Age: The Victorian Perspective

In his Cambridge Prize poem, *Timbuctoo*, written in 1829, Tennyson laments that as a city of the imagination, like the lost Atlantis and Eldorado, Timbuctoo must 'render up' the 'glorious home' of poetry and myth 'To keen Discovery' (239-40). When the modern explorers finally reach the fabled city, they discover only 'Low-built, mud-walled, barbarian' huts (244). In an age which worships at the Vatican of 'keen Discovery,' in which scientific methods of empirical verification occupy the same place in the kingdom of thought as did theology in the Middle Ages, Tennyson is resolved like most Victorian poets to justify Wordsworth's faith that 'poetry is the breath and finer spirit of all knowledge; ... the impassioned expression which is in the countenance of all science.'[1] But if this is the poet's function, in what sense is his 'impassioned expression' true? How can his language give us knowledge?

Lying at the heart of the debate which Arnold and Huxley waged over the virtues of a literary as opposed to a scientific education, these questions have been central to Northrop Frye's investigations, and they seem to me as important today as they were a hundred years ago. In this essay I study changing conceptions of poetic truth by examining the impact on Victorian poetics of three scientific models. I begin with Mill's account of scientific induction in his *System of Logic*, then examine two later doctrines: Huxley's theory of the physicist's symbolic fictions and John Tyndall's theory that the scientist makes use of pictorial analogies to mediate between direct description of physical nature and a mere symbolic shorthand designed to economize mental labour. I conclude the essay by analysing F.H. Bradley's critique of scientific abstraction. I show that whereas earlier Victorian theories subordinate poetry to a scientific model of induction, later neo-Hegelian thought subordinates science to a poetic theory of universals which, unlike the universals of the scientist, are concrete rather than abstract. Bradley's ultimate postulate of faith is that only the concrete universals of his poet and metaphysician can describe the structure of a world we are entitled to call real.

I

In his *System of Logic* J.S. Mill offers the most comprehensive Victorian account of scientific induction. Postulating the validity of a correspondence theory of truth, Mill argues that every scientific inference is a form of judgment, or what he calls 'belief grounded on evidence.' In cases of scientific inference the mind compares its many past sensations of tawny colour, heavy weight, large jaw, and shaggy mane with its present sensations of such qualities to determine with accuracy whether the animal now before it is in fact a lion. But 'if a poet describes a lion,' Mill argues, 'he does not describe him as a naturalist would ... He describes him by imagery ... which might occur to a mind contemplating the lion, in the state of awe, wonder, or terror, which the spectacle naturally excites. Now this is describing the lion professedly, but the state of excitement of the spectator really.'[2] In his literary essays of the 1830s Mill repeatedly implies (like Bentham) that poetry, as the language of emotional assertion, is devoid of cognitive value: it should not be assimilated to the judgmental inferences of science.

We may say that science (in Mill's view) is a language of true-or-false propositions, whereas poetry is a language of more or less felicitous proposals. When the geologist identifies the stones of the hill as terminal moraine, he proceeds to classify the hills by providing a scientific explanation of their glacial origin. We judge the geologist's classifications as true-or-false judgmental inferences, capable of being empirically tested. In *In Memoriam*, however, we judge Tennyson's classification of the solid lands as mist and clouds by different criteria.

There rolls the deep where grew the tree.
　O earth, what changes hast thou seen!
　There where the long street roars, hath been
The stillness of the central sea.

The hills are shadows, and they flow
　From form to form, and nothing stands;
　They melt like mist, the solid lands,
Like clouds they shape themselves and go.　　　(*In Memoriam* CXXIII.1-8)

Tennyson's lines have all the immediacy of wonder and dread passed through an idea of terrifying dissolution in which everything solid and definite seems to slip away into the void. No reader can respond to Tennyson's powerfully restrained proposals to see land as mist and hills as shadows unless he has been properly educated by metaphor. By metaphor I mean the association of ideas, not by contiguity, but by similarity – or, as Mill would argue, by the logic of their emotional as well as their conceptual links.

But even in freeing poetry from a correspondence model of truth, Mill is not prepared to concede that poetry is untrue. Eager to defend the cognitive value of poems by Wordsworth and Tennyson, Mill is not long satisfied with the simple emotive theory of poetry he formulates in the two essays of 1833. If we study his theory of intuitive inferences in *A System of Logic*, we can see how he is trying to retain as a form of inference – and hence of knowledge – metaphoric associations of hills with shadows and of solid lands with clouds. Sensations of awe and terror which Tennyson experiences simultaneously rather than successively in the presence of the hills are compounded under the influence of powerful feelings. But far from losing all correspondence to their sequence in nature, the alternation of fluid and solid elements – the displacement of the tree by the deep and of the central sea by the roaring street – correspond to a sequence in time that could actually be observed if we were to study a time-lapse photograph of the earth extending over billions of years. Mill believes that there is much in our knowledge (including perhaps the emotional knowledge of the poet) which may seem to be intuited, but which is actually inferred. By showing how Tennyson can check his sensations of mingled awe and dread against phenomena which cannot be observed directly, but which a study of Lyell's *Principles of Geology* can indirectly confirm, Mill's doctrine of intuitive inference allows him to restore a correspondence theory of truth in an altered form.

Mill's theory of inference is capable of one further refinement. In section CXXIII of *In Memoriam* there seem at first to be no sensations in nature which correspond to Tennyson's curiously elated sense of being invulnerable to change.

> But in my spirit will I dwell,
>    And dream my dream, and hold it true;
>    For though my lips may breathe adieu,
> I cannot think the thing farewell.          (*In Memoriam* CXXIII.9-12)

If Tennyson's feeling of elation and release corresponds to no phenomena he is now conscious of experiencing, there is only one way in which it can be a valid intuition, or a disguised form of inference; it must correspond to forgotten or evaded sensations, to experiences repressed in the poet's memory. There are indeed several earlier experiences in *In Memoriam* which arouse the same curious amalgam of dread and exaltation. I am thinking of frightening sensations of lucid veils and glimmering gravestones, or of the strange experience of dim light waging battle against boundless day. In finally submitting to the geological truths, and allowing the dizzying depths of duration to be dispelled before his eyes, Tennyson is bringing to consciousness a truth about the soul's fragile hardihood, about its power to create its own enduring worlds. Though the poet's conjunctions of dread and exaltation are disguised or intuitive forms of inference, which his earlier experiences confirm, the truth to which they point – the soul's sovereignty over nature – has formerly been repressed, perhaps because it seemed too daring to acknowledge.

So far I have tried to make as strong a case for Mill as I can. I have argued that Mill's doctrine of intuitive inferences is designed to confer an emotive freedom on the poet without making poetry descriptively untrue. But I believe even Mill's revised version of a descriptive theory has serious limitations when applied to poetry. Mill posits the priority of pre-existing data of sensation: the poet's language must correspond to these data. As Tennyson realizes, however, all description is interpretation. Independent of an observer's perception of the world, there exists no world with which either the scientist's judgmental inferences or the poet's intuitive inferences can be said to correspond. Tennyson, we know, was a student of metaphysics, and an admirer of J.F. Ferrier, the shrewdest of the early-Victorian idealists. As Ferrier asserts, 'the whole universe by itself,' which Mill would make the test of his correspondence theory, 'is absolutely unknowable.' 'The object of knowledge' is always 'the object with the addition of oneself ... Object ... plus subject is the *minimum scibile per se.*'[3]

No object or thought can ever be unhinged from a self-conscious observer. Not even Tennyson's imagination of the world's grand annihilation – 'When all that seems shall suffer shock' (*In Memoriam* CXXXI.2), – can entail the supposition of the poet's own extinction. The problem with Mill's correspondence model of truth is that it obscures the counter-truth that the sovereignty of Tennyson's self-conscious mind prevents the poet who 'dream[s] [his] dream, and hold[s] it true' (*In*

*Memoriam* CXXIII. 10) from experiencing his own dissolution. Despite the soul's apparent fragility in a world always on the edge of fragmentation, always on the verge of dissolution and collapse, the impossibility of unhinging Mill's sensory data from a perceiving subject gives Tennyson's soul a rocklike durability (*In Memoriam* CXXXI.1-3). As Ferrier concludes, 'we cannot, and we do not think [our death]: we only *think that we think it.*' 'In the real thought of [our death] we should be already dead.' But 'in the mere illusive imagination of the thought,' we 'are already an immortal race.'[4]

II

Mill's correspondence theory of truth remains a dominant interpretative model until 1870. But in later Victorian thought it is replaced by two other theories: by Huxley's teaching that scientific theories are a mere symbolic shorthand and by John Tyndall's less sceptical teaching that they are pictorial analogies, not purely descriptive but not mere symbolic fictions either. Both theories have important consequences for poetry, and I should like to examine each of them briefly.

The extreme form of the first theory, enshrined in Karl Pearson's *The Grammar of Science*, stands in the same relation to the descriptive postulates of an early-Victorian scientist like John Herschel[5] as the late-Victorian formalism of Arnold or Pater stands to the earlier mimetic postulates of G.H. Lewes, say, or Ruskin. John Herschel may not have been 'very confident of a close connection between current [scientific] theories and unseen Nature.' But as David B. Wilson observes, 'he regarded such a correspondence as [in principle] *attainable.*'[6] By contrast, Karl Pearson in *The Grammar of Science* treats physical theories as mere '"shorthand" methods of distinguishing, classifying, and resuming phases of sense-experience.'[7] With comparable candor T.H. Huxley confides that all scientific hypotheses are 'more or less imperfect and symbolic.' If the symbolic language of science still refers to phenomena, it refers to them at two removes, the way the earthly paradise of Morris discloses formal principles that seem to stand behind the brazen world of nature, but which (in Huxley's words) are 'neither self-evident' nor 'strictly speaking, demonstrable.'[8]

The non-ontological status of such a theory provides Matthew Arnold with a belated scientific justification of Wordsworth's claim that poetry is 'the impassioned expression which is in the countenance of all science.' If poetry is truly 'the breath and finer spirit of all knowledge,'[9] as Arnold polemically reasserts in *The Study of Poetry*, it is presumably because Arnold's poet can design elegant symbolic structures, because he can express with more emotion than the scientist (but with as much concision and clarity as the laws of mathematical physics) the rules that govern an ideal world. Unlike Bacon's poet, he is not simply submitting the shows of things to the desires of the mind. He is remoulding nature, but always like the nineteenth-century physicist in accordance with analogies and models that make it possible to speak intelligibly (and in the case of physics, even correctly) about phenomena that are not basically known.

To retain vestiges of Newton's mechanical model of simple substances and their qualities, which had been systematized by Locke, nineteenth-century scientists had tried to explain sound and light by postulating the model of a mechanical wave moving through a semi-rigid medium called the ether. But after Clerk Maxwell had translated Faraday's fields of force into mathematical form and developed them into a theory of electromagnetic waves, the postulate of the ether comes to be viewed by theorists like Helmholtz, Huxley, and Karl Pearson as mere symbolic shorthand, no more descriptive of external reality than the obsolete concept of phlogiston in chemistry. The pictures of a universe of atoms 'floating in ether,' says Pearson, 'do not exist in or beyond the world of sense-impressions, but are the pure product of our reasoning faculty.'[10]

A close reader of Helmholtz and Huxley as well as John Tyndall, an agnostic physicist and former colleague of Faraday, Tennyson[11] explores the doctrine of the merely fictive status of all scientific and philosophic concepts in his late poem *The Ancient Sage*. Since all thought 'Break[s] into "Thens" and "Whens" the Eternal Now' (104), the sage warns the sceptic that it is a mistake to confuse with an ultimate reality 'unshadowable in words' (238) a language which deals in logical antinomies. Science's 'counter-terms,' as Tennyson calls them (*The Ancient Sage*, 250), make clear that the reality which lies beyond space, time, and atoms, beyond the antinomies 'Of this divisible-indivisible world' (*De Profundis*, 43), is 'unconceivably' itself, ultimately unknowable and hence, in Tennyson's phrase, 'unshadowable in words.' Huxley's idealist critique of the Newtonian mechanical models is also exactly analogous to Tennyson's critique of the atomic philosophy in an earlier poem, *Lucretius*. In that monologue Tennyson shows how the atomistic model of a physicist like Tyndall, who quotes extensively from Lucretius in his Belfast Address,[12] fashions a mechanical mythology that is just as fantastic an exaggeration of partial knowledge as the religious mythology it supplants and a good deal less consoling.

The parallel between Huxley's theory of symbolic fictions and the unreality of all concepts, of all antinomies which fashion 'This double seeming of the single world,'[13] is explored not only by Tennyson in *The Ancient Sage* but also by Browning in his monologue *Mr. Sludge, 'The Medium.'* The hypotheses of the spiritualist, Sludge argues, which may have originated as poetry or mere 'novel-writing of a sort,' are not to be confused with the strictly true-or-false propositions of Mill's inductive logician. But then neither are the supreme postulates of the theologian or the molecular hypotheses of the biochemist and physicist. Like Pascal's two immensities, the unknowable God of the theologians comes close behind a 'stomach-cyst' (*Mr. Sludge, 'The Medium,'* 1117). He permeates in an infinite regress the least of the scientist's atomic models, which (as Mr Sludge observes) 'turns our spyglass round, or else / Puts a new lens in it' (1110-11). An X-ray machine may photograph a 'stomach-cyst' or tumour. But no microscope or lens has ever allowed the eye to see an atom, which remains a mere chemical hypothesis, mere 'novel-writing of a sort.' When reading Jowett's comments on Plato's *Republic* in the volume Jowett gave him, Browning would have encountered a remarkably similar formulation. The model world of Plato – and, by implication, of much modern poetry – illuminates natural phenomena in much the same way as do the hypotheses and model worlds of chemistry and physics. The poetic 'anticipations or divinations' of Plato, Jowett concludes, 'stand in the same relation to ancient philosophy which hypotheses bear to modern inductive science.'[14]

III

I have suggested that the reluctance of mathematical physicists like Clerk Maxwell to claim that even their experimentally confirmed theories offer a faithful picture of the world as it 'really' is parallels the aggressively 'non-ontological' kind of poetic theory that after 1870 tends increasingly to celebrate the poet's power to fashion and inhabit autonomous model worlds. Like Sidney's unfallen golden world, Morris' earthly paradise stands behind and slightly apart from nature: the fall into time and history has not yet occurred. In the physical theories of John Tyndall, a physicist whose works Tennyson owned and apparently read with interest, we find a third tradition based upon the mind's picture-making power to fashion and use concrete analogies. Equally critical of the empirical theory that the real is identical with all appearances in nature and of the idealist theory that the real sits apart from phenomena as a mere heuristic fiction, Tyndall argues that the scientist's pictorial models, however fragmentary, accurately reveal a concrete feature of the real world.

Tyndall sets forth his theory most persuasively in an essay entitled 'Scientific Use of the Imagination,' which he originally delivered as an address to the British Association at Liverpool in 1870. A member of the Metaphysical Society Tyndall attended, Tennyson owned a copy of this essay, which is now in the Tennyson Research Centre at Lincoln. Praising imagination as 'the architect of physical theory,' Tyndall argues that though the scientist, like the poet and the theologian, must use his imagination to penetrate the world of sense, he must always operate with concrete particulars which can be supported and verified by sense experience. Tyndall's scientist will begin with some familiar sensory phenomenon: the propagation of waves through water, for example, which Tennyson describes in vivid detail in *Timbuctoo* (119-29). To explain less obvious effects the scientist will then use the propagation of waves in water as a pictorial analogy of the transmission of sound waves through air and of light waves through a medium, the ether, which (though invisible) the scientist is forced to imagine or invent. Tyndall argues that these pictorial analogies are 'not less real than the world of ... sense.' As adjectives of the real, the wave motions of light in ether, like the lines of force connecting magnetic poles, may be veiled from view. But since 'the world of sense itself is the suggestion' of these analogies, 'and, to a great extent [their] *outcome*,'[15] Tyndall insists that they are not only real entities. They are also the living 'garment of God,' as he provocatively calls them, quoting Goethe and Carlyle.[16]

Tyndall's pictorial model of light waves in ether is precisely the form of divine vesture Tennyson uses a year earlier to endow the sacramental cup in *The Holy Grail* with real existence. Like Tyndall, who argues that the conception of ether, trembling with waves of light, bears the same relation to the observable phenomenon of ordinary wave motion that the theological postulate of a Universal Father shaping nature to his own will bears to 'the ordinary actions of man upon earth,'[17] Tennyson gives to the sacred object a base in such optical phenomena as the surging waves of the aurora borealis. The splendour of the Holy Grail, solidified like the 'gateways' of the New Jerusalem 'in a glory like one pearl' (*The Holy Grail*, 527), is a containing form of nature that Tennyson describes with scientific accuracy in the glorious auroral transformation of earth and nighttime sky. The great gusts of auroral light, startling and ephemeral as shooting stars, and of constantly shifting shape, are adjectives of the real that veil the Grail from view. But the Grail also gleams radiantly through the shimmering auroral waves. Tennyson is claiming to define in the volatile fire that imitates the spiritual change in Galahad a principle that, as Tyndall argues, underlies nature, that gives metaphysical as well as physical laws a local habitation and a name. Without the auroral fire and the characteristic accuracies of Tennyson's descriptive notation, there would be no vision of the spiritual city. The accomplished miracle of the Grail's simultaneous appearance and withdrawal would be lost.

Tennyson's poem *De Profundis*, which was completed only in 1880, after Tyndall's 'Scientific Use of the Imagination' had already appeared, may well reflect the influence of Tyndall's thought. Unlike the Ancient Sage, the poet of *De Profundis* is resolved, in Tyndall's words, to 'degrade neither member of the mysterious duality' which Tennyson celebrates in the 'main-miracle' of his poem: the indissoluble marriage of the soul to matter. In 'this divisible-indivisible' (43) conjoining of the material and spiritual universes which constitute the two halves of *De Profundis*, Tennyson's stirring account of the human embryo's remarkable ability to recapitulate the evolution of the whole race 'for a million aeons' (3) draws adventurously, as Tyndall says, upon 'the power of matter to divide itself and distribute its forces.' As his mind runs back with awe over the whole length of biological succession, Tennyson channels through subtly varied caesural pauses and carefully placed trochaic inversions his marvelling sense that, in Tyndall's phrase, matter and spirit are 'Equally worthy, and equally wonderful, ... two opposite faces of the self-same mystery.' As in the psalm by which Tennyson is inspired, a discipline is imposed upon the poet by the perfect parallelism of his phrasing: 'Out of the deep, my child, out of the deep' (1, 26), and by the many felicities of his syntax – by the way, for example, each successive epithet proves more expansive than the one preceding it: 'million,' 'vast / Waste,' 'multitudinous-eddying' (3-4). Exalting the material universe of part one from its abasement, and repealing as Tyndall would say 'the divorce hitherto existing between [the two universes],'[18] Tennyson moves through a spacious sequence of expanding clauses and phrases, relieving the overflowing emotions he expresses too directly in the coda, *The Human Cry*.

But like Tyndall, Tennyson is still at a loss to explain the 'main-miracle' (55). In his Belfast address, which he delivers four years after his lecture on 'Scientific Use of the Imagination,' Tyndall proclaims his faith that the two universes, material and spiritual, 'go hand in hand. But we try to soar in a vacuum,' he admits, 'the moment we seek to comprehend the connection between them. An Archimedean fulcrum is here required which the human mind cannot command.' In *De Profundis* the evolutionary atomic and physical models of the first half of the poem and the evolutionary spiritual models in the second half seem to run in tandem as parallel phenomena. But because man the physical object is still separated by an impassable gulf from man the subject Tennyson finds he cannot quite command Tyndall's 'Archimedean fulcrum.' The near-hysteria of the coda betrays that sense of failure.

> Hallowed be Thy name – Halleluiah!
>   Infinite Ideality!
>   Immeasurable Reality!
>   Infinite Personality!
> Hallowed be Thy name – Halleluiah!           (*De Profundis*, 57-61)

It seems incredible that a poet of such fertile metrical invention as Tennyson could write a stanza so obdurately heavy-footed and graceless. The three-line clump of banal rhymes, framed by unintegrated quotation from the Lord's Prayer, provides too little resistance to the poet's impulse to vent affirmations he would not venture on in prose. If the clichés of hymn-singing are recalcitrant materials, it is not because their emphatic metres are too resistant, but because they yield too readily to an uncritical formulation of Tennyson's pre-existing faith in a mysterious unity of matter and spirit he cannot quite compass or express. Once launched on his primitive raft of Sunday-school faith, the poet rides the deep buoyantly. But what he really seeks, I suspect, is not the assurance of the Lord's Prayer. Nor is it the uncertain consolation provided by the evolutionary atomic model of the two universes – physical and spiritual – he has just explored. In God's Incarnation Tennyson seeks an answer to the question that bewilders both himself and Tyndall: how from the combination and separation of mere insensate atoms can the miracle of human consciousness come to birth?

The Incarnational faith of the Christian is not a solution available to the agnostic Tyndall. And I think even Tennyson would welcome a less dogmatic answer. Recalling in his Belfast address that even 'the great Leibnitz felt the difficulty' of explaining how consciousness can arise from matter, Tyndall strains to envisage a new cosmology, a world in which dead atoms will be replaced by self-conscious monads all capable of functioning as 'more or less perfect mirrors of the universe.'[19] But it is not, I believe, to Leibnitz's monadology but to neo-Hegelianism that historians of Victorian thought must turn for a metaphysical model of the kind Tennyson and Tyndall are seeking. Tennyson was familiar with neo-Hegelian thought in the writings of Edward Caird: he owned a copy of Caird's monograph *The Problem of Philosophy at the Present Time*. The most systematic exposition of such thought is to be found, however, not in Caird himself, but in the writings of his fellow Idealist, F.H. Bradley, which I must briefly consider in the concluding section of this essay.

IV

In *The Principles of Logic* Bradley argues that the abstract universals and the abstract particulars of science and logic are unreal. Through the exercise of logic alone Bradley shows how the mind is tricked into constructing paralogisms which establish the truth of opposite conclusions: nothing that is real is universal; everything that is real is universal – no real is particular; most reality must be particular.[20] Bradley is equally insistent that reality is not to be confused with the abstract universals and the abstract particulars of science. 'What is real is the individual,' the unique item, 'the patch, matchwood, immortal diamond' that Hopkins celebrates (*That Nature is a Heraclitean Fire*, 23). But because Hopkins' 'Jack' or 'joke' is an allotrope, because he retains his identity as carbon even in being turned from a 'patch,' a piece of 'matchwood,' into 'immortal diamond' (23-4), he endures as a concrete *universal* as well.

Bradley recognizes that in the world of appearances logicians and scientists find it difficult to sustain this notion of a concrete universal. If they predicate of A what is different, they ascribe to the subject what it is *not* (a piece of coal, after all, is coal, not diamond): and if they predicate what is *not* different, they say nothing at all. They limit themselves to the one kind of proposition which we never make: the tautology that A equals A (coal is coal, diamond is diamond). The deadlock results from philosophers' attempts to extend the law of non-contradiction – the law that A cannot be both *a* and *non-a* – from the realm of logic, where it is valid, to the realm of concrete particulars and facts, where it may be possible, as Hegel argues, for unity to exist only through multiplicity, for A to assume the nature of C and D, allotropes of being like Hopkins' coal and diamond, without ceasing to be itself – a concrete particular distinctive as the taste of alum.

> In a flash, at a trumpet crash,
> I am all at once what Christ is, since he was what I am
> This Jack, joke, poor potsherd, patch, matchwood, immortal diamond,
> Is immortal diamond.
>
> (*That Nature is a Hercalitean Fire*, 21-4)

The recovery of the self's archetypal identity is marked by Hopkins' strong reversion to truncated three-stress half-lines:

> In a flash, at a trumpet crash (21)
> Is immortal diamond. (24)

The repeated strokes and lift of the internal rhymes (21) show the firmness of the soul, staunch under attack. Linking solidity with finely faceted beauty, identification with Christ, a concrete universal who has lived through the same destiny, alchemized from death to life, confers on Hopkins the only identity he has: 'I am all at once what Christ is, since he was what I am.' Though there is a jump from the concrete particular to the concrete universal, the individual is not blotted out. Alchemized from coal to diamond, the poet reaffirms the mystery of archetypal identity – a mystery laid out, not just in biblical myths, but in all the ancient fertility myths of resurrection and rebirth.

The power of a concrete universal to contain particulars as the Word contains the world can be studied to advantage in Hopkins' hermeneutical sonnet from *New Readings, Although the letter said*. All nature's indifference and stupidity, Hopkins argues, are redeemed and gathered up in two of the great containing forms of nature, the bread and wine of the Eucharist.

> From wastes of rock He brings
> Food for five thousand: on the thorn He shed
> Grains from His drooping Head;
> And would not have that legion of winged things
> Bear Him to heaven on easeful wings.
>
> *(Although the letter said,* 11-15)

Hopkins shows how, in a spiritual alchemy more rare than any Ovidian metamorphosis, the banquet of grain and wine harvested by Christ from the thorns of his death and resurrection transforms the meaning of the parable of the sower by surrounding the nature the parable describes and by putting that nature inside a body, a being at once individual and infinite, in which the whole universe can be contained.

It is less accurate to say that Hopkins' banquet of grain and wine describes nature than to say that nature, in such concrete particulars as the 'Grapes,' the 'drops of wine,' the 'Food for five thousand' (*Although the letter said,* 2, 5, 12), describes and foreshadows the archetype. Like Hopkins' Christ, the Holy Grail that Tennyson describes at the hour of Galahad's passing or the talking breeze that he evokes at the climax of *In Memoriam* turns nature itself into the content of a concrete universal. In *The Holy Grail*, for example, the elusive chalice that Tennyson projects as a Symbolist metaphor upon the heavens fashions itself out of pulsing stars and celestial visions of the New Jerusalem, and turns even the flickering whorls of red auroral light into an infinite containing form more human than inanimate.[21] A similar phenomenon occurs in section xcv of *In Memoriam*, where Tennyson describes a fugitive spiritual principle which builds its boundless day out of the merging of the afterglow of sunset with the early glow of dawn on midsummer nights in northern latitudes. If reality is a concrete universal, as Bradley maintains, then it must be intuited from such concrete manifestations of its power as Tennyson's description of the rocking of the full-foliaged elm trees, the throwing into wavelike motion of the scents that stream from the rose and the lily, and the final astonishing apparition of the speaking breeze, which seems to materialize out of the looking-glass world of *Maud*'s talking flowers, then just as mysteriously vanishes (*In Memoriam* xcv.53-64).

In his last book, *Essays on Truth and Reality*, F.H. Bradley confesses that he does 'not know whether this in my case is a mark of senility, but I find myself now taking more and more as literal fact what I used in my youth to admire and love in poetry.'[22] Bradley's metaphysics assumes that the more truth the mind attains, the more it can lay aside Mill's correspondence model: instead of evolving poetry from the world, the world can be evolved from poetry and its coherence model of truth. Because the real is both concrete and universal, it is less accurately defined through Mill's scientific inductions, through Huxley's symbolic shorthand, or even through Tyndall's pictorial analogies, than through analogy with a vast containing metaphor or poem. But if reality is poetic in its structure, is the converse proposition not equally valid? Are statements about poetry not also statements about the structure of a world we are entitled to call real? And if they are, is any scientist likely to accept this poetic model of truth?

It might appear at first that Bradley's metaphysics provides exactly the solution Tyndall and Tennyson are looking for. We have seen, for example, that Tyndall believes it is just as accurate to say that the world itself is deduced from our pictorial models of the world as to say that a metaphorical proposal about the wave properties of light is directly inferred from ready-made facts. The scientist's pictorial analogies resemble Keats's metaphor for the poetic imagination: they are like Adam's dream – he awoke and found it true. But we must not underestimate the widespread scientific hostility to Hegelianism. Though many scientists acknowledge their indebtedness to Kant, their contempt for Hegel is well expressed by Helmholtz, who observes that Hegel's 'system of nature seemed, at least to natural philosophers, absolutely crazy.'[23] It is true that in the later nineteenth century the distinction Mill originally draws between a scientific language of true-or-false propositions and a poetic language of metaphoric proposals ceases to be valid for all but the most uncritical materialists like Büchner. But the increasing approximation of scientific to poetic models does not mean that scientists are prepared to subordinate science to a poetic model of truth. Like most Hegelian systems, Bradley's *Appearance and Reality* must have struck most Victorian scientists as an abdication of intelligence. We should not, after all, expect philosophers of science like Pearson and Huxley to expose the merely fictive status of the scientist's models only to embrace with open arms the massive reification of such fictions in the kind of poetical ontology which turns the merely formal and logical account of the concrete universal that Bradley offers in his *Principles of Logic* into a metaphysical theory that makes existential claims as well.

On the contrary, for Huxley the strict truth or falsity of a scientific model, like its ontological status, is never really at issue. The symbolic shorthand of the physicist is conceived solely for the mind's convenience or delight, like a tool we might use or a poem we might admire for its verbal economy. In *The Grammar of Science* Karl Pearson completes the Kantian deconstruction of theology and ethics by deconstructing the theories of science itself. We may recall that in his *Critique of Pure Reason* Kant had developed a theory of the conceptual understanding designed to defend the validity of the scientific method against Hume's critique. Kant argues that the scientist's propositions are both true and cognitive: they are true because they are a priori: they organize experience according to spatial and temporal forms that the mind itself supplies. But unlike the analytic a priori propositions of mathematics, the propositions of science also give us knowledge of the world, because they are *synthetic* propositions that add information in the predicate that is not given in the subject. The truths of ethics and religion, by contrast, are mere postulates of the practical reason. Once Pearson and Huxley, however, show that science itself is only a tool or a convenience, an invention of the practical reason, then Kant's influential distinction between the pure and practical reason, designed to preserve the ultimate authority of science, is found to be invalid. Nor can theologians any longer argue, as did the neo-Kantian Dean of St Paul's, H.L. Mansel, in his Bampton lectures for 1859, *The Limits of Religious Thought*, that the primacy of our practical reason requires us to believe in a God whose conceptual definitions are riddled with the logical contradictions that are generated whenever a concept like the infinite or the absolute is not directly convertible into sense impressions, as are the concepts of the scientist.

Having completed the deconstruction of scientific theory, late Victorians like Karl Pearson and Huxley are likely to be deeply suspicious of F.H. Bradley's attempts in book two of *Appearance and Reality* to reconstruct their world by baptising the poet's concrete universals in the name of the Real and calling them the Absolute. Like later philosophers, these scientists are far more sympathetic to Bradley the deconstructionist, who in book one of *Appearance and Reality* systematically unmasks the abstractions and contradictions of conceptual thought. All abstract thinking is relational, he argues, and the relational is unreal. More relentlessly and incisively than any other Victorian, Bradley exposes what Whitehead calls 'the major vice of the intellect' – 'the intolerable use of abstractions.'[24] He provides the most searching critique of the fatal tendency of all conceptual thought to strip away and abstract, producing only a dissection of the warm and living world the poets know. For this reason alone scientists and humanists alike owe a lasting debt of gratitude to Bradley.

I have shown how John Tyndall, in his essay 'Scientific Use of the Imagination,' tries to remove science's heel of Achilles, its tendency to impoverish concrete reality, to make its models too generic and abstract. For despite the efforts of late Victorians to minimize the differences between science and poetry, thinkers as dissimilar as Tennyson, Tyndall, and F.H. Bradley all recognize that in order to retain their ability to control and predict events the models of the scientist are condemned to be incomparably more attenuated, more naked and skeletal than the poet's. The atomic theories of the scientists disclose only 'some spectral woof of impalpable abstractions,' as Bradley says, 'or unearthly ballet of bloodless categories. Though dragged to such conclusions, we cannot embrace them. Our [scientific and logical] principles may be true, but they are not reality. They no more *make* that whole which commands our devotion, than some shredded dissection of human tatters *is* that warm and breathing beauty of flesh which our heart found delightful.' To escape from the Fallacy of Misplaced Concreteness, from the tendency of science to invest atoms and ether with a reality they do not possess, many Victorians find they must turn away from the abstractions of science to the delights and pains of the affective life, which are preserved for them, as they were for F.H. Bradley and for J.S. Mill after his mental breakdown, in the imagination of the poets. Only the poets seem able to repair the sense of injustice that we feel whenever our individual experiences, which we believe to be unique to ourselves, are described in the abstractions of the scientist, who uses concepts common to everyone. Because the poet's representations are wholly individual, he may greatly diminish Bradley's sense of loss, his sense that 'the sensuous curtain is a deception and a cheat,'[25] by countenancing the belief that in all its idiosyncratic detail – single, unrepeatable, compelling – a poem like *In Memoriam* or *The Prelude*, even in speaking to and for our common humanity, is speaking to each of us alone.

NOTES

1 'Wordsworth's Prefaces of 1800 and 1802,' *Lyrical Ballads: Wordsworth and Coleridge*, ed. R.L. Brett and A.R. Jones (London, 1963), 253.

2 Mill's two essays of 1833, originally published in the *Monthly Repository*, 7 (Jan., Oct. 1833), 60-70, 714-24, are reprinted as 'Thoughts on Poetry and Its Varieties,' in Mill's *Dissertations and Discussions*, 2 vols. (London, 1859), I, 63–94. The quotation is from 'Thoughts on Poetry and Its Varieties,' in *Autobiography and Literary Essays*, ed. J.M. Robson and Jack Stillinger, *Collected Works of John Stuart Mill*, I (Toronto, 1981), 347.

3 J.F. Ferrier, *The Institutes of Metaphysics: Theory of Knowing and Being* (Edinburgh and London, 1854), 93, 106.

4 J.F. Ferrier, 'Berkeley and Idealism,' *Blackwood's Magazine*, 51 (June 1842), 819.

5 Author of *A Preliminary Discourse on the Study of Natural Philosophy* (London, 1831). For the comparison of Herschel and Pearson I am indebted to David B. Wilson, 'Concepts of Physical Nature: John Herschel to Karl Pearson,' in *Nature and the Victorian Imagination*, ed. U.C. Knoepflmacher and G.B. Tennyson (Berkeley, 1977), 201-15.

6 'Concepts of Physical Nature,' 207.

7 *The Grammar of Science* (London, 1892), 214.

8 The first quotation is from 'Science and Culture' (1880), *Collected Essays of T.H. Huxley*, III (London, 1893), 150. The second quotation is from 'The Progress of Science' (1887), ibid., I, 61. A more complete account of science's symbolic shorthand can be found in Huxley's essay 'On the Physical Basis of Life' (1868), ibid., I, 165: 'With a view to the progress of science, the materialistic terminology is in every way to be preferred ... But the man of science, who, forgetting the limits of philosophical inquiry, slides from these formulae and symbols into what is commonly understood by materialism, seems to me to place himself on a level with the mathematician, who should mistake the $x$'s and $y$'s with which he works his problems, for real entities.'

9 Matthew Arnold, *The Complete Prose Works*, ed. R.H. Super, IX (Ann Arbor, 1961), 162.

10 *The Grammar of Science*, 214-15.

11 Tennyson's abiding interest in the philosophy of science and in its implications for poetics, theology, and for a theory of knowledge is evident from his owning such works as John Tyndall's *Scientific Use of the Imagination* (London, 1873), F.L. Büchner's *Force and Matter* (London, 1864), and Samuel Brown's *Lectures on the Atomic Theory* (Edinburgh, 1858). Tennyson owned Tyndall's *Six Lectures on Light Delivered in America in 1872-1873* (London, 1873) and pamphlets by Tyndall on cometary theory and on Helmholtz's theory of ice and glaciers.

12 Delivered before the British Association, 19 August 1974. 'The Belfast Address,' *Fragments of Science: Essays, Addresses, and Reviews by John Tyndall*, II (London, 1889), 162-9, 144.

13 *The Ancient Sage*, 105. Besides reflecting Huxley's influence, Tennyson's exposure of such logical antinomies may also owe something to Victorian neo-Kantian thought. Whereas the nineteenth-century German Idealists develop the constructive side of Kant's epistemology, the Victorian neo-Kantians tend to develop its critical side. Beginning with Sir William Hamilton, they emphasize the inaccessibility of God to the conceptual understanding. They show that our ideas of an absolute and infinite deity are in logical contradiction with each other. Having put God in the test-tube, Mansel and Hamilton discover that God's names and attributes have no sensory content with which a science of God can deal. On the implications for poetic langauge of H.L. Mansel's agnostic theology see my essay, 'The Agnostic Imagination in Victorian Poetry,' *Criticism*, 22 (1980), 116-39.

14 *The Dialogues of Plato* (Oxford, 1871), II, 80. According to the Sotheby Catalogue of the Browning library, which was dispersed in 1913, Jowett presented his edition of Plato to Browning in 1875.

15 'Scientific Use of the Imagination,' *Fragments of Science*, II, 104, 107.

16 'Scientific Use of the Imagination,' 132. The doctrine of moral vocation which Tyndall cites with approval in Goethe, Fichte, and Carlyle is to mere hedonism what Tyndall's doctrine of pictorial analogies is to the materialism of Büchner. And Tyndall's Carlylean doctrine of salvation through work is to the eviscerated theism of spiritualists like the Ancient Sage what his scientific theories of 'the picturing power of the mind' are to the imperfectly incarnated symbolic fictions of a Huxley or Pearson. For 'the kingdom of science,' Tyndall avers, 'cometh not by observation and experiment alone, but is completed by fixing the roots of observation and experiment in a region inaccessible to both, and in dealing with which we are forced to fall back upon the picturing power of the mind' ('Apology for the Belfast Address,' 208).

17 'On Prayer as a Form of Physical Energy,' *Fragments of Science*, II, 43.

18 'Scientific Use of the Imagination,' 126, 132.

19 'The Belfast Address,' 194, 168.

20 F.H. Bradley, *The Principles of Logic* (London, 1883), 174-5. Of course, Hopkins' allotropes are *my* illustration of the logical doctrine, not Bradley's. In *The Principles of Logic* Bradley leaves open the question whether the individual is 'finite' or 'absolute.' 'Metaphysics,' he concedes, in anticipation of his resumption of the inquiry in *Appearance and Reality*

(Oxford, 1893), 'would have to take up these questions, and in any case revise the account which is given in this chapter' (*Principles of Logic*, 177).

21 For a more complete account of Tennyson's lifelong poetic use of auroral phenomena see the essay I wrote in collaboration with the geophysicist Carl W. Gartlein, 'The Aurora: A Spiritual Metaphor in Tennyson,' *Victorian Poetry*, 3 (1965), 213-22.

22 F.H. Bradley, *Essays on Truth and Reality* (Oxford, 1914), 468.

23 H. Helmholtz, *Popular Lectures on Scientific Subjects*, trans. E. Atkinson, introd. John Tyndall (London, 1873), 5. Helmholtz criticizes Hegel for launching out 'with unusual vehemence and acrimony, against the natural philosophers, and especially against Sir Isaac Newton, as the first and greatest representative of physical investigation. The philosophers accused the scientific men of narrowness; the scientific men retorted that the philosophers were crazy.' Helmholtz himself retains great respect for Kant's 'Critical Philosophy,' and argues that scientists have much to learn from philosophical 'criticism of the sources of cognition, and the definition of the function of the intellect.'

24 A.N. Whitehead, *Science and the Modern World* (New York, 1925), 18.

25 Bradley, *Principles of Logic*, 533. As authoritative today as when it was first written, Antonio Aliotta's classic study, 'Science and Religion in the Nineteenth Century,' trans. Fred Brittain, in *Science Religion and Reality*, ed. Joseph Needham (New York, 1925), 151-86, is still the single best essay on the subject I have explored. For excellent discussions of the concrete universal and its relation to the anagogic phase of symbolism, Northrop Frye's *Anatomy of Criticism* (Princeton, 1957), 119-28, is also indispensable. The best comments on the subject of Tennyson and late-Victorian science are to be found, I think, in F.E.L. Priestley, *Language and Structure in Tennyson's Poetry* (London, 1973), esp. 166-8.

**JENNIFER
LEVINE**

# Reading 'Ulysses'

*Finnegans Wake* ... is the chief ironic epic of our time ... Who then is the hero ... ? No character in the book itself seems a likely candidate ... Eventually it dawns on us that it is the *reader* ... the reader who ... is able to look down on its rotation, and see its form as something more than rotation.
Northrop Frye, *Anatomy of Criticism*

When a text quotes and requotes, with or without quotation marks, when it is written on the brink, you start, or indeed you have already started, to lose your footing. You lose sight of any line of demarcation between a text and what is outside it.
Jacques Derrida, 'Living on: Border Lines'

We can begin with 'Oxen of the Sun.' Of all the episodes in Joyce's *Ulysses* it seems the most appropriate by which to mark the enduring power of Northrop Frye's dialogue with literature. As so much of Frye's work has done, it addresses itself to 'literature as a whole.' It speaks to our sense that individual works exist within a tradition, that they are caught up with each other in an ongoing play of imitation, translation, acceptance, and rejection, and that they derive much of their meaning from such encounters. I choose the comment from the *Anatomy* as one of my epigraphs even though its explicit reference is to *Finnegans Wake*, because it suggests an entry to *Ulysses* as well.[1] It stresses, first of all, the crucial work of the reader.[2] It also alludes, through the rubric of irony, to that refusal of a final authorizing language which is already present in *Ulysses*. Finally, it signals to Frye's profoundly visual imagination, an imagination which maps the reader's relationship to texts and the relationship of texts to each other in a spatial way.[3] 'Oxen of the Sun' translates itself easily – perhaps too easily – into a visual shape before our eyes. As we recognize the succession of styles 'quoted' in the episode, the straight line of chronology locks each element into place. But then, the very act of recognition which achieves that line also fractures it into a much more complicated and precarious arrangement – as Derrida's comment tells us: 'When a text quotes or requotes ... you start ... to lose your footing.'[4]

In my own discussion of *Ulysses* I will focus first on 'Oxen of the Sun,' then on 'Ithaca.' I shall adopt a visual metaphor of sorts, tracing out the shifting distances between the reader, language, and the fictional world. Both episodes tantalize us with an offer of meaning or revelation, and yet deny that possibility. Both suggest that the world is the product of interpretation and of language. My sense of *Ulysses* is that it partakes of the mode Frye has called ironic, and that post-structuralist criticism has articulated more fully as modern, writerly, or interrogative.[5] Although I am not persuaded that the reader's work in *Ulysses* is heroic, I am convinced it is essential, and my argument takes the experience of reading as its focus.

Leopold Bloom and Stephen Dedalus have tentatively impinged on each other at a number of points in *Ulysses*. But it is not until 'The Oxen of the Sun,' when both find themselves at the Maternity Hospital during Mrs Purefoy's long labour, that they mutually acknowledge each other's presence. Bloom watches paternally over Stephen as questions of creation (both physical and literary) are bandied about. Stephen's sympathy for Bloom is rather more limited. (When Lynch turns to him to ask 'Who the sooty hell's the fellow in the black duds,' Stephen answers with histrionic flair: 'Hush! Sinned against the light and even now that day is at hand when he shall come to judge the world by fire.')[6] Nevertheless, Stephen does stand Bloom a drink – even if it is only ginger cordial.

Characteristically in a text that chooses not to record other crucial encounters (Molly and Boylan's in particular), the episode allows us no sense of direct access to the meeting of Bloom and Stephen. Style after style interposes itself as the voices of English prose from its Saxon and Latinate beginnings to the anarchic present parade before us. It is a virtuoso performance. But the response to 'Oxen of the Sun' has not been unanimous. For some, it is a brilliant platform for Joyce's skill; for others a pretentious flop. Approving readers raise the banner of mimetic form.

After her long labour Mrs Purefoy is eventually delivered of a child, and so the development of writing mirrors the gestation and birth of a human being. 'The process ... begins in a murk of chaos' and ends 'in the manner of a dithyrambic American super-hot gospeller.' The long travail brings forth 'a grinning golliwog ... the language of the future.'[7] For Stuart Gilbert the analogy between language and biology is so powerful that even deviations from literary chronology are acceptable. More than that: they confirm his interpretation. He makes the point of noting certain anachronisms with the comment that the growth of an embryo is not uniform either, that an eye, for example, may develop 'out of its term.'[8] Other readers have not been able to share Gilbert's conviction. Harry Levin writes that though we may be admonished (even by Joyce himself) that the parodies 'illustrate the principle of embryonic growth,' we cannot take the claim very seriously.

To call in so many irrelevant authors as a middle term between the concepts of biology and the needs of the present narrative is to reduce Joyce's cult of imitative form to a final absurdity. For what organic reason, if any, must Lyly represent the foetus in the third month, and Goldsmith in the sixth? And what's Bunyan to Mrs. Purefoy, or Mrs. Purefoy to Junius?[9]

Levin pushes the analogy to its logical conclusion, not just accepting it as a general hypothesis, but working it out in the smallest details. The model is expected to fit at every point. Perhaps he demands more from a reading such as Gilbert's than was ever intended. But he does put his finger on an important difficulty: the parallel between the growth of a foetus and the growth of a language is not maintained consistently. Somewhat grudgingly he admits that the pastiche of styles 'does offer Joyce fair field for his technical virtuosity,' and, indeed, the chapter is saved for many readers in the same way.[10] Levin takes a step back from the claims of mimesis and from the strictly 'internal' coherence which links the development of style to the development of human life, and adopts a larger overview which now includes the writer and the act of writing. Thus the development of styles is not so much a metaphor (literary history is biological history), as an index to Joyce's skill, and to his status in the literary tradition. Anthony Burgess' response is interestingly poised between a reader's impatience and a fellow writer's admiration. Of all the episodes in *Ulysses*, he says, this is the one he would most like to have written.

It is an author's chapter, a dazzling and authoritative display of what English can do. Moreover, it is a fulfilment of every author's egotistical desire not merely to *add* to English literature but to *enclose* what is actually there. Literary history is a line; Joyce wants to see it as a series of concentric circles, himself the outer ring ... But it is a pity that Stephen and Bloom have to get lost in the process of glorifying an art that is supposed to be their servant.[11]

This, then, is the episode in which Joyce's skill as a writer becomes most obvious – ironically perhaps because he was unable or unwilling to sacrifice literary exuberance to literary economy. And yet by the very rules of the game he has chosen to play, it is also the episode in which he defers most obviously to the reader. The joke falls flat, the game becomes an absurd solitaire, if readers do not play their part. A whole set of recognitions is at stake in 'Oxen of the Sun.' We must first of all notice the shifts in language. We must recognize specific pre-texts. We must recognize the chronogical order. And we must recognize the extent of distortion between each text and its original.

Even without the special knowledge that for Joyce the episode was the most difficult in *Ulysses*, readers are quick to sense that a bravura performance is taking place.[12] But the focus on the writer alone (Joyce as the conqueror of the past, the man who can do all the styles, and see through them) ends up immobilizing the reader. We stand aside, watch, admire. At best we recognize the shots as they spin off the writer's pen, and in that brief moment of complicity we might share a rush of power. This scenario would be appropriate if we really were kept in an attitude of respectful admiration, but the parodic onslaught is very uneven. Some scenes bear the master-mimic's touch: the Swiftean account of the Irish bull in an English china shop, or Mulligan as 'le Fecondateur' and a Sterne-like Lynch discussing the French fashion for cloaks which keep 'a lady from wetting.' Other parodies are less convincing. The Dickensian moment, for instance, is so caricaturized that without the insistent 'Doady' readers might think themselves in a pulp-fiction interlude. The advantage of reading 'Oxen of the Sun' through a perspective of 'Joyce the Prodigy' is that, though it immobilizes the reader, it organizes the multiple voices into a shape (the line of history which culminates in Joyce or, as Burgess suggests, the circles of history which Joyce encompasses). But if we insist on that characterization we have to conclude that Joyce was not quite the prodigy we would like to think, and that the chapter is an embarrassing lapse: better to read through it quickly on the way to better things. And yet it is worth noting at this point that subsequent versions of the first long paragraph changed it from a fairly straight copy of Tacitus to something much closer to pastiche, and that Joyce's sources throughout were less often the originals themselves than mediating texts like Saintsbury's *History of English Prose Rhythm* and Peacock's study of literature from Mandeville to Ruskin.[13] Already in the writing, it would seem, there is a sense of seeing things by choice at second or third remove – as though through a variable and distorting medium of interpretation and not through the transparent glasses of imitation. In spite of the reassuring structures we build up (the straight line of literary history is the most obvious) our position in the text is never fixed. On the contrary, the episode is memorable because of the ways it keeps us off balance. In this, I would argue that 'Oxen of the Sun' speaks for and with *Ulysses* as a whole. And, of course, we must not be too serious: our instability is part of the fun in the episode. My reading of 'Oxen' is made not so much to save the episode from accusations of failure as to indicate its place within the larger project of the novel. I see in *Ulysses* an increasing move away from the kinds of writing (interior monologue, mimetic or expressive form) that suggest that language can become transparent, giving us 'the thing itself' without distortion.

It is worth exploring further how the scene in the Maternity Hospital engages us in its labour. The metaphor is deliberate. If we speak of the reader's work in a text, in this episode we might more appropriately call it a labour: we are taken up by an irrevocable logic, thrust forward by history toward 'the utterance of the Word' (404) and the cry of the newborn child. Nevertheless this illusion of irreversibility, however powerful, is only an illusion. We are not giving birth. We are reading a book, which means we are always free to stop, to turn the pages back and forth, and consider what is happening to us. When we do so we find that the movement of 'Oxen of the Sun' is not simply a linear one. Like any parodic text, it is constantly directing us out beyond its margins to other languages, other sources. It is surely ironic that in the attempt to stabilize the episode we introduce a whole Pandora's box of unbalancing factors. We recognize the gaps between successive languages in the text and bridge them with a knowledge of literary history, but in each recognition of a pre-text a new gap opens up. The very nature of parody keeps us off balance: we are kept at a distance by the imitation (because to imitate is also to measure and to judge), and yet we are drawn in by memory (which seems to promise, again, an entire fictional world).

'Oxen of the Sun' engages us in a double reading, reading both text and pre-text. I have already noted the inconsistent parodic distances – the different gaps between, say, Joyce-Swift and Swift, and Joyce-Dickens and Dickens. My purpose in doing so was to question the usual formulation of the writer's authority and the reader's static passivity. It is also important to see how these shifting gaps make it even more difficult to sustain a simply linear organization. With each new style we have to reposition ourselves in time. We also have to reposition ourselves in relation to whichever pre-text is invoked. At certain times the gap between them is considerable; at others, when we feel the imitation is exact, the gap almost disappears. Every new quotation makes us lose our footing in a new way. The two-dimensional line moves out into a third dimension: it goes forward from past to present, and also in and out in its relation to literary history. The episode is further complicated because not only the Joycean text shifts ground – so does each pre-text invoked by memory as it inscribes a different distance to the reader and to the fictional world. 'Pepys'' language, for example, might seem the spontaneous expression of reality, rendering words transparent and the reader invisible. 'Swift's' positions us in quite a different way, demanding our intervention as decoders. It makes it obvious that the relationship between words and meanings is not direct – that the story it tells of Lord Harry, farmer Nicholas, and the gelded bull is more than a pastoral interlude. Reading 'Oxen of the Sun' we find ourselves in a kaleidoscopic space where every 'shake' of the writing creates a new cluster of relationships between language and its origins, language and its reference, language and its interpreter.

Let us return to the straight line of history. In spite of all the refracting elements that enter into our reading, and which I have been discussing, the force of that first linear organization remains an inevitable one for the episode. Indeed, our whole way of thinking about history encourages it. If, as Augustine suggests, human history is a sentence whose meaning is only revealed (or, conversely, a culprit whose sentence is only decreed) when the final syllable is uttered[14] – that is, if it only becomes intelligible when read in its entirety from beginning to end in that very specific and non-reversible order, and closure and disclosure are simultaneous – what, then, to make of the final scenes of 'Oxen of the Sun'? Things certainly seem more intelligible as we progress toward the present but we do not simply move out of the murk of early time into a final clarity. At a certain point – ironically after 'the utterance of the Word' – the writing reverts to opacity. Obviously the verbal confusion matches the increasing drunkenness of Stephen and his friends. But the voice of mimesis does not take us far enough. It does not answer the main question: why plot a history that returns to incoherence of action and of language?

The final pages play on our sense of an ending as the call of closure for those in the pub is heard through the raucous blend of voices. 'Keep a watch on the clock. Chuckingout time ... Ten to ... closing-time gents ... Time ... Time all ... Night. Night' (406-9). Even more notably, the last paragraph announces the apocalypse: 'Even now that day is at hand when he shall come back to judge the world by fire ... *Ut implerentur scripturae*' – that the scriptures might be fulfilled (409). The hot-gospelling diatribe that follows pulls out all the stops, invoking the prophetic entrance of Elijah (Matthew 17:9-11), the blood of the lamb (Revelation 7:14 and 5:6-8), and the final gathering in of sinners that marks the Day of Judgment:

Elijah is coming washed in the blood of the lamb. Come on, you winefizzling ginsizzling booseguzzling existences! Come on, you doggone bullnecked, beetle-browed ... weaseleyed fourflushers ...! Come on ...! Alexander J. Christ Dowie, that's yanked to glory most half this planet from Frisco Beach to Vladivostock. The Deity ain't no nickel dime bumshow ... He's the grandest thing yet and don't you forget it. Shout Salvation in king Jesus. (409)

But this is a mock apocalypse. The second coming is utterly carnival-ized. The revelation at the end is denied. And whereas the final verses of the Book of Revelation promise the quenching of thirst by the word of God, the Dubliners' indulgence in drink has quite another effect: writing is not so much fulfilled as thrust before us in its opaque materiality. In its final gesture, the episode moves away from Stephen and Bloom. The last paragraph says very little about them (except by suggesting that Bloom is the occasion for Elijah's second coming – but then, has he really sinned against the light?). We do not meet them again until some pages later when Stephen, announced as 'the parson' and 'flourishing the ashplant in his left hand' (412), crosses the stage followed by Bloom 'flushed, panting, cramming bread and chocolate into a side pocket' (414). Something has happened at Westland Row Station, but neither 'Oxen of the Sun' nor 'Circe' chooses to reveal clearly what it is.

Indeed, throughout 'Oxen of the Sun' the parodic voices refract and distort the possibility of any direct access to meaning. The function of language is questioned – comically so in the account of the bull of Ireland and his seduction of every 'maid, wife, abbess and widow':

and the end [of the story] was that the men of the island ... made a wherry raft, loaded themselves and their bundles of chattels on shipboard, set all masts erect, manned the yards, sprang the luff, heaved to, spread three sheets in the wind, put her head between wind and water, weighed anchor, ported her helm, ran up the jolly Roger, gave three times three, let the bullgine run, pushed off in their bumboat and put to sea to recover the main of America. (383)

There is such sheer exuberance in the writing: but to what effect? Instead of each additional phrase enhancing the expressive power of language (as each additional brush stroke on a canvas might increase our illusion of 'the real'), the accumulation of phrases is such that language itself is reified, and meaning (i.e. the thing 'out there' that language points to) recedes into the background. Before they even got out of the harbour, the men of Ireland are nearly drowned in a full sea of words. Is the description a failure? The phrases are not carelessly redundant: they quite specifically invoke the larger paradigm within which each individual phrase acquires significance. But the delight is in the world of signs themselves and in the richness of the paradigm – not in particular meanings. We may or may not agree with Burgess' rueful judgment that 'it is a pity that Stephen and Bloom have to get lost in the process of glorifying an art that is supposed to be their servant': he is nevertheless right to see that the expected hierarchy between words and a fictional world has been overturned. Closing time in 'Oxen of the Sun' discloses the loud and empty rhetoric of salvation – a twist on the biblical Elijah who learns that God's rule is established in a 'still, small voice' (1 Kings 19:12). Perhaps, after *A Portrait of the Artist*, Joyce no longer sees himself as a kind of God, aloof, detached from his handiwork, paring his fingernails, and capable of revealing the world in all its meaning.[15] If we want to invoke an authorial presence when we speak of *Ulysses*, my own reading of 'Oxen of the Sun' would see not so much a Joyce parodying the past to proclaim his superiority to it as a Joyce who involves the reader in the dilemma of language.

For a number of readers the episode suggests that the styles of the past are all, in different ways, inadequate – but that precisely by collecting so many of them Joyce transcends their limits and achieves a new fullness of meaning.[16] My sense of the episode is rather the reverse. I see in each parodied style a renewed evocation of the power and pleasure of language. But cumulatively the experiment speaks to a more limited sense of what is possible. With each style another light goes on, illuminating another corner of experience. Yet the illusions of access end in frustration. The rhythm of change is relentless. Each 'voice' has only just enough time to establish itself before it is dispatched by its successor, placed swiftly and irrevocably in the past (which is the double past of this particular episode and of an entire literary tradition). Of course, this is only dramatizing the implications of any parodic structure. Parody always attempts to subvert and deny one discourse in favour of another – to make us wonder how we could ever have taken it seriously instead of as the absurdity or sheer falsehood it so patently represents. Parody achieves this by replacing its target (either implicitly or explicitly) with another language, a 'truer' one. Parody does not question the possibility that such a language can be located. On the contrary, it sees the task as both possible and necessary, and as the essence of the writer's work. 'Oxen of the Sun' is made up of parodies and yet its cumulative effect is very different. There is no one language that is allowed to take up and retain a special position vis-à-vis the truth (as there is no final resting point that holds all the voices together). The moments of privilege for each style are only that – moments, and they are dissolved in the ongoing reading of the episode. The parodic voice presupposes a fixed centre, a point from which and to which the play of reference and judgment can be anchored. But in 'Oxen of the Sun' each parodic assault is undermined by the one that follows in an endless deconstruction. Frye's account of irony as a way of seeing that – in contrast to satire – refuses any authoritative perspective is useful here. We are dealing with irony, he says, 'whenever a reader is not sure what the author's attitude is or what his own is supposed to be.'[17] The distinction is echoed in recent discussions of fiction, most notably in Roland Barthes' paradigm of the readerly versus the writerly text: *le lisible/le scriptible, écrivance/écriture*, the text of classical realism/the modern 'limit text.'[18] (Indeed, Barthes' account of the multivalent or writerly text and its strategy of quotation recalls the procedures of 'Oxen of the Sun.' 'A multivalent text [he writes] can carry out its basic duplicity only if it subverts the opposition between true and false, if it fails to attribute quotations ... to explicit authorities, if it flouts all respect for origin, paternity, propriety, if it destroys the voice which could give the text its ("organic") unity ... For multivalence ... is a transgression of ownership.'[19] Barthes develops his central paradigm so that the readerly is identified with a concept of language as transparent, with a commitment to the signified and to a hierarchy of meanings. The writerly depends on a self-reflexive play with language, on the elaboration of the signifier and a concomitant plurality of meanings. In the later episodes of *Ulysses* the voice of the writerly is heard more and more strongly.

'Oxen of the Sun' already speaks for *Ulysses* in a number of ways. Perhaps more often than any other episode (because of the insistent and continuous shifts in style) it keeps its readers in a state of disequilibrium, never able to sustain a consistent relationship to the language or to the fictional world inscribed within it. It plays on the themes of closure and disclosure but at the end of the line reveals very little, shifting its attention (and that of its readers) from the signified to the signifier. We are refused that moment of clear vision, 'as though face to face,' promised by Revelation. The episode tries out style after style, discarding each in turn, never allowing one to take more than temporary precedence over another. And because there is no single language which will provide and authorize a meaning (neither one of the voices of the past nor the voice of Joyce standing above his creation) meaning can only be relational, produced in the space between languages. 'Oxen of the Sun,' like *Ulysses*, is not a text of revelation but of interpretation.

As *Ulysses* proceeds it moves further away from the norms of transparency established at the beginning in the interior monologues of Stephen and Bloom. 'Oxen of the Sun' continues that movement. It is in 'Ithaca,' at the end of Stephen's and Bloom's journey, that we find the most consistent refusal to reveal. The scenario here is typically subversive, for 'Ithaca' speaks in the double voice of Science and Religion. The two languages our culture privileges most highly, because they seem to provide an access to Truth, are overlapped in a long game of question and answer. The catechism, though, leads to unorthodox conclusions. In the early chapters the insistence on a scrupulously accurate language eases our movement through the sign, makes the object signalled more accessible. Thus when Bloom's cat rubs against his leg she is heard to say not 'Meow' but 'Mrkgnao,' asserting the real truth of her cry as against the conventions of mere writing. A similar insistence in 'Ithaca' suggests that rendering the world accessible through words is no longer such a compelling task. On the contrary, it seems that the project itself has become the butt of 'Ithaca's' considerable humour. After a long and detailed description of the 'phenomenon of ebullition,' the question is

posed: 'What announced the accomplishment of this rise in temper-
ature?' and the answer given: 'A double falciform ejection of water vapour
from under the kettle-lid at both sides simultaneously' (634). Similarly,
some pages later,

What suddenly arrested his ingress?
The right temporal lobe of the hollow sphere of his cranium came into contact
with a solid timber angle, where, an infinitesimal but sensible fraction of a
second later, a painful sensation was located in consequence of antecedent
sensations transmitted and registered. (666)

Nothing is taken for granted in descriptions such as these. Every detail
has been reconsidered through the pseudo-scientific accuracy of the
writing. Unlike the sense of rediscovery in 'Mrkgnao' (of course ... that
really is the sound a cat makes), in 'Ithaca' we encounter a resistance, as
though language were deliberately pushing us away from its object. Is
the episode deliberately courting our impatience? We want to shout
(and giggle) 'steam!' or 'he hit his head,' reasserting normal discourse
and normal access to the world. The opacity of the language is
ambivalent enough that we feel we can circumvent it, replace it with
our own more straightforward answers. Thus reading becomes (in the
crudest sense) a mode of rewriting. But how to distinguish between a
language that misses its mark deliberately, and one that does so out of
sheer incompetence? The only answer is that the failure of language
must be seen to succeed in another way. By turning away from the
imagined world of 7 Eccles Street, *Ulysses* can open onto the com-
municative act itself. With mixed delight and frustration the text
explores the materiality of language.
    The patterning of 'Ithaca' is important. What it reveals, however, is
the precoded nature of signs. Just as every question in 'Ithaca' has an
answer, so too every word seems locked into a paradigmatic chain
which is made explicit in the text. If a door is a 'door of egress' (for
Bloom and Stephen) it must also be a 'door of ingress' (for the cat) (659).
And 'concerning the respective percentage of protein and caloric energy
in bacon, salt ling and butter,' the information will be given as 'the
absence of the former in the lastnamed and the abundance of the latter
in the firstnamed' (634). Words do not approach us as free agents, ready
to do our bidding as pointers to the real world, but already compromised
by their own internal relations. When Bloom contemplates the passing
of time, and the inverse relationship betwen his 'individual develop-

ment' and his 'interindividual relations,' they are linked as follows: 'From inexistence to existence he came to many and was as one received: existence with existence he was with any as any with any: from existence to nonexistence gone he would be by all as none perceived' (628). And after two more questions: 'Why was he doubly irritated? Because he had forgotten and because he remembered that he had reminded himself twice not to forget' (629). How to read these ostensible glimpses into Bloom's head as glimpses *into* anything when the words keep directing us out of their own explicit patterning? Except as they are already related by the paradigms of language (many/one, all/none, forgotten/remembered, reminded/forgot), the words remain hard, gem-like, separate: they seem to repel further combination. When readers describe their experience of 'Ithaca' (as they often do) as one of detachment or even boredom, or when they interpret it as transcending the human level,[20] they are responding to the episode's precoded quality, and to an opacity which keeps them at a distance. Transparent language creates the illusion of identity between the sign and its meaning. Opacity forces a recognition of the gap between them. Perhaps what we learn in 'Ithaca' is what Merleau-Ponty says we have learned from Saussure, 'that, taken singly, signs do not signify anything, and that each one of them does not so much express a meaning as mark a divergence of meaning between itself and other signs ... language is made of differences without terms ...'[21]

As far as language is concerned, it is the lateral relations of one sign to another which make each of them significant, so that meaning appears only in the interval between words. This characteristic prevents us from forming the usual conception of the distinction and the union between language and its meaning ... Signs are supposed to be no more than monitors which notify the hearer that he must consider such and such of his thoughts. But meaning does not actually dwell in the verbal chain or distinguish itself from the chain in this way. Since the sign has meaning only in so far as it is profiled against other signs, its meaning is entirely involved in language ... There is thus an opaqueness of language. Nowhere does it stop and leave a place for pure meaning ...[22]

In a crucial way 'Ithaca' turns the catechismal mode on its head. Instead of revealing through the exhaustive patterning of its responses an ultimate patterning of all experience into Truth (God's will, pure meaning) these responses and their questions undermine the notion that language can be totally revealing, that it can ever give unmediated access to the world. The classical commitment to mimesis, like the concept of a scientific or objective language and like the religious hope of revelation, has a sense of the sign as something to be moved through toward a meaning other than itself. The revelations of 'Ithaca,' however, are of another kind. 'Through the transparent kitchen panes' Stephen sees 'a man regulating a gasflame ... a man lighting a candle, a man removing ... his two boots, a man leaving the kitchen ...' (630). We guess that this is Bloom; but the scientific rigour of the language will not allow Stephen (or us) to assume any such thing. And yet what, after all, is Bloom but the discourse that names him as such? The unity of character disintegrates here: character may or may not be the sum of certain gestures. The specificity of language interposes itself ('a man ... a man ... a man ... a man'). It forces a break in our movement through the sign as it interrogates our natural apprehension of the world.

There is a strange and contradictory quality in the chapter. Everything is de-naturalized, and yet we do not usually have a sense of shock, of suddenly seeing something anew – or do we? 'Ithaca' distances us from the objects of discourse in order to focus our attention on discourse itself. What we do see new are the possibilities, and impossibilities, of access through language. If a pussycat's 'Mrkgnao' in 'Calypso' makes us believe the world is fully available, transparently there, the tea kettle's 'double falciform ejection of water vapour' in 'Ithaca' fogs up the glass of language. As Merleau-Ponty writes,

if we rid our minds of the idea that our language is the translation or cipher of an original text, we shall see that the idea of *complete* expression is nonsensical, and that all language is indirect or allusive – that it is, if you wish, silence. The relation of meaning to the spoken word can no longer be a point for point correspondence that we always have clearly in mind.[23]

We are more likely to grant the truth of his insight to poetic and symbolic language than to the language of the novel. (Perhaps this is what lies behind Frank Budgen's comment on 'Oxen of the Sun' and 'Ithaca' – the two chapters in which, as we have seen, language becomes most obviously opaque. Budgen writes that '*The Oxen of the Sun* is, with the exception, perhaps of *Ithaca*, more symbolical than any episode in the book.')[24] Is this invocation of a symbolic mode not, in essence, a contingency plan for the reader? For when the expected relations between sign and meaning do not apply, it allows extraordinary measures of recuperation. To talk of symbolic meaning is to grant the sign the freedom of indirect mediation and to grant ourselves as readers the freedom to make the silence speak.

If language is silence, how do we make it speak? In a strange reversal, it is sometimes the absence of words, the silence of the thing unsaid, that speaks to us with a certain meaning. At various points in *Ulysses* the fact that Bloom is neither acknowledged nor mentioned becomes more significant than those acknowledgments that are recorded.[25] And yet at other times we feel the presence of words as an overwhelming silence. We might consider the account of 'what lay ... [in Bloom's] kitchen dresser,' presenting the objects in all their opaque, unsymbolic, and untranscendable 'thereness':

On the middle shelf a chipped eggcup containing pepper, a drum of table salt, four conglomerated black olives in oleaginous paper, an empty pot of Plumtree's potted meat, an oval wicker basket bedded with fibre and containing one Jersey pear, a half-empty bottle of William Gilbey and Co's white invalid port, half disrobed of its swathe of coralpink tissue paper, a packet of Epp's soluble cocoa, five ounces of Anne Lynch's choice tea at 2/- per lb. in a crinkled leadpaper bag ... [etc., etc.] (635-6)

The paragraph might well stand at the beginning of a traditional short story: the point of the narrative to follow being to demystify each item, to make us see its meaning. The story itself, in other words, will bring a whole world out of silence and into speech. But this account comes at the *end* of a full day in Dublin, and whatever speech is to be heard will be articulated by the reader. Our impulse throughout the paragraph it to recognize the objects in the dresser, to know more about them than what this language tells us. Only at certain points can we do so. If we remember the scene in 'Wandering Rocks', for instance, when Boylan buys them for Molly, we will see through the wicker basket and the Jersey pear. We can break their silence so that they speak to us about Boylan, Molly, the assignation at four. In turn, the 'bottle ... half disrobed,' the basket 'bedded,' will bespeak Molly herself. In comparison most of the other items on the shelf remain apart, silent. Despite the meticulous attention with which they are presented, what we sense in the description is the resistance of the world to our demand for access. The words themselves take us only so far. Beyond a certain kind of knowledge they will not, or cannot, venture. It may well be the heterogeneity of languages that makes it more obvious in *Ulysses* as a whole, but it is the reader who has greater authority, and greater access to meaning, than any single language in the text. It is an access, however, which we ourselves construct across the silences. And since there is no metalanguage (except our own as we read) the whole process of 'filling in,' of making the silence speak, becomes much more problematic.

And yet ... And yet ... Although 'Ithaca' takes us as far away from transparency as anything in *Ulysses*, 'Ithaca' does not have the last word. Instead, 'Penelope' claims its privileged position at the end, and punctuates everything that leads up to it in a double sense. It closes the Dublin Odyssey. But, like the little hen in *Finnegans Wake* clawing holes into the letter, it also punctures it.[26] It reopens the novel because it reasserts the possiblity of making the world (Molly's thoughts, feelings) transparently available though language. Full of wonderful vitality, 'Penelope' persuades us we are inside Molly's head.

When we stand back from *Ulysses* and see it as a whole it is clear that the novel refuses a final commitment to opaque and self-reflexive writing. But at the same time it makes sure we can no longer have a naive faith in the translatability of things into words. We lose our footing so often and in so many different ways that we cannot take the ground of language for granted. What Frye might call the ironic perspective of *Ulysses* plays itself out not only in the larger relationship between 'Penelope' on the one hand and 'Ithaca' or 'Oxen of the Sun' on the other (with *Ulysses* choosing not to choose between them), but also in all sorts of small ways throughout the novel. 'Ithaca' itself is not as simply opaque as I have made out; the ironic hesitation is voiced within that chapter as well when Stephen and Bloom exchange stories. After some thought of the similarities and differences between himself and Stephen, and after Stephen's education and artistic temperament have been alluded to, Bloom goes over his own area of expertise – 'the modern art of advertising.' He lists ads to be admired and ads to be avoided, and ends with his own idea, rejected by his employers but still cherished by him, to advertise stationery with 'an illuminated showcart ... in which two smartly dressed girls were to be seated engaged in writing' (645). Bloom has thought of the scheme earlier in the day as well. In 'Lestrygonians' the cart is specifically a transparent one, tantalizing the viewer with a glimpse of secrets to be laid bare: 'Smart girls writing something catch the eye at once. Everyone dying to know what she's writing' (143). This image of a woman writing captures Stephen's imagination, and he begins to tell a story. The scene is constructed for us:

Solitary hotel in mountain pass. Autumn. Twilight. Fire lit. In dark corner young man seated. Young woman enters. Restless. Solitary. She sits. She goes to window. She stands. She sits. Twilight. She thinks. On solitary hotel paper she writes. She thinks. She writes. She sighs. Wheels and hoofs. She hurries out. He comes from his dark corner. He seizes solitary paper. He holds it towards fire. Twilight. He reads. Solitary. (645)

He reads and discovers 'What?' Writing at its most opaque, paralysed: 'In sloping, upright and backhands: Queen's hotel, Queen's hotel, Queen's Ho ...' (645). This then is the hidden meaning: the elaboration of signs cut off from meaning, black lines on a white surface – not communication but penmanship. It is a fitting tale from Stephen who, as 'Telemachus' suggests and 'Ithaca' makes clear, distrusts 'acquacities [transparencies?] of thought and language' (633). However, just as *Ulysses* does not end with 'Ithaca' but goes on to 'Penelope,' this account does not leave us here. Bloom too constructs a scene, and it responds to the limits of Stephen's answers. Bloom's imagination rushes back to 1886, filling the Queen's Hotel with the story of a suicide and an inquest. It becomes 'The Queen's Hotel, Ennis ... where Rudolph Bloom ... died on the evening of the 27 June 1886 ... in consequence of an overdose of monkshood ... after having, though not in consequence of having, purchased ... a new boater straw hat ... (after having, though not in consequence of having, purchased ... the toxin aforesaid) ...' (645). And in spite of the obstructing legalese, or perhaps because of it, what is striking in this small narrative is the anxiety to understand, to establish the proper relationship between chronology and motive ('after ... though not in consequence of ...'). In the telling, Bloom struggles for access to the past. He may know when his father died. He also needs to know why. On the one hand, then, Stephen with his celebration of opacity and his delight in opposing our expectations of meaning. (He has played a similar game earlier in the day in 'Nestor' with his riddle of the fox burying its grandmother, and in 'Aeolus' with his Parable of the Plums. Nor can we help but wonder, while enmeshed in 'Scylla and Charybdis,' whether his account of paternity is ever meant to be unravelled.) Often with Stephen language both resists and seduces. That is to say, access to the signified is resisted, while the materiality of the signifier is seductively thrust before us. Here in 'Ithaca' the repetition of 'Queen's Hotel' fulfils the requirements of Stephen's anti-plot, but also invokes the incantatory power of the words. On the other hand we have Bloom, with his transparent showcart, his fondness for both mysteries and revelations (the revelation of the advertiser's name and product is, after all, the point of the exercise), and his alternative to Stephen's story, which rushes to fill in the vacuum left by the mysterious calligrapher. Stephen and Bloom's little narratives articulate two very different notions of what fiction should – or perhaps only can – do.

What Bloom does for the Queen's Hotel suggests a connection with the reader, because for those of us on the other side of narrative reading is also a demand for access. Indeed, *Ulysses* invites us to know its characters, their motives and actions, more intimately than most other texts. In a very real sense it is a monument to what language can do. Yet at certain points it raises a barrier between us and the fictional world. Words stubbornly point us back to our encounter with language. No text could sustain its readers' interest and affection, as *Ulysses* does, if it consistently denied the demand for access. *Ulysses* challenges its readers – it does not turn its back on them. John Berger's remarks on landscape painting, and on the nature of clarity and obscurity, are worth noting here.

The legibility of the image is something which must be approached with extreme caution. The cult of obscurity is sentimental nonsense. But the kind of clarity which two centuries of art encouraged people to expect, the clarity of maximum resemblance, is irrevocably outdated. This is not the result of a mere change of fashion, but a development in our understanding of reality. Objects no longer confront us. Rather, relationships surround us.[27]

Perhaps most clearly in 'Oxen of the Sun,' we see how relationships, ever-shifting relationships, surround us. Our movement through literary history is no longer one in which we simply confront the great voices or 'objects' of the past. Similarly, with the much more prosaic objects detailed in 'Ithaca' we are strangely distanced from what is set so carefully before us. The legibility of the image in Joyce's novel is put into question: the representation of reality is itself thematized. It would indeed be 'sentimental nonsense' to argue that *Ulysses* celebrates obscurity as a sufficient end: either *pour épater le bourgeois* or, given the hermetic fascination of the art work, as a self-engrossed refusal to engage with public meanings. On the contrary, the novel is large and complex enough to reward our desire for meaning. Still we are faced with silences, opacities, contradictions. What kind of knowledge, then, is available? How can we make the silences speak? These are the questions which *Ulysses* poses and to which it offers not a single answer but a number of possible alternatives, each of which questions and modifies our temporary solutions.

The overarching irony of *Ulysses* is its hesitation between a language that wishes to reveal the world (as Bloom's does in 'Ithaca') and one (like Stephen's) that makes its self-reflexive turn away from meaning. Most of my discussion has focused on this second mode. But to use Barthes' word, *Ulysses* 'plays' between the two alternatives. It refuses to sacrifice its pleasure in either one for the sake of the other, while it explores the space available to each. *Ulysses* celebrates the power of language. It also indicates its limits, and in this second gesture it sets the activity of the reader into relief. In marked contrast, the text of Revelation recalled by 'Oxen of the Sun' is authoritative: nothing shall be added to it and nothing shall be taken away.[28] It has no need for an interpreter because meaning is already plangent in the utterance. *Ulysses* depends on the intervention of a reader: in this it speaks most powerfully for fiction.

NOTES

1 The paragraph that precedes the quotation makes it clear that, for Frye, *Ulysses* is also ironically constructed, and that Penelope 'constantly affirming but never forming [choosing?] presides over the ironic cycles of the text' (*Anatomy of Criticism: Four Essays* [New York, 1966], 323).

2 An implicit concern with the reader characterizes much of Frye's work. The *Anatomy* suggests that a text's significant context is not simply the one brought to it by the writer. The relevant tradition for any work is defined by the reader's experience of other fictions. Thus, for example, Shakespeare is to be read 'against' both his precursors and his followers. The traditional question of influence is not of much interest to Frye, and I suspect he would like Borges' reformulation of it in 'Kafka and His Precursors.' More specifically, for a discussion of literature as process, and of the reader's work, see 'Towards Defining an Age of Sensibility,' *Fables of Identity: Studies in Poetic Mythology* (New York, 1963), 131, 137.

3 I am thinking of the way in which modes of fiction are defined according to the distance/difference between the hero's power of action and the reader's, so that, moving from myth through romance, high and low mimetic to irony, the initially vast gap shrinks to nothing, and finally becomes a negative distance, with the reader looking down on the ironic hero (*Anatomy*, 34-5). Genres and modes themselves are often spatially aligned – above, below, and merging into each other. 'Irony descends from the low

mimetic: it begins in realism ... But ... it moves steadily towards myth ...
Our five modes evidently go around in a circle' (42).

4 'Living on: Border Lines,' in *Deconstruction and Criticism*, ed. Harold
  Bloom et al. (New York, 1979), 81-2.

5 Roland Barthes, *S/Z*, trans. Richard Howard (New York, 1974), 5: 'in this
  ideal [writerly] text, the networks are many and interact, without any of
  them being able to surpass the rest ...' Catherine Belsey speaks of an
  'interrogative' text which 'differs from the classic realist text in the
  absence of a single privileged discourse which contains and places all
  the others' (*Critical Practice* [London, 1980], 92). I am aware that
  Barthes' use of the term 'irony' does not coincide with Frye's. On the
  contrary, for him it 'acts as a signpost, and thereby destroys ... multivalence' (*S/Z*, 44). He is thinking of the way one might quote a statement, ironically, in order to put it in its place and, implicitly, to place
  oneself above it in a hierarchy of truth or value. Obviously I am not
  using 'irony' in the same sense. Rather, I have adopted Frye's distinction
  between irony and satire, so that the first is aligned with what Barthes
  calls 'multivalence' (or the writerly), the second with its opposite,
  'univalence' (the readerly).

6 James Joyce, *Ulysses* (London, 1949), 409. Further references will follow the
  quotations in the text.

7 Stuart Gilbert, *James Joyce's Ulysses* (Harmondsworth, 1969), 257, 268, 269.

8 Ibid., 258.

9 Harry Levin, *James Joyce: A Critical Introduction* (London, 1960), 95. For
  Joyce's account of his method and intention, see his letter to Frank Budgen,
  *The Letters of James Joyce*, I, ed. Stuart Gilbert (London, 1957), 138-9.
  Although Gilbert (1931, rev. 1950) and Levin (1941) are both early readers
  of *Ulysses* their arguments for and against the episode have largely been
  followed by later critics.

10 Levin, 95.

11 *ReJoyce* (New York, 1968), 156.

12 *Letters*, I, 137.

13 J.S. Atherton, public lecture on 'The Oxen of the Sun,' Cambridge University, 5 March 1974. The information on Saintsbury and Peacock is reiterated in 'The Oxen of the Sun,' in *James Joyce's Ulysses: Critical Essays*, ed.
   Clive Hart and David Hayman (Berkeley, 1974), 315.

14 Saint Augustine, *Confessions*, IV, 10. I am indebted to Patricia Parker for this
   reference. See also her *Inescapable Romance: Studies in the Poetics of a
   Mode* (Princeton, 1979), 52, 225, 231.

15 *A Portrait of the Artist as a Young Man* (Harmondsworth, 1969), 215.

16 See, for instance, Wolfgang Iser, *The Implied Reader: Patterns of Communication in Prose Fiction from Bunyan to Beckett* (Baltimore, 1974), 186-7, and C.S. Peake, *James Joyce: The Citizen and the Artist* (Stanford, 1977), 262. Both Iser and Peake see 'Oxen' as a microcosm of *Ulysses*, in that its multiplication of perspectives achieves a fuller degree of reality.

17 *Anatomy of Criticism*, 223.

18 *S/Z*, passim, and *The Pleasure of the Text*, trans. Richard Miller (New York, 1975), passim. One need not accept the historical claims for Barthes' paradigm (and I do not) in order to acknowledge its usefulness.

19 *S/Z*, 44-5. My point about Barthes' use of the term irony is very much at issue here (see n. 5). The closing sentence in its entirety reads: 'For multivalence (contradicted by irony) is a transgression of ownership.'

20 Levin, 108: 'Here, if anywhere [influenced by an astronomical film], Joyce contemplates his characters *sub specie aeternitatis*, from the scope of planetary distances ... and we shudder, like Pascal, before the eternal silence of infinite spaces.'

21 Maurice Merleau-Ponty, 'Indirect Language and the Voices of Silence,' in *Signs*, ed. and trans. Richard K. McCleary (Chicago, 1972), 39.

22 Ibid., 42.

23 Ibid., 43.

24 *James Joyce and the Making of 'Ulysses'* (London, 1972), 221.

25 See, in particular, *Ulysses*, 118, 304.

26 *Finnegans Wake* (London, 1971), 124.

27 *Selected Essays and Articles: The Look of Things* (Harmondsworth, 1972), 174.

28 Revelation 22:18–19.

**ELI**
**MANDEL**

# Northrop Frye and the Canadian Literary Tradition

Northrop Frye's writing on Canadian literature has been extraordinarily influential in both criticism and poetry but, despite widespread admiration for his achievement, the nature of his influence and the character of his work continue to be controversial and unclear in certain aspects. It is by no means surprising that his achievement is paradoxical: peripheral to his major critical work, his Canadian writing nonetheless remains, or so he tells us, oddly central to his writing career, 'always ... rooted in Canada and drawing its essential characteristics from there.' Cogent and powerful, it still is puzzling, widely misunderstood. Misreadings of it form one of the fascinating chapters of Canadian literary history. Strangely too, his criticism now reveals itself as at once coherent and inconsistent, systematic and contradictory, perhaps not entirely surprisingly so, considering the length of the period its concerns involve, but nonetheless disturbingly difficult to explain or resolve. And widely regarded as comprehensive, even exhaustive, the Canadian writing turns out to be for the most part occasional and only briefly sweeping in essays or surveys, 'episodes,' as Frye himself says, 'in a writing career which has been mainly concerned with world literature and has addressed an international reading public.'[1]

No doubt it is possible to explain away contradictions by reference to his poetic style and method (the end to which this essay does resort). 'The imagination,' Frye reminds us, 'is occupationally disposed to synthesis,'[2] and so, just as it seeks to put together a country that seems to be coming apart, it seeks as well to resolve apparent critical discontinuities and disorder. It is difficult if not impossible to believe that so witty and urbane a commentary as Frye's could be dismissed as confusion rather than retrieved as poetry.

I

His writing on Canadian subjects takes shape in two ways: first, as what he calls 'field work,' the ten essays he wrote for the annual survey of Canadian poetry in the 'Letters in Canada' section of the *University of Toronto Quarterly* through the decade of the nineteen-fifties; second, as a series of essays of cultural criticism. The essays, written from 1943 to 1965, and the reviews, are collected in *The Bush Garden*, subtitled 'Essays on the Canadian Imagination.' Aside from these, the only work of note I take account of is his little book on modernism, which puts Canadian writing in the context of contemporary internationalism and Canada in the post-national world, *The Modern Century*; his survey of poetry of the fifties, 'Poetry' for *The Arts in Canada*, edited by Malcolm Ross; and his essay on contemporary romanticism in Canadian poetry, 'Haunted by a Lack of Ghosts' in *The Canadian Imagination*, edited by David Staines.

Frye's cultural essays form the basis of his theory of a literary tradition in Canada. That and the questions his position pose occupy the major portion of my essay. It seems adequate to note here that the theoretical formulation develops first out of Frye's earliest critical article, a review of A.J.M. Smith's *Book of Canadian Poetry* (1943), that the alternating rhythms of Canadian life that occupy him in his extraordinary 'Conclusion to a *Literary History of Canada*' first came to his attention through Canadian painting, and that he extends his discussion of the major themes of the first and last essay in his discussion of narrative form and his imaginary anthology of Canadian poetry. His version of the literary tradition of Canadian poetry we note, not entirely by the way, turns out to be a version of the romantic fall into modern consciousness, the wilderness or labyrinth of space and time, and the antithetical quest for a return to an integrated being. Obviously, it is a matter of some critical consequence as to where one chooses to put the emphasis in reading Frye's work: whether, for example, on his romanticism or his nationalism. This essay seeks to acknowledge his romantic reading of a Canadian literary tradition while placing its emphasis on critical problems arising from questions having to do with a definition of a national literature.

Frye's 'field work' is especially interesting and important for several reasons. It provides one of the most extensive reviews of Canadian poetry of the fifties, a period less closely noted or discussed elsewhere. It views that poetry both particularly and in the light of a developing theory of considerable importance in Canadian thought. It is probably the period most consistently misread in Frye's work and is certainly the period which raises the vexed question of his influence as a reviewer and critic. Probably of least interest is the fact that some of the contradictions within his work appear at this point. We are told, for example, that 'The representational tendency in poetry is sophisticated and civilized: the formal tendency is primitive'; yet, 'In our day, the primitive tendency is reached through a further refinement of sophistication,'[3] a puzzle less bothersome than his shifting attitude toward the values of regionalism in art.

It is during this period that Frye reviews a poetry beginning to articulate its modern concerns through new methods and conventions. In a peculiar way, the fifties is a slack period of Canadian writing, a sort of post-war depression. Yet during the fifties, the modernism of the thirties and forties took new directions and a characteristic set of concerns took shape. Reading Frye's reviews of this period, one becomes aware of certain recurrent phrases, imaginative keys to the sound he is hearing and reading: repeatedly, one encounters phrases about symbolism or 'a symbolic language of the poet's own,' 'erudite, elegiac and allusive,' 'mythical and metaphorical,' and notably, 'typically formal poetry, mythical, metaphorical, and apocalyptic.' There is nothing sloppy in the repetition. It points to a poetic recurrence, a pattern or design of the kind of poetry the fifties is providing and Frye is reading in his reviews; the range is wide and various, the interests diverse: James Wreford, F.R. Scott, A.J.M. Smith, Kay Smith, Irving Layton, Louis Dudek, Raymond Souster, Alfred Bailey, R.A.D. Ford, John Glassco, Al Purdy, Ron Bates, Fred Cogswell. But it does not take long to sense where Frye's interests lie and in what poetry. He writes major essays on E.J. Pratt's *Towards the Last Spike*, Earle Birney's *Trial of a City*, James Reaney's *A Suit of Nettles*, Jay Macpherson's *The Boatman*, Anne Wilkinson's *The Hangman Ties the Holly*, George Johnston's *The Cruising Auk*, and Wilfred Watson's *Friday's Child*. He tells us 'One can get as tired of buttocks in Layton as of buttercups in the *Canadian Poetry Magazine*,' but soon notices that with Layton we are in the presence of 'a poetic mind of genuine dignity and power.'[4] Reading *The Boatman*, he is moved to observe a growing professionalism among younger Canadian poets, which 'has nothing to do with earning a living,' but a lot to do with the view of poetry 'as a craft with its own traditions and discipline.'[5] He introduces an essay on Patrick Anderson with a discourse on the technical development of a lyric poetry (from obscurity to simplicity) and a review of a retrospective Carman with an account of the characteristic development of a romantic poet's mind (from impressionism to myth-making). He prefaces a review of Indian mythical poems and a selected Charles G.D. Roberts with an astute comment on the poles of poetry: primitivism and representationalism. In short, the reviews are occasion for both practical criticism, evaluation, *and* theoretical speculation. The latter is, in some ways, the most intriguing.

His 'field work,' Frye tells us, was carried on while he was working out a comprehensive critical theory. The theory, we now know, can be found as the *Anatomy of Criticism*, in turn developed from *Fearful Symmetry*, where his conception of three great mythopoeic periods of English literature emerged in the last chapter of that book. 'I was fascinated to see how the echoes and ripples of the great mythopoeic age kept moving through Canada and taking a form there that they could not have taken elsewhere.'[6] Myth to Frye means not 'an accidental characteristic of poetry' but 'a key to the poem's real meaning,' 'the structural principle of the poem itself.'[7] The theory, says Frye, was 'widely misunderstood,' for 'I was thought – still am in some quarters, evidently – to be advocating or encouraging a specific mythological school of academic, erudite, repressed and Puritanical poetry, in contrast to another kind whose characteristics were undefined but which was assumed to be much more warm-hearted, spontaneous and soul brother to the sexual instinct.'[8] The confusion to which Frye points has not been cleared to this day[9] though it is obvious that in discerning mythopoeia in Canadian writing, it was not his own influence that he was seeing but the language and poetics of a time. Watson, Wilkinson, LePan, P.K. Page, Birney, Pratt, Anderson, and Layton, not to say Reaney, Macpherson, and Cohen (whose first book is significantly entitled *Let Us Compare Mythologies*), all were articulating the poetics that Frye sensed in 'the echoes and ripples of a great mythopoeic age,' as that wave washed across Canadian poetry of the fifties. As to his own influence on poets, few have spoken of it more gracefully, accurately, or easily than Frye himself:

These reviews are too far in the past to do the poets they deal with any good or harm, not that they did much of either even at the time. In any case the estimates of value implied in them are expendable, as estimates of value always are. They may be read as a record of poetic production in English Canada during one of its crucial periods, or as an example of the way poetry educates a consistent reader of it, or as many other things, some of them no doubt most unflattering to the writer.[10]

As to Frye's influence not upon poets but critics, the reading of his work as a 'pharmacopoeia' or of Frye himself as 'the great white whale of Canadian criticism'[11] suggests some of the grosser distortions possible in a misreading, but the development of what has been called 'thematic criticism,' particularly in the work of D.G. Jones in *Butterfly on Rock*, and Margaret Atwood in *Survival*, suggests also that younger critics were quick to sense the establishment in Frye's work of the nationalist and literary contexts within which it would be possible to speak of a Canadian literary tradition. Recently, one of these younger critics spoke directly to this point:

Frye's influence on Canadian criticism, on me anyway, had less to do with his own criticism, which obviously I admire, than with his cultural generalizations, which made me feel good. Frye and the whole tenor of the 1970's led me to write systems criticism in spite of myself. I tried very hard to be a functionalist, but everything kept relating to the larger argument. To sex and violence, to isolation, to regional consciousness, irony. It was historically necessary to go through this, to establish contexts and connections. In retrospect it seems like we were defining the perimeters of the garrison.[12]

Elsewhere, John Moss speaks of a 'very parochial school of criticism' and touches there on the irony and paradox of Frye's criticism: seeking to enlarge the field, to move the parochial into the wider world of international concerns, he in fact locates the 'systems, contexts, connections,' to use Moss's language,[13] in a narrower context. The process of that narrowing is what we trace now.

The larger context of Frye's study of Canadian poetry, then, is the Canadian literary tradition, the literary context of Canadian writing. The first task of the critic, in these terms, is the locating of a literary tradition. The second (as we shall see) is the very difficult one of justifying its national existence, to name it as a *Canadian* tradition, and the third, to rename (or review) it.

II

One would expect that 'Canada and Its Poetry,' a truly extraordinary imaginative feat, would provide a major account of the literary context of Canadian writing. But oddly Frye seems preoccupied there by geographical and political (or at least, national) questions. In 'The Narrative Tradition in English-Canadian Poetry,' as the title suggests, he picks up the question not in political or geographical terms but in terms of language. This has the advantage of suggesting at once the literary connections that need to be examined. A double Canadian poetic 'nature' then appears: nineteenth-century in its employment of customary, routine forms, but much older in spirit, Anglo-Saxon in fact. The argument is not complex: 'it is at least possible that some of the poetic forms employed in the earlier centuries of English literature would have been more appropriate for the expression of Canadian themes and moods than the nineteenth-century romantic lyric or its twentieth-century metaphysical successor.'[14] So it is that the narrative poem has a surprising role in the Canadian literary tradition. The argument points to an uneasy fusion of form and theme that we encounter in a more serious and difficult version later, but it also suggests an even more surprising aspect of the literary tradition.

In his 1952 review of Pratt's *Towards the Last Spike*, Frye fastens on a poetic question raised by narrative, a question that becomes central to the contemporary modernist poet, manifesting itself in both Michael Ondaatje's edition of *The Long Poem Anthology* and Robert Kroetsch's article on the contemporary long poem, 'For Play and Entrance'.[15]

I have a notion that the technical problems involved in *Towards the Last Spike* are going to be central problems in the poetry of the future. And I think that the ingenuity with which these problems have been met would make the poem a historical landmark even for readers who disliked it as a poem ... (Some younger writers who are interested in the theory of 'composition by field' may see an important aspect of it in this poem.)[16]

Frye tends to speak of prophecy as vision, the fully aroused senses, certainly not fortune-telling, but the remark above is uncanny in its prescience. More than the acute awareness that Pratt's 'mosaic' technique links with 'composition by field' and so with contemporary experimentalism, the prophetic vision of a tradition from pre-Chaucerian time to contemporary primitivism provides an astonishing overview of Canadian literary tradition and its significance. This was written in 1946, but it still resonates today:

... the lyric, if cultivated too exclusively, tends to become too entangled with the printed page: in an age when new contacts between a poet and his public are opening up through radio, the narrative, as a form peculiarly well adapted for public reading, may play an important role in reawakening a public respect for and response to poetry. There are values in both tradition and experiment, and in both the narrative has important claims as Canadian poetry hesitates on the threshold of a new era.[17]

Insight of this order can be found thoughout this brilliant criticism, fusing literature, society, the cultural order we strive to discern. Signals, codes, messages flash across poetry to criticism to the social and cultural order, each illuminating the other like the network of lights linking the outposts of civilization in this vast land, itself a mirror of the cosmic night lighted above, perhaps a metaphor of the meaning of tradition.

Frye's incidental comments on tradition sometimes prove even more illuminating than his articulated argument. Certainly, in 'Canada and Its Poetry,' he is taken up with more incidental questions than he can handle easily and even the more articulated 'Preface to an Uncollected Anthology' loses some focus in trying to sort out the literary question from the social and historical ones with which the critic must 'settle uneasily.' It has long seemed to me that a passage in his 1954 review of *The Selected Poems of Bliss Carman*, edited by Lorne Pierce, serves as the best summary of his sense of the literary tradition in Canada, its context of romanticism, its development from impressionism to myth-making poetry.[18] In these terms Canadian poetry in its lyric phase begins with Roberts' *Orion*, develops through elegiac or at least wistful and nostalgic impressionism in Carman to a kind of fusion of subject and object in Lampman's visionary *City of the End of Things* and D.C. Scott's ancestral voices that suggest the appearance of the mythic in nature. Pratt's devotion to narrative, as Frye puts it, suggests a deep, albeit unconscious, affinity with the Canadian tradition exemplified in Sangster, Heavysege, and Howe earlier, and in the post-Confederation period in Mair, Crawford, and Duvar, besides important narrative works by Lampman and Scott. The development to modernism is both documentary and urban (in Pratt and F.R. Scott) but continuous from Carman to Smith in plangent elegies of the death and resurrection myth. In brief, the romantic mode defines the Canadian tradition from its beginning to its modern mythopoeia, from Carman's *Sappho* to Layton's *Birth of Tragedy*. Two complementary aspects of this myth, the tragic identity of the sinister and terrible with man's death wish and the comic fusion of human life and life in nature, are not inconsistent with each other but together account for the unity of impression in Canadian writing, perhaps best summed up as a pastoral quality. For Frye, an emblematic summary of the argument from tradition would be two famous primitive American paintings, *Historical Monument of the American Republic*, a vision of the technological will to power, and *The Peaceable Kingdom*, where the lion lies down with the ox.[19]

So far we have been tracing a tradition that is romantic and pastoral and that because it is linear shows a tendency to look obsolete (an objection urged against it by modernists who tend to see it as academic and 'ancient'). Recently Frye chose to note a shift in attitude toward tradition from viewing it in linear terms to a 'more kaleidoscopic and simultaneous affair.'[20] Everything happens at once: from echoes of Spenser, to descent themes from Ishtar and Boris Karloff movies, to prosodic devices from Old English to concrete poetry. We noted earlier the curious contemporaneity of Pratt's 'mosaic' techniques in narrative; now with this same mode of vision appearing in an account of tradition, we might wonder about the cultural forces at work. Imagery of descent (a contemporary vision of the solitude of the wilderness) ends, Frye comments, 'not in introversion but in an intensely centered vision,' a reflection as it happens on the effects of modern technology.[21]

III

Northrop Frye's criticism, then, in its formal and literary aspect, appears to provide a fusing link between poet and critic (criticism and creativity – idea and image) and – to use James Reaney's phrase – 'an electrifying organizing effect with regard to the imagination.' His account of tradition shows no tendency to become dated or obsolete but rings a contemporary note, as the line from Frye to Reaney to bp Nichol suggests. But the effort to hold the discussion of Canadian writing at the formal or literary level produces an oddly strained effect. 'The critic of Canadian literature' Frye himself notices, 'has to settle uneasily somewhere between the Canadian historian or social scientist, who has no comparative value-judgments to worry about, and the ordinary critic, who has nothing else.'[22] The problem of naming a *Canadian* literary tradition (that is, discerning *Canadian* literary forms) is not only exceedingly difficult, but virtually impossible.

What follows is necessarily rudely schematic, given the range of ambiguities and possibilities. First, one admits that few social commentators, if any, have been so perceptive or illuminating as Frye about this place and its conventions (his famous image of entering the country by

sea as if being swallowed by a leviathan might serve as one example).
Second, if we accept that turning society into a series of literary
conventions were to resolve the major dualities of this discussion, all
would fall into place in the argument. But the terms prove to be slippery.
I note one example. In his 'Preface to an Uncollected Anthology,' Frye
states the major premise of his argument:

We spoke at the beginning of certain principles that become important in the
study of Canadian poetry. One of these is the fact that while literature may have
life, reality, experience, nature or what you will for its content, the forms of
literature cannot exist outside literature, just as the forms of sonata and fugue
cannot exist outside music. *When a poet is confronted by a new life or
environment, the new life may suggest a new content, but obviously cannot
provide him with a new form. The forms of poetry can be derived only from other
poems ...*[23]

This is firmly stated and as always lucid. But what are its implications?
First, because there is a problem of identity in English Canada
associated with the question of language and poetry (i.e., the political
self-identification of Canadian vis-à-vis British and American poets),
there has developed a feeling that Canadian poetry needs a defence or
manifesto: 'The main result of this has been that Canadian poets have
been urged in every generation to search for appropriate themes, in
other words to look for content.'[24]

But a poet's concern or quest is not for content, but form, the
informing or shaping principle of the poem. Of these, the most
important is metaphor, at its purest and most primitive in myth. The
second – and most critical – implication follows. 'When we look for the
qualities in Canadian poetry that illustrate the poet's response to the
specific environment that we call Canada, we are really looking for the
mythopoeic qualities in that poetry.'[25]

We may be looking for myth, but we won't, I submit, find it. We will
find only content. Frye's much-praised account of the romantic myth in
Canadian poetry – a symbolic response to the environment, the riddle of
the unconscious, the confrontation between the poet and a blank,
pitiless, indifferent nature – is not a myth but a theme, an idea, content.
So in the famous review of Smith's *Book of Canadian Poetry*, 'Canada
and Its Poetry,' we are told: 'And the winter is only one symbol, though a
very obvious one, of the central *theme* of Canadian poetry: the riddle of
what a character in Mair's *Tecumseh* calls "inexplicable life." It is

really the riddle of inexplicable death: the fact that life struggles and suffers in a nature which is blankly indifferent to it.'[26]

There is a passage in the 'Preface to an Uncollected Anthology' that suggests Frye's uneasiness with the context of nationalism and prefigures the argument of his 'Preface' to *The Bush Garden*. At the close of his 'Conclusion to a *Literary History*,' there is a stunning meditation on the disappearance of Canada in a post-Canadian world and the reappearance in the foreground of its old rival as the eternal frontier, the first thing the writer's imagination must deal with.[27] The poetry of the future has been written in Pratt's *The Truant*, a science-fiction poem about the quarrel between an imp and a sky-god that has strange echoes in bp Nichol's *The Martyrology*, though, in Nichol's version, language not machines provides the landscape. The argument of the 'Preface to an Uncollected Anthology' and the 'Conclusion to a *Literary History*' is repeated in *The Modern Century*, along with an apology for once holding a romantic folklore version of culture.[28] But the main attempt at a resolution to the dilemma raised by shifting from a literary to an environmental or nationalist context is to alter it again. Either it has disappeared, as *The Modern Century* suggests, or it reappears as locality and region.

IV

The Alice-in-Wonderland sense of Frye's critical world is partly a matter of altered contexts, partly the result of the appearance and disappearance of figures repeating identity questions we thought had been answered. 'Who am I?' 'Where is here?' Environment and politics reappear in the 'Preface' to *The Bush Garden*, now in somewhat changed forms from their appearance in the earliest essay about 'Canada and Its Poetry' or in *The Modern Century*. The political argument here is impeccable, a defence of a multicultural society against those centrifugal and centripetal forces (called separatism and nationalism) that threaten to destroy it by implosion or explosion. The environmental argument, less tidy, depends on a version of what has been called the geographical fallacy (the flatness of prairie poetry and the soaring lines of B.C. mountain writing), but defining region as place leaves it open to the flanking attack of linguistic regionalism (not to say ethnicity).

Frye's position, of course, restructures his earlier argument about Canadian writing by shifting the question of identification (the central literary question of his work) from its Canadian context: 'the question of Canadian identity, so far as it affects the creative imagination, is not a "Canadian" question at all, but a regional question.'[29] But that shifts the political terminology too. Identity is not a political term, but a cultural one. The political question of Canada is a question of unity. 'Identity is local and regional, rooted in the imagination, and in works of culture; unity is national in reference, international in perspective, and rooted in political feeling ... The tension between this political sense of unity and the imaginative sense of locality is the essence of whatever the word "Canadian" means.'[30]

It is difficult to offer less than admiration for this critical performance. An apparently insoluble tension, beginning at the point where theory descends to practice, appears to have been solved or re-solved. Along the way, Frye has taken us through history and literature – wedding a Laurentian theory of Canadian history with a romantic myth of a descent to the interior, through cultural history – ranging across folk-culture theories of nation to modernist internationalism, through the distinctions between romanticism and modernism, quest and antithetical quest, art and anti-art, structure and composition by field. If indeed the question a survey of this kind should address itself to is the vexed one of influence, it now seems fair to say that the real influence of Frye is to have shown the precise points where local creation becomes part of the civilized discourse he speaks of as criticism and creativity, the world of wonder, the universe of words.

To close by entering a reservation may seem not only graceless but ungenerous. But I would enter two, if only to suggest the more important reply that might be made. One is that the vegetable form of regionalism of Frye's 'Preface' ('there is always something vegetable about the imagination') sorts oddly with the equally Blakean vision he consistently urges: 'All human forms identified.' The other is to note how younger contemporary regionalists (Kroetsch, Bowering, Marlatt, Hodgins) locate their landscape not in place but in story, in word, in language.

It may very well be, then, that a profoundly true critical instinct told Northrop Frye that his Canadian anthology had to remain an uncollected one, and in his own words an 'ideal,' one he 'imagines,' 'with no difficulties about permissions, publishers, or expenses.'[31]

NOTES

1 'Preface,' *The Bush Garden* (Toronto, 1971), i.
2 Ibid., x.

3 Ibid., 44-5. Contradiction in Frye seems to have more to do with historical change than logical inconsistency. Occasionally, too, it springs from his
love of paradox. For example, he speaks of 'a quality in Lampman,'
surely the least adventurous of our writers, 'which links him to our great
Canadian explorers, the solitary adventurers among solitudes' (ibid.,
147). It might be useful to think of paradox as a structural principle of his
work: genesis as apocalypse, for example, in his definition of tradition
(the past) as origin ('Originality largely a matter of returning to origins, of
studying and imitating the great poets of the past' [ibid., 136]).

4 Ibid., 8, 41.

5 Ibid., 75.

6 Ibid., viii.

7 Ibid., ix.

8 Ibid.

9 An important exception can be found in Frank Davey's comments in
*From There to Here*, which provides a startling rereading of Frye in the
light of modernist theories of composition, 'correcting' the long-held
misreading of 'myth criticism' Frye points to here: 'A ... misconception
about Frye is that his theories of poetry require a conscious effort by
the contemporary poet to incorporate mythology into his writing ... Far
from resembling the conscious myth-usage of the "Frygians" ..., Frye's
theory of composition – based on Blake's dictum, "The authors are in
eternity" – resembles that of such contemporary pre-reflective writers
as Gerry Gilbert, Daphne Marlatt, George Bowering, Victor Coleman,
bp Nichol, and Bill Bissett' (*From There to Here* [Erin, 1974], 111).
Elsewhere Davey notes that a misconception about the 'other worldli-
ness' of this theory of literature as dream and mythology as well as his
preference for 'consciously literary' writing unfairly links him 'with an
aestheticist and formalist tradition in Canadian writing.' Davey's
rereading is, itself, problematical, as his version of Reaney's *Suit of Nettles* and Macpherson's *The Boatman* makes evident. He cannot have
read Frye's reviews of the two books.

10 *The Bush Garden*, viii. This comment in the 'Preface' is picked up again
in the last review of the decade: 'The reviewer knows that he will be read
by poets, but he is not addressing them, except indirectly. It is no part
of the reviewer's task to tell the poet how to write or how he should have
written. The one kind of criticism that the poet himself, *qua* poet,
engages in – the technical self-criticism which leads to revision and
improvement – is a criticism with which the reviewer has nothing to
do' (ibid., 124).

11 Ibid., ix.

12 *Books in Canada*, 10.9 (November 1981), 39. Moss identifies 'thematic criticism' with what he calls 'systems criticism.' This misreading of Frye's view of myth as 'systems criticism' appears to reflect a confusion about the principles of criticism to which Frye refers, and Frye's account of Canadian romanticism (the fall into modern consciousness) for the advocating of a specific 'mythological school' of poetry.

13 Ibid.

14 *The Bush Garden*, 148-9.

15 Robert Kroetsch, 'For Play and Entrance: The Contemporary Canadian Long Poem,' *Dandelion*, 8.1 (1981), 61-85.

16 *The Bush Garden*, 11-12.

17 'The Narrative Tradition in English-Canadian Poetry,' *The Bush Garden*, 155.

18 Frye's review of Carman appears in *The Bush Garden*, 34-5. The outline of the tradition that follows is suggested variously throughout his reviews in 'Letters in Canada' and in his articles in *The Bush Garden*.

19 'Conclusion to a *Literary History of Canada*,' *The Bush Garden*, 247-9.

20 'Haunted by a Lack of Ghosts,' *The Canadian Imagination*, ed. David Staines (Cambridge, Mass., 1977), 45.

21 Ibid., 44.

22 'Conclusion to a *Literary History of Canada*,' *The Bush Garden*, 215-16: 'of the general principles of cultural history we still know relatively little'; 'We do not know what the social conditions are that produce great literature, or even whether there is any causal relation at all.'

23 'Preface to an Uncollected Anthology,' *The Bush Garden*, 173.

24 Ibid., 176.

25 Ibid., 178.

26 Ibid., 139. Theme, we note, is content.

27 Ibid., 250.

28 *The Modern Century* (Toronto, 1967), 53.

29 'Preface,' *The Bush Garden*, i, ii.

30 Ibid., iii. Compare especially Ramsay Cook's comments in his own preface to the second revised edition of *The Maple Leaf Forever* (Toronto, 1977).

31 To argue that Frye's criticism is 'fictional' is not entirely fanciful. Frye himself distinguishes between experiential and traditional (that is, literary) poetry in 'Canada and Its Poetry' in *The Bush Garden*, and resolves the criticism/creativity duality in 'The Road of Excess,' *Contexts of Canadian Criticism*, ed. Eli Mandel (Toronto, 1971), 125-39. Miriam Waddington, among others, insists on the purely metaphorical nature of thematic

criticism, hence its limitations as a kind of fiction (see her 'Literary Studies in English,' *Supplement* to the *Oxford Companion to Canadian History and Literature* [Toronto, 1973], 206). In 'Criticism as Ghost Story,' *Another Time* (Erin, 1977), 145-50, I argue that Atwood's *Survival* is a ghost story, that is, a fiction.

**JAMES
REANEY**

# Some Critics Are
# Music Teachers

At the end the witch appears again, and on being asked what is really the truth, answers: 'The truth, my children, is that we are, all of us, acting in a marionette comedy. What is important more than anything else in a marionette comedy, is keeping the ideas of the author clear. This is the real happiness of life ...'
Isak Dinesen, 'The Roads Around Pisa,' from *Seven Gothic Tales*

What the critic whose birthday book this is has to say about plays, particularly Shakespeare's, could really make a big difference in their performance. There's a new theatre in such works as *Anatomy of Criticism* and *A Natural Perspective*. Its being there in fragments may be why it has none of the polemical menace of Artaud's or Brecht's theatre theories or those of that sixties and early seventies group, much touted in the *Village Voice*, whose actors used to jump down from the stage and embrace the audience. I prefer to think, though, that the reason what I see as a new theatre is so modestly put forth is because Frye wouldn't dream of calling it new. It simply and casually results from his poetics, which deal with the verbal universe on a great many other fronts as well.

Some critics are ministers, some are archival burrowers, and some are music teachers. These last named can give you, for one thing, some indication of how quickly the work is to be played. So far as I remember, the first time I became conscious of the problem was in my first year at University College, when during a class on Homer Professor E.T. Owen announced that of course for the proper effect the *Iliad* had to be read at the same speed you read Dickens; otherwise the power drives of the various narrative lines wouldn't mesh properly. This notion has stuck with me ever since, particularly with regard to the matter of producing, acting, and directing plays. With plays, all is lost unless the director makes the mechanism or organism in front of us move at the correct tempo – with, naturally, the nuances, rallentandoes and rubatoes that make the noting of 'correct speed' more than just the results of buying a metronome. After Professor Owen I went across the park and took lessons from Professor Frye; what he added to the former's observation was the fact that you cannot arrive at the correct rhythm of a play's performance until you have discovered its design, its patterns, quite often hidden under distracting mounds of content or wrongheaded playing traditions.

Accordingly, if you think of a critic as a music teacher and literature as music, then the critic gives you a metronomic goal and also shows you the design your practising must bring out more and more clearly as you pick up steam. I once heard of a director who went backstage during the first intermission of *Man and Superman* and shouted into the dressing rooms, 'Go faster! Faster!' I think the actors did, but since they weren't on the wavelength of the play anyhow it didn't help. There is something to be said for a brute rush-through of a piece just for the sake of overview, but that much comes very early in the rehearsal schedule; then must follow the analysis of character and plot design, then the final decisions about tempo. When I see a play particularly well directed, I sometimes at the same time hear a tune that has nothing to do with the actual music or imagery of the play, but everything to do with the way the director has built up tension and relaxed it, made, as a matter of fact, the silences of the play into a sinuous, flowing subtext. I first heard a play do this in Winnipeg, years ago; it was Giraudoux's *The Enchanted* directed at the Playhouse Theatre by a youthful John Hirsch. To explain what I was delighted by in that long-ago evening demands attention to certain implications in the works of the two critics mentioned above.

I should now like to say more about how a critic or 'music teacher' can influence the production of a play to such an extent that an audience member might say, 'This must be a new idea of what theatre is all about.' First of all, let's go to your local regional theatre and see plays by Chekhov, Ibsen, James and Shaw. But, before the curtain even rises, we perhaps inspect the shape of the theatre we have just entered. What relationship does it bear to the play produced tonight? Such a critic as Francis Yates in *The Art of Memory* shows how the symbolism of the Globe Theatre's architecture echoed the order of the Shakespearean universe. At Stratford, Ontario, the Festival Theatre there does have such overtones. A theatre in the round with a hierarchy of playing areas that go from trap-door to balcony and even higher, it works well with the Shakespeare productions and creates such feelings about the Chekhov and Ibsen produced on its boards that one longs for more variety and adventurousness in other theatres visited, most of whose architects seem to have been content with the usual picture stage. Now the 'music teacher' critic in me keeps saying that the physical theatre itself makes a big difference with regard to effective production of all plays and that certain playwrights might definitely profit from having their works produced in a theatre that echoed their world-picture. With regard to Shaw, for example, what would a theatre look like whose architect knew of this dramatist's desire, as he says in *Back to Methuselah*, to provide an iconography for creative evolution? The curtain goes up; we must be thankful that we are in a theatre at all, but one cannot help thinking of how wonderful a real union between literature and architecture might some day be.

We are watching a Chekhov play. In *Anatomy*, Frye suggests that Chekhov wrote ironic *comedies*. What we're watching, however, seems to be the usual lugubrious, slow-paced nightmare mistaken for a Chekhov production in our society. Doesn't someone say in *The Seagull* that 'It's a dream'? Still, I'm not sure I want the audience to laugh very much; isn't it just that everything should move more quickly? Then, perhaps, the effects of such typical Chekhovian events as self-stifling, lingering suicide, and failure to get out of Perm would actually be quite moving. I hesitate to use this quotation because its original speaker gave genre criticism such a send-up, but would not the audience then 'by indirections find directions out'? Somewhat the same problem arises with productions of Ibsen's *The Wild Duck*. Despite the fact that in his *Anatomy* the music teacher indicates 'Quixotic Comedy' as the tempo for this score, most directors insist on *lento maestoso* and the feeling of tragedy's muffled drums. As a result we in the audience are not being asked to think; there's no *serio ludere*, no sense of the absurdity of Hedvig's death, the possibility of bitter *laughter* at a manipulator trapped in his Judas illusions. Now this literal-minded approach to certain Chekhov and Ibsen plays is not good for theatre's reputation. Theatre becomes a place where you fall asleep beside your wife while she grits her teeth and watches foreign masterpieces through to the bitter end. But Ibsen and Chekhov might have intended to keep you awake with the contrast between miserable reality and the rhythm of contrasting dramatic form. To direct their works along the lines of this hypothesis would probably cause some audience members to say, 'Why this is a new idea of what theatre is all about,' and yet it is nothing more, in a way, than simply upping the tempo.

Next, let us imagine that we are attending a dramatic adaptation of James' *The Turn of the Screw*; it has appeared in film, stage and operatic versions but always without the surround that James purposely gives to it, the surround of a ghost story that is told to a select circle of listeners at the end of the year. In other words, ghost stories are stories, and they are designed to make you shiver with delight: dread as pleasure, not dread as pain. *Anatomy* tells us that ghost stories show a comic society dissolving into the knights-and-dragons world of romance. We're inside Prospero's head and through his eyes we see how a magic world makes pleasure and pain the same, parts of a story, not parts of reality as we usually know it. But in the adaptations of *The Turn of the Screw*, the ghost story aspect is lost sight of and what emerges instead is a satyr play where the Marlon Brando valet, rather the worse for wear, lurches through the window to grab the child-actor playing Miles. This is too literal and too horrible. The so-called lighter approach where we are firmly warned that this is a story would actually be more moving.

It's not that the plays discussed are just stories; it's that they are stories. Emphasis on that can allow a director to understate matters with telling effect. This fact leads to some strange discoveries, one of them being that literary criticism can save a theatrical producer quite a bit of money. For quite often, in the society I live in, the bigger the playhouse and the bigger its budget, the worse its handling of the critical problems outlined above, the less its directors are willing to tell stories and the more they are unfortunately able to hide this failure with expensive sets and 'serious' acting and 'grave' pacing. But last year I saw a puppet version of *The Tempest* which outshone all other productions previously seen simply because puppets have so few resources for acting their roles that the little they can do stimulates the observer to complete the process for them. So, calling the above-mentioned works 'comedies,' emphasizing their story and encouraging an approach aslant from their content would probably have the same exhilarating and completing effect.

Where the music lessons would result in the most spectacular effect on our society would be in theatres producing our greatest and most popular playwright. So the next thing I would like to focus on is Shakespeare plays as they have actually and recently been produced for the most part at Stratford, Ontario. I say 'actually produced' because everyone seems too relaxed about closing the gap between what goes on at a university and what seems to be going on at a popular classical theatre. What does closing the gap involve? It involves thinking about a small city in the centre of Southwestern Ontario and its thirty-year-old Shakespeare Festival.

The reader may be wondering if the writer has ever seen anything he was satisfied with. The writer wonders if, so far as our Canadian theatre is concerned, it's not just a matter of time. Because at a theatre in Dublin, the Gate, with two or three more decades of its history than is the case with most theatres here, I once saw an excellent *Doctor's Dilemma*. With memories of an awkward and unconvincing Toronto production in my mind, I didn't expect to be so entertained, for the Toronto actors had made such a slow symposium for medical purposes out of the Shavian arguments. Every idea had been carefully underlined, and what strong ideas they are too. Given time, you can chew them. But the Irish actors kept the plot foremost; they played the plot for all it was worth over and against the medical parts. As a result, you saw the play's shape for the first time and enjoyed hearing the arguments as well. Given Shaw's early milieu, the aesthetics involved should not be too strange. Dublin knows how to tell stories; Toronto, a first cousin of Belfast, only knows how to preach sermons. The next step for the Dublin Gate Theatre is to get *Back to Methuselah* resurrected, a challenging task. Meanwhile, the theatres whose implied presence lurks above need to be more theatrical; that is, they need more music lessons.

After years of naming some of its streets and all of its schools after Shakespearean character – for example, King Lear Public School! – the citizens of my home town, Stratford, Ontario, beheld the gods pouring incense on such sacrifices in the form of a Shakespeare Festival, which has ever since the early fifties annually caused cultivation, furore, delight, and education as well as making possible for the first time in central North America close acquaintance with the canon of Shakespeare in performance. Quite early on, a Guthrie *Merchant of Venice* surprised viewers by reserving some of its energies for the last scenes at Belmont. Someone had taken a trip to a music teacher and learned that the play wasn't just about Shylock, but about lovers overcoming his disturbing influence, for Shylock's performance had been curbed and, to those who could let go of the notion that the play is about Shylock, the evening made a satisfying whole. Never mind that a new can of worms was opened at the very end by the presentation of Antonio in purple shot silk brooding over Bassanio's deserting him for Portia. Should this be the last image of this play, *Merchant of Venice* though its title be? Just excise that, however, and what you had was a well-balanced *Merchant* quite different from the productions where Shylock steals the show. I'll discuss the first two *Twelfth Nights* later on; note the sombre first *Measure for Measure* after which people came away, shattered, murmuring, 'It's not a play, it's an experience'; and skip to that part of the Festival's story where a director finally dared to tackle the late romances. The first *Winter's Tale* Stratford did wins the prize; it actually believed (unlike the second production) that spring was better than winter, gave us actors who believed what they were doing, and made us believe in the statue scene. *Pericles* and *Cymbeline* – likely no one, even the critics, had seen them before – ran into trouble. For these two plays represent extreme cases of what Antoinine Maillet, the Acadian author of *La Sagouine*, calls *raconter pour raconter*, and Canadians still are not sure that pure story is really as serious as sermon with a story in front of it. Perhaps because it's hard to find the sermon in such excessively plotted plays as *Pericles* and *Cymbeline*, either something in the productions or the audience reactions or both together suggested that these were silly plays, which they quite definitely are not. By silliness I mean such things as the cardboardy silver moon in the Diana sequence of the former play and the send-up of the wicked Queen in the latter. However, the same company turned out an excellent *Troilus* and a wonderful *Titus*, two plays whose tunes seem easier for this rusty age to get the hang of than any of the other plays in the canon. What practical effects can the music teachers' view of plays have on our classical theatre if its most spontaneous successes are Shakespeare's most bitter and ironic plays? *Titus* works so splendidly with audiences that it must have been originally intended for TV. The other kinds of plays should be just as successful, though – what available adjustments in perception and stylization should be given a trial?

I say 'should be given a trial' because just about everything else has been. Some samples will serve as a sort of anti-masque to my proposed 'adjustments' – not all of them even appearing in my native town. I have seen a *Twelfth Night* where Malvolio sat on a swing, chatting and swinging at us with such indecent pleasure that I fully expected his conventicle to rush in and tie him to a cutty stool; an *Antony and Cleopatra* as well as a *Beggar's Opera* where the Antony and the Macheath seemed positively indifferent to their ladies; a *Macbeth* where when Ross enquires of Macduff if he will to Scone he holds up a baked scone; a *Tempest* where Ariel kept stumbling. I have heard of (but not seen) an all-male *As You Like It*. Yes, yes, boy actors originally played the parts of Rosalind, Celia, and Audrey, but such big hefty ones? Parts for women are already rare enough in Elizabethan plays without a director's underlining the fact so decisively. However, one hears of an actress who played Portia and could not be fired when she kept insisting that Portia was really a man. Yesterday morning the *Village Voice* brought news of a Joe Papp *Tempest* in which Trinculo was dressed as W.C. Fields and Stephano as Mae West. Finally, there is the A-frame *Macbeth* in which *every* actor was shorter than the star of the piece – Lady Macbeth.

No doubt a convulsive and bored society is quite capable of shredding its traditional classics, as in the 'bold' experiments of Charles Morawitz in which *Merchant* and *Macbeth* are disembowelled and reassembled. But the above procession of grotesqueries results surely from superficial directors having run out of superficially different things to do, while newspaper critics who should know better goad them on. What very few of them realize is that what would be really novel and shocking these days would be to see a classic text directed from its own viewpoint, not that of existentialists or Marxists or fashionable trendists but its own.

To illustrate: Frye says that from its own point of view *Macbeth*

is not a play about the moral crime of murder; it is a play about the dramatically conventional crime of killing the lawful and anointed king. The convention gives a ritual quality to the action, and the element of reversed magic to the imagery that enables the poet to identify the actors with the powers of nature. The lawful king has his place in the 'great bond' of nature: he has mysterious powers of healing, and is linked to everything in nature that keeps its rightful place and order. The usurper becomes linked with all the powers of chaos and darkness: not only is his deed accompanied by prodigious portents, but he himself becomes an incarnation of tyranny, an evil spirit that Malcolm must recognize and cast out of his own soul before he can become the lawful successor ... If we keep this mythical and conventional element in Duncan's sovereignty at the centre of the play, every word of it fits together into the gigantic and terrifying tragic structure that we know so well. Take it away ...'

And we have the usual *Macbeth* production where all the casting and directorial energies have been lavished on Macbeth. Both Duncan and Malcolm usually seem rather pinched and unattractive, the speech about Edward the Confessor is often cut as a piece of tediousness, and, because Macbeth is not reflected in the eyes of actors who are skilled and alert, we see so much of him that we can't see him at all. I think a production that made Duncan a vigorous symbol of spiritual health and shot some adrenalin into all the good characters, particularly Malcolm, would probably cause a furore. But in the end what might seem like a new play would settle down as having finally recovered its ensemble qualities at the expense of the same star system that frequently mars performances of *Merchant*, a problem which Stratford solved in its early days. However, it really seems a matter of reading the text of *Macbeth* and letting all of its parts and images have their effect on you. But, of course, what is obvious seldom seems attractive to directors in pursuit of novelty.

Not so obvious perhaps is an adjustment that could be made when *Romeo and Juliet* next is played. Frye uses canonical counterpoint to link Juliet's appearing on a platform (balcony) with similar appearances of Cressida and Cleopatra doing so on Walls of Troy and Tomb respectively. All three women are seen as being love goddesses for whom men die. By no means is Juliet the sexual siren that the others are, but her 'Gallop apace' speech makes her a Queen of the Night, a demi-goddess whose sensual, dangerous energies Mercutio celebrates in the Queen Mab Speech. Now these insights could revolutionize the casting for Juliet. Directors seem always to read 'She's not fourteen,' think 'teenager,' and cast a variety storekeeper's daughter; in fact, a recent film version boasted of casting a grocer's daughter from Birmingham. But suppose, in line with the mention of the Queen of the Night, you asked Botticelli to provide you with one of his innocent but not naive, fragile but dangerously posed women from *Primavera*? There again you'd have an apparently new play.

As I listened to the Tamblyn Lectures Frye gave at Western last year on the theme of reversal, a new *Measure for Measure* appeared: not a *maestoso*, shattering experience of deepening gloom, but a much more quickly paced tricky comedy. It does so, of course, if the director picks it up by its reversal, a carefully signalled prose passage where the absurd, initial tragic themes are turned back. Most directors seem to prefer picking up this play by its cowl. Looking at *Natural Perspective*, the reader finds a *Timon* that is not a tragedy but a comedy: '... the sense of the play as a comedy of humour with no focus for a comic development.' Some day in this age of Beckett, a certain kind of ironic character actor is going to light up at the implications of 'with no focus' and an accompanying phrase '*idiotes* role,' find an intelligent director and have a hit. Turning some more pages, have we ever seen a Coriolanus who is an awkward adolescent? No, the actors who get this role are tougher, older birds, or if slimmer, too sophisticated. And so on, for there are a great many more such insights whose effect would be the freshening of both audiences and plays. Instead, directors use designers to do the freshening with period fiddling, such as putting Shylock in a Rothschild frock coat. This is the result of too much money. No, where the new-looking Shakespeare will first arise is probably at some starving liberal arts college where physical innovations are expensive but mental ones are not.

Let us now leave the various auditoria we've been complaining in, and go back through the green room and into the rehearsal hall. Let us go back in time as well to the point when the director was laying the groundwork for the performance we have just seen. Ten to one, if there has been a groundwork laid it's been that of naturalism. I once saw an incredibly dissatisfying *Importance of Being Earnest* in which the actors must have been told to imagine themselves not as patterns of words, gestures, and intonations but as *real* people. As a result the evening moved with repellent balkiness. Familiar results are a Hotspur or a Mark Antony who cannot be understood, but certainly is grunting like the gentleman in question. The actors have found the character in the context of their own egos, but they haven't found it yet in the context of the play's words. One young actor recently told me that he was so used to doing psychopaths in plays where the director let him depart from the text in order to dig within himself for more psychopathia that he was quite unable to stick to an author's words any more. This modern inability to accept any stylization save that of naturalism and ego means that ensemble acting involving five or even more types of clowns, churls, misanthropes, and cunning servants, in short the masks of *Commedia*, is rather hard to get off the ground. For instance, there was a *Twelfth Night* at Stratford with Siobhan McKenna in which Feste, the clown with the little drum, took a whip and larruped the blazes out of the trap door under which Malvolio had just been confined. This completely destroyed the delicate balance between buffoon, *idiotes* (Malvolio) – well, the comic masks just mentioned. For the Fool, Feste, has quite suddenly lost all of his charm and become a psychopath with a bullwhip. We begin to sympathize with poor old Malvolio so much that even Viola and Sebastian begin to unravel. But, surely Malvolio is heavy, straight, and somewhat morbid; all the others must be shades lighter than he or they can't bounce off him, and this bouncing of character types off each other is one of the delicious things about a comedy. So, how do we get actors and directors interested in getting outside of themselves, out from under their hatfuls of rain and into the masks of *Commedia*? These masks, too, are given half their meaning by other actors' skill in playing against, not playing at all, playing up to, etc. So there's selflessness involved as well as skill. Indeed, I think *Anatomy* implies that there should be a theatre where actors specialize in character conventions.

In the rehearsal hall, let us go through the following modulatory etude, basing our exercise on a passage from *Anatomy*: 'For children's drama or romance – you can be a Knight, you a Dragon, you a helpful Dwarf, and you a Witch.' Change the focus to comedy, and the Witch who supported the Dragon becomes: 'a Churl. You who were the Dwarf become now a Buffoon, you who were a Dragon become the Self-Aggrandizer, and you who were the Knight become the Self-Deprecator with the Buffoon on your side.' Change the filter to tragedy and: 'you who were the Dragon now become the Knight or the Tragic Hero. You who were the Knight now become the Villain.' This last part of the role-playing game is very important because it reminds the participants just how closely they are related to their opposites. Without a Dragon there'd be no Knight. Without Malvolio, there'd be no Belch, Ague-cheek, Maria, and Feste; they'd have nothing to do except laugh at Sir Andrew, which doesn't take long. No Malvolio, no clown. To my mind this kind of groundwork in convention produces a more buoyant play, partly because the actors now know what the other actors are thinking. There are, in Shakespeare at least, some dazzling variations on the above patterns, and some day the sizzling chess patterns of *Cymbeline* will seem fun to both audience and actors, not silly and bewildering, simply because a rehearsal technique has been found for them. If our society wants it, the theoretical groundwork has been laid for a new classical theatre.

For the last twenty-five years I have been often involved in practical theatre, usually in workshops where embryonic plays are being baked in ovens made up of children and actors at the end of their tethers; or warming ovens, just lately, of quite old actors for whom proper dramatic rhythm and timing means a sense on the director's and playwright's part of where the next toilet break should be. Yes, and increasingly I become aware of how practical literary criticism is. On the basic level of keeping the audience unbored and in their seats, the critic as music teacher has so much to say that it amounts to a vision of what a theatre should be.

From the windows of the rehearsal hall we look down on the crowds going home from shopping, school, or work or, these days, simply going. Eventually, if the music we're playing for them is played correctly and effectively, their lives will be better. If they are watching what is alive, what is truly itself, then they themselves become more alive. I think of this as listening for the tune, although I suppose it could also be called listening for the breathing and heartbeat of a play. Let's stick to 'tune.' I know that one day every member of the passing crowd will be a music teacher, but until that day arrives we should listen to what music teachers we've got.

**HAROLD
BLOOM**

# Reading Freud: Transference, Taboo, and Truth

Jean Laplanche concludes his *Life and Death in Psychoanalysis* with a brief meditation upon what he finds to be most problematic in the transference:

... it was above all in its metaphorical dimension – that of *as if*, of misperception, of an error in addressee – that transference was first understood and, as a result, interpreted.

And yet, think of the situation: are we prepared to reduce the working of therapy to the generating of an illusion in order to dissipate it? Is it conceivable that its effectiveness can be reduced to so little? And that even more so nowadays when everyone entering analysis is well aware that he will 'have a transference.' If a transference takes on the dimensions of an event capable of changing something for someone, it is indeed because, in one of its dimensions, it transcends the phantasmagoria to which it has occasionally been reduced ...[1]

Unfortunately Laplanche has no suggestion as to this dimension of transcendence, beyond another of those exercises in the supposed differences between metaphor and metonymy of which the common reader rightly wearies. Yet he does state one burden that must afflict any rational consideration of the psychoanalytical transference. Why should it be genuinely therapeutic to generate an illusive relationship merely in order to dissipate it? Is there any analogue available to us that might illuminate so odd a transaction? How has psychoanalysis won social acceptance of so knowing an illusion, of so imaginary and consciously deceptive a false connection? A misleading and artificially induced infatuation is exploited in order to create a pseudo-neurosis which soon enough is real enough, and such a *praxis* is both applauded and indeed remunerated by civil society. Do the teachers of religion, philosophy and the art of poetry ever transgress in any way nearly so outrageous? Karl Kraus wickedly remarked that psychoanalysis itself was the disease of which it purported to be the cure. Is his remark truly wicked, if its reference is to the cause and the 'cure' of that imaginary illness, the transference neurosis?

Freud's only mode of transcendence was what he, perhaps unjustifiably, called 'reality-testing.' What then is transcendent or true about the transference, what in it *is* other than phantasmagoria? And if, as I will insist, Laplanche is mistaken, and the transference is only phantasmagoria, what kind of phantasmagoria is it? does it belong to poetry? to religion? Or is it Freud's own mythic formulation, his poem or his faith as to the right use of the wrong kind of love? Finally, in this litany of questions, what truly *are* the dynamics of the transference? Are they what Freud asserted them to be in his papers on therapy and technique, or are we to look elsewhere in his writings for their true account? And if we are to look elsewhere, and to find what we seek, was Freud then not truthful with us? Did he dissimulate?

The answer to all of these questions will be found in the reading of *Totem and Taboo*, by which, I hasten to add, I *do* not mean *my* reading of *Totem and Taboo*, but indeed in anybody's reading once they start with the sad, simple, and truthful translation of totem into psychoanalyst and of taboo into transference. But such a start itself depends upon an initial realization of the curiosity that *Totem and Taboo* represents, both as a book, and more particularly as a book *by Freud*, the first of his full-length 'cultural' works, and unmatched for gorgeous nonsense among them until his last, *Moses and Monotheism*, a quarter-century later.[2]

The origins of *Totem and Taboo* in Freud's work precede his 1907 essay on 'Obsessive Acts and Religious Practices,' but Freud's reader needs to start with that essay's description of 'religion as a universal obsessional neurosis'[3] in order to surmise some of the motives behind the excess that marks the book published six years later. Everything about the book, as of its descendant, *Moses and Monotheism*, is marked by excess and by surprise, Freud's own surprise, akin to the surprise he insisted he experienced at each fresh instance of the analytical transference. As with the book 'on' Moses, Freud was more than hesitant about publishing *Totem and Taboo*, supposedly yielding only to the urgings of his disciples. Yet again, in regard to both books Freud himself was unusually dogmatic, perhaps because the foundation of each was so palpably dubious.

Is psychoanalysis itself only (or also) a universal transference neurosis? Unfair as the question must be, it can be posed cogently because of the curious juxtapositioning in Freud's work of two fundamental mythopoeic notions, taboo and transference, neither of which means what Freud meant it to mean. Freud himself was obsessed with questions of priority, and since transference is the first of the two figurations in his work an account of transference has to precede the story of the later tangles between the two in January 1912, when each leaped to a first full formulation.

The early Freudian uses of *Übertragung* have surprisingly little to do with his matured sense of the term. 'Transference' in *The Interpretation of Dreams* refers to the process that enables unconscious ideas to enter the preconscious, a process of 'connection' that Freud identifies as a transferring of intensity from the repressed to an idea already preconscious.[4] More relevant to the later concept of analytical transference is the 'false connection' between patient and Freud described in the *Studies on Hysteria*, yet even this seems more an allusion to a 'compulsion to associate' than a proper symptom of a therapeutic eros.[5] Historians of psychoanalysis accurately point to the 'Postscript' of the 'Dora' case as the true start of the Freudian transference, yet it is only a start, if we examine the metaphor by which the transference is there represented:

What are transferences? They are new editions or facsimiles of the tendencies and phantasies which are aroused and made conscious during the progress of the analysis; but they have this peculiarity, which is characteristic for their species, that they replace some earlier person by the person of the physician. To put it another way: a whole series of psychological experiences are revived, not as belonging to the past, but as applying to the person of the physician at the present moment. Some of these transferences have a content which differs from that of their model in no respect whatever except for the substitution. These, then – to keep to the same metaphor – are merely new impressions or reprints. Others are more ingeniously constructed; their content has been subjected to a moderating influence – to sublimation, as I call it – and they may even become conscious, by cleverly taking advantage of some real peculiarity in the physician's person or circumstances and attaching themselves to that. These, then, will no longer be new impressions, but revised editions.[6]

New editions, facsimiles, revivals, new impressions, reprints, but above all, revised editions: the anterior texts of the psyche retain so much priority in all of these that transference itself is devaluated.

Indeed, the transference has not yet come to its painful birth. To chart that birth we need to abandon the writing of Freud for that of his most gifted disciple, Ferenczi, who compelled his master to move on in transference theorizing by an audacious breakthrough in 1909. Surely no other paper by a psychoanalyst other than Freud was so repressedly influential upon Freud himself. Ferenczi's great essay, 'Introjection and Transference,' begins by a pious citation from the 'Postscript' to 'Dora' but then proceeds rapidly to a marvellous leap that Freud would not take until three years later, in 1912. Nothing that Freud had written up to 1909 associated the primal ambivalences and emotive confusions of the Oedipal conflict with the vicissitudes of the transference. It was reserved for Ferenczi to state this true connection, while carefully, indeed anxiously, paying tribute to Freud on a just-about-every-other-paragraph basis throughout:

With the extraordinary significance that attaches (according to Freud's conclusion which is confirmed daily) to the repressed 'Oedipus-complex' (hate and love towards the parents) in every case of neurosis, one is not surprised that the 'paternal' air, the friendly and indulgent manner, with which the physician has to meet the patient in psycho-analysis gets so frequently used as a bridge to the transference of conscious feelings of sympathy and unconscious erotic phantasies, the original objects of which were the parents. The physician is always one of the 'revenants' (Freud) in whom the neurotic patient hopes to find again the vanished figures of childhood. Nevertheless, one less friendly remark, reminding him of a duty or of punctuality, or a tone that is only a *nuance* sharper than usual, on the part of the analysing physician is sufficient to make him incur all the patient's hate and anger that is directed against moralising persons who demand respect (parent, husband).

The ascertaining of such transferences of positive and negative affects is exceedingly important for the analysis, for neurotics are mostly persons who believe themselves incapable either of loving or of hating (often denying to themselves even the most primitive knowledge about sexuality); they are therefore either anaesthetic or else good to a fault, and nothing is more suited to shatter their erroneous belief in their own lack of feeling and angelic goodness than having their contrary feeling-currents detected and exposed *in flagranti*. The transferences are still more important as points of departure for the continuation of the analysis in the direction of the more deeply repressed thought-complexes.

Ridiculously slight resemblances also: the colour of the hair, facial traits, a gesture of the physician, the way in which he holds a cigarette or a pen, the identity or the similarity in sound of the Christian name with that of some person who has been significant to the patient; even such distant analogies as these are sufficient to establish the transference. The fact that a transference on the ground of such petty analogies strikes us as ridiculous reminds me that Freud in a category of wit shewed the 'presentation by means of a detail' to be the agent that sets free the pleasure, *i.e.* reinforces it from the unconscious; in all dreams also we find similar allusions to things, persons, and events by the help of minimal details. The poetical figure 'pars pro toto' is thus quite current in the language of the unconscious.

The sex of the physician is in itself a much-used bridge for the transference. Female patients very often attach their unconscious heterosexual phantasies to the fact that the physician is a man; this gives them the possibility of reviving the repressed complexes that are associated with the idea of masculinity. Still the homosexual component that is hidden in everyone sees to it that men also seek to transfer to the physician their 'sympathy' and friendship – or the contrary. It is enough, however, that something in the physician seems to the patient to be 'feminine' for women to bring their homosexual, and men their heterosexual interests, or their aversion that is related to this, into connection with the person of the physician.[7]

Remarkable as these paragraphs were in themselves, *at the time that they were written*, more remarkable still is Freud's failure to have written them. What accounts for Freud's long delay (1895-1912) in formulating the psychoanalytic concept of the transference? And what, besides Ferenczi's catalytic intervention, made it possible for Freud to break through his reservations or inhibitions, and compose the three essays on the transference from 1912 to 1914?

The first clue to answering the second question comes in the 1911 'Notes' on the visionary paranoid, Dr Schreber, in the extraordinary 'Postscript,' where Freud broods upon his own mythological associations as set going by Schreber's 'delusional beliefs' concerning his relation to the sun.[8] As he speculates on the sun as Schreber's sublimated 'father-symbol,' Freud for the very first time in his work cites the phenomenon of totemism, and then links it in a footnote to his own early paper on 'Obsessive Acts and Religious Practices.' This brief but absolutely crucial Freudian meditation upon the totem, at the end of the Schreber Case, will lead directly to the writing of *Totem and Taboo*, a leading that, as I shall show, in turn liberated Freud into writing upon the transference as a version of taboo and the analyst as a version of totemism.

The title-page of *Totem and Taboo* carries as subtitle: *Some Points of Agreement between the Mental Lives of Savages and Neurotics*. Should we add: *and between the Therapeutic Functions of Totems and Psychoanalysts*? Freud's original, September 1913 'Preface' expresses more confidence in his treatment of taboo than of totem:

The analysis of taboos is put forward as an assured and exhaustive attempt at the solution of the problem. The investigation of totemism does no more than declare that 'here is what psychoanalysis can at the moment contribute towards elucidating the problem of the totem.' The difference is related to the fact that taboos still exist among us. Though expressed in a negative form and directed towards another subject-matter, they do not differ in their psychological nature from Kant's 'categorical imperative,' which operates in a compulsive fashion and rejects any conscious motives. Totemism, on the contrary, is something alien to our contemporary feelings – a religio-social institution which has been long abandoned as an actuality and replaced by newer forms ... (x)

The still-existent form of taboo Freud presumably thought of as the obsessional neurosis, just as those 'newer forms' of a religio-social institution would have included the Roman Catholic Church in Austria. Or did Freud know, on whatever level, that his true model for taboo was what he soon came to call 'the transference neurosis,' and that the truly contemporary replacement for totem and for bishop was to be the Freudian psychoanalyst? Certainly the book's first essay, 'The Horror of Incest,' is untroubled by such possibilities, and the reader encountering it now may well wonder what function it fulfils in the text of *Totem and Taboo*. Its two fundamental concerns, totemism and incest, seem yoked together not so much by textual violence as by textual yearning, and the totem, at first appearance, seems already to be a metaphor not so much for the phallic father, or for a Nietzschean ancestor-god, as for Freud himself as founder of a therapy and a doctrine, ancestor of the psychoanalytic clan. How aware was Freud of the apposite and sardonic humour of this metaphor?

... In the first place, the totem is the common ancestor of the clan; at the same time it is their guardian spirit and helper, which sends them oracles and, if dangerous to others, recognizes and spares its own children. Conversely, the clansmen are under a sacred obligation (subject to automatic sanctions) not to kill or destroy their totem and to avoid eating its flesh (or deriving benefit from it in other ways). The totemic character is inherent, not in some individual animal or entity, but in all the individuals of a given class. From time to time festivals are celebrated at which the clansmen represent or imitate the motions and attributes of their totem in ceremonial dances. (2)

Translate experimentally 'totem' as 'Freud,' and 'the clan' as the psychoanalytic profession, and the passage takes on very dark overtones in regard to such clansmen as Adler and Jung having violated their 'sacred obligation.' There are also delicious nuances as to psycho-analytic festivals where the more loyal clansmen perform their repre-sentative and imitative 'ceremonial dances.' More interesting than these interpretive possibilities are those oracles, 'dangerous to others,' but amiable to the clan. How are we to translate what Freud goes on to describe as the totemic characteristic that most engrosses psychoanal-ysis? 'In almost every place where we find totems we also find a law against persons of the same totem having sexual relations with one another and consequently against their marrying' (4).

We could say, modifying Hamlet, that this law is almost more honoured in the breach than in the observance, except that Freud may have shifted his perhaps unconscious metaphor here, so that the focus has moved from the vicissitudes of the analytic clan on to the social tact of the analytic transference. Freud should have called the chapter not 'The Horror of Incest' but something like 'The Interest of Incest' because it is both the aesthetic piquancy and analytic centrality of incest that dominates as Freud concludes by noting 'the writings of Otto Rank which have brought more and more evidence to show the extent to which the interest of creative writers centres round the theme of incest and how the same theme, in countless variations and distortions, provides the subject-matter of poetry' (12). Shelley had called incest the most poetical of circumstances, but by 'poetical' he meant something more than 'emotional ambivalence,' which informs the great Freudian reduction that is the Oedipal conflict.

Such reduction is vital to the second chapter of Totem and Taboo, the superb essay, 'Taboo and Emotional Ambivalence,' which is Freud at his strongest, but also at his uncanniest. Coleridge's 'holy dread' is also Freud's, when he declares that: 'Taboo prohibitions have no grounds and are of unknown origin.' Freud asks why we should concern ourselves with the riddle of taboo, but evades an answer by again falling back upon the Kantian 'categorical imperative' as our supposed version of taboo. But the clues, conceptual and verbal, make Freud's actual design transparent. Approaching taboo, Freud cites the angle of vision or stance of the psychoanalyst as being uniquely appropriate to judging the phenomenon:

> He has come across people who have created for themselves individual taboo prohibitions of this very kind and who obey them just as strictly as savages obey the communal taboos of their tribe or society. If he were not already accustomed to describing such people as 'obsessional' patients, he would find 'taboo sickness' a most appropriate name for their condition ... (26)

But, would he also find 'taboo sickness' to be an appropriate name for that 'artificial illness,' the transference neurosis? A certain anxiety about the very word 'transference' (*Übertragung*) in this context clearly drifts through Freud's text:

> ... Obsessional patients behave as though the 'impossible' persons and things were carriers of a dangerous infection liable to be spread by contact on to everything in their neighbourhood. I have already drawn attention to the same characteristic capacity for contagion and transference in my description of taboo. We know, too, that anyone who violates a taboo by coming into contact with something that is taboo becomes taboo himself and that then no one may come into contact with *him*.
>
> I will now put side by side two instances of the transference (or, as it is better to say, the *displacement*) of a prohibition ... (27)

Yet transference keeps coming back, as Freud develops the relations between emotional ambivalence and the obsessions of undoing and the 'touching phobia.' An extraordinary passage, prophetic of the mutual contamination of the ideas of defence and the drive in the later Freud, serves in this essay as a bridge to the transferences and extensions of the concept of taboo:

> As a result of the repression which has been enforced and which involves a loss of memory – an amnesia – the motives for the prohibition (which is conscious) remain unknown; and all attempts at disposing of it by intellectual processes must fail, since they cannot find any basis of attack. The prohibition owes its strength and its obsessive character precisely to its unconscious opponent, the concealed and undiminished desire – that is to say, to an internal necessity inaccessible to conscious inspection. The ease with which the prohibition can be transferred and extended reflects a process which falls in with the unconscious desire and is greatly facilitated by the psychological conditions that

prevail in the unconscious. The instinctual desire is constantly shifting in order to escape from the *impasse* and endeavours to find substitutes – substitute objects and substitute acts – in place of the prohibited ones. In consequence of this, the prohibition itself shifts about as well, and extends to any new aims which the forbidden impulse may adopt. Any fresh advance made by the repressed libido is answered by a fresh sharpening of the prohibition. The mutual inhibition of the two conflicting forces produces a need for discharge, for reducing the prevailing tension; and to this may be attributed the reason for the performance of obsessive acts. (30)

This intricate paragraph packs into itself everything which is most problematic about *Totem and Taboo*. But I want now to isolate from it only a single emphasis, and that one is between the lines. Strength and obsessiveness are ascribed as a doublet to taboo and to neurosis; weakness and randomness conversely belong to 'intellectual processes' which cannot diminish unconscious desire. Ease of transference and extension therefore are assigned to the emotive ambivalences of taboo and neurosis. Implicit throughout the passage is the hint that strength to combat strength must be sought in the taboo's transferences and obsessions, so as to turn taboo against taboo, transference neurosis against obsessional neurosis. It is thus no accident that Freud suddenly makes the leap from taboo to totem, anticipating what will become the fourth essay in the book, 'The Return of Totemism in Childhood,' which we are compelled to read as a barely concealed study of psychoanalysis itself:

The most ancient and important taboo prohibitions are the two basic laws of totemism: not to kill the totem animal and to avoid sexual intercourse with members of the totem clan of the opposite sex.

These, then, must be the oldest and most powerful of human desires ... the wording of these two taboos and the fact of their concurrence will remind anyone acquainted with the findings of psychoanalytic investigations on individuals of something quite definite, which psychoanalysts regard as the centre-point of childhood wishes and as the nucleus of neuroses. (31-2)

Again, what matters most here is to be read between the lines. If the Oedipal intensities of ambivalence are at the centre of neuroses, then the Oedipal intensities of ambivalence in the taboos can be summoned as an opposing power. How? The path of the transference is sketched in a cento:

This transmissibility of taboo is a reflection of the tendency, on which we have already remarked, for the unconscious instinct in the neurosis to shift constantly along associative paths on to new objects ...

If the violation of a taboo can be made good by atonement or expiation, which involve the renunciation of some possession or some freedom, this proves that obedience to the taboo injunction meant in itself the renunciation of something desirable ...

... The magical power that is attributed to taboo is based on the capacity for arousing temptation; and it acts like a contagion because examples are contagious and because the prohibited desire in the unconscious shifts from one thing to another ... (34-5)

The reader who experiments by substituting 'analytical transference' for 'taboo' in that cento will do only scarce violence to Freud's text. Towards the end of the curiously repetitive discourse that follows, Freud abruptly ceases from analogizing taboo and neurosis and seeks instead the difference: 'But after all taboo is not a neurosis but a social institution. We are therefore faced with the task of explaining what difference there is in principle between a neurosis and a cultural creation such as taboo' (71).

But the difference, whether in principle or particle, does not show up in Freud's subsequent discussion. In neurosis, he tells us, there is a 'preponderance of the sexual over the social instinctual elements,' but the very next sentence reminds us that the social instincts have their erotic components. That Freud pursues larger quarry is suddenly made apparent in one of his most aggressive declarations:

The neuroses exhibit on the one hand striking and far-reaching points of agreement with those great social institutions, art, religion and philosophy. But on the other hand they seem like distortions of them. It might be maintained that a case of hysteria is a caricature of a work of art, that an obsessional neurosis is a caricature of a religion and that a paranoic delusion is a caricature of a philosophical system. (73)

But what about that great social institution, psychoanalysis? Might it be maintained that a transference neurosis is a caricature of psycho-analysis? Freud would have frowned darkly upon the question, but then in 1912 psychoanalysis was not yet a major social and cultural institution. Nearly seventy years later, Freud's own patterns of displace-ment and transference seem much clearer. Art, religion, and philosophy all have their taboos, and so does psychoanalysis, which names it not as the displacement but as the transference, the carrying-across or metaphor that sometimes even substitutes itself for the entire therapeutic process that is Freud's legacy. Freud actually thought that religion was nothing but an obsessional neurosis, and that philosophical systems scarcely could be distinguished from paranoic delusions. His ambivalence towards the art of literature precluded his confusing a poem and a case of hysteria, except that if a poem attempted to be taken as more than a beneficent illusion, Freud would have called that attempt an hysteria.

Precisely such an attempt was the program of Romantic poetry, which sought to assert the power of imagination or creative mind over what John Milton had called 'the universe of death,' the natural world. But just that power Freud deprecated, from at least 1909 on, as 'the omnipotence of thoughts,' the greatest of narcissistic delusions. The uneasy third chapter of *Totem and Taboo*, 'Animism, Magic and the Omnipotence of Thoughts,' centres on the genesis of this supposed delusion. Freud begins with the assertion that the human race has developed three comprehensive 'systems of thought – three great pictures of the universe: animistic (or mythological), religious and scientific.' Animism Freud defines most basically by following Hume: 'There is an universal tendency among mankind to conceive all beings like themselves, and to transfer to every object those qualities with which they are familiarly acquainted, and of which they are intimately conscious' (77).

Yet Freud is not interested in the natural history of animism, or even in magic, supposedly 'the animistic mode of thinking,' but in obsessional neurosis, and in its uncanny tendency towards 'the omnipotence of thoughts.' Animism, for Freud, is the earliest version of obsessional neurosis, and shares therefore in what is the centre of obsessional neurosis: the fear of death. The next phase, Freud insists, is religious, where men transfer their belief in the omnipotence of their thoughts to the gods, and thus do not abandon their own narcissistic overestimation of themselves. When Freud goes on to state the third phase as being scientific, we know that he means *his* science, which is to replace Christianity (and Judaism) even as they, in his view, superseded animism. What abides, even in this third phase, of the narcissistic overestimation of psychical acts, is: 'The state of being in love, which is the normal prototype of the psychoses.' Art, like love, is then added to this archaic survival, and Freud proceeds to conclude his third chapter by hinting that love at least must be renounced in certain restrictions that make possible 'difficult or responsible work.' Again, the prohibitions that may be invoked in psychoanalytic work are darkly prefigured in the patterns of taboo (89).

But it is chapter IV, 'The Return of Totemism in Childhood' (I would add: 'And in Analysis'), which is the true centre not only of this book, and of the transference, but in some sense of all Freud's work. After two sections of the merest shadow-boxing, half-heartedly summarizing the supposed range of theories of totemism, Freud forcefully considers animal phobias, demonstrating the displacement of fear from the father on to the animal. Ambivalence, fearing castration, substitutes: this is the formula, grimly persuasive, and Freud is quick to relate it to the Oedipal conflict:

If the totem animal is the father, then the two principal ordinances of totemism, the two taboo prohibitions which constitute its core – not to kill the totem and not to have sexual relations with a woman of the same totem – coincide in their content with the two crimes of Oedipus, who killed his father and married his mother as well as with the two primal wishes of children, the insufficient repression or the re-awakening of which forms the nucleus of perhaps every psychoneurosis ... (132)

Who among Freud's readers in 1912 could have anticipated the leap from this to the extraordinary story compounded out of the myths of the totem-meal and the primal horde? Here are the central passages of Freud's most extravagant invention:

... One day the brothers who had been driven out came together, killed and devoured their father and so made an end of the patriarchal horde. United, they had the courage to do and succeeded in doing what would have been impossible for them individually ... The totem meal, which is perhaps mankind's earliest festival, would thus be a repetition and a commemoration of this memorable and criminal deed, which was the beginning of so many things - of social organization, of moral restrictions and of religion. (141-2)

... the tumultuous mob of brothers were filled with the same contradictory feelings which we can see at work in the ambivalent father-complexes of our children and of our neurotic patients. They hated their father, who presented such a formidable obstacle to their craving for power and their sexual desires; but they loved and admired him too. After they had got rid of him, had satisfied their hatred and had put into effect their wish to identify themselves with him, the affection which had all this time been pushed under was bound to make itself felt. It did so in the form of remorse. A sense of guilt made its appearance, which in this instance coincided with the remorse felt by the whole group. The dead father became stronger than the living one had been – for events took the course we so often see them follow in human affairs to this day. What had up to then been prevented by his actual existence was thenceforward prohibited by the sons themselves, in accordance with the psychological procedure so familiar to us in psycho-analyses under the name of 'deferred obedience.' They revoked their deed by forbidding the killing of the totem, the substitute for their father; and they renounced its fruits by resigning their claim to the women who had now been set free. They thus created out of their filial sense of guilt the two fundamental taboos of totemism, which for that very reason inevitably corresponded to the two repressed wishes of the Oedipus complex. Whoever contravened those taboos became guilty of the only two crimes with which primitive society concerned itself. (143)

A.L. Kroeber, in 1939, reflected that *Totem and Taboo* was at most the representation of a prevalent human dream or nightmare, a reflection developed by Lévi-Strauss into a damaging verdict upon Freud's Primal History Scene:

The failure of *Totem and Taboo*, far from being inherent in the author's proposed design, results rather from his hesitation to avail himself of the ultimate consequences implied in his premises. He ought to have seen that phenomena involving the most fundamental structure of the human mind could not have appeared once and for all. They are repeated in their entirety within each consciousness, and the relevant explanation falls within an order which transcends both historical successions and contemporary correlations. Ontogenesis does not reproduce phylogenesis, or the contrary. Both hypotheses lead to the same contradictions. One can speak of explanations only when the past of the species constantly recurs in the indefinitely multiplied drama of each individual thought, because it is itself only the retrospective projection of a transition which has occurred, because it occurs continually.

As far as Freud's work is concerned, this timidity leads to a strange and double paradox. Freud successfully accounts, not for the beginning of civilization but for its present state; and setting out to explain the origin of a prohibition, he succeeds in explaining, certainly not why incest is consciously condemned, but how it happens to be unconsciously desired. It has been stated and restated that what makes *Totem and Taboo* unacceptable, as an interpretation of the prohibition of incest and its origins, is the gratuitousness of the hypothesis of the male horde and of primitive murder, a vicious circle deriving the social state from events which presuppose it.[9]

Why did Freud invent the gratuity of the male horde and of primitive murder? This is quite a different and perhaps less important question than why, once invented, the Freudian dialectics of taboo and totemism freed him to formulate the transference neurosis. The totemic system, as Freud conceived it, is a covenant with a surrogate father, in which the surrogate's 'protection, care, and indulgence' is exchanged for the child's obedience to the taboo, so that the father, once triumphed over, will now prevail over all ambivalences. The longing for the father, the root of all religion as Freud insists, confers upon the totem the authority that Freud himself possesses, and which he seeks for his analytical followers, not of course in regard to *their* father, himself, but certainly in regard to *their* sons and daughters, their patients. When Freud reaches his conclusion, and insists that 'the beginnings of religion, morals, society and art converge in the Oedipus complex,' we can wonder legitimately why he does not add psychoanalysis to that list of beginnings. We have made the crossing to the dynamics of the transference when Freud moves towards a formula that will allow the analyst's unconscious to interpret the ambivalences of the patient's unconscious: 'psychoanalysis has shown us that everyone possesses in his unconscious mental activity an apparatus which enables him to interpret other people's reactions, that is, to undo the distortions which other people have imposed on the expression of their feelings' (156, 159).

The 1912 essay on 'The Dynamics of the Transference' is, as we should now expect, one of Freud's most curious and reticent theoretical performances, requiring a certain reading between the lines, particularly as regards its relationship to Ferenczi, who receives only one rather displaced reference towards the end of the text. Freud begins by saying that his subject is 'almost inexhaustible' but that he seeks to clarify the *inevitability* of transference in analysis, and this quality of the inescapable immediately is found in the exercise of every individual's 'capacity to love.' The neurotic individual, whose 'passion for transference' Ferenczi had described, is viewed as being very susceptible indeed: 'Expectant libidinal impulses will inevitably be roused, in anyone whose need for love is not being satisfactorily gratified in reality, by each new person coming upon the scene, and it is more than probable that both parts of the libido, the conscious and the unconscious, will participate in this attitude.'[10]

In one of those agile leaps that characterize his authentic genius, Freud surprisingly is able to devote his paper *to the transference itself,* and *not to the patient,* whose status is thoroughly devaluated throughout. Partly this is because Freud is driving hard for authority, but partly also his suddenly overt theory of the transference is being informed covertly by the principle of redundancy or overload, rhetorical and dialectical, that dominates *Totem and Taboo.* For what, according to the paper 'The Dynamics of the Transference,' are the stigmata of the transference? Why, that it is marked by excess, in character and degree, over what is rational and justifiable. Once he has stated this excess, Freud ponders three grand questions: why is this excess so much greater under analysis, why does it provide the strongest resistance to the cure, and why does a balked free association revive when the analyst is indeed the subject of the patient's repressed thought and emotion? Freud answers the first question unconvincingly, by simply denying it. He answers the second by invoking the infantile imagos, and by demonstrating forcefully that any return of these from repression *must* both provoke resistance and appear as resistance. But the third question, which marks the true scandal of the transference, Freud does not answer, and he passes instead into the supposed distinction between 'positive' and 'negative' transference. Precisely where Freud stops pondering, and insists that he must turn to analytical evidence, is where his exegetes should begin. I choose to begin with a question of my own, to which I shall return later. Has any other discipline or *praxis* dared the hubristic spiritual authority that psychoanalysis has usurped?

Is this not the centre of any meditation, in whatever intellectual context, upon the relationship of psychoanalysis to truth? Who but an analyst, in what after all is an erotic (as distinguished from a sexual) situation, would so diminish the dignity of the other by insisting that any silence or blockage *must* have the analyst himself as object? That a social and professional institution has been erected upon so outrageous a presumption is the lasting tribute that Western history has paid to Sigmund Freud. The poet Yeats allows his hero, Cuchulain, to proclaim: 'I make the truth!,' but that is the High Romantic intensity of a fiction proceeding knowingly towards its own imminent death. How can we justify Freud's unanswered questions, which are not fictions, since they touch everywhere upon the pragmatics of human misery, necessary and unnecessary?

One truth about the transference rests upon the Freudian dynamics at their most persuasive, as here in the reduction of every positive transference to an ultimately sexual basis:

Positive transference can then be divided further into such friendly or affectionate feelings as are capable of becoming conscious and the extensions of these in the unconscious. Of these last, analysis shows that they invariably rest ultimately on an erotic basis; so that we have to conclude that all the feelings of sympathy, friendship, trust and so forth which we expend in life are genetically connected with sexuality and have developed out of purely sexual desires by an enfeebling of their sexual aim, however pure and non-sensual they may appear in the forms they take on to our conscious self-perception. To begin with we knew none but sexual objects; psychoanalysis shows us that those persons whom in real life we merely respect or are fond of may be sexual objects to us in our unconscious minds still.

So the answer to the riddle is this, that the transference to the physician is only suited for resistance in so far as it consists in *negative* feeling or in the repressed *erotic* elements of positive feeling. As we 'raise' the transference by making it conscious we detach only these two components of the emotional relationship from the person of the physician; the conscious and unobjectionable component of it remains, and brings about the successful result in psychoanalysis as in all other remedial methods. In so far we readily admit that the results of psychoanalysis rest upon a basis of suggestion; only by suggestion we must be understood to mean that which we, with Ferenczi, find that it consists of – influence on a person through and by means of the transference-manifestations of which he is capable.[11]

But is there then a truly 'positive' transference at all? Evidently not, since there cannot be a useful degree of resistance to be overcome, without the heightened affect of ambivalence, or shall we not accurately call it 'taboo,' in the precise sense of the second chapter of *Totem and Taboo*? For taboo, in Freud's sense, is only another version of the *agon*, of the struggle between analyst and patient, between Freud and his reader, between Freud and anteriority, and ultimately between the later and the earlier Freud. The extraordinary closing sentences of 'The Dynamics of the Transference' depict this *agon*:

This struggle between physician and patient, between intellect and the forces of instinct, between recognition and the striving for discharge, is fought out almost entirely over the transference-manifestations. This is the ground on which the victory must be won, the final expression of which is lasting recovery from the neurosis. It is undeniable that the subjugation of the transference-manifestations provides the greatest difficulties for the psychoanalyst; but it must not be forgotten that they, and they only, render the invaluable service of making the patient's buried and forgotten love-emotions actual and manifest; for in the last resort no one can be slain *in absentia* or *in effigie*.[12]

Whom does Freud wish to conjure up, that he may slay them? Surely in the first place the patient's parents, but truly he has reversed the pattern of the totem-feast here, and the totem-analyst slays the primal horde. How far are we here from what will become the second of the transference-essays, the paper on 'Recollection, Repetition and Working Through' of 1914? The difference, or distance traversed, is principally in the boldness with which the 1914 essay sets forth that dismaying disease of love, the 'transference neurosis.' This boldness is evident also in Freud's overt war against the past: 'The past is the patient's armory out of which he fetches his weapons for defending himself against the progress of the analysis, weapons which we must wrest from him one by one.'[13]

Against these weapons, Freud adopts as a final wresting-technique 'an artificial illness,' the transference neurosis itself, darkly confirmatory of Karl Kraus's bitter jest that psychoanalysis was the disease of which it purported to be the cure:

The main instrument, however, for curbing the patient's compulsion to repeat and for turning it into a motive for remembering consists in the handling of the transference. We render it harmless, and even make use of it, by according it the right to assert itself within certain limits. We admit it into the transference as to a playground, in which it is allowed to let itself go in almost complete freedom and is required to display before us all the pathogenic impulses hidden in the depths of the patient's mind. If the patient does but show compliance enough to respect the necessary conditions of the analysis we can regularly succeed in giving all the symptoms of the neurosis a new transference-colouring, and in replacing his whole ordinary neurosis by a 'transference-neurosis' of which he can be cured by the therapeutic work. The transference thus forms a kind of intermediary realm between illness and real life, through which the journey from the one to the other must be made. The new state of mind has absorbed all the features of the illness; it represents, however, an artificial illness which is at every point accessible to our interventions. It is at the same time a piece of real life, but adapted to our purposes by specially favourable conditions, and it is of a provisional character. From the repetition-reactions which are exhibited in the transference the familiar paths lead back to the awakening of the memories, which yield themselves without difficulty after the resistances have been overcome.[14]

The 'transference neurosis,' properly manipulated through interpretation, will work through from repetition to true recollection, at least if we are to credit Freud's design. But we have met the transference neurosis before, throughout the second chapter of *Totem and Taboo*, but under the name of primal history and its ambivalences. Freud's anxieties about this hidden pattern both produce and vex the third and most remarkable of the transference essays, the 'Observations on Transference-Love' of 1915, a paper in which Freud justly took an especial pride. His overt centre here is the female patient who falls in love with her analyst, but his true concern is the counter-transference of the analyst, which may interfere with the Freudian insistence 'that the psychoanalytic treatment is founded on truthfulness.'[15] Fearful of jeopardizing his authority, Freud forgot how vulnerable his immediate formulations were. Is the transference after all true love? Is *Totem and Taboo* true? Freud wisely says that the analyst must neither fulfil nor suppress the patient's craving for love, while taking up a stance towards the patient's love 'for which there is no prototype in real life.' Indeed, Freud's ideal analyst 'must face the transference-love boldly but treat it like something unreal.' This analyst, 'proof against every temptation,'[16] is curiously like the biblical Joseph confronting Potiphar's wife, which prompts me to the wish that Freud had followed the grand injunction of Nietzsche's favourite author, Emerson: 'Leave thy theory, like Joseph his coat in the hand of the harlot, and flee.'[17] Instead, Freud splashes into the swamps of love, attempting vainly to distinguish between transference-love and 'normal love' by the supposedly greater power of transference-love to achieve results. A startling paragraph upon the embattled stance of the analyst instantly puts this power into question:

> The analytic psychotherapist thus has a threefold battle to wage – in his own mind against the forces which would draw him down below the level of analysis; outside analysis against the opponents who dispute the importance he attaches to the sexual instinctual forces and hinder him from making use of them in his scientific method; and in the analysis against his patients, who at first behave like his critics but later on disclose the over-estimation of sexual life which has them in thrall, and who try to take him captive in the net of their socially ungovernable passions.[18]

However eloquent, this is rendered coherent only by its hidden reliance upon Freud's mythopoeic creation, *Totem and Taboo*. The forces of the counter-transference that might pull down the analyst are less those of Eros than of Thanatos, for they are the forces, now internalized, that destroyed the totem-father. Outside opponents truly dispute not so much the sexual thesis as that of the Primal History Scene, perpetually repeated in the taboo restrictions that analysis places upon the patient. Most crucially, the patients pass from their dark sources in the Primal Horde to the posture of the guilty brothers, for whom the slain ancestor has become a numinous shadow, loved with that fearful Eros that only God and the gods provoke. The truth of the transference is the truth of Primal Ambivalence, no more, no less, and finally of Freud's own Primal Ambivalence towards tradition.

NOTES

1 Jean Laplanche, *Life and Death in Psychoanalysis*, trans. Jeffrey Mehlman (Baltimore and London, 1976), 138.

2 Sigmund Freud, *Totem and Taboo: Some Points of Agreement between the Mental Lives of Savages and Neurotics* (1912), Vol. XIII of *The Standard Edition of the Complete Psychological Works of Sigmund Freud*, trans. James Strachey, *et al.* (London, 1953). Hereafter *Standard Edition*. Subsequent references to *Totem and Taboo* will appear in parentheses in the text.

3 Freud, 'Obsessive Acts and Religious Practices' (1907), *Standard Edition*, IX, 127.

4 Freud, *Interpretation of Dreams* (1900), *Standard Edition*, V, 562-6.

5 Freud and Josef Breuer, *Studies on Hysteria* (1895), *Standard Edition*, II, 303-4.

6 Freud, 'Fragment of an Analysis of a Case of Hysteria' (1905), *Standard Edition*, VII, 116.

7 Sandor Ferenczi, 'Introjection and Transference,' *Sex in Psychoanalysis*, trans. Ernest Jones (New York, 1950), 41-3.

8 Freud, 'Psycho-analytic Notes on an Autobiographical Account of a Case of Paranoia' (1911), *Standard Edition*, XII, 80-2.

9 Claude Lévi-Strauss, *The Elementary Structures of Kinship*, ed. Rodney Needham (London, 1969), 491.

10 Freud, 'The Dynamics of the Transference' (1912), *Collected Papers*, trans. Joan Riviere (London, 1924), II, 313.

11 Ibid., 319.

12 Ibid., 322.

13 Freud, 'Recollection, Repetition and Working Through' (1914), *Collected Papers*, II, 371.

14  Ibid., 374-5.
15  Freud, 'Observations on Transference Love' (1915), *Collected Papers*, II, 383.
16  Ibid., 385.
17  Ralph Waldo Emerson, 'Self-Reliance,' *The Complete Works*, ed. E.W. Emerson (Boston and New York, 1903-4), ii, 57.
18  Freud, 'Observations on Transference Love,' 390.

**ANGUS FLETCHER**

# The Image of Lost Direction

The labyrinth – Frye's *Anatomy* calls it 'the image of lost direction' – appears in literature as just that, an image. Generally it suggests an inextricable tangle. The image has such power that, while it often merely conveys an impression of pleasant or unpleasant intricacy, it also may inform narrative structure at large. *Tristram Shandy*, for example, is not only about a labyrinthine situation (life in the Shandy family); its story too is told through endless mazy digressions, quirky slithers of narrative sequence, which Sterne happily called 'the sunshine.' Many other works, ancient and modern, share in the rhythms of labyrinthine movement. Frye properly considers the labyrinth an archetypal, rather than casual image. Yet owing perhaps to its inherent complexity and its many metaphoric transformations into other mazy shapes (is the fog in *Bleak House* a labyrinth?), 'the image of lost direction' has only recently begun to receive the attention it deserves.

Frye's ringing epithet occurs in a discussion of demonic imagery; the idea is already present in *Fearful Symmetry*; *The Critical Path* attacks its problematic directly. The essay 'Towards Defining an Age of Sensibility' observes the oracular discontinuities preferred in such periods, when narrative and lyric forms come apart, under pressure from a now familiar type of anxiety whose mark is that 'pity and fear become states of mind without objects.'[1] Perhaps because such flux is typical of 'Gothic' fictions, where terror is a stock in trade, the modern reader will readily assent to a negative, demonic reading of the image. Yet even in the much larger perspective of the *Anatomy*, Frye is able to locate the labyrinth on the downside of mythic vision. Its converse tends to be some apocalyptic heaven, temple, Eden, resolving cadence, home. With twentieth-century literature the labyrinth almost always has negative or at least unsettling associations.

The main advantage of analysing the labyrinth is that this is a directional image, as Frye observed. The image geometrizes some problems of state of mind. The *Odyssey* has a number of such images, and indeed the whole poem may be conceived as a vastly extended labyrinth, but the iconography of the labyrinth proper can focus on a precise range of shapes of the *space of passage*, to clarify the ways in which we can feel lost, or found. The archetype raises the question: what is a sense of direction in any case?

Frye's account draws for us the traditional crux of lost and found. 'Here too are the sinister counterparts of geometrical images: the sinister cross, and the sinister circle, the wheel of fate or fortune ... Corresponding to the apocalyptic way or straight road, the highway in the desert for God prophesied by Isaiah, we have in this world the labyrinth or maze, the image of lost direction, often with a monster at its heart like the Minotaur' (*Anatomy of Criticism*, 150).

Losing the 'straight road' can occur for various reasons, but common to all is a psychological component. The presumption is that the road does exist, but one has lost sight of it. The loss of direction is a lost *sense* of direction. The reader is asked to share in this mental experience, with all its attendant anxiety. We are not misled when sometimes the experience is vaguely pleasant or titillating as when, in the Renaissance and the seventeenth and eighteenth centuries, landscape becomes a high art and the maze becomes an adjunct to the formal garden.[2] The literature describing this art, or using its associations for metaphoric purposes, tends always to emphasize the wandering, meandering, errant aspect of passage through the labyrinth. This wandering is subject to a mental bafflement. One does not pass through a mazy scene unless one thinks one's way through it. The thinking of the labyrinth is the problem of the labyrinth. It is not so much a trial of strength as a kind of perceptual skill. The meandering passage promotes always a thinking into one's state of mind. To a degree the labyrinth leaves its traveller with nothing much but state of mind. As Marvell says, in his poem of the countermaze, *The Garden*,

> Meanwhile the Mind, from pleasure less,
> Withdraws into its happiness ...
> Annihilating all that's made
> To a green thought in a green Shade.

If then, with delight or pain, the experience of the labyrinth is that of thought experiencing itself, some *object* or *aim* or some two *points* defining a straight line will have ceased to provide orientation. Yet orientation is always a resource of cosmic dimensions. What could these objects, aims, and points possibly be?

The poets have suggested an answer, which at first seems no answer at all. They compare the labyrinth to life itself. Marvell's contemporary, Bishop Henry King, says: 'Life is a crooked Labyrinth, and wee / Are dayly lost in that Obliquity.'[3] Michael Drayton, an intermediary between Spenser and those poets, asks: 'for what liker to a Labyrinth, than the Maze of Life?'[4] Spenser initiates the action of his immense epic by introducing his essential hero, the Redcrosse Knight, into the Wood of Error, which the poet calls a 'labyrinth,' in order that we shall see the whole career of the hero as a doubtful traverse of 'so many paths, so many turnings seene.' This Wood conforms to Frye's account of the labyrinth: at its heart resides the monster of Error itself, a terrifying, self-consuming dragoness of convoluted, deformed thoughts. Before he can proceed, the hero must kill this monster – the monstrous source of error. He manages this, but not before we realize that his life will be devoted to deciphering monstrous error wherever he meets it. He finds that error persists, unavoidable in life, if not elsewhere. The epic rhythm of continuity of *The Faerie Queene*, as of the *Odyssey*, is lifelike, because each poem mirrors the eternal recurrence of directions lost and found, found and lost.

That life is a labyrinth might seem an unduly empty notion, however obvious or natural. Yet even such a precise poet as Dante sees the archetype this way. His *Commedia* begins in a maze: 'In the middle way of this life, / I found myself [lost] in a dark wood.' Literally Dante says, 'of *our* life,' of the life of man in general. In the midst of 'living,' he says, we find we are lost – that, in terms of his poem of the discovery of direction, is what being 'in the midst of things' really means. By definition, being in the middle implies that there are too many optional possible paths, so many indeed that the sense of reachable goal is baffled by excessive 'freedom.' As if a goal that can be reached by too many paths will vanish, to be replaced by the mere activity of pathfinding. Discovery and curiosity become ends in themselves; the means becomes the end.

Viewed in a certain light, a definition of human life, as lifetime, would have to include at least some reference to the idea that a life that is lived is primarily a process and therefore that for living to be 'really living' the means *must* become the end. Thus far it seems a reasonable archetypal connection to say that man's life is a labyrinth. But then we shall have to reckon with all the negative aspects of the maze that Frye identified in the *Anatomy* and that poets have so persistently recognized, especially in the modern era. Modern mazes are relentlessly frightening. This being so, for the most part, we need to get a clearer notion, in regard to the labyrinth, of the distinction between ends and means.

Again the archetype and the ideas of 'lost direction' will come to our aid. The traditional account does suggest some useful limits to the troublesome openness of the life/labyrinth equation.

So far as the labyrinth has a *mythos* attached to it, western literature returns to the story of Theseus, Ariadne, Daedalus, Minos, and the Minotaur – the story of the Cretan Labyrinth. Theseus' adventure is clearly a heroic initiation into his destiny as protector of a people. He volunteers to kill the Minotaur, and he succeeds. Whereas, however, many a dragon-slaying encounter could form part of the hero's initiation into manhood, this particular story enhances what Victor Turner would call the 'processual' aspects of the achievement.[5] Theseus is 'separated' from his folk, he 'passes through' a set of thresholds in the initiatory midphase of the labyrinthine hunt for the Minotaur, and he is rejoined with the folk at the end (the *aggrégation* as it is called in Van Gennep's classic terminology). On such a plan Mircea Eliade would say that all labyrinth-passages are myths of initiation ritual.[6] If such accounts hold up, then it would appear that the life/labyrinth metaphor is based on the idea that all of life is a series of initiations. Every intelligible goal or direction will be defined by the particular initiation appropriate to the hero at a given time of life. Life becomes an experience, unfolding in time, of secondary labyrinths. A sense of 'the next thing,' the experience of the next labyrinth in some due course, will bring order to the larger pattern of existence. So life is organized in primitive societies, as well as advanced societies, though in the latter the profusion of apparent choices makes it often virtually impossible to discern what ought to come next. The only large-scale error would be to believe that there are no labyrinths, no Minotaurs, for then there would never be any beginnings, any possibilities, in a ritual sense, of initiation into any significant actions.

The denial that the labyrinth exists has a curious result: everything becomes labyrinthine. The processual flow of life cannot, in fact, be stopped, as life goes on; it can only be subdivided, more or less fluently, with more or less discipline. The Cretan Labyrinth provides the original literary model for such subdivisions. Theseus enters and leaves a walled enclosure. As a result, the situation changes for the doomed Athenian youths and maidens – they are saved from death – and, more important to our story, the situation changes for Theseus himself. He is now certifiably a hero, a 'culture-bringer.' Some have argued that the Minotaur is not just a monstrous engine of tyranny, but rather that he is the hero's dark shadow, his own evil self, which he kills to liberate his own heroic virtue. Before any further great exploits may be achieved, this initial enlightenment must occur, so that the hero may possess 'vision' to perceive the natural sequentiality of his heroic career. For him the idea of the labyrinthine terror can no longer cloud *all* of life's unfolding. Theseus can now always subdivide the maze.

The reader of modern literature may well at this point begin to wonder if this Cretan model is not too neat and optimistic, with its guaranteed escape system. Spenser's Blatant Beast, his Minotaur in one of its shapes, is the typical modern case: the beast cannot be imprisoned, nor can we avoid him. Shakespeare and La Fontaine create the inverse myth from the Cretan, in their poems of Adonis;[7] there the monster kills the hero. Gothic and Oriental romance,[8] 'Graveyard,' and much Romantic poetry push this threat even further.

Negativity increases until in our century Kafka invented virtually boundless, cosmic, bureaucratic mazes; size and boundary are always dubious in Kafka. Borges, a somewhat more cheerful author, because more elegiac, stretches the allusiveness of his labyrinths until he has constructed a universal text larger than our known physical universe.[9] Calvino's invisible cities so proliferate in number, size, and kind that finally they exist only as dots on the pages of an infinite atlas.[10] As Frye observes in a review entitled 'The Nightmare Life in Death,' Beckett employs 'a shaggy-dog type of deliberately misleading humor, expressing itself in a maddeningly prolix pseudologic ... The most trivial actions of Watt, most of which are very similar to those we perform ourselves every day, are exhaustively catalogued in an elaborate pretense of obsessive realism, and we can see how such 'realism' in fiction, pushed to so logical a conclusion, soon gives the effect of living in a kind of casual and unpunishing hell.'[11] The modern attempt to break out of this bland inferno through the 'freedom' of drugs leads equally to a frightening prolixity, the endless 'hide and seek' chronicled by Henri Michaux' *Cannabis Indica*.[12] A classic title would be Lowry's *Under the Volcano*, whose hero, the Consul, sees himself 'balancing, teetering over the awful unbridgeable void.'[13] The classic shape of the modern story of obsession is a journey to the end of the night, perfect in the sense that night is the very form of the boundless. It is as if the modern form of hell is labyrinthine, the humour is absurdist, every exit a blind alley. Our literature has tended to discover most of its most hellish pains in the workings of social systems organized on plans of 'maddeningly prolix pseudologic.'

How this modern twist of fate relates to the ancient image of lost direction is the business of the historian. If worlds have changed to such a degree over the millennia, the critic faces two related tasks. He can reconsider the archetypes and myths, as given in their earlier forms; and he can notice what appear to be epochal changes of sensibility, as the virtually unchanged archetypes bend to accommodate the pressure of historical impact.

Here it is possible to note only a few dimensions of the critical problem. It will help, first of all, to distinguish three main uses of the term 'labyrinth,' following the work of Hermann Kern, who in turn follows, among other guides, the prior work of William Henry Matthews and Paolo Santarcangeli. Kern's monumental *Labirinti* describes the 'forms and interpretations of 5000 years of the presence of an archetype.'[14]

Kern begins by observing that in current usage the term 'labyrinth' has three main meanings: (1) as *metaphor* for any inextricably difficult situation where the very structure of the difficulty cannot be discerned; (2) as any *intricate system of paths* [*intrico de vie*], usually in the form of buildings or gardens, presenting the traveller with a choice among many alternative routes, yet always leading him down blind alleys (this second sense has enormous range: it is used by Herodotus in referring to the necropoli of the ancient Egyptians, and by German horticulturalists and landscapers in referring to the ornamental *Irrgarten*), and finally, (3) as *labyrinth in the proper sense of the word*, i.e., as shown in the design of the 'Cretan labyrinth,' which appears on the face of ancient coins.

There are no blind alleys in the pure Cretan design; thus it differs sharply from the *intrico* (no. 2). The form of movement within is, however, tortuous in one sense: from a single point of entrance the traveller twists and turns between 'walls' round and round, but also back and forth. The Cretan traverse does *not* offer any choices of path, but direction in it does keep changing, whether the overall design is circular, rectangular, or polygonal. The Cretan traverse takes the traveller from an outside to a middle area, and then, without any possibility of getting lost as long as he progresses, into a centre.

Similarly, by retracing his steps he has only one way back out to the edge.

In this labyrinth the traveller has only two choices, and neither has anything to do with choosing a correct path into another correct path (and so on). He can choose only to keep moving or to stop, moving inwards or outwards; and he can choose to stop at the centre, stay there forever, and refuse to come back out from that central point. In effect these two choices reduce to one choice: he must decide whether or not to keep moving. The Cretan labyrinth gives him absolutely no choice of direction.

Unlike the metaphoric sense, and the intricate structural sense, the third, proper sense of the term labyrinth as given in Kern is extremely puzzling to contemplate. For this reason: such a maze forces the traveller to follow the one sole correct path to the centre, and back out. In effect he cannot 'get lost' here. The question at once arises: why then does Theseus need Ariadne's thread? The immediate answer is one given in ancient lore, namely that the Cretan labyrinth of the coins is not the one Theseus entered. Instead, he entered a vast, intricate structure akin to the Palace at Knossos – an *intrico*. But then the 'correct' coin-design would seem an absurdly simple-minded equivalent of the scene of Theseus' adventure, and would have to refer us to some other conception. Perhaps the true Cretan maze symbolized an astrological theory of planetary movement; Kern believes the design has, among other meanings, a calendrical significance.[15] Comparative research indicates that the Cretan model could well be the choreographic plan of a ritual dance, going back to the 'dance of the cranes' on the Island of Delos.[16] Such a use would be related to the 'Troy Town' games of Northern Europe, to the stone labyrinths found near Scandinavian fishing villages, to the labyrinthine rock carvings of the American Southwest Indians.[17] How such a radical choreographic design could travel almost round the whole world is puzzling, but one thing is certain: the pure Cretan labyrinth of the coins is, in terms of essential complexity, the very opposite of the *intrico*. One could get lost in the Egyptian necropolis or the Palace of Minos, or in any such 'megastructure,' simply because there were too many corridors, stairs, illusionistic recesses, and blind turns. But to 'find oneself lost' in a labyrinth of iron determinism, like the Cretan, is to suffer a quite different sort of disorientation. The Cretan model is therefore, I believe, the more important case, since it is truly enigmatic. The fact that, on the surface at least, it is impossible to 'get lost' in the Cretan maze makes that maze a very peculiar device for its stated mythic purpose.

If it were not the case that the Cretan maze is associated with dance movements following its form – that is, its structure has an objective choreographic function – we might wish to argue that the ancient coins and other designs strictly following their layout were merely emblems for a much more complex kind of structure, of Kern's Type 2. But the Cretan design passes down the centuries as an intact geometrical shape, as if its significance depended upon its seven 'rings,' with their permutations to larger numbers, with varied angular shapings (e.g., rectangular shapes, or polygons) yet never losing the one cardinal property of preventing the traveller from straying from the single possible path to the centre. This one severe limit placed upon the design seems to be its essential attribute. Oddly, as we have said, it is a limit that should in principle make it absurd to speak of getting lost in such a labyrinth.

There seems to be no way to explain the paradox except to account for it in psychological terms. Something happens in the Cretan maze that so disturbs the traveller's mind that he is, in some deeper sense, 'lost.'

The story of Theseus, told and retold, gives us some clues. From these a line of speculation may proceed. Theseus must move in large arcs of a circle, each arc tighter than the one before it. Before each arc can form a full circle, it swings back (Kern says, with 'pendular' motion)[18] to shift the traveller to the smaller arc. What often looks to the casual glance like a spiral is not one, for there the radius of the arc being travelled would be *continuously* diminished. In the Cretan maze we have *two* kinds of movement, the one circular or constricting (the case with rectangular mazes, etc.), the other a backswing or reversal of direction. This backswing is a diametrically reversing movement. A first speculation might then be that in the Cretan maze Theseus suffers a vertiginous loss of clarity as to what 'forward' means; to go 'forward', he must keep reversing his direction, that is, he must go backward. The tighter the arcs as he approaches the centre, the more frequent will be this enforced 'undoing' of the idea of forward motion. We might label this process 'the peril of reversing convolutions.' Whereas a spiral maintains continuous forwardness, the Cretan maze enforces a discontinuous forwardness at best, and if the pendular reversals have indeed a psychological effect, this forwardness will seem to Theseus always more and more *questionable*.

The mounting centripetal tension of this back-and-forth movement leads no doubt to questions that only a psychologist could begin to answer. The effect appears, however, to be that of a certain type of vertigo.

A second line of psychological speculation would equally take off from the basic elements of the old story. Of these perhaps the most intriguing is Ariadne's thread. Everything said so far would suggest that her 'silken string,' as Hawthorne calls it,[19] would serve no orienting purpose during the hero's passage to the centre of the maze. It would clearly serve such a purpose if he were doomed to enter and traverse a vast, reticulated structure of merging, angling corridors, stairs, tunnels, etc., that is, a true *intrico*. Such, following the tradition given in Plutarch, is Hawthorne's version of the maze: 'Theseus had not taken five steps before he lost sight of Ariadne; and in five more his head was growing dizzy. But still he went on, now creeping through a low arch, now ascending a flight of steps, now in one crooked passage and now in another, with here a door opening before him, and there one banging behind, until it really seemed as if the walls spun round, and whirled him round along with them.'

Hawthorne adds a delicate touch to the story, to indicate a basic implication of the silken cord. She holds the other end of the cord in her hand at all times, so that 'every little while' Theseus is made aware of her presence outside the maze; he is 'conscious of a gentle twitch at the silken cord.' Hawthorne's narrator expatiates on the emotions attached to the word – 'Oh, indeed, I can assure you, there was a vast deal of human sympathy running along that slender thread of silk.' Human sympathy is perhaps a critical motif in the Theseus story; certainly for Hawthorne that is so. Yet the twitching tug at the cord indicates something more basic even than the bonds of sympathy. In effect the cord becomes an extrusion of Ariadne's hand and implies that, with it in hand, the hero suffers no discontinuity with the outside of the maze. He never, in effect, leaves the outside. Radically reducing the image of the cord to the idea of continuity in space (despite distance), Hawthorne's version suggests that the *intrico* is designed to produce discontinuity, quantal gaps in the hero's perception of his own movements and direction. It is as if, without the silken thread of Ariadne, the hero would suffer from a breaking, a splintering, a rupturing of *continuous* awareness. We may not be able to say what such a flow of consciousness would consist in. But we can assert that the *intrico* disturbs it to the point of vertigo, or rather, Theseus' dizziness is saved from taking effect by the artifice of the cord of continuity.

At once, without elaborating much, it becomes clearer how the Cretan story is tied to Dionysian myth.[20] The Dionysian whirl is not solely that produced by the 'peril of reversing convolutions,' nor solely that produced by reticulated, Daedalian numerosity of choice-points (though these contribute powerfully). The Dionysian whirl is part of a ritual of discontinuous change of spirit. Of conversions of soul so complete that they amount to rebirth. Ariadne in this scheme, as scholars observe, is an earth goddess whose subsequent fate is to go through a sacred marriage with Dionysus. The god of discontinuous conversion marries the goddess of continuous flow. This myth stands apart and around the heroic story of Theseus, giving that story a hieratic ritual framework and 'meaning' in a larger cosmic scheme of things.

Yet our interest here cannot be in that larger schema, however tempting its Nietzschean resonance. The cord is a human artifice permitting the defeat of discontinuity. Without it, there would be an unbridgeable chasm between the inside and the outside of the maze; it bridges that gap. The problem of the labyrinth is to bridge such gaps. The result of not bridging them is 'lost direction.' The cord works because it restates the hero's problem. He no longer needs a sense of direction; all he needs is continuity with the outside, with Ariadne's hand. By definition, anyway, a sense of direction is what the labyrinth forces one to lose. There may be direction in the original Daedalian map of the maze, but there is none in the lived experience of the maze.

In an essay, 'Ariadne's Thread: Repetition and the Narrative Line,' Hillis Miller describes a paradox of the thread, according to which 'that thread maps the whole labyrinth, rather than providing a single track to its center and back out. The thread is the labyrinth, and at the same time it is the repetition of the labyrinth.'[21] Miller means by this paradox the fact that the thread 'threads' a space marked out by the 'walls' of the maze, which, following Ruskin's insight, are conceived as 'spectral,' not real walls. Ruskin says, '*Had* the walls been real, instead of ghostly, there would have been no difficulty whatever in getting either out or in, for you could go no other way. But if the walls were spectral and yet the transgression of them made your final entrance or return impossible, Ariadne's clue was needful indeed' (*Fors Clavigera*, XXIII).

The experience of the labyrinth, ghostly and spectral in its channelling, requires, on Miller's view, a full acceptance of endless doublings and 'repetitions' within that scene of trial. As with the discernment of a 'line of narrative' in a novel, here one must somehow read through multiple reduplications of an originally clear design, or map. What one reads for is continuity. But we ask, what is this continuity? How, given increased complexity of maze-forms, does continuity increasingly evanesce?

The literature and art of the labyrinth (of virtually any type) indicates that a sense of direction implies a continuous linkage with the past. The 'faculty' that fails to work in the maze is memory. Proverbially, those who cannot remember the errors of the past are doomed to repeat them. The maze induces this forgetting. The story of Theseus makes much of forgetting, and not just the forgotten 'way out.' On two critical occasions after his escape from the labyrinth, Theseus forgets: he forgets Ariadne on the island of Naxos – he just leaves her there, forgotten; and he forgets to hoist the white sail to signal victory to his father, Aegeus. This act of forgetting drives Aegeus mad with despair; he does not wait to witness the disembarcation from the returning ship, and dives to his death in the sea which is thence named for him, the Aegean. Two forgettings, one of the Mother Goddess, Ariadne, the other of the actual father. A detour into the psychoanalytic history of the hero's destiny would clarify these mental separations from the parent; such separations (though not always through a process of mental repression) would seem necessary for the heroic career to proceed.

One might say that Theseus first experiences his own forgetting in the labyrinth, but because Ariadne gives him the clue, he is, without needing to know how, saved from knowing that experience in full. He begins his true heroic progress by a saving oblivion; after the escape, it is a question whether he does have this oblivion drawn to his attention. On the other hand, the 'lost direction' of his labyrinthine oblivion was superseded by a 'found direction,' discovered on a higher level, that of pure continuity with the past, with the place *outside* the maze. The maze, it would seem, has an excessive presentness; it is a scene of too many instants, too much linear complexity.

This last is a critical factor in the imagery of the Cretan maze. In its pure form it is a flat layout, a plane figure, in which all choices of change of direction are made in a two-dimensional space. Daedalus, the inventor of the maze, knows about this inherent property of his invention. Thus, when imprisoned there by Minos, he adds a knowing third dimension, and flies out. What he gets, by adding the third dimension, is perspective *on*, to replace direction *in*. With every added dimension of perception of the maze, there will be an increase of power over the system of perilous convolutions. These perspectival distancings are mechanisms for achieving what direction alone must always lack, namely orientation. When a fourth dimension of time is added to the thinking of the maze, the traveller is able to know where he entered, what directional changes he has made by following the thread, what is the orientation of these changes, and what is the amount of the total sum of movements. This is precisely the kind of information required by any ocean voyager, if he is to travel toward any destination across the vast, undifferentiated plain of the sea. With such information in hand, the pilot knows where he is, a knowledge of present position entirely dependent upon a continuous link with the past.

It may be that the labyrinth, as image, goes thus quite beyond the phenomenal impression it makes, which is that of 'lost direction.' It suggests lost origin, lost direction, lost plan, lost orientation, lost position, in fact almost total loss of all controlling awarenesses of the complete manifold of any presentness. If one possessed the present completely, one would possess a summing mechanism in full and perfect operation, and that mechanism would be total memory. For the present in theory is a summation of an infinite past.

At the outer edge of the mythology of the maze there will always be found an insistent theme of the gaining and losing of a more or less complete remembrance.

A number of modern writers have leaned hard upon this theme. Borges imagines a highly 'literary' cosmos, in which present narratives are composed of quotations, including quotations of literary styles, as when he imitates the inner cadences of some favourite author (Chesterton, Browne, Beckford, the Arabian Nights, etc.). Calvino always studies the reduplication of signs, motifs, narrative doublings, no matter what the scene of his fictions. With such authors the encounter with the Minotaur is endlessly varied in outward circumstances, but common to all such encounters is a projected yearning for an increase of dimensions of perspective, as the key to the loss of memory (and the regaining of the meaning of the memorious).

Modern authors, authors at least since Cervantes, Montaigne, Swift, and Sterne, agree that the original model (and 'the point') of the labyrinth is the process of thinking itself, when that process is subjected to any deeply disorienting stress. Hawthorne is quite clear on this matter. His narrator, like his hero, treads 'boldly into the inscrutable labyrinth. How this labyrinth was built is more than I can tell you. But so cunningly contrived a mizmaze was never seen in the world, before nor since. There can be nothing else so intricate, unless it were the brain of a man like Daedalus, who planned it, or the heart of any ordinary man; which last, to be sure, is ten times as great a mystery as the labyrinth of Crete.'

Hawthorne chose his words carefully. In theory a perfectly designed automaton could thread the process of even a Daedalian brain. But the human heart is a metaphor for an essentially undecidable yearning. And this spiritual 'machine,' the heart, is the only guide in the valley of human, ordinary indecision. To allude to the heart is to allude to a dimension of perspective even beyond the summing dimensionality of perfect memoriousness. To allude to this sixth sense is to allude to the domain of spirit, an area beyond technology. To enter upon any discussion of such an area would be to mystify criticism, and we may draw back.

The struggle of recent critical theory has been unusually painful, perhaps because there exists a climate in which it is embarrassing to speak openly of the domain of spirit. Yet, what else has Harold Bloom been talking about, if not *spiritual* 'crossings?'[22] What else has given Frye's work its continuing force, if not its connection with that vast, intersecting verbal system of Strange Loops, the Bible? What else gave Milton's poetry its sublime signifying tension, if not the collision (the leap?) between Classical and Christian myth? Similar discontinuous leaps of level, similar Gödelian/Escherian undecidables occur throughout the Romantic tradition, which plays a naturally precursive role in the drama of our critical thought. Our critics have been variously seeking to prevent the illusion that the entrance into the centre of the pan-textual maze is an infinite regress. Instead, as Hofstadter has shown, there may be natural perspectives available to the hero in the maze, of 'what is, and is not.' Hofstadter sketches the idea of the Strange Loop as a phenomenon where 'by moving upwards (or downwards) through the levels of some hierarchical system, we *unexpectedly* find ourselves right back where we started.'[23] A system of Strange Loops is called a 'tangled hierarchy.' That is the perfect definition of a maze, whether of the pure Cretan type or the extended *intrico* type. It would appear, then, that a return to Frye's 'image of lost direction' will prove particularly fruitful in times like our own, where hierarchies appear nothing if not tangled. The exit into light is sure to be unexpected.

NOTES

1 *Anatomy of Criticism*, 150. *Fearful Symmetry*, 221, 369-70, 380. *The Critical Path* (Bloomington, 1971) begins with an account of the way Frye experi-

enced the Dantesque labyrinth of *Inferno*, canto i: 'About twenty-five years ago, when still in middle life, I lost my way in the dark wood of Blake's prophecies, and looked around for some path that would get out of there ... The critical path I wanted was a theory of criticism which would, first, account for the major phenomena of literary experience, and, second, would lead to some view of the place of literature in civilization as a whole' (13). The same desire to get a perspective *on* literature, while remaining in touch *within* it, is apparent in such essays as 'Towards Defining an Age of Sensibility,' reprinted in *Fables of Identity: Studies in Poetic Mythology* (New York, 1963), 130-7.

2 In this essay I deliberately understate the difference between 'maze' and 'labyrinth.' The latter is a term from building, or architecture. The former has a stronger etymological overtone of *psychological* sense, since it derives from Middle English *masen*, to confuse, puzzle; the word is akin to the Norwegian, *masa-st*, to fall into a slumber, to lose one's senses and begin to dream (Skeat). Thus Marvell says, 'How vainly men themselves amaze.'

3 Henry King, *The Labyrinth*, Poems (Oxford, 1965), 173.

4 Michael Drayton, *Works* (Oxford, 1961), II, 138.

5 Victor Turner, *The Ritual Process* (Chicago, 1969); *Dreams, Fields and Metaphors* (Ithaca, 1974); Arnold van Gennep, *The Rites of Passage*, trans. M.B. Vizedom and G.L. Chaffee (Chicago, 1960).

6 Mircea Eliade, *Patterns in Comparative Religion* (Cleveland and New York, 1963), 381. See my discussion of these comments in *The Prophetic Moment*, 33-4.

7 The boar in *Adonis* is 'a tyrant of the forests,' an 'enormous and cruel monster, who sullies [i.e., contaminates] the fountains [natural springs?]' (*monstre énorme et cruel, qui souille les fontaines*). Like a bandit, he lives in a tangled, inaccessible fortress. La Fontaine identifies the boar with contagion: in the depths of the forest there is a poisonous pool of stagnant water, where the monster drinks in the vapours it exhales. See the French text in the *Oeuvres diverses*, ed. Pierre Claran (Pléiade Edition; Paris, 1948). Paul Valéry's famous essay, 'Concerning *Adonis*,' in *The Art of Poetry*, trans. Denise Folliot (Bollingen Edition; New York, 1958), does not probe the implications of the labyrinthine monster, but observes that 'Adonis, about to become intelligent, hastens to order a hunt. Death rather than reflection.'

8 William Beckford's Gothic/Oriental romance, *Vathek*, ends at the Hall of Subterranean Fire. The story weaves its way there through a series of high camp episodes, whose formal dependence on coincidental happenings

makes the story as a whole mazy. Beckford's later account of the book suggests, to use his own word, that it was a visionary account of an actual house party of his youth, a party occurring in the 'labyrinth' of his father's home. In Gothic and Oriental romances it appears that the idea of the labyrinth gives the author the plan of the narrative form as a whole. Cf. Maturin's *Melmoth the Wanderer*, where the whole narrative consists of nested sub-narratives, deliberately coiling in upon themselves, so that the form of the book projects the disorientation of the hero and narrator.

9 In Kafka psychological terror frequently is the result of a deformity, a metamorphosis, or even a slight physical defect of the body. There is always an assault on the integrity of the body-image. This discomfort over the body then expands obsessively to the point where there is no 'world' in which the body will be at home. Gregor Samsa's insect-body has many terrors, but perhaps the most acute is that it is too large; as insect, he cannot fit through the door in his house (end of Part I, *Metamorphosis*). The house becomes an inappropriate universe – for an insect. Space is always, in Kafka, on the verge of becoming too large or too small for any given body in it. Thus, in the final chapter of *Amerika*, Karl's quest takes him to a scene of ingrown cosmic expansion, 'the nature theater of Oklahoma': 'only now [as he journeys West] did Karl understand how huge America was.' The obsession with cosmic expansion is characteristic of all major labyrinth-authors, Borges as much as Kafka. Thus Borges' *Lottery in Babylon*, where the 'Company' grows like a cancer, until its location, Babylon, expands to universal dimensions; the final speculation of its Babylonian interpreters is that the Lottery 'is nothing else than an infinite game of chance.' This story is reprinted in *Labyrinths*, ed. D.A. Yates and J.E. Irby (New York, 1964).

10 Italo Calvino, *Invisible Cities*, trans. Warren Weaver. This 'bestiary' of labyrinthine structures and phenomena returns over and over to the question: how can one tell whether a limit (as produced by city walls, gates, etc.) is a benign or malign constraint? Thence, in Calvino, arises the further, continuous speculation: how can one tell the difference between an 'inside' and an 'outside'? This latter is the basic formal question to be asked about the process whereby, in labyrinth-literature, temples transform into labyrinths, and vice versa. Of his city, Penthesilea, Calvino's Marco Polo asks: 'Outside Penthesilea does an outside exist? Or, no matter how far you go from the city, will you only pass from one limbo to another, never managing to leave it?' The indeterminacy of space is paralleled by indeterminacies of time. Thus, of Berenice, the final invisible

city, Marco Polo says: 'all the future Berenices are already present in this instant, wrapped one within the other, confined, crammed, inextricable' (*avvolte l'una dentro l'altra, strette pigiate indistricabile*). The ultimate indeterminacy of limit upon space and time is provided by the dialogues, interpolated, between the Great Khan and Polo; even these are unable to decide what semiotic system would capably mark, designate the placement and extent of each city, relative to every other. To a degree they exist only in the mind, invisibly, and share in the final lack of edge which characterizes thought (as distinct from action).

11 Frye, 'The Nightmare Life in Death,' in *On Culture and Literature: A Collection of Review Essays*, ed. R.D. Denham (Chicago, 1978), 222.

12 Henri Michaux, *Cannabis Indica*, in *Light through Darkness*, trans. Haakon Chevalier (New York, 1963), 61-128. See also Michaux, *Miserable Miracle*, trans. Louise Varèse (San Francisco, 1972; 3rd printing). Virtually all the literature of drug experience, from Coleridge and De Quincey to the Americans writing in the fifties and sixties, not to mention Aldous Huxley, explores an artificially induced vision of the dialectic of temple and labyrinth.

13 The phrase is embedded in a Hermetic passage: 'Or do you find me between Mercy and Understanding, between Chesed and Binah (but still at Chesed) – my equilibrium, and equilibrium is all, precarious – balancing, teetering over the awful unbridgeable void, the all-but-untraceable path of God's lightning back to God? As if I ever were in Chesed! More like the Qliphoth' (*Under the Volcano* [New York, 1947], 39). Douglas Day, *Malcolm Lowry: A Biography* (New York, 1973), 344, glosses the Cabbalistic terms as follows: *Chesed* is Mercy; *Binah* is Understanding; *Qliphoth* is the realm of husks and demons. Day's fine biography goes far to rescue Lowry from the misfortune of becoming an underground cult hero.

14 Hermann Kern, *Labirinti*, trans. Libero Sosio (Milan, 1981). Kern includes an extensive bibliography of the subject. *Labirinti* was written for exhibitions in Munich and Milan, the latter held, with a symposium, in June 1981. For this symposium I presented a paper entitled 'Definitions of Threshold for a Theory of Labyrinths' (forthcoming in a volume of theoretical essays edited by Richard Milazzo).

15 Kern, 27-30. See also Kern, *Kalenderbauten: Frühe astronomische Grossgeräte aus Indien, Mexico und Peru* (Munich, 1976).

16 See Hubert Damisch, 'La Danse de Thesée,' *Tel Quel*, 26 (Summer 1966), 60-8. For Damisch the labyrinth is 'the metaphor, or figure' of an aboriginal recess, the aboriginal 'cave' of unformed matter. He notes that even Daedalus does not provide a plan of the labyrinth for Ariadne, since

'l'auteur lui-même ignorait le plan.' Here lost direction is involved with the loss of design; the labyrinth is 'the image of the lost map.'

17 Kern, *Labirinti*, 393-7.

18 Ibid., 13. The Italian reads 'questo movimento pendolare.'

19 Nathaniel Hawthorne, 'The Minotaur,' in *A Wonder Book, Tanglewood Tales, and A Grandfather's Chair* (Boston, 1883; Riverside Edition), 238.

20 On the obscure question of the role of Ariadne as Dionysian goddess/heroic maiden, see Giorgio Colli, *La nascita della filosophia* (Milan, 1980), ch. 2, 'La signora del labirinto.'

21 *Critical Inquiry*, (Autumn 1976), 70.

22 In Harold Bloom's studies of poetic anxiety, the critic attempts to analyse, and to analogize, the many ways in which the poetic act, at its most powerful, involves cata-strophic turnings against some figure of overpowering authority, be it the earlier pre-text, or image of the earlier poetic master, or some earlier phase within the poet's own work or experience. All poetry on this account appears to be 'revisionist.' The great value of Bloom's work is its emphasis on a psychoanalytic perspective, however gnostified, mystified, cabbalized that perspective may be. A significant comment, relating to the labyrinth, would be from *Agon: Towards a Theory of Revisionism* (New York, 1982), 110: 'Freud's revised account of anxiety is precisely at one with the poetic Sublime, for anxiety is finally seen as a technique [i.e., a defence] for mastering anteriority by *remembering* rather than *repeating* the past' (Bloom's italics).

23 Douglas R. Hofstadter, *Gödel, Escher, Bach: An Eternal Golden Braid* (New York, 1979), 10. Hofstadter points out that the concept of 'level' is among the most elusive, as it is among the commonest, we employ, to indicate sub-routines in a larger program of problem-solving. A typical case would be: what is happening when a melody is replayed, in a fugue or sonata, in a different key? What are the 'levels' of modulation doing? This question leads, for instance, to the essential theoretical studies of Heinrich Schenker, among modern musicologists; it has much to do with the way certain pieces need to be played – perhaps the most obvious being the extended instrumental works of Schubert. Hofstadter's cases are chiefly drawn from Bach, one being the 'Little Harmonic Labyrinth.' In general, each loop in a program may or may not work at a different 'level' within the whole structure. The strangeness of loops results from the fact that while each level may, on one view, mark a separable stratum, the strata are not always experienced as distinct from each other, on some other view. Hofstadter gives the example from Escher, *Drawing Hands*, where each of two hands draws the other hand emerging from a plane which, as plane,

exists only by virtue of being drawn by one hand or other. The two hands and their products are distinctly separate – but which of the two draws *the* plane which establishes a base for the whole image? The question is undecidable. On the surface, a strangeness results, since it follows that each hand is both plane and three-dimensional at once. Hofstadter resolves the paradox by showing that there is a third hand at work, Escher's own actual hand. That hand remains 'invisible' and yet provides us with the 'higher' way out of the tangled hierarchy. Generally this resort to an invisible source of perspective on the tangle will be found at every moment when a labyrinth is suddenly transformed into a temple-like structure, a place of clarified vision. The trick is to increase the number of dimensions in which the puzzle is seen. Thus, in my essay, 'Definitions of Threshold for a Theory of Labyrinths,' cited above, n. 14, I attempt to show that all complex labyrinths require a capability of 'reading' threshold-passages (choice-points of shift from one loop to another) in at least *five* dimensions, the last of which assumes the virtual undecidability of knowing if one is making a progressive move toward exit. Topographically, I believe, decision-making in the maze always comes down to a question: what at a given moment is the edge between inside and outside? In literature we seek a parallel type of decision: what at a given moment is the 'sense' of symbolic terms, what is included and excluded, for without making these cuts we cannot proceed in our reading. To proceed means to let some puzzle of meaning merely continue in a state of continuous looping. The looping is not a repetition; it is a 'remembering' (see n. 22, above). And an odd, strange kind of remembering, since the reader now allows a specific 'memory' within the text of its web of allusions to other texts to be 'forgotten,' bypassed as the whole program moves forward. Any system with an inadequate number of dimensions of decision-making, cut-making, will not be able to forget steps previously passed through (as an event remembered is passed through), but will attempt to repeat and repeat that passage, never jumping up or down within the system. The reader will behave as a viewer of Drawing Hands would behave, fixating on the drawn hands, instead of asking: but which hand is doing the drawing? The ingenious aspect of Escher's print, as Hofstadter points out, is that the third hand, Escher's own, is a mental as well as physical fact for a complete response to the picture. Final cuts are then 'invisible,' as thought is.